Singing about It

Folk Song in Southern Indiana

Singing about It

Folk Song in Southern Indiana

George List

Indianapolis

Indiana Historical Society

1991

The paper in this publication meets the minimum requirements of American
National Standard for Information Sciences—Permanence of Paper for Printed
Library Materials, ANSI Z39.48-1984.

Library of Congress Cataloging-in-Publication Data

Singing about it: folk song in southern Indiana/[transcribed] by George List.
    p. of music.
    Unacc. melodies.
    Transcribed principally from recordings in the Indiana University Archives of
Traditional Music.
    Includes bibliographical and discographical references (p.) and index.
    ISBN 0-87195-086-3 : $32.00
    1. Folk songs, English—Indiana. 2. Folk music—Indiana. 3. Folk songs,
English—Indiana—History and criticism. 4. Folk music—Indiana—History and
criticism. I. List, George, 1911-   . II. Indiana University, Bloomington. Archives
of Traditional Music.
    M1629.7.I39S5   1991   91-16566
                                                               CIP
                                                                M

To the singers of the songs

TABLE OF CONTENTS

LIST OF TRANSCRIPTIONS

Key

Song information is given in the following format:

Number of Transcription   Title of song   Page number
Performer(s), place recorded, date recorded.

Last name(s) of recorder(s)/ATM accession number/ATL number, Cassette (Cass.) number, or Earliest Copy (EC) number. (If number is not preceded by an abbreviation, it is an ATL.)

The ATM accession number is the finding number given to the original tape in the Indiana University Archives of Traditional Music. It consists of three parts: year accessioned—serial number within that year—indication of status of recording (B = broadcast; C = commercial; F = field).

ATL (Archives Tape Library) numbers refer to the copies of tapes available to the general public in the Archives Listening Library. If no ATL copy is available, a Cassette number or Earliest Copy number is given, if applicable. Cassette and Earliest copy numbers refer to original cassette tapes and the first copy made of any Archives deposit, respectively. These are not available to the general public. However, listening copies of most original materials, Cassettes, and ECs will be made upon request at the Archives Listening Library, depending upon restrictions placed upon the Archives by the depositor of the material.

Names of Recorders

BUCKLEY	Bruce Buckley
DICKEY	Quentin Lotus Dickey
HALPERT	Herbert Halpert
HOSKINSON	Isabel Saulman Hoskinson
KAPLAN	Jean Kaplan (now Kaplan Teichroew)
LIST	George List
LOMAX	Alan and Elizabeth Lomax
MAY	Phyllis May (now May-Machunga)
MEADE	Guthrie T. Meade
NETTL	Bruno Nettl
ROSENBAUM	Arthur Rosenbaum
SCHREIBER	Dale Schreiber

Names of Collectors or Compilers

BREWSTER	Paul Brewster (See Brewster 1936 in Bibliography.)
WOLFORD	Leah Jackson Wolford (See Wolford 1916 in Bibliography.)

ILLUSTRATIONS

INTRODUCTION

This volume offers a representative sampling of folk song as sung in southern Indiana from the Civil War to the present. Whenever possible I have endeavored to relate each song to its social and historical context. Toward this end I have provided photographs and short biographies of the individual singers and histories of their families. I have described the activities during which the songs were sung and the incidents or historical movements which they reflect. Also, to give the reader a sense of and a feeling for the emotions, customs, and ideas expressed in these songs I have reproduced articles and clippings from old newspapers, old broadsides of the song poems, and a few early editions of the songs with both words and music. Discussion of the structural and stylistic characteristics of the songs has not been neglected, but the primary focus has been placed upon the social aspects.

I have transcribed the bulk of the songs, both words and the melodies, from recordings on deposit in the Indiana University Archives of Traditional Music, of which I was director from 1954 to 1976. To this there are two exceptions. The first is the inclusion of three transcriptions of girls' clapping songs made by Phyllis May from a videotape which was later deposited in the Archives. The second is the reproduction of a number of transcriptions of play-party songs published in Leah Jackson Wolford's *The Play-Party in Indiana*, and one published in an article by Paul Brewster, "Game-Songs in Southern Indiana" (1936). The inclusion of these was made necessary by the lack of sufficient representation in the Archives' collections to document fully this genre.

Until early in this century singing in the Anglo-American folktradition was of a single unaccompanied melodic line. Then this began to change, and folksingers could be heard accompanying themselves with the guitar or, more rarely, with the banjo.

> The guitar had been present in America since the colonial period but was originally perceived mainly as a polite upper class instrument. It seems to have moved into the hinterlands very slowly. Virginia mountain folksinger, Hobart Smith, told Alan Lomax that he saw his first guitar about the time of World War I when a Black construction gang laid rails into Saltville, Virginia.[1]

In some of the recordings from which the songs transcribed were taken, the singer accompanies himself with the guitar. Almost without exception these songs were sung earlier without accompaniment, and sometimes there are in the Archives performances of the same song with and without guitar accompaniment, in one case by the same singer. I therefore have not considered a guitar accompaniment, when present, as an indispensable element in the performance, and I have transcribed only the melody sung. However, in such cases I have indicated that the song was accompanied by the guitar.

The transcription of at least one stanza of the melody and its associated text is offered for each song. This is usually the first stanza but may be the second if the recording of the first is imperfect. The first performance of a chorus, when there is one, is also transcribed. When variation occurs in subsequent stanzas, which is not merely the repetition of a pitch to accommodate additional syllables or the slight shortening or lengthening of particular notes, a later stanza will also be transcribed as well, usually the second. The variation(s) illustrated may consist of change(s) in form, meter, rhythm, and/or pitch. The entire text of the song then follows.

Beneath the title of each numbered transcription is given the name or names of the singer or singers and the date and place the song was recorded. The name or names of the recorder(s) or collector(s) of the song and its finding numbers in the Archives of Traditional Music are given in the List of Transcriptions as are bibliographic references to those songs published by Wolford and Brewster. Superscripts found in the running text in the Introduction and Chapters refer to the Notes at the end of the volume. A complete reference for each publication cited will be found in the Bibliography. In cases where commercial recordings are referred to, the record company and number will be given.

The ballad, the narrative form of folk song, has been the most studied. There are four works which might be described as catalogs of the ballad in the English language. Unfortunately, no similar works exist for other genres of folk song. Since folksingers often give different names to the same ballad, it is useful to refer to the generic name and the symbols by which it is identified in these four "catalogs." These are *The English and Scottish Popular Ballads* by Francis James Child; his earlier collection, *English and Scottish Ballads*; *American Balladry from British Broadsides: A*

Guide for Students and Collectors of Traditional Song by George Malcolm Laws; and *Native American Balladry: A Descriptive Study and a Bibliographical Syllabus*, also by Laws. Should any ballad transcribed in this volume be cataloged in one of these four works, the appropriate reference will be given in parentheses following the title given above the transcription. Child's later collection will be indicated only by his name, the earlier collection as Child ESB. *American Balladry from British Broadsides* will be identified as Laws BR, and *Native American Balladry* as Laws AM. Thus references may appear as (Child ESB, The Children in the Wood), (Child 4, Lady Isabel and the Elf Knight), (Laws BR N 20, The Golden Glove), or (Laws AM G 17, The Silver Dagger), etc. When such a title is the same as that of the TR, it is not repeated. Laws applies a rather restricted definition to the ballad in *Native American Balladry* but offers a list of ballad-like pieces which he does not find to satisfy fully his definition. A number of items on this list are included in this volume. Since in these cases there is no identifying symbol, the page number will be given instead in the running text.

Since I was principally working with recordings made by other collectors, and the greater number of singers were either deceased or otherwise unavailable for consultation, the transcriptions of some words and phrases presented difficulties. The problems presented could be solved often by reference to other published variants of the song, in particular those in Brewster's *Ballads and Songs of Indiana* (1940). Many of the singers recorded by Alan Lomax for the Library of Congress had previously sent written copies of the texts of some of the songs recorded to Brewster. He printed many of these in his volume. The transcriptions, however, represent what I could hear in the recording. The texts written down by the singer and sent to Brewster do not always duplicate in every particular the recorded performance.

In the recordings one can also hear slips of the tongue, mispronunciations, elisions, errors in grammar, and at times what appear to be archaic words. As seems necessary, such phenomena are discussed in the running text. In the song poems I am not attempting to reflect regional dialect or accent, but such obvious usages as "cain't" and "growed" are written as heard. The dropping of the "g" in the final "ing" is common, but the singers are not consistent in this omission. Therefore "ing" is always written out in full. Other elisions of individual letters are indicated by apostrophes. Words which I have good reason to believe have been omitted are inserted within brackets [ ]. Words which are obviously incorrect as, for example, the use of "she" to refer to a male, are followed by [*sic*] to indicate that this is what is actually sung. When there is some doubt in my mind that a word or phrase is correct I have placed it in parentheses ( ). Finally, when no determination can be made by any means as to what is being sung, the ellipsis (. . .) is employed.

When in the poem there are repeated lines, these are written out in full for the first two stanzas, but in following stanzas are indicated by (etc.). Such repetitions can occur within a stanza or at its end. Should the repetition not be exact as, for example, when "lay" is substituted for "lie" in st. 5 of TR 76, "Six Kings' Daughters," the repetition will be written out in full.

Guide to the Transcriptions

Should a transcription be given a metrical signature this indicates that the song displays a fairly steady pulse or underlying beat. This applies whether or not changes in metrical signature occur. If the transcription is assigned no metrical signature it is declamatory in nature, having free rhythm, and is marked "parlando rubato," a term originally applied to folk music by Béla Bartók.

For purposes of comparison, all but two of the melodies have been transposed so that they end on g^1, the second line of the treble clef. These two, TRs 7 and 61, are clearly in the major mode and have been transcribed in G Major. However, they end on the second and third scale degree, respectively. Further, it should be noted that TR 15 (first part) does not remain in the same tonality throughout. Nevertheless, it has been transposed so that it ends on g^1.

Symbols Employed in the Transcription

Stemless black note in parentheses indicates the actual final pitch of the performance.

(Note that in all cases the transcriptions were made from copies of the original recordings, sometimes even from second-generation copies. Since tape recorders can vary considerably in speed, the "actual pitch" given can vary by as much as a semitone from that of the original recording. The actual pitch is therefore not necessarily exact but is instead a close approximation.)

 Upward-pointing arrow indicates that the note marked is as much as, but not more than, a quarter-tone sharp.

 Downward-pointing arrow indicates that the note marked is as much as, but not more than, a quarter-tone flat.

 The note so marked is slightly longer in duration than written.

 The note so marked is slightly shorter in duration than written.

 The lines above the staff indicate a short break in the continuity.

The Accompanying Cassette

The cassette accompanying this volume offers the reader the opportunity to listen to a selection of copies of the recordings from which the transcriptions of the song tunes and texts were made. The performers are not trained singers but the individuals described in Chapter 1. Their memories at times fail them, and they may pause or repeat. Nor are these studio recordings. They are field recordings, made by a number of individuals in varying circumstances over a period from 1938 to the present. The original recordings are found on acetate and aluminum discs and on open reel or cassette tape. They were made with different types of portable equipment with varied microphone arrangements. Some of the recordings are worn or have other defects. Every attempt was made to retain or even to improve the quality of the original recordings. However, what the reader will hear is history in sound, not acoustical perfection.

Should the reader have difficulty in understanding the words of a song he should refer to its transcribed text. The contents of the cassette are given on the J-card that accompanies it. The transcription number is given to the left of the song title, and the page upon which the transcription of the music is found is given to the right. The full text follows immediately thereafter.

Indiana University, Bloomington

July 1991

ACKNOWLEDGMENTS

During the several years spent in the preparation of this volume I was fortunate in having the assistance of a large number of individuals, institutions, and agencies. My appreciation must first be extended to the individuals who recorded folk songs in southern Indiana, deposited them in the Archives of Traditional Music, and gave me permission to use them. Among these are Arthur Rosenbaum, University of Georgia, Athens; Herbert Halpert, Professor Emeritus at St. John's University, Newfoundland, Canada; Guthrie T. Meade, formerly of the Library of Congress (now deceased); Bruno Nettl, University of Illinois, Urbana; Bruce Buckley, formerly of the Farmers' Museum, Cooperstown, New York; Phyllis May-Machunga, formerly at the Smithsonian Institution and now at Moorhead College, Minnesota; and Jean Kaplan Teichroew, National Geographic Society.

I acknowledge with thanks the assistance of a number of colleagues at Indiana University. I received references and other data concerning the Anglo-American ballad from W. Edson Richmond and Mary Ellen Brown. Richmond also provided me with a computer printout of items concerning music in his bibliography of the ballad, later published as *Ballad Scholarship: An Annotated Bibliography* (New York: Garland Publishers, 1989). From Walter Meserve I received information concerning practices in American theater in the nineteenth century. Stephen Stein offered data and references concerning American religious practices in the last century, and Donna L. Eder provided references to sociological studies concerning the relationship of boys and girls in American schools. Other scholars to whom I am indebted for references and other materials include Joseph Hickerson of the Archive of Folk Life of the Library of Congress, John Hasse of the Smithsonian Institution, and Phyllis May-Machunga, who also at the time was at the Smithsonian Institution. I am also indebted to Joseph Hickerson for sending me the notes made by Alan Lomax while recording in Indiana in 1938. Guthrie T. Meade provided me with invaluable information concerning hillbilly recordings of traditional songs. Thus Meade is represented in this volume as scholar, collector, and singer. W. K. McNeil, folklorist at the Ozark Folk Center of

Mountain View, Arkansas, kindly shared with me his wide knowledge of the background and history of Anglo-American song.

I am grateful to three members of the staff of the Monroe County Community Schools for sharing with me their knowledge of gender relationships on the playground. Sara Estabrook teaches music in the elementary grades; David Ebeling is now a member of the administrative staff but related his experiences in a two-room schoolhouse thirty years in the past, and Carol Darling teaches in a one-room schoolhouse in Benton Township.

I owe a large debt of gratitude to the staff of the Archives of Traditional Music, an institution of which I was director for twenty-two years. Anthony Seeger, who was director during the first two years of this study, extended me many courtesies, as did his successor, Ruth Stone, and the associate director, Dorothy Lee. I made constant use of the Archives' library, where I received invaluable assistance from Mary Russell and Brenda Nelson-Strauss. Marilyn Graf, the Archives' secretary, assisted me in more ways than I can enumerate. Glenn Simonelli, recording technician, was also very helpful. I am particularly grateful to Norah Dial, technical specialist at the Archives of Traditional Music, for her painstaking work in preparing the master tapes for the cassette which accompanies this volume.

I acknowledge with thanks the aid which many librarians at Indiana University have offered me. Among those who can be named are three in the Graduate Library: Polly Grimshaw, folklore librarian; Ann Bristow, reference librarian; and Thomas Glastras, associate librarian (now retired). At the Lilly Library Josiah Quincey Bennett, associate librarian emeritus (now deceased), was also of assistance. In addition I wish to express my gratitude to the many anonymous librarians of the Reference Department, the Circulation Department, the Interlibrary Loan Department, and the Microforms and Periodicals Department of the Graduate Library, the Circulation Department of the Undergraduate Library, the Circulation and Reference departments of the Music Library, and the staff of the Lilly Library of Rare Books.

A number of graduate students at Indiana University were of inestimable help in preparing this study. Mary Fechner was my highly competent research assistant during the early stages of the work and also typed first drafts of several chapters into the computer. This post was then taken by Marc Satterwhite, who worked with me until the final draft was completed. He was unusually diligent and effective and served far beyond the call of duty. He was also responsible for the word processing of the final draft and for the preparation of the visuals. He has displayed his skills as a music copyist in preparing the final versions of the music notations. For part-time assistance I am also indebted to Nancy C. McEntire, Paulette Gissendanner, Cheryl Keyes, Rebecca Jemian, Nancy Totten, and Carlos Fernández. I am further grateful to Nancy McEntire for making available to me the bibliography she prepared for the class in Indiana Folk Music she had taught for the Collins Living Learning Center, Indiana University.

I owe thanks to Jennie Rathbun, Houghton Library, Harvard University, for assistance in securing copies of broadsides from that library and to John L. Selch, newspaper librarian, Indiana State Library, Indianapolis, for help in securing copies of old Indiana newspapers. Copies of old published songs were secured through the Photographic Service of the British Library, London, and the Music Division of the Library of Congress. The map illustrating the Hoosier Apex was prepared by the Graphic Arts Service, and all photographic copying was done by the Photographic Service, both divisions of the Audio-Visual Center, Indiana University Learning Resources Department.

I acknowledge with appreciation the help of a number of individuals who provided obituaries and other information which led to contacts with the relatives and friends of the singers and sometimes to the singers themselves. The largest contributions in this direction were made by Erin Cornish of the Indiana Room of the Monroe County Public Library and Helen Reeve of the Brown County Historical Society. Others who contributed in this manner are Thelma Whaley, Genealogical Room of the Monroe County Museum, Jack Scott of the Jackson County Genealogical Society, and the following librarians: Chris W. Cullnane III, Founders' Memorial Library, Oakland City College; Joan M. Elliott, Willard Library, Evansville; John W. Barlow, Alexandrian Public Library, Mt. Vernon; Starr DeJesus, Bedford Public Library; Lesa L. Griffin, Rushville Public Library; Jewell Sears, Crawford County Public Library, English; Bernice Lanman, Perry County Public Library, Cannelton; Starr Skirvin, Brown County Public Library, Nashville; Linda Leipold, Princeton Public Library; and Benita K. Mason, New Albany-Floyd County Public Library.

I am deeply indebted to the following individuals for providing information leading to the development of biographies and/or family histories of the singers indicated:

BRYANT: Margaret Harper, Oakland City; Patsy Kixmiller, Evansville; Esther Bryant (Frazier) Scales, Dixon, Tennessee; Lowell McNeely, Indianapolis; and Russell Bufkins, Denton, Texas.

COLLIER, John W.: Mrs. Robert Allender, Monroe County; Bramble Stogdill, Monroe County; Leona Stogdill, Freetown; and Ursula Scott, Brownstown.

CURRY: Orpha Mae Curry, Bloomington; Richard Hopper, Clayton; William M. Jones, Nashville; Mary Jane Head, Bloomington; Laura Coia, Bloomington; and Irma Hendricks, Bloomington.

DICKEY, Quentin Lotus: Quentin Lotus Dickey.

DIXON, Samuel Clay: Clinton Maurer, Mt. Vernon; Marion Oschmann, Newburgh; Winola Henry, Harper Woods, Michigan; and Sue Becknell, El Paso, Texas.

ELLIOTT, Phoebe: Josephine Elliott, New Harmony; and Constance Crossen, St. Louis, Missouri. The latter permitted me to use material from her unpublished book, "Wabash Scrapbook."

FIELDS, Albert J.: Ruel W. Steele, Bedford; Lois Shipman, Riverview, Florida; and Nancy Fields Fadum, Raleigh, North Carolina.

GARY, Abraham Lincoln: John N. Hughes, Rushville.

HOSKINSON, Isabel: Sara Hoskinson Frommer, Bloomington; Isabel Hoskinson, St. Louis, Missouri; and Arthur Heckman, Bloomington.

KIRK, Jacob Oatman Forester: Wendell P. Wiggs, Oakland City; and Victor M. Evans, Alexandria.

LINDSEY, David: Charles D. Glass, Bloomington; and Don Thompson, Spencer.

MEADE, Guthrie T.: Guthrie T. Meade, Frankfort, Kentucky.

PARKS: Charles Parks, Milltown; Lucille Faulkner, Davenport, Iowa; and Bertie Parks Underhill, Marengo. Charles Parks was contacted under the assumption that he was a relative. He was not, but as a genealogy buff he volunteered to drive to English to secure names of the Parks' relatives from the county authorities.

SANDAGE/UNDERHILL: Ira Anderson, Siberia; Bertie Parks Underhill, Marengo; and Mr. and Mrs. Clarence Underhill, English.

SCHREIBER: Guthrie T. Meade, Frankfort, Kentucky; Dale Schreiber, Ellettsville; and Hazel Schreiber Merry, Bedford.

SMELSER, Vern: Gerald Stout, Bloomington; Otis Stout, Paoli; Kenneth Smelser, Orange County; Nellie Smelser, Orange County; and Vance Smelser, New Albany.

SOUTH/KING: Guthrie T. Meade, Frankfort, Kentucky; Harold South, Anchorage, Alaska; Lula South, Monroe County; Dorothea South Rampley, Bloomington; and Carmen Ritter (now deceased), Bloomington.

STOGDILL, Marion: James Wilkerson, Brown County; Mrs. Robert Allender, Monroe County; Bramble Stogdill, Monroe County; Adolph Beauchamp, Brown County; and Dorothy Lutes, Monroe County.

WARD, Isie Dora McMurtry: William P. Ward, Princeton.

WEVER (WEAVER), Nellie Rebecca Butler: Paul B. Wever, Jr., Evansville.

I am much indebted to the staff of the Indiana Historical Society for the various tasks involved in the preparation of this volume for publication. This work was under the general supervision of Thomas A. Mason, director of publications. Paula Corpuz was a painstaking copy editor and was a most patient and cooperative collaborator in working out all details of publication. Kathy Breen and Megan McKee, editorial assistants, contributed immensely to every phase of the production of this volume. Frank Personett is responsible for the interior design and Tony Woodward for the cover design.

Finally I must express my appreciation to the agencies and the divisions of Indiana University whose funding made this study possible. The largest contribution came from the Indiana Historical Society, Peter Harstad, executive director, and Raymond L. Shoemaker, assistant executive director. I also was the recipient of a summer fellowship for July through August 1988 from the Indiana Humanities Council, Kenneth Gladish, director. This agency also funded the preparation of the cassette which accompanies this volume. Thanks also goes to the following divisions of Indiana University, Bloomington: from the Office of Research and Graduate Development, Albert Wertheim and Helen Nader, associate deans, I received research grants-in-aid and a special grant to be applied to the preparation of this volume. The Graduate School, George Walker, associate vice president, gave me a grant for a similar purpose. The College of Arts and Sciences, John Lombardi, then dean, provided me with fee remissions to be applied to my graduate assistants.

CHAPTER 1   FOLK SONGS AND FOLKSINGERS

When in 1938 "Aunt" Phoebe Elliott of New Harmony, then in her eighty-third year, was asked where she had learned "Pretty Sarry" (TR 42) she replied:

> I learned it from this great aunt of mine. She lived up on what's called McCary's Bluff, up on the Wabash River, and I was sent there as a little girl to recover from the measles. And we all sat around the fire at night, around the fireplace, and, of course, singing was a diversion. And Polly always sang this song and I acquired it from Polly . . . [It was] in 1866 that I acquired the song and the aunt was then 80 years old and she knew it as a girl, you see. She gave it from memory to her daughter.

The incident upon which the ballad, "Pearl Bryan," (TR 97-98) is based occurred in 1895. According to Oscar "Doc" Parks, who was recorded singing it in 1963 in Alton:

> It was out when I was just a little boy. I'm 71 . . . I remember my Daddy coming from Livingston riding--he had to ride to Livingston ev'ry Saturday evening, you know--and I remember him coming from Livingston one Saturday evening and setting down by the fireside after he got his horse put up and tell Mom that story about Pearl Bryan and about them killing her. And years after that, not too many years after that, the song came out. You see, they back out in them hills never got any news unless they went to town. Newspapers didn't float out in the country. They had to go to some town before they could get any.

This is a collection of old songs. Most of them come from the last century or before. In most cases they were sung by old people, many of whom are now deceased. They had learned the songs when they were young and when singing was a common form of recreation. Most were learned from family or friends, some from phonograph records, radio, or in school. They became part of the singer's repertory. If he or she had known who had written the words or who had composed the music of a song this was soon forgotten. They sang it for others who listened and learned it and, in turn, passed it on in the same way. Lyricist and composer became anonymous, and the song passed into what is known as the "oral tradition." It became a folk song.

As the folk song was passed along, changes occurred due to lapses in memory or differences in taste. One could hear it sung differently in one place than in another or by two different singers. It had developed what folklorists call "variants," a common characteristic of folk song and one of its most interesting aspects. Frequently throughout this book I have given more than one variant of a song so that through comparison the reader can see what changes have taken place, how the words and music have been varied.

The words of the songs often appeared in print. In England beginning as early as the seventeenth century, and later in the United States, they were printed on single sheets known as "broadsides," which were hawked through the streets. Later they were published individually or in groups in newspapers, or small collections were made into what were called "chapbooks" or "songsters" and sold. In order to preserve the texts, some singers wrote them down in scrapbooks or in the eastern United States in personal collections called "ballets" (pronounced "ballots"). These were used to refresh the memory, or at times the songs were actually sung while looking at the words, although most of the time songs were sung from memory.

Many of the songs offered in these pages entered the oral tradition or were maintained in that tradition through hillbilly or early country music recordings. (The two terms, "hillbilly" and "country music," seem to be used interchangeably.) These recordings began to appear in the 1920s, and their issue continued through the 1930s and 1940s and even into the early 1950s. The singers, Vernon Dalhart and the Carter Family being some of the best known, invariably accompanied themselves with one or more instruments, guitar, fiddle, or banjo, and often the songs were sung in harmony. Wherever such performances seem to have prolonged the carrying of a song in the oral tradition, and the data is available, I have listed one or more such issues.

The oral tradition is no respecter of class. As learned from family or friends, a folk song might be sung by a washerwoman or a lawyer, a farmer or a postman. These singers sang for the pleasure thereof. They were not minstrels singing for their living. But little by little the phonograph, the radio, the cinema, and, finally, television began to make most of us into a nation of listeners rather than singers. At the same time professional "folksingers" arose, individuals who earned their living through singing folk songs on the radio, in concerts, at folk festivals, and on phonograph records.

Some, like Jean Ritchie, had learned their traditional songs from members of the family. Others, like Pete Seeger, came from a professional background and learned their songs purely as an avocation, then, in some cases, as a vocation.

Some rural folk with a repertory of traditional song became semiprofessionals, earning part of their living by singing folk songs on the radio and at various types of gatherings. Simultaneously, beginning in the 1930s and flowering in the 1950s there arose what is often called the "folk song/folk music revival." In this movement many of the young, inspired by Pete Seeger and others, began to learn to strum the guitar or pick the banjo and to sing folk songs which they had learned from Folkways Records or other issues. Some searched through the countryside to find old-time fiddlers and singers to record and thus to better imitate their styles. Some practitioners of popular music became influenced by folk revival music, and styles such as "folk rock" developed.

All this produced a modern scene in which a few years ago I heard a radio program in which two young women, both schoolteachers, sang what they called folk songs. They composed the songs themselves, sang in harmony, and accompanied themselves with guitars. When asked, they said a folk song was one with a good story, heartbreak, human interest, and a good melody to back it up, a song that would last. This is probably a good description of the average person's concept of a folk song. But the songs these young women sang could not be included in this volume. If a song is sung by its composer it obviously has not entered the oral tradition and therefore cannot be considered a folk song.

Remnants of French and German songs have been recorded in southern Indiana, but they are not included here. Nor is there representation of black folk songs. There are well established black communities in southern Indiana, and studies have recently been published concerning their economic and cultural contribution to the state.[1] However, the only recording of black music in the Archives of Traditional Music is of a church service in Bloomington. There are no recordings of black folk songs, and therefore none will be found in this volume, although their occasional stylistic influence will be noted. Thus this book primarily represents the song traditions of the English-speaking European and his English-speaking descendants.

There are very few recordings in the Archives from northern Indiana of the type presented in this volume. The bulk of recordings from the northern part of the state are either of instrumental music or of ethnic music of various types, mostly from the Calumet region. Southern Indiana has therefore been selected since it has a much richer repertory of this type of folk song, due, in good part, to its southern heritage.

Early settlement in most states moved from east to west, while in Indiana the initial movement was from south to north. The state was first settled by southerners who crossed the Ohio River and pushed north as war and treaty opened Indian lands. Although many moved still further north, they tended to settle below the National Road, which ran east to west through Indianapolis. Birthplace data collected in the 1850 Federal Census indicated that:

> Southerners accounted for 44.0 percent of all Hoosiers native to the United States but born outside of Indiana, a far greater proportion of the population than the 28.3 percent southern average for the entire Old Northwest and nearly 10 percent higher than in any other state in the region.[2]

On the basis of the 1850 census it has been estimated that adult Hoosiers born in the South, plus their children, most of whom had been born in Indiana, may have totaled 40 percent of the entire population.[3]

The bulk of the southerners who moved north into Indiana had come from the Upland South. The upland/lowland division of the South occurs at the fall line dividing the Piedmont from the coastal plain. The lowland consists of the coastal plain, while the upland includes the Piedmont, Blue Ridge, the Shenandoah Valley, the Appalachian Plateau, and smaller interior plateaus. The culture of the lowland and upland southerners differed in many respects: in agriculture and economic systems, in the holding of slaves, and in ethnic origins.[4]

An analysis of the surnames in the 1790 census indicated that English surnames predominated in the American population as a whole. The upland population was ethnically distinctive, there being a greater proportion of Celtic and German names than in the lowland South or the remainder of the country. Most of those with English surnames were native born and moved to the uplands from the lowland South, or from southeastern Pennsylvania. Many of the Scotch-Irish and Germans had arrived only recently and moved directly into the uplands in search of inexpensive and fertile land.

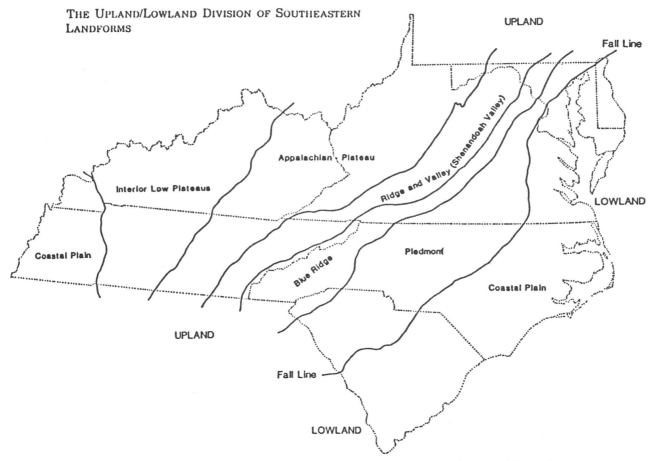

THE UPLAND/LOWLAND DIVISION OF SOUTHEASTERN LANDFORMS

Gregory S. Rose, "Upland Southerners: The County Origins of Southern Migrants to Indiana by 1850," *Indiana Magazine of History* 82 (September 1986): 250

Fig. 1

At this point it will be useful to offer a short history of the Scotch-Irish, a people known by this nomenclature only in the United States. The Southern Uplands culture was an amalgam of Scotch-Irish, English, and German, but the Germans soon abandoned their native language for English. (At least there are few, if any, secular songs in German from the United States in the Indiana University Archives of Traditional Music.)

Following the Reformation, England established its own official church, the Church of England, Anglican, or Episcopalian, but many English remained Catholic. The northern half of Scotland, the Highlands, remained Catholic as, in general, did the southern quarter, the Upland. Between these two regions, occupying a quarter of Scotland, and the most urbanized quarter, are the Lowlands. Here most Scots accepted Calvinist doctrines and slowly developed the Presbyterian faith. Ireland, with its own great Roman Catholic monastic tradition, remained almost entirely Catholic.

The king of England controlled Scotland and not only persecuted the Catholics but also attempted to force aspects of Anglican practices upon the Scottish Presbyterians. The English conquered the north and northeastern part of Ireland, gave the land to English landlords, and opened this area for settlement. Although some English and Scottish Catholics settled there, the bulk of the immigrants were Lowland Scots who hoped not only to improve their economic condition but also to find the freedom of religion denied them at home.

Most of the Scottish immigration into Northern Ireland occurred during the seventeenth century. James II, the last of the Stuart line of kings, converted to Catholicism before he ascended to the throne of England in 1685. He attempted to ameliorate the conflict between competing religions, but with little success. In 1688 powerful members of Parliament secretly invited William, the Dutch Prince of Orange and the son-in-law of James II, to come to England to succeed the latter. James was unable to withstand William's invading army since a good part of his own army defected to William's. James fled to France, which still recognized his right to the throne. His unsuccessful attempt to regain the throne is discussed in relation to the ballad, "The Battle of the Boyne" (TR 87). Similar attempts by his descendants are related in connection with the song, "Weevily Wheat" (TR 38).

By the end of the seventeenth century the Scots living in Northern Ireland were beginning to emigrate to the United States because of adverse economic conditions and political restrictions. The absentee English landlords demanded high rents, and laws passed by the English Parliament forbade the exportation of wool from Ireland, thus rendering sheep raising unprofitable. Presbyterians were excluded from civil and military offices, although they were simultaneously taxed to support the Anglican church. Waves of Scotch-Irish crossed the Atlantic. Although no exact figures are available, it is estimated that in 1790, 6 percent of the entire population of the United States was Scotch-Irish or of Scotch-Irish extraction, a total of 225,000 people. All, of course, did not move to the Southern Uplands.

Just before the Revolution migrants from Virginia and North Carolina began moving through the Cumberland Gap into eastern Kentucky. After the war so many settlers migrated through the Gap to the bluegrass region of north central Kentucky that this area rapidly became a trans-Appalachian extension

6

of the Upland South. It formed a crescent reaching from north central Maryland south to North Carolina and southern Indiana.[5] In this northern movement most settlers lived for a time in Kentucky before crossing the Ohio into Indiana.

In the early part of this century large bodies of folk song were collected from those who had remained in the isolated Southern Uplands. The singing of ballads and other folk songs was an integral part of these people's lives, as it had been in that of the Scotch-Irish and English yeomen whose descendants formed the bulk of this population. They sang not only the old ballads but also newly invented ones. However, in the most famous collection of this period, Cecil Sharp's *English Folk Songs from the Southern Appalachians*, one can find primarily ballads and lyric folk songs which were English in origin.

Upland singing which has been recorded is often characterized by an ornamented style not caught in Sharp's transcriptions, which were made by ear rather than from recordings. This song repertory and style, like other aspects of upland culture, flowed across the Cumberland Gap with the migrants following the Wilderness Trail to Boonesboro, to Lexington, to the northern bluegrass region, and finally into Indiana.

Some migrants from New York and Pennsylvania reached southern Indiana by floating down the Ohio River. Others from the Middle Atlantic and New England states moved westward into Indiana either cross-country or through the Great Lakes. Most of the latter settled in the north of the state, but some moved south, following the White River and minor drainage areas into the southeastern part of the state.[6]

According to the 1850 census only 7 percent of the inhabitants of the Hoosier state had been born abroad, principally Germans, farmers and craftsmen, and Irish, primarily diggers of canals and layers of rails.[7] In most cases these immigrants soon blended with the English and Scotch-Irish, and the population of Indiana remained remarkably homogenous for the remainder of the century, receiving fewer immigrants from abroad than almost any other state. In 1880, when Indiana ranked sixth in population among the states, foreign born made up only 7.3 percent of the population, contrasting with 44 percent of foreign born in Wisconsin, 24 percent in Michigan, 23 percent in Illinois, and 14 percent in Ohio. Although immigration into the United States raised to flood tide, the percentage of foreign born in Indiana actually decreased. In 1920 Indiana had the lowest proportion of foreign born of any state in the Union.

This continued homogeneity of the population undoubtedly had the effect of preserving cultural conservatism, including the retention of customs and oral traditions such as songs and stories. The strength of this phenomenon can be measured by the fact that even today southern Indiana displays more southern cultural influence than any of its neighboring northern states. In establishing a general boundary between southern and northern speech habits, linguists follow the Mason-Dixon line west and then generally the Ohio River, but as it reaches Indiana the line moves considerably northward and then returns to the Ohio through the Little Egypt region of Illinois. Thus in most dialect maps the boundary delimiting north and south in Indiana has an apex-like contour. However, Craig Carver finds the region to be a transitional zone. Although culturally and linguistically it is part of what he terms "the lower North," he recognizes a linguistic extension of "the upper South" into this region which he dubs "the Hoosier Apex." It should be noted that Carver's conclusions are based upon word count and lexicon rather than accent, although boundaries based upon the latter linguistic feature usually roughly parallel those of the former.

In Fig. 2 the Hoosier Apex as drawn by Carver has been enlarged and superimposed upon a map of Indiana. On this map only the towns and localities where the singers represented in this volume were recorded are indicated. It can be seen that all of these fall within the Hoosier Apex.[8]

Short biographies of thirty-one of the singers whose songs are included in this volume follow. Singers with family connections are grouped together. Only two children, each of whom sang several songs, are included. I have no biographical data concerning children who sang only one song or who sang as a member of a group.

In each case I have endeavored to provide some family history or genealogy which might explain how or why the singer acquired the particular repertory of song he or she possessed.

Whenever documentation accompanied the recordings on deposit in the Archives of Traditional

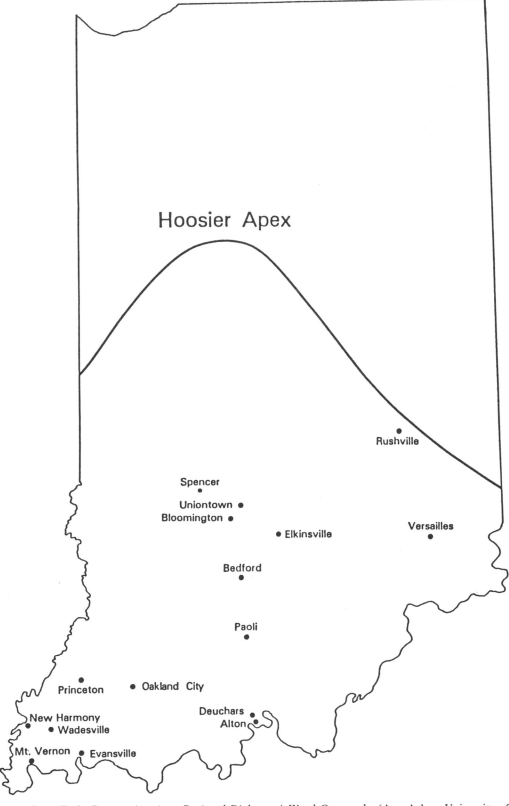

Hoosier Apex

Rushville

Spencer

Uniontown

Bloomington

Elkinsville

Versailles

Bedford

Paoli

Princeton

Oakland City

Deuchars

New Harmony

Alton

Wadesville

Mt. Vernon

Evansville

Adapted from Craig Carver, *American Regional Dialects: A Word Geography* (Ann Arbor: University of Michigan Press, 1987), 348

Fig. 2

9

Music, whether written or in the form of interviews within the recordings themselves, this has been partially incorporated into the bio-histories given below. Thus material has been taken from the notes, some fairly full but often scanty, made by Alan Lomax during his 1938 field expedition into southern Indiana, from the extensive interviews in Herbert Halpert's 1941 recordings, from the descriptive notes provided by Guthrie T. Meade for his recordings of 1956 and 1960, and from the excellent notes accompanying Pat Dunford's and Arthur Rosenbaum's 1964 Folkways album *Fine Times at Our House*.[9] The recordings made in 1955 by Bruce Buckley and Bruno Nettl unfortunately only include announcements of place, date, name of the singer, and titles of the songs sung.

Without exception, I have added some material concerning each singer in addition to that offered by the collectors. At times my contribution forms the bulk of the bio-history offered. A small part of my information has been secured from published sources, but most is based upon correspondence and recorded interview either in person or by telephone with those singers who are still alive and in other cases with close relatives, descendants, or friends. Memory is fallible, and it cannot be assumed that every detail offered here is historically accurate. Nevertheless, it is my hope that these short bio-histories will not only offer the reader some perspective concerning the personality of each singer presented but also will assist in placing the songs in their social and historical context, and thus make them more meaningful.

Although the information was not given to me in confidence, as a matter of courtesy I am not including in the following bio-histories material concerning the activities of individuals whom the families considered to be "black sheep." One of the singers, for example, spent considerable time in a penitentiary. Then there was the grandfather, a teacher who "jumped the fence" with an eighth-grade pupil, leaving his wife "flat." The father of another was a "woods colt," a local term applied to a child born out of wedlock. Then there is the grandfather who was a preacher and who "became disillusioned with religion, turned around and made very embarrassing remarks about anyone who had any faith. He took up the promotion of Russian philosophy and Communism and made speeches all over the country and embarrassed us to death."

BRYANT: Bryant, Mary Vandora McNeely (1876-1948) TR 12, 76, 82, 84, 96; Frazier (Scales), Esther Bryant (1901-   ) TR 78; (Clemens), Kathleen Bryant (1903-   ) TR 91; Niemeyer (Daganhart), Ethel Bryant (1913-   ) TR 59.

When on 8 April 1938 Alan Lomax walked into the comfortable, pleasant home of Thomas M. Bryant on East Gum Street in Evansville he found more music than he had anticipated. He and his wife, Elizabeth, were on a field trip collecting folk songs for the Archive of American Folk Song of the Library of Congress. They had come to see Mrs. Bryant at the recommendation of Paul Brewster, to whom she had sent many texts of British and American ballads which she sang and which he later published in his *Ballads and Songs of Indiana* (1940). Besides Mrs. Bryant there were her husband, who played the fiddle, and three of her four daughters, who sang ballads they had learned from their mother.

Lomax set up his Presto instantaneous disc machine, plugged in the microphone, placed an acetate disc on the turntable, and began to record. Song succeeded song, intermixed with an occasional fiddle tune until late in the morning. Lomax returned again on 11 April, and when he left he still felt that there were more ballads that Dora, as she was usually called, could have sung for him. Actually, he had recorded twenty-eight songs, of which a dozen or so were old British ballads and of which at least three were fairly well known American ballads.

Dora told Lomax that she had never been a good singer and that her family never allowed her to sing when she was young. She had learned the songs from her mother and aunts and had always sung them around the house under her breath. This no longer applied when she had her own family. In the house on Gum Street two of her daughters, who were divorced, had their children with them so she sang not only to her daughters but also to her grandchildren.

Esther's daughter, Patsy Kixmiller of Evansville, remembers well Dora Bryant's ballad singing. Dora often sang ballads to the children as lullabies. "Some of the songs were absolutely, Oh, my! they were brutal and harsh," she told me. "But when she sang them they were beautiful lullabies." Asked about this, Esther said that Dora's songs always seemed to deal with death. "People drowned, froze, were stabbed, or had their heads cut off with a sword. I don't think we thought much about the words. They were lullabies, they just put you to sleep at night."

11

Dora's parents, Elijah Allen McNeely (1854-1904) and Lucinda Adaline Camp McNeely (1858-1927) had six children, four girls and two boys, all musically inclined. Her brother, Dale, for example, was a folk guitarist who accompanied himself while singing ballads. Dora was born and reared on a farm near Tennyson in Warrick County, where her father was not only a farmer but also a justice of the peace. Her mother was reared in Spurgeon in Pike County, daughter of Andrew Jackson Camp (1834-1866) and Hannah Louisa Powers McNeely (1839-1907). The family later moved to Linsville in Warrick County, where the father died and Hannah married William Stephen Cox (1835-1916) in 1868.

According to Russell Bufkins, son of Dora's sister, Nellie Viola McNeely Bufkins, Dora and his mother learned their ballads from their mother, Lucinda, and their aunts, and in particular from Lucinda's half sister, Mary Jane Cox. Lucinda and Mary Jane in turn learned their ballads from their mother, Hannah. Dora, at least, also learned songs from her stepgrandfather, Stephen Cox. When Lucinda came visiting she would sing ballads to the Bryant family. She mailed many written variants of the songs as she sang them to Dora, as did Mary Jane Cox.

Russell Bufkins recalls as a six- or seven-year-old hearing Nellie and Lucinda, his mother and grandmother, singing as they quilted. The songs he remembers them singing are "Barb'ry Allan" (Child 74, TR 80-82), "The Two Lovers" or "The Cambric Shirt" (Child 2, TR 46), "Charles Giteau" (Laws AM E 11, TR 102), and "Young Charlotte" (Laws AM G 17, TR 91-92). He also remembers their singing some "commercial songs." According to Esther Scales, Dora and her daughters sang "After the Ball Is Over" and "She's Only a Bird in a Gilded Cage," both popular songs of the latter part of the nineteenth century. Later came "St. Louis Blues," "The Birmingham Jail," and "St. James Infirmary." Esther does not specify whether these "blues" were sung by both Dora and her daughters or by the latter only, which seems more likely. Patsy, Esther's daughter, remembers her mother singing "St. James Infirmary" to her as a lullaby.

Dora's husband, Thomas M. Bryant, was his mother's fifth child, and she died at his birth. He was reared by a stepmother and two sisters. He worked on his brother's farms, and his children helped. "We always had gardens to hoe, animals to feed, pumpkin seeds to plant, walking behind the corn planter, and plenty of white beans, potatoes, and corn bread and milk to eat. That's the reason

12

for our long lives," Esther Scales wrote to me in March 1988. At that time her brother, Clarence, was ninety-one and the three sisters were eighty-seven, eighty-five, and seventy-five, respectively. "We were poor," she wrote, "but we didn't know it."

The children attended elementary school in Oakland City, and later their father became a blacksmith and horse trader, and the family moved to Evansville, where the children attended high school. Thomas soon had to give up his horses, however, and went to work at the Hercules Buggy Plant. When Lomax visited them they had lived in Evansville for approximately twenty-three years. He noted that all four daughters were working as "cashiers, stenographers, etc." Thomas did not sing ballads. He preferred fiddling, but his brothers had reputations as singers.

Neither Thomas nor Dora Bryant read music, but their eldest child, Clarence, studied music at Oakland City College and at the State College at Terre Haute. For a while he was choir director of the First Baptist Church in Evansville, where for years all the Bryant girls sang in the choir. In addition, Ethel performed with a local band and on the local radio station, WGBF, as the "Baby Blue Blonde," making her broadcast debut with the song "My Man," popularized by Fanny Brice. During Lomax's recording sessions the girls sang from written copies, but Dora sang her ballads from memory.

Russell Bufkins, who holds a B.A. in history from Indiana University, has traced the McNeely family back to Barra and Gigha, both islands in Scotland. The family was a member of the clan McNeil. Later the family settled in Northern Ireland, in County Antrim near Carrickfergus. Starting about the middle of the seventeenth century, the Scotch-Irish began to migrate to America, many of them settling in Lancaster and York counties in Pennsylvania. Between 1734 and 1736 Reverend Michael Wood brought a group of families into Albemarle and Augusta counties, Virginia. Robert McNeely, who died in Albemarle County in 1757, was among Michael Wood's Presbyterian flock.

From Albemarle and Augusta counties the McNeelys moved south to Botetourt County, Virginia, where they appear in the militia list of 1782-83. They probably moved to Madison County, Kentucky, about 1786. An ancestor, John McNeely, appears in Madison and Lincoln County tax lists but vanishes after 1810. About 1815 or 1816 George McNeely, his wife, Sarah, and his unmarried children moved from Logan County, Kentucky, to Spencer County, Indiana. The McNeelys' great-grandfather, William Barnett

13

McNeely, is shown in the 1820 census a few names from Thomas Lincoln's family. There is no record of family members having known young Abe, but it is possible that they did. Lucinda Adaline Camp's parents also came to Indiana by the Appalachian-Virginia-Kentucky route.

COLLIER, John William (n.d.) TR 65.

Lomax met Collier in the office of the Federal Recreation Project in Bloomington. The project was sponsoring square dances, handicrafts, and other forms of amusement around the city. For this purpose the project had gathered together a group of folk musicians of whom John W. Collier was one. He told Lomax that he had been a fiddler "all his life" and that for fifteen years he had worked with "a colored minstrel show" in which he was "end man, rattle bones, tambourine, and violinist." The show had taken him through the small towns of forty states.

Lomax described him as "a wizened fellow of about forty years," but when he asked Collier where he had "found" a song which he sang Collier replied, "Where did I find it? In the sticks, in Jackson County, Indiana. I made that song thirty-five years ago."

Bramble Stogdill, one of Collier's cousins, referred to Collier as "John Will." I interviewed Bramble at the home of Mr. and Mrs. Robert Allender in Monroe County during one of his occasional visits to the area in June 1988. Born and reared in Brown County, Bramble had left for the West in 1920 and at the time lived in Fresno, California. Although ninety-one years of age, he had vivid recollections of his youth in Brown County. Bramble's father, James Stogdill, had two brothers, one of whom, Marion, was also recorded by Lomax (see STOGDILL), and four sisters. One of these sisters, Sarah, married Richard Collier and moved to Jackson County where John Will was born in Vallonia.

John W. Collier married Jemena Akers in 1896. They had four children: Alvin (b. 1901); twins Marshall and Herschel (b. 1906); and Etta (b. 1909). His wife died soon after the birth of Etta, and Collier reared the children himself.

According to Mrs. Leona (Paul) Stogdill of Freetown, daughter of Mrs. Hettie Collier Fields, a half sister of John W. Collier, "John was self-taught on playing musical instruments and taught his sons to play also." Another daughter of Hettie Collier Fields, Mrs. Ursula (John) Scott of Brownstown,

14

remembers that her Uncle John was on the go and never had anything. He and his family would live with them when they were in these parts. She said that in the 1920s and 1930s her Uncle John and his children would put out a cup on the street in Brownstown and would play for the money that people would put in the cup.

Bramble Stogdill recalls Collier and his children visiting the Stogdill family in Brown County for about a week when Bramble was a child of seven or eight. Some of Collier's children were about his age. Collier had never learned to read or write, but according to Bramble he was a fine fiddler. He had taught his three boys to play on cigar box fiddles and his little girl to play the triangle. They played every night for the Stogdills while they were staying there and, according to Bramble, played "almost everywhere." Since Collier no longer had a wife, he apparently took the children traveling with him. "Dad said he would never amount to nothing because all he does is play music." And while they were visiting, Bramble's father asked Collier, "How do you get by on the train?"

"Well," said Collier, "I get my fiddle out and go to playing and send my little girl down the line to get a collection. Sometimes we got more money than the fare cost." According to Bramble, Collier's little girl played the beat on a small triangle when the group played or when she was making a collection.

The story goes that John Will could play anything on the fiddle after he had first heard it. Some time before the First World War he went to an old fiddler's contest in Chicago. After playing everything they had requested, they placed a piece of music in front of him. He could not read it, so he asked them to tell him what it was and he would play it. They disqualified him for being unable to read.

Bramble thought that John Will had died somewhere around Brownstown in Jackson County, but I have been unable to verify this. Collier had told Lomax that he was born in Jackson County, was raised partially in Brown County, and that his ancestors had come from Scotland where they were shepherds. They had first moved to Virginia and then to Kentucky where his father was born and, finally, to Jackson County, Indiana.

CURRY: Curry, Patricia "Patty" Elaine (1947-   ) TR 14, 15, 18, 19; Curry, Orpha Mae Hopper (1913-   ) TR 3.

In August of 1955 while I was living on East Second Street in Bloomington I invited a number of neighborhood children to come into my home for a recording session. Of all the children, Patty knew the greatest number of songs and was the most ready to sing them for me. A number of these are included in Chapter 2. Toward the end of the session her mother, Orpha Mae Curry, came in and at my request sang "Two Babes in the Woods" (TR 2-3), which she said she had learned from her father. The songs I recorded from Patty were both those that she had learned on the playground from other children and those she had learned in school. I have not included the latter.

Both Patty and her mother were born in Bloomington. Patty's father, James Ralph Curry (1916-   ), comes from a family of old settlers in Bloomington. Orpha Mae's parents were born in Brown County but married in Bloomington. Orpha Mae Hopper and James Ralph Curry were married in 1940. After several periods of separation they were divorced in the late 1970s.

Patty was attending Elm Heights School at the time that I recorded her. She graduated from University High School and received a B.A. from Indiana University with a double major in English and French in 1968, and later her M.A. in English. In 1973 she received a Ph.D. in political philosophy, also from Indiana University.

She has been a member of the faculties of Georgetown University, University of Indianapolis, Purdue University, Indiana University at Indianapolis, and the University of Houston. While in Houston in 1988 she was in a severe automobile accident and is still partly incapacitated and undergoing physical therapy in Bloomington.

Orpha Mae Curry joined the staff of Indiana University in 1936 and was a member of the university staff for forty-four years, taking off six years to have Patty and take care of her during her early years. While at the university she held a number of responsible positions, including administrative secretary of the president's office, office superintendent in the chancellor's office, and administrative secretary in continuing education. She retired from the university in 1984.

Her husband, James Curry, also held positions of trust at Indiana University. From 1946 through 1952 he was an assistant manager of the Indiana Memorial Union and from 1958 through 1970 was controller of inventory successively in the controller's and accountant's offices. He was also known as a jazz trumpet player and played professionally with the Bourbon Philharmonic in Indianapolis.

Orpha Mae Hopper Curry is the daughter of Gurnie E. Hopper (1890-1949) and Cora Eunice Wyse (1889-1918). They married in Bloomington in 1911. Cora Wyse died during the influenza epidemic of 1918 and left four children, three girls and a boy, the eldest Orpha Mae, being six years of age. In 1919 Orpha Mae's father, Gurnie, married Edith Guy Hazel who, according to information available, had been married to a lineman for the electric company who had been electrocuted at work. She brought one son to the marriage. Thus Orpha Mae was raised in a family including a number of stepchildren.

Gurnie's father, William Marmaduke Hopper (c. 1832-1901), was a schoolteacher who was instrumental in incorporating the village of Nashville. He separated from his first wife, Nancy, whom he had brought with him from Noble County, Ohio, and around 1878 married Martha Emmaline Percifield, who was Gurnie's mother. Cora Wyse's mother was Cordelia Arnes, date of marriage to Ben Wyse unknown. In 1892 Cordelia married Myars Bush (what happened to Ben Wyse is not known), so Orpha Mae's mother, Cora, was also a stepchild.

Among the Hoppers who were the offspring of William Marmaduke's first marriage were twins Mildred Lucille and Mark. Mildred played the guitar and had a fine soprano voice. She sang at musical gatherings at home, at musical plays, and in church. She had a miscellaneous repertory, which of the ballad tradition included only "Two Babes in the Woods." Other songs she sang seemed to be of Irish or Western extraction. Brother Mark was also very musical and composed ballads. He conducted the town band, consisting mainly of his seven children, which played at parades and other musical festivities.

William Marmaduke Hopper was the son of James and Margaret Hopper of Sharon Village, Noble County, Ohio. He was first active as a blacksmith but in the census of 1870 gave his occupation as engineer. By the 1860 census he had moved to the Belmont area of Brown County with his wife, Nancy, and several children. His father, James, had come to Noble County in 1830 as a blacksmith. According to the first National Census of 1790, James's father, Robert, had lived in Prince Georges County, Maryland, before moving to Ohio where he bought one hundred acres on Wheeling Creek, Belmont County. The

17

Hoppers' ultimate American ancestor is believed to be a Marmaduke Hopper who was transported as an indentured servant in the 1660s, thus required to give three years of free labor to the individual who paid his passage. The middle name, Marmaduke, was common among the Hoppers. Not only was the grandfather named William Marmaduke but also his son, his grandson, and his great-grandson. According to a British book of Christian names, Marmaduke is primarily a Yorkshire name first recorded in the *Domesday Book* and is believed to be derived from one of two Celtic names, Maolmadoc, "servant of Madoc," or Meriadoc, "sea leader." The popularity of the name in Northern England indicates a strong survival of Celtic stock there.

(Much of this information was obtained from an article by Dick Hopper in the *Indianapolis Star* of 18 March 1984.)

DICKEY, Quentin Lotus (1911-1989) TR 70, 71.

Lotus, as everyone called him, was a folk fiddler and singer, and he could chord on the guitar. He lived in a log cabin on a small farm in Orange County, six miles southeast of Paoli on the top of Grease Gravy Hill on Grease Gravy Road. Lotus had a large repertory of songs, most of which he learned from his father, and he composed his own as well. In 1981 he was "discovered" by an active folklorist, Dillon Bustin, who has published a book on folklore in Brown County.[10] According to Lotus, Bustin launched him on his present semiprofessional career, performing at state parks, folk festivals, and workshops in Indiana, Massachusetts, Washington, and California. He also appeared in a film made by Bustin. In addition, Lotus received two grants from the Indiana Committee for the Arts, one to record the songs he had learned from his father and the other to record his own songs.

In selecting material for this volume, I discovered that the Archives of Traditional Music had no representation of a common genre of the last century, songs protesting drunkenness, such as "The Drunkard's Dream," "The Drunkard's Wife," "The Drunkard's Doom," etc. We had recordings of these songs from other states but not from Indiana.

Several individuals suggested that I get in touch with Lotus Dickey, which I did by telephone. He, indeed, knew "The Drunkard's Dream," having heard his father sing it many times. Lotus had memorized one stanza of the text and had the remainder written down. He said that his father had used two tunes in singing the song, so he sang the song over the telephone for me, each time employing a different tune. I asked him if he would then sing the entire song for me to both tunes if I would send him a cassette. He readily agreed to do so. Some time after I had received this cassette he telephoned me to tell me that he had remembered a third melody, which was the one that his father had most commonly sung the song to. He again sang a stanza over the telephone, and finding this melody more interesting than the other ones I requested that he sing the song again to this melody, which he was quite willing to do. A few days later he and Dillon Bustin dropped into my office with the new recording.

Lotus Dickey was a modest, generous man who was continually apologizing for his lack of "training," as though this were a necessity for a folk musician. His father sang ballads and taught his children the rudiments of music, primarily from old hymnals which he called "gospels." His mother also sang, and between them they managed all the parts. His sister, Bunnie, fifteen years his senior, could read the music and play it on the old pump organ. "Just sort of singing was a way of life when we had idle time, winter nights after work, Sundays, etc."

Lotus was the fifth and youngest child of Marion Dickey (1860-1952) and his second wife, Sarah Jane (Jennie) Reck (1873-1961). Marion was born in Darke County, Ohio, near North Star, and was reared on an eighty-acre farm belonging to his father. Lotus's mother was born near Clinton, Missouri, and moved to Ohio with her parents when she was two. They were married in 1896. They moved to Alexandria, Indiana, and then to Muncie, where Marion worked in a rolling mill. When this factory moved to Middletown, he followed it. After Marion worked in two other factories, the family moved south and settled on a small farm near Paoli, where they grew strawberries and weathered the depression. Lotus walked two miles to elementary school and five and a half miles to high school in Paoli. After graduating from high school he worked in a sweatshop making baskets. Later he worked in construction in Bloomington.

Lotus married Dorothy May Johnson in 1943 in English, Crawford County. His wife was born in 1927 on Rock Castle Creek near Livingston, Kentucky. Her father, Nelson Johnson, was born in 1897 in

Bell County in the Kentucky mountains and reached age ninety-one in 1988. He married Matilda Jane Summers (1901-1987). After their marriage they resided in Bell County and in Harlan, Kentucky. When Dorothy May was nine or ten years of age, they moved to Crawford County, Indiana, near a little town called Fredonia, overlooking the Ohio River.

Lotus and Dorothy May had eight children, six boys and two girls. Dorothy May died in 1972. Lotus did not remarry. As of 1988, he had twenty-eight grandchildren and seven great-grandchildren.

Lotus's ancestry is primarily English, German, and Irish. According to Lotus, his earliest ancestor named Dickey was born in England in the 1700s and emigrated to the American colonies, possibly settling first in Florida (a British possession from 1763 to 1783). He then moved to Kentucky and helped Daniel Boone in the settlement of Boonesboro in 1775. Following this he fought in the Revolutionary War against the British, riding with the brigade of Henry "Light-Horse Harry" Lee, the father of Robert E. His son, Alexander Dickey, probably born around 1790 in Kentucky, died in Ohio in 1877.

On Lotus's mother's paternal line, Christian Reck, born between 1710 and 1720, emigrated from the Palatinate or Gutenburg to the colonies with his sixteen-year-old son, Christian, Jr., and settled in Pennsylvania. His grandson, Samuel Reck (1809-1883) moved from Adams County, Pennsylvania, to Darke County, Ohio. A further descendant, William Henry Harrison Reck (1837-1909), served in the Civil War, enlisting on the Northern side in 1861. He married Catherine Murphy (1838-1915). Catherine's paternal ancestor, given name not known, emigrated from Northern Ireland to Montgomery County, Ohio, in the 1700s.

DIXON, Samuel Clay (1901-1978) TR 1, 2, 8, 37, 89.

One of the singers Lomax had been advised to contact during his field trip in Indiana was Samuel Clay Dixon of Mount Vernon. He finally found Clay, as he was usually called, at choir practice at a German Lutheran school in the country and recorded quite a bit of Clay's large repertory. Clay was the oldest of eight children, two boys and six girls, all of whom were reared on a large farm in Posey County near Mount Vernon. Clay's father, General Grant Dixon, had inherited the farm from his grandfather, also Samuel Clay Dixon, who had homesteaded the land when General Grant was five. When

General Grant was old enough to take over, the grandfather moved to Mount Vernon, where he was active in politics and was sheriff for many years.

General Grant Dixon was a successful farmer who took pride in providing for his family. Those who wanted to take piano lessons were given the opportunity, and those who wished to attend college were helped. Clay attended Evansville College for three years and then began to teach in the rural schools near Mount Vernon.

He married Fannie Carl Schwinn (1900-1985), who was born in Boonville, Indiana, a daughter of Charles Schwinn and Susan Burris Schwinn. Fannie's father was a coal miner and then the keeper of a general store. Her mother became ill early in life, and Fannie stayed home to take care of her. Thus she did not graduate from high school until she was twenty-one. After two years of study at the State Teachers College at Terre Haute she also began to teach school. She and Clay met while teaching in a rural school in Mars Township, Posey County. They had one child, Sue Carol, now Mrs. Becknell of El Paso, Texas.

In 1988 Mrs. Winola Dixon Henry of Harper Woods, Michigan, was the only survivor of General Grant's eight children. She had left home in 1934. According to Winola it was a family custom in the summertime to gather on the front porch after all the chores were done and to relax by singing. The family was musical, and the family members would sing in harmony by ear. Clay could accompany with guitar or banjo, both of which he played well, mouth organ, or almost any other instrument he could pick up. The family sang old popular songs such as "Tenting Tonight on the Old Camp Ground," "She's Only a Bird in a Gilded Cage," "A Bicycle Built for Two," and songs commonly sung in harmony such as "Down by the Old Mill Stream" and "Sweet Adeline," as well as an occasional old folk song like "Old Dan Tucker." Two of Clay's favorites were "Whoa, Mule, Whoa" and "Where Has My Little Dog Gone?"

Clay learned many of his songs from his mother and his grandmother, Missouri David Lilleston, who lived with the family for many years. Concerning the latter, Winola wrote:

> She became widowed during the Civil War and lived in a little town called West Franklin. During the war, Morgan's Raiders would cross over the Ohio River and ravage the area where she lived. The residents would hide out in the hills--she got weary of this and refused to leave her home. The Raiders came and she was

asked to cook for the officers, which she did, and when they left, they supplied her with ham, bacon, vegetables, etc. and instead of being molested, she thought she was more blessed.

Winola remembers being rocked to sleep by her mother, Lulu Lilleston, with "Go Tell Aunt Rhody" (TR 1) and "Two Babes in the Woods" (Child ESB, The Children in the Wood, TR 2-3). "I rocked my child and grandchildren to 'The Wyoming Lullaby' and 'Poor Babes in the Woods' many, many times. A few tears would be shed over 'Poor Babes in the Woods' but still they would insist upon hearing it."

Clay was a bit of a comedian, and in high school he did an act in blackface, accompanying himself upon the banjo at a high school fair. A scout from Field's Minstrels was there and offered him a job, but his parents would not let him go. "But this gave him ideas, and he formed a group of his own and every winter for a number of years they would put on a minstrel that would run for two or three nights. It was an event that was looked forward to by the public."

Clay, his younger brother, two of his sisters, and his mother were in great demand to sing at church affairs throughout the area. "Of all the relations," Winola wrote me, "our family had the talent. Those that had piano lessons were all talented at playing by ear. One sister in particular could hear a song and then play it by ear."

According to Sue Carol, Clay's daughter who was born in 1937, both her mother and her mother's sister, Anna, also sang as well as played the piano. "Singing was a tradition in both families. It seemed that they could never, ever, ever get together without singing. . . . They always sang at Christmases . . . and Sunday family reunions. They always wound up singing. It was mostly done by ear . . . they all sang and had a really wonderful time."

Clay had been a member of the National Guard and entered the army when the Guard was mobilized in 1941. After a short period of service in Mississippi, he was sent to Officers Training School in Florida, then assigned to camp duty in Wisconsin. There followed occupation duty in Yokohama, Japan, and stints at camps in El Paso, Texas, and Anchorage, Alaska. Wherever he went his family went with him. He retired from the army at the rank of major with a medical discharge in 1955, and the family returned to Indiana, all three members attending college.

Clay went to Evansville College to finish his bachelor's degree, Fannie completed her junior year at the State Teachers College at Terre Haute, and their daughter, Sue, went for her freshman year at Indiana University at Bloomington. The next year they all enrolled at Terre Haute, remaining there until Clay had his M.A. and his wife her bachelor's degree. They then moved to Evansville where Sue finished her bachelor's degree. In 1959 Clay and Fannie moved to El Paso to teach in that school system and Sue to teach in Colorado.

Neither Clay nor Fannie did much with music after they began teaching in El Paso. Clay taught science and math in Henderson Junior School. Only Sue to some extent continued the family singing tradition by teaching many of the old songs and accompanying them on the guitar. The two lullabies Sue remembers Clay singing to her are "Go Tell Aunt Rhody" and "The Wyoming Lullaby."

Marion Oschmann, whose mother was Clay's sister, sent me the following genealogical information which he culled from her scrapbook. According to his mother, the family's ancestry was a mixture of Scottish and German. Dixon was originally "Dickson," and the Dicksons were a branch of the Keith clan. The family's earliest traced ancestor, Hendrich Casselberry, came to the United States from Germany before 1691 and died in 1729. A further German ancestor, Paul Casselberry, born in 1767 in Montgomery County, Pennsylvania, moved to Indiana in 1806. In the South another ancestor, Charles Carson (possibly an English name), served in the Revolutionary War as an ensign in a Virginia regiment. Originally from Delaware, he moved to Virginia in 1793 and then to Indiana in 1806. A Samuel L. Dixon, who was born in 1805 in North Carolina, also moved to Indiana, and at one point he was a colonel in the Indiana Infantry. Samuel L. Dixon married Paul Casselberry's daughter Elizabeth. Clay's grandfather was a son of this union and was married to Mary Carson. His maternal grandfather was Samuel Lilleston.

DODSON, Viola (1860-1952) TR 93.

Mrs. Dodson told Lomax that she had learned her songs from schoolgirls she had taught in Rummersfield, Bradford County, Pennsylvania, fifty years before he visited her in Bloomington. She was seventy-eight at the time he recorded her, so she would have been in her late twenties when she taught at that school. She sang her songs from written copies.

Her daughter, Mrs. Estella Dodson Stevenson, was at the time a WPA field-worker and was later assistant music librarian at Indiana University. In May 1988 I located Mrs. Stevenson at the Bloomington Convalescent Center, but she was too ill to be interviewed. She apparently had no living descendants since her card was marked "no family."

ELLIOTT, "Aunt" Phoebe Stoker (1855-1940) TR 4, 6, 9, 10, 11, 42.

Of his visit to New Harmony in 1938 Lomax wrote, "The oldest living inhabitant, 'Aunt' Phoebe Elliott, still vigorous and witty at eighty-four, treated Elizabeth and myself to a glass of cherry wine and several beautiful songs." As a precocious child of five, she had a short period of schooling during which, according to Lomax, she had learned to cross-stitch, to sing songs concerning the multiplication table and the capitals of the states, and nothing much else. However, she made up for her restricted education by omnivorous reading and by keeping up with current events and politics. Lomax commented on the considerable size and variety of the library in her little home.

"Aunt" Phoebe's paternal grandfather, Benjamin Stoker, Sr., had emigrated from Virginia to Gibson County, Kentucky, and then to Posey County, Indiana. Her parents, Benjamin Cooper Stoker, Jr., and Malinda Aldridge, had five children, only two of whom, Phoebe and Mary D., survived infancy. Phoebe married Charles D. Elliott, who had served as a captain in the Civil War and who died in 1927. They had two sons, Willard and Charlie, both of whom died in 1942.

"Aunt" Phoebe was an original. Born in New Harmony, she lived most of her life in a log cabin built by her father in 1838. The small, one-story structure was later covered with clapboard but not otherwise modernized. Its inhabitant was a participant in most of the activities of the community, including those of the New Harmony Thespian and Literary societies. For years she wrote a weekly column, mostly concerning her personal activities, for the *New Harmony Times*. The following is an excerpt from an article about Mrs. Elliott which appeared in that newspaper on 25 November 1933.

> Modern standardization has not spoiled her. She has not permitted a dubious progress to mould her into a conformity of habit of mind or of speech. This dear little woman, whose features hold not only the charm of an old daguerreotype, but also the impish eagerness of Puck, has a magnetism felt by old and young alike.
> New Harmony neighbors and many from Evansville, St. Louis, Mount Vernon, New-

burg and numerous other towns seek her society. What is this rare quality belonging to Aunt Phoebe[?] It is something intangible but nevertheless compelling. Why do people of all ages and conditions count themselves fortunate if numbered among her friends? She does not barter rare viands or luxurious household gadgets in return for their attentions. In her modest frame dwelling, frankly devoid of electricity and plumbing, is found a simple table of plain wholesome food.

If you have been among her friends you will remember their freely flowing laughter, and the obvious enjoyment of the lady of the house.

FIELDS, Albert Jeremiah (1879-1966) TR 48, 49, 50, 83.

Albert J. Fields was born in Lawrence County in a log house built in 1817 by his great-grandfather, George Sheeks. The house was located near the present Spring Mill State Park and has since been moved and preserved as part of Spring Mill Village.

He graduated from the Indiana University Law School in 1904 and began practice in Bedford in September of that year. The same year, as a volunteer coach, he organized the first basketball team at Bedford High School, and for three years his teams were undefeated.

In 1910 he was elected mayor of Bedford and was reelected in 1914. He was the first mayor of either party to be reelected and to bring a Democratic council in with him. Among his achievements as mayor were the installation of the first modern water purification system and the establishment of the first city park. He also served for thirteen years as Bedford City Attorney and was admitted to practice before the Supreme Court. Although he never again sought elective office, he remained active in city and county affairs. He was one of the founders of the committee that initiated the movement which resulted in the acquisition of Spring Mill State Park.

He married Alma Doris Braden in 1915. They had two daughters, Eleanor and Nancy, both of whom became attorneys.

His paternal ancestor, Jeremiah Fields, emigrated from England to what is now North Carolina in 1765. The family resided in Rowan and Guilford counties in the Piedmont region of North Carolina. Jeremiah's grandson, Absalom, who was born about 1788, migrated to Lawrence County, Indiana, in 1817 and was one of the earliest settlers in the county. He was Albert's great-grandfather. His ancestors on his mother's side also came from Rowan County, North Carolina. His maternal great-grandfather, George Sheeks, was born there in 1744 and also moved to Indiana in 1817. George Sheeks's son, David L.

Sheeks, who was Albert J. Fields's maternal grandfather, owned a large portion of Lawrence County, at his death being the owner of four thousand acres of land.

I could find no record of ballad singing in the family, but considering their Southern Uplands history it must have existed. Nancy Fields Fadum, Albert's daughter, wrote me that she had no specific memory of her father singing ballads but noted that before she left home at age seventeen "we were very much into the age of radio at that time." She thinks it possible that her father learned the ballads from an uncle, William Fields, who was a well-known folk fiddler and the leader of a family band.

(Much of the information for this bio-history was taken from the following printed sources: *History of Lawrence and Monroe Counties*, 2 vols. [Indianapolis: B. F. Bowen & Co., 1914], 1:560-62 and the *Bedford Daily Times-Mail* of 26 and 27 May 1966.)

GARY, Abraham Lincoln (1868-1953) TR 38.

Abraham Lincoln Gary was born in a log cabin and reared on his family's farm in Rush County. His father was the Reverend Thomas B. Gary, a minister of the Methodist Episcopal church and a circuit rider who had charges throughout Wayne, Fayette, and Rush counties. His mother was Phoebe J. Ball of pioneer stock. The couple had nine children of whom Abraham Lincoln was the fifth.

He had his elementary schooling in the neighborhood's district school of Frog Pond and at the graded school at Carthage. He then attended the Cyrus Hodgin Normal School in Richmond, Indiana, and in the fall of 1886 began to teach school, farming in the summers. After a few years of teaching school he entered DePauw University and graduated in 1895. He earned part of the funds which enabled him to complete this degree acting as a guard at the World Columbian Exposition at Chicago in 1893.

In 1897 he was elected superintendent of schools in Rush County. He resigned this position in 1902 in order to take charge of the Indiana State Reading Circle in Indianapolis. (The Reading Circle was based on the Chautauqua method and was supported by the State Commission of Education as a means of further educating schoolteachers, particularly those living in rural districts. The teachers were assigned lists of books to read and later met in groups to discuss them.) Gary was manager of the Reading Circle for five years. During this period he also enrolled in the Indiana Law School, carrying on his studies and his Reading Circle work simultaneously. In 1907 he received his law degree and moved to Rushville, later taking as a junior partner Anna L. Bohannan. He continued his practice in that city until his death.

In 1908 he married Jessie E. Spann, daughter of Jesse J. Spann, a lawyer and former state senator. They had one child who died in infancy.

Gary was legal advisor to Wendell Willkie, Republican presidential candidate in 1940 under the slogan of "One World," and assisted him in the purchase and management of Rush County farmland.

On the maternal side Abraham Lincoln Gary was descended from an old colonial family. An ancestor of the Rush County Balls was Colonel Joseph Ball, one of the seven brothers who settled on the east bank of the Rappahannock River in Lancaster County, Virginia, in the early part of the seventeenth century. One of his descendants later moved to Washington County, Pennsylvania. Of this line a Jonathan Ball was born in Washington County in 1797 and in 1820 married Asenath Moore, who was born in the same county.

In the fall of 1836 Jonathan Ball, his wife, and seven children came to Indiana, driving an ox team and a "Democrat" wagon, arriving at Rushville after about four weeks of travel. For the first year in Rushville, Jonathan Ball, who had learned the tailor's trade, supported his family with his needle. Later he purchased a farm on Little Blue River, and by clearing the forest by day and working at his needle by night he gained further holdings until he possessed approximately a thousand acres. His daughter, Phoebe J., became Reverend Gary's wife and Abraham Lincoln Gary's mother.

(Much of the information for this bio-history was taken from A. L. Gary and E. B. Thomas (eds.), *Centennial History of Rush County, Indiana*, 2 vols. [Indianapolis: Historical Publishing Co., 1921], 2:440-42.)

HOSKINSON, Isabel Saulman (1911-   ) TR 22.

Isabel Saulman was born on a farm in Posey County that was the property of David Alcorn. Her father, Arthur Saulman, was a farm laborer who lived in the hired man's house along with his wife Eva, his children, and his wife's mother and sister. One day while working in the field Mr. Saulman had a sunstroke. The doctor who was called in said that he must never work in the field again, but must find another occupation.

Saulman's only work experience had been farming, but he thought he might turn that to advantage by becoming a veterinarian. Mr. Alcorn was a good friend and his wife a distant relative of the Saulman family, so he made it possible for Saulman to study toward this field at the no-longer-existent Terre Haute Veterinary College. Once Saulman had been certified as a veterinarian, he moved his house to the neighboring unincorporated village of Wadesville to begin his practice. Through this he was able little by little to repay Mr. Alcorn for his financial outlay in his behalf.

Isabel used to accompany her father on visits to the farms and at times helped him in one way or another. As she grew to maturity, she decided to become a nurse and acquired this profession by working her way through the Welborn Baptist Hospital in Evansville. A student at the Northern Baptist Seminary in Chicago, Charles Hoskinson, came once a month to Wadesville to serve the General Baptist Church. He stayed at the home of Mrs. Saulman, who by this time was a widow, and there met Isabel. The two were married, and after his graduation Hoskinson served in several pastorates and finally settled in St. Louis, where at the time of this writing he and his wife are retired.

Her daughter, Sara Hoskinson Frommer, lives in Bloomington and sang the children's song, "Playmate," for me. She said she had learned it from her mother, who in turn had learned it from her mother, Eva Saulman, who lived from 1882 to 1934. At my request Mrs. Hoskinson self-recorded the song on a cassette and sent it to me (TR 22).

KING (see SOUTH/KING)

KIRK, Jacob Oatman Forester (1872-1952) TR 87.

When Lomax visited him in Oakland City in 1938 Kirk gave his given names only as O. F. He was described by Lomax as "an old time Baptist minister who had been a very fine singer, particularly of religious songs, but when I met him he was quite faint voiced." Kirk knew only three songs that Lomax considered folk songs.

Kirk was born in Wheeling and died in Oakland City, both in Gibson County, Indiana. His first wife died of tuberculosis, and afterward he married Jennie Evans. They had no children but later adopted Victor M. Evans, Jennie's nephew, as a foster son. He had come from a broken home and was reared by his grandparents until they died and he was taken in by the Kirks. He now lives in Alexandria, Indiana.

According to Wendell P. Wiggs of Oakland City, who had known Kirk in the 1920s, the latter had been active as a minister, veterinarian, and justice of the peace. The first two professions were carried on in Union, Pike County. According to Victor Evans, at one point Kirk lived in and operated a general store in Effingham, Illinois, and then moved to Oakland City around 1918 where he "did some work as justice of the peace." Kirk never talked to Evans much concerning his past but did tell him that he had had an uncle who was a minister in southern Ireland.

LINDSEY, David (1891-1974) TR 74.

David Lindsey had been married four times, but when his obituary was published in the newspaper no family was mentioned. In 1956 I placed a notice in a column of the *Bloomington Herald-Telephone* in which I asked individuals who knew old songs and who would permit me to record them to contact me. Lindsey was one of those who did so. I recorded him singing two songs, both items from the nineteenth-century popular repertory. Lindsey lived in Spencer at the time, but had an insulation business in Bloomington.

Born in Ohio, he moved to Indiana where he had a somewhat varied career, mixing farming and business. Of his first two marriages, both of which ended in divorce, I know little except that he had a son named Harry from the first. Harry inherited a farm on Hardscrabble Road near Spencer from his father. In 1977, while living in Richmond, Virginia, he sold the farm to Don Thompson of Spencer. I was unable to locate Harry Lindsey in Richmond.

Charles D. Glass, a stepson of Lindsey's third marriage, told me that his mother married Lindsey in 1941 or 1942 in Anderson. Glass was in the third grade at the time. They moved to a farm north of Martinsville in Morgan County and remained there for two years while Lindsey continued his activities as a soap salesman in Anderson and elsewhere. They then moved to a farm near Quincy in Owen County and later to the farm on Hardscrabble Road. A year or two later Lindsey began an insulation business in Bloomington where he sold siding and other materials. His two stepsons from his third marriage managed the farm, raising cattle and selling timber. Both left the farm after graduating from high school, and in 1956 their mother divorced Lindsey.

He then married for a fourth time, this time to a woman who was a pianist. According to Don Thompson, for some time they operated a music store in Spencer at which pianos were sold and tuned and music lessons given. The tuning was done by a blind man who came down from Martinsville.

According to Charles Glass, Lindsey was survived by his fourth wife who buried him in Washington, Indiana, which was apparently her home.

LIST, Amanda Joan (1974-   ) TR 17, 26, 27, 28.

Mandie is my granddaughter. She was twelve when she was recorded in 1986 and at that time was in the seventh grade in Bachelor School in the Monroe County School District. However, she had learned the songs she sang for me at an earlier age while she was attending Harmony School, an alternative school in Bloomington.

MEADE, Guthrie T. (1932-1991) TR 57.

Gus Meade was born and reared in Louisville, Kentucky, and, like Arthur Rosenbaum, was as much, if not more, a collector than an informant. (The latter term is applied by folklorists to individuals whom they interview or record.) Both are products of the urban folk music revival movement of the 1950s (see p. 3). After completing high school in Louisville, Meade moved to Bloomington where he secured his B.A. in anthropology at Indiana University in 1958. He then began graduate work in the folklore program which, however, he did not complete. Instead he moved to Washington, D.C., where until his retirement he worked at the Library of Congress and the National Archives as a computer programmer and later as a systems analyst. At the Archives he developed a system for indexing, retrieving, and producing finding aids for research purposes.

Meade was working on a project which he began when he was in Bloomington, an annotated discography of traditional music from 1921 to 1942, supported by two grants received from the National Endowment for the Arts. This project consists of the listing of songs that he terms "traditional" found on country music recordings. For the last fifteen years he and a friend had been researching and recording fiddlers and fiddle music in Kentucky, where he moved after his retirement.

Upon my inquiry he wrote that "my ancestry is of the Heinz 57 variety." His father was born and reared in Henry County, Kentucky, and his father's parents and grandparents had resided there back to the early 1800s. His mother was born in Crawford County, Indiana, and lived an unsettled life in her early years, moving into localities in Kentucky and Tennessee until her mother died when she was twelve. Then she was sent to Arkansas where she was reared by an aunt. His maternal grandfather's family were Quakers who lived in Lynchburg, Virginia, and then moved to Grayson County, Kentucky. The "Heinz 57 variety" theme is illustrated by his father's ancestry, which is primarily Dutch, but also English, Welsh, Scottish, and Italian. His mother's ancestry is primarily English and Irish but also includes German, Swedish, and Amerindian. None can doubt that Gus Meade is truly American.

PARKS: Parks, Oscar "Doc" (1892-1971) TR 39, 80, 81, 97, 103; Parks, Sudie Summers (1899-1979) TR 44.

The Parkses had the distinction of being the only informants recorded by two collectors, and they sang a number of the same songs for each. Rosenbaum contacted them by letter in his search for informants previously recorded by Lomax. Of Oscar, Lomax wrote in 1938:

> He is certainly the most vigorous folk singer that I encountered in Indiana. Mr. Parks we found feeding the horses at his daughter's barn in Perry County. His daughter had come down with the measles and he had come over to help with things.

Deuchars, where Parks lived, and his house

> turned out to be the same thing. They both consisted of one little log shanty, one room of which had been partitioned off, the partition representing the boundary of the United States Post Office.
> At Deuchars there lived Mrs. Parks, postmistress . . . and a whole string of tow-headed, charming Parkses from six feet on down to two in stair step fashion.

The Parkses had followed the timber out of Rock Castle, Kentucky, and had settled at Deuchars because it looked so much like Kentucky. Many years later they moved to Alton, where in 1963 they were recorded by Rosenbaum who wrote:

> Doc Parks is a garrulous Kentuckian of near 70 with a head full of old songs who has made his home for the last thirty years in the hilly, thinly settled back country of Crawford County, just over the Ohio River from his home state. He was born in the westernmost tip of Virginia in a round-log shack . . . near the town of Rose Hill. When he was a year and half old his father, a native of Tennessee, and his mother, a Virginian, moved the family up to Livingston, Kentucky. As he grew up here, he learned his great store of ballads, lyric songs, and ditties, and his classic highland singing style from his father [John Wesley Parks].[11]

Should we judge only from what the Parkses recorded for Lomax and Rosenbaum, they knew only two Child ballads, "Barb'ry Allan" (84, TR 80-81) and "The Lass of Roch Royal" (76). On the other hand, their repertory of American ballads, especially those related to local incidents and in some cases not listed in Laws AM, was quite large. This is also true of their stock of lyric and humorous songs, many of which formed common Appalachian repertory.

Before moving to Indiana, Oscar had worked as a wagoner and a crosstie cutter. He was one of eleven children. He and Sudie also had eleven, but only seven lived to maturity. Oscar could read and write--having had a fourth-grade education--but he usually left such chores to his wife, whose education had been more extensive. However, when he found that his neighbors were suspicious of the motives of the Lomaxes, when they wondered whether they were really from the Library of Congress or were just stealing his songs, he took pen in hand. On 19 April 1938 he wrote to Mr. and Mrs. Lomax as follows:

> Will say there was some people around here didn't seem to have any confidence that you folks was what you claimed to be so we just wrote into the Congressman and got the return letter from him so I just took it on to myself to read the return letter we received to some of them. As you I guess know some folks have to be sited [sic] about matters this day and age of time.

According to one of his daughters, Eliece, his nickname was something his dad had started when he was little. "Grandpa called him 'Docky Diddle' and it got shortened to 'Doc' and stayed with him."

The Parkses went through the depression and had four burnouts, but their troubles did not keep them from being a close family. While both the parents were living, all seven children would return home every year for a reunion. Then, according to their youngest child, Mrs. Lucille Faulkner of Davenport, Iowa, "they would bring out their music and we would get out in the shade in the yard and have what we called our 'whing ding.' That was standard procedure." Lucille was four when Lomax came to record her parents, and she can still "see the curls piling up" from the recordings.

After their parents' deaths the children continued to have reunions in which they sang and played the old songs and music. Between them they played guitar, mandolin, and autoharp. The last reunion at which all were able to be present was in September 1985.

SANDAGE/UNDERHILL: Underhill, Anna Sandage (1905-1973) TR 46, 60, 69, 75, 79, 95; Sandage, Virgil (1897-1972) TR 94, 99.

Anna and Virgil came from a large family, their father having had nineteen children by three wives. The land they lived on, a tract in Perry County near Doolittle Mills and the Ohio River, had very poor soil, so poor that "you couldn't raise more than a fuss on it." But they made a go of it. It was a family with a singing tradition. Both their father, Mose Sandage, a veteran of the Civil War, and their mother, Emerine Taylar Sandage, were fine singers as were their Aunt Safron Taylar and Uncle Jack Taylar.

Singing songs was common entertainment after dinner, as well as on Sunday afternoons when there might be company. In common with other families discussed in these pages, in the evenings the children would gather around the pump organ and sing to their mother's playing. Anna learned to play this instrument by ear. Virgil branched out a little and played breakdowns and waltzes on the fiddle. He also played the banjo, and his wife, Ida Mae Miller, the accordion. The two made some money playing folk music on a radio station in Louisville.

Anna lived her entire life in Perry County, as did her parents. As far as Clarence, a son from her first marriage, knew, all their ancestors had lived in Indiana. Anna had never been to a dance but had attended play-parties as a youngster. Rosenbaum recorded her singing a few of the songs she had learned from the play-party, but I could find none of them associated with known play-party games. She married Earl Underhill in 1923, and they had two children, of whom only Clarence survived. Earl died in 1958, and in 1960 Anna married Sigler Underhill. In the latter part of her life she lived in Uniontown. According to Clarence Underhill, Sigler was a farmer. After Anna's death Sigler married Bertie Parks, a daughter of Oscar Parks.

Virgil Sandage was a carpenter by trade, and at various times he and his wife lived in Tell City and Uniontown in Indiana, and also in Louisville and Florida. They had no children.

In 1930 Anna and Virgil wrote down the words of some of the ballads and songs they sang as a means of preserving them. A friend of the family, Dr. Claude Lomax of Dale, sent a few of these to Paul Brewster who later incorporated some of them in his *Ballads and Songs of Indiana*. Anna's repertory included not only old English and American ballads but also sentimental songs from the last century, such as "The Orphan Girl" (TR 69) and "The Dying Nun" (TR 75). She also liked to sing religious songs such as "In the Sweet Bye and Bye."

Virgil, who played as much as he sang, preferred American ballads such as "The Texas Rangers" (TR 99) and "Did the *Maine* Go Down?" and more earthy items such as "Sugar Babe" and "Birmingham Jail."

SCHREIBER: Schreiber, Dale (1924-   ) TR 21, 45, 58, 61; Schreiber, Clara Belle Smith (1892-1971) TR 41; Schreiber, Paul Emmet (1891-1965) TR 72 with Schreiber, Walter (1889-1972).

The Schreibers were a family in which everyone sang or played a musical instrument: mother, father, uncle, and six children, of whom the oldest two were girls. They sang while they were living at home and later in family reunions, which they held yearly until the Second World War.

Dale was the youngest of the children and was born in Bedford. The family seems to have moved as often as the Lindseys but remained one family, the parents celebrating their golden wedding anniversary. During Dale's childhood they lived not only in Bedford but also in Loogootee, Bryantsville, and Pin Hook in Lawrence County, and finally in South Union in Monroe County. Paul Emmet, Dale's father, worked as a car blocker in stone mills in Bedford. (A car blocker packs limestone blocks into railway cars for shipment. They use wooden paddles to force excelsior down between the stone segments so they will not break in shipment.)

As the Great Depression set in, Paul could find less and less work at the mills and turned his hand to what carpentry jobs he could find, a field in which he was skilled. The family did a modest job of farming on a small rented acreage near Bryantsville, mostly devoted to gardening plus raising a few pigs and cows. As Dale relates, "We didn't have any horses or any machinery so we borrowed everything we used. We waited until the first of May when everyone else's plowing was done to borrow a horse and plow." At the lowest point they lived in a four-room house at Pin Hook, where they heated and cooked with wood and had to carry water from a spring a thousand feet away.

Pin Hook has an interesting history. It is named after a subterfuge bootleggers used to circumvent the law. They sold you a pin and gave the whiskey away free. If you paid enough for the pin you got a good, big bottle of whiskey.

The father again found work at a stone mill, and the friendly owner, who owned a house in South Union, let Schreiber have it just for the upkeep. "It was the first house I had lived in," Dale told me, "where you could see paint on the walls." In South Union, Paul Emmet also began to grow strawberries and continued this later when he retired and was living at 440 Clear Creek Drive in Bloomington.

Dale finished grade school in a one-room schoolhouse in South Union and then traveled by bus to Bloomington for high school. During the Second World War he was stationed in Northern Ireland and was surprised to find that the inhabitants of Ulster were unfamiliar with what he thought were Irish songs, such as "Danny Boy." Returning, he became a barber and later a custodian for one of the city's school buildings. He lives with his wife, Joyce, in Ellettsville.

Dale's great-grandfather, Heinrich Schreiber, emigrated from Hamburg, Germany, to the United States and settled in Floyd County, Indiana. They were farmers, and the men of the family had reputations as carpenters. Some of the barns they built are still standing, although they are held together by pegs. Walter Schreiber, Dale's uncle, was also a carpenter by trade.

Paul Schreiber was one of the first in his neighborhood to own an Edison cylinder player,

35

"one of those little jobs with a big morning glory horn." It cost seventeen dollars, and later he traded it for a pony. After he was married he bought an Edison Amberola. (This was Edison's final attempt to compete with the disc turntable. The plastic cylinders were long-playing and of high acoustic quality.) At Loogootee they had a Cheney disc player.

The older Schreibers learned most of their songs from the phonograph. Dale learned most of his songs from his brothers and sisters, particularly from Hazel, ten years his senior, who used to sit in the porch swing and sing to the younger children. The three boys formed a trio, and when Dale was thirteen he joined the trio and made it a quartet. They participated in several local talent contests and won first prize in two. They formed a hillbilly band as well as a singing quartet and twice performed on a truck outside of grocery stores, receiving groceries as their pay. They sang together until the Second World War and once or twice afterwards. Their repertory consisted primarily of material taken from the black tradition or imitations thereof as heard in minstrel shows. They sang "I Been Working on the Railroad," "Mandy Lee," a "Jubilee Medley," and some real black spirituals.

In 1959 Gus Meade lent Dale Schreiber a tape recorder and a roll of tape, and he recorded the older members of his family and himself at their home at Clear Creek Drive in Bloomington. In 1988 I recorded more songs from Dale during an interview.

SMELSER, Vern (1910-1974) TR 7, 43, 47, 51, 56, 62, 64, 92, 101.

Vern was born in Blountsville near Muncie, the son of Frank Smelser (1877-1949) and Emma Iola Chapman Smelser (1888-1957). They had four children, three boys and a girl, of whom Vern was the second. When the parents were married in Delaware County, Frank Smelser was working as a section hand on the Baltimore and Ohio Railroad. Then they moved to Hanover, Indiana, where Smelser scooped up mussels from the Ohio River and sold them to a button factory in nearby Madison. In 1913 they moved back to Muncie where Frank worked for the Griffith Furniture Company, maker of wooden chairs, porch swings, etc. Vance Smelser, the eldest son, wrote, "The wages then were a dollar a day, six dollars for a six day week. . . . When work became more plentiful during World War I Griffith raised wages to $1.50 a day and $9 for a six day week."

36

In 1922 when Vern was eleven the family moved south to a farm in Orange County near Paoli. "My father drove a covered wagon, my mother drove a horse and buggy" on the twenty-day trip.

It was a musical family. The father, of German extraction (the family name was originally Schmeltzer), played both guitar and banjo and the mother the piano, which she taught "all over the country." Vern learned most of his songs from his maternal grandmother, Rhoda Carver Chapman (1861-?), who used to sing to her grandchildren from the porch swing after supper. He also learned a few songs from his grandfather, Arthur Chapman (1862-1942). Both came to Indiana from Kansas in 1919. He was born in Boonville, Warrick County, Indiana, she in Kansas. They died in Orange and Delaware counties, respectively.

Vern learned to play the guitar at the age of twelve, and by age sixteen he was entertaining at parties along with his brother, Kenny, who both played the fiddle and sang. The family, mother, father, three brothers, and a sister also made music as a group. "Our favorite pastime . . . was gathering around the organ after supper, our mother learning each one of us our part of the song, and then putting all the parts together in order to harmonize." The family also performed in musical plays mostly put together by Olin Stout, a local schoolteacher. These were given in the early 1920s at Young's Creek south of Paoli, primarily for the benefit of surrounding communities. No admission was charged.

In 1932 Vern married Nellie Mae Bickleburger, with whom he had two daughters. The latter used to join him in singing at church gatherings, homecomings, and at the Farm Bureau. A gracious, generous man, Vern entertained at these various affairs for the pleasure it afforded the listeners, not for pay. For a living he worked for the woodworking factories of the area and did some farming.

He had a very large repertory of songs, which he picked up wherever he could find them. They included three Child ballads, "Barb'ry Allan" (84), "John Came Home" (274, TR 56), and "Hangman, Hangman" (95). He also sang a number of American ballads such as "Young Charlotte" (Laws AM G 17, TR 92), "The Little Mohea" (Laws AM H 8, TR 51), and "The Johnstown Flood" (Laws AM G 14). Among the other items in his highly mixed repertory was a very old Scottish song, "Mr. Grumble," which he unaccountably called "The Old Man in the Woods," and a number of pathetic and humorous popular songs from the latter part of the nineteenth century, such as "In the Green Fields of Virginia" and "The Jolly Burglar Boy" (Laws AM H 23, TR 62).

When asked by Rosenbaum how many songs he knew, he replied:

> Now I never just did count them up but I imagine I know about 125. I know that at one time I started singing at nine o'clock in the morning . . . and I sung until four o'clock that evening and never sang the same songs twice.

Like a good entertainer he calculated his effects:

> Part time I had them laughing, part time I had them crying. I mixed them up a little bit, you know, I'd sing a sad song and then a funny one, you know. First thing I'd have them laughing and then crying the next thing you'd know.

Vern's paternal grandfather, Adam Smelser (1830-1895), was a veteran of the Civil War. He was born in Fayette County, Indiana, and died in Delaware County. He enlisted in 1862, and his Civil War papers list his occupation as "farmer." He was wounded at Gettysburg and mustered out in Washington in 1865 for disability. His wife, Margaret Keezling (1833-1921), was born in Indiana and died in Delaware County.

Two brothers, Valltin and Johann Adam Schmeltzer, sailed from Rotterdam on the ship *Royal Union* and arrived in Philadelphia in 1750. They had emigrated from Germany to Holland, but their place of origin is unknown. Upon becoming a citizen in 1750, Vern's ancestor, Valltin Schmeltzer, changed his name to Valentine Shmeltzer. When his son, Peter, moved to Bourbon County, Kentucky, he changed the family name to Smelser.

SOUTH/KING: South, Garland "Jack" (1897-1962) TR 67, 85, 86, 100; South, Lula Beard (1905-) TR 40; King, Roxie South (1880-1970) TR 68, 73, 90, 98, 102.

The Souths were a singing family. According to Lula South, whom I interviewed in May 1988 in her farmhouse three miles west of Ellettsville, "I've always been singing. I would start a song in the kitchen and Garland and Hal would pick it up in the living room. I would sing while I was hanging out the wash; I was singing all the time." She was eighty-two and her son, Hal, who was there during the interview, was sixty. We talked of the recordings Gus Meade had made of the singing Souths in 1956 and 1970. The recordings were of Garland, Lula, and Roxie King, Garland's aunt. Garland and Lula's son Hal (Harold) and his wife, Louise, were also recorded, but as they generally sang in very close harmony with guitar accompaniment their songs were not appropriate for inclusion in this volume.

In addition to Hal, Garland and Lula had three other children: Garland William South, by then deceased; John E. South, retired from twenty-five years in the Navy; and Dorothea South Rampley, the only one of the children who lives in Bloomington.

Garland was born on a farm in Monroe County, son of Charles Edward South and Margaret Estella Tungate South. His parents separated when he was a small boy, and he went to live in Sullivan County near Paxton with his grandparents, Thomas and Susanna Boatman South. Thomas was a veteran of the Civil War. After twelve years the parents became reconciled and settled near Gosport, Owen County, on a dairy farm. Garland, by then seventeen, joined them to help with the farm. While there he became a member of the National Guard and in 1916 was called up and sent to the Mexican border to fight under General John Joseph Pershing against the troops of Pancho Villa. When he returned, the United States had declared war on Germany, and he was sent to France where he stayed for the remainder of World War I. After the war he worked for a short time on the Missouri National Road and then rejoined his parents, who had moved to Mahalisville, Morgan County, where he operated a sawmill.

Lula was born in Barbersville, Johnson County, Indiana, daughter of James William Beard and Hattie Stewart Beard. In 1905 and 1906 her father was employed in the building of the Illinois Central Railroad, and they moved from town to town following its route.

When Lula was about four years old her parents separated and both remarried, her mother marrying John Thompson, who had a farm near Mahalisville, where Lula was reared. It was here that she met Garland South in 1922 and married him in 1923.

Later the Souths moved to Bloomington to a house on West Fifteenth Street, and beginning in 1937 Garland worked in a sawmill located on East Fourteenth Street along with Ike Ritter, a son-in-law of Roxie King. Following this, Garland worked for many years as a machine operator at the Allison's General Motors Plant in Indianapolis, commuting daily by automobile. In 1950 he bought a large farm, the bulk of which is in Owen County and the house in Monroe County. It is primarily forest, but they did raise some cattle, hogs, and chickens. Dorothea and her husband lived there for two years, and then Garland, who was beginning to have some health problems, and Lula traded residences with them.

Garland and Lula remained on the farm for six years while the former went through a series of cancer operations. In his notes of the recordings Meade writes:

> [Garland] has, however, been able to take care of the farm stock and run his own sawmill. As a young man, he was known for his great strength, which may account for his remarkable ability to stay active in spite of his health.

The sawmill referred to was a small one which Garland had set up primarily for his own recreation.

After six years on the farm Garland and Lula moved back into Bloomington, living in a house on Dunn Street, where Garland finally died. Lula then moved back to the farm. When she retired after having worked in the housekeeping department at Indiana University for twenty years, she concentrated on her hobbies of quilting and canning fruit.

Roxie South King was eighty years of age when she was recorded in 1960 and said into the microphone that she had been married for sixty years. She had reared seven children. Her husband, John King, worked at various times as a farmer, in a stone quarry, and for the Showers Furniture Factory.

Garland was reputed to have a remarkable memory. It was said that he only had to hear a song once or twice and then could repeat it exactly, as well as tell you where he had learned it. Most of his songs he learned from his Aunt Eve, who was already deceased at the time he was recorded, and from his Aunt Roxie. Other songs he learned from the phonograph and the radio. Lula learned most of her songs from her mother, Hattie Thompson. Lula wrote, "My mother was like many young women at the time, like Roxie South King, collecting ballads to sing." Her mother also played the organ, and Aunt Roxie played the piano.

Dorothea South Rampley remembers her father singing to her when she was a small child. He sang "Barb'ry Allan" (Child 84), "Go Tell Aunt Rhody," and "Two Babes in the Woods" (Child ESB, The Children in the Wood) as lullabies. She loved "Two Babes in the Woods," but the first thing she would say was "Daddy, sing 'Barb'ry Allan.'" She sang "Two Babes in the Woods" to her own little girl. Another song that Garland used to sing to her was "The Rosewood Casket," a sentimental song dating from the previous century.

Garland sang a few old British ballads such as "The Hangman Song" (Child 95, TR 86), "The House Carpenter" (Child 243), and "Brennan on the Moor" (Laws BR L 7, TR 85). He also knew a number of American ballads such as "Young Charlotte" (Laws AM G 17) and "The Cowboy's Lament" (Laws AM B 1, TR 100), as well as many songs derived from the popular field. Lula had a somewhat similar repertory as her husband, but the repertory of Roxie King, if we can judge from the songs she recorded, consisted primarily of American ballads such as "Charles Giteau" (Laws AM E 11, TR 102), "The Jealous Lover" (Laws AM F 1, TR 90), and many sentimental songs from the popular repertory.

STOGDILL, Francis Marion (1852-1939) TR 77.

Marion Stogdill was born in Jackson County, Indiana, the son of William Sherman Stogdill and Mariah Elkins, but lived most of his life in Brown County in or near Elkinsville, where he died. This little town was named after one of his mother's ancestors, and he was buried in the Elkinsville Cemetery.

He was married three times and survived all three wives. With his first wife, Eliza Jane Crider, whom he married in 1874, he had three children, two girls and a boy, the latter dying in infancy. At maturity the two girls left the hills to find work in Illinois. He had no children in his subsequent marriages to two widows, Amanda Purtlebaugh in 1917 and to Matilda Bush in 1927. The last marriage was the third for both parties.

Lomax was taken to visit Stogdill in Elkinsville by John W. Collier (see COLLIER), who was Stogdill's nephew. Stogdill had been a rural postman since 1917, and although somewhat deaf and feeble was still carrying the mail daily on the route from Elkinsville to Cripple Creek.

> At first Stogdill protested he had forgotten all his songs, but little by little he began to recall them.
> Stogdill kept repeating that he had had an easy life but he had to work hard all the time and he was furious against the Government for not granting him an old age pension. He couldn't get one because he wouldn't say he was too old to work.

41

Although some of his variants were quite fragmentary and full of errors in memory, Lomax felt them important because, as Stogdill said, "His people came to Brown County when there wasn't but one house in Columbus and 'ev'ry holler was full of Indians.'"

Four of the seven songs recorded by Stogdill, "William Hall" (Laws BR N 30), "The Oxford Girl" (Laws BR P 35), "Lord Baker" (Child 53), and "Six Kings' Daughters" (Child 4, TR 77) are indeed old English ballads. Much of his singing also displayed the old Appalachian ornamented style. Marion played the fiddle, but according to his nephew, Bramble Stogdill, "he couldn't hold a candle" to John W. Collier.

Education in the Brown County hills at the turn of the century took place in a one-room school-house built of split logs pegged together. As Bramble remembers it, every child had only three books, a McGuffey speller, a McGuffey reader, and a geography. Bramble did not know what it had been like in his uncle's day. Obviously Marion had acquired some skill in reading and writing or he could not have become a postman.

Marion's life could not have been too easy before he became a postman. In earlier days Brown County folk had no difficulty in raising enough to feed themselves but had no surplus to sell. About the only source of money was selling timber and its bark for tanning. Oak and hickory trees were cut down, their bark peeled off and sold to a tannery in Martinsville. There was also a furniture factory in Martinsville which would buy hickory poles. Or one could hew out crossties for the railroad, which brought forty cents apiece.

Even the postman's life presented some difficulties. In good weather and with a light load Marion could negotiate the Brown County hills in a cart drawn by one horse. When the snow piled in drifts, and especially when the Sears-Roebuck and Montgomery Ward catalogs had to be delivered, he had to work his way through with a heavily loaded wagon pulled by four horses.

Marion, whom everyone liked, and who in turn had considerable liking for whiskey and women, made some cash in the early days by bringing in whiskey and selling it. But, according to Bramble, if Marion had a dime in his pocket and a chaw of tobacco he could get along.

Marion Stogdill was related to another large Brown County family, the Wilkersons, through his third wife. However, the Stogdills and Wilkersons were so closely related, as Bramble put it, "some of us were double cousins." Marion died at the home of a near relative, Isom Wilkerson.

When Elizabeth Lomax asked Marion where his forebears had come from he said, "Kentucky." The Wilkerson line can be traced back not only to Kentucky but also to North Carolina and Virginia. The earliest Wilkerson whose existence had been documented for the Brown County Historical Society was born in 1735 in King County, Virginia.

UNDERHILL (see SANDAGE/UNDERHILL)

WARD, Isie Dora McMurtry (1874-1962) TR 63, 66.

Dora Ward's granddaughter, Elaine Ward Miller, always considered her grandmother the epitome of a pioneer woman. She was, indeed, a "tough old gal," who carried on through all difficulties while singing and writing verse and managed to live to the ripe old age of eighty-eight.

Dora McMurtry was born in Kansas in 1874. Her mother died a few months later, and her father brought her to Indiana in 1875. On his death in 1879 she was taken West by her uncle and aunt; they returned to Indiana in 1883, where she lived the rest of her life. Dora married James Henry Ward in 1894. To this union were born eleven children, five girls and six boys, nine of whom grew to maturity. One girl died of pneumonia at age one, a second of appendicitis at age nine. In 1914 the father, James Henry, grew ill and died at the age of fifty. Only seven weeks had elapsed since the birth of his last child.

When the father died, the family was living on a small farm east of the town of Princeton. The farm was mortgaged for more than it was worth, so Mrs. Ward gave it up to the man who held the mortgage and with her nine children moved into Princeton. There Dora supported her family as best she could, taking in washing and cleaning people's houses. Soon the two older girls married and left home. The remaining children helped in any way that they could. Two younger girls began to work in a factory after a year or two of high school. All five boys had newspaper routes until they were old enough to hold other jobs.

When Lomax visited Dora Ward in 1938 she, too, turned out to know more songs than she had sent in by mail to Paul Brewster. Lomax noted:

> She was a very difficult person to work with, because, I think, she felt ashamed of her poverty and her profession--that of washerwoman. I felt sorry that I had only a few hours to spend with her and her friends, because I think that from her and through her acquaintances more information about the ballad in Indiana could be collected than from any other source I encountered. She lives in half of a little frame house in one of the poorer parts of Princeton.

The change in status from that of the wife of an independent farmer to that of a domestic would indeed have been difficult for one of Dora Ward's strong character to bear, but perhaps Lomax was not a model of tact.

William P. Ward, Dora's ninth child, remembers the circumstances of his birth as told to him by his mother:

> When they were expecting me and the time was near, [she told me] that my dad wanted to take the horse and buggy and go get the doctor. There was a big snow on the ground, being January. The drifts were very deep, so Mom said no, you may get in a drift, so he stayed with Mom and was the midwife under her direction. Must have been some guy!

Another incident which Ward remembers is his mother walking the ten or twelve blocks to town, having all her teeth extracted, then stopping on the way home to do a lady's wash on the rub board. Mrs. Ward was a widow for forty-eight years and was often asked why she never remarried. She always replied, "I was too busy raising my family. It was a full-time job."

She delighted in singing Irish songs to her children and often spoke in what they considered to be an Irish brogue. She told them that both her mother and father were Irish and that she was all Irish. Unfortunately, Lomax did not record any of her Irish songs.

Dora Ward's father was Benona Fuller McMurtry (1848-1879), and her mother was Mary McReynolds McMurtry (1847-1875), both born in Warrick County. The mother was buried in Kansas; the place of burial of the father is unknown. Her paternal grandfather was Isaac McMurtry, who was born in Ohio, date unknown. He died at age sixty-two and was buried in Kansas. Her paternal grandmother was Mary Elizabeth Stephens McMurtry.

WEVER (Weaver), Nellie Rebecca Butler (1884-1970) TR 88.

Nell Butler was born in Crawford County. Her husband, Frank Warren Wever, was born in 1887 in Leesville, Lawrence County. He worked there for a number of years as a grocer until he was dismissed by his employer for refusing to join the Ku Klux Klan. After a short period of working in Bedford, he moved his family to Bloomington where he began to work for Showers Brothers, at that time one of the largest furniture factories in the United States. He was hired at Showers because the owner was impressed by the fact that he had refused to join the Klan. The Showers Company had been founded by a circuit-riding minister, James, and his brother, William. When William died, his son, Edward, took charge, so it was still a family business at the time Wever was employed.

Wever worked at Showers until he suffered a stroke, which eventually led to his death in 1942. His wife therefore found it necessary to find means of supporting the two of them. They had a large home on Atwater, which she first used as a child care center. Later she organized nursing care, both at home and elsewhere, for women who had broken their hips. She had had a normal school education and at times substituted in the public schools.

She was manager of the Third Street swimming pool until it was closed by the Parks Department in 1937. From 1946 through 1956 she was employed by the Children's Unit of the Indiana University Speech and Hearing Clinic in capacities as housemother, supervising clinician, and clinician of a dormitory. After several illnesses she moved to the Four Seasons Home in Columbus in 1968 at age eighty-four. When she moved to the Four Seasons, Elmer Guy Smith wrote a lengthy article in the "Senior Citizens Corner" of the *Bloomington Herald-Telephone* of 14 February 1968, commending her for her many civic activities.

Mrs. Wever told Lomax that she had formerly known a number of ballads which she had learned as a child from her mother. According to Lomax, her mother, who was still living,

> recalls fragments of songs but could scarcely carry a tune. She was a niece of Governor Crawford of North Carolina and came to Indiana when she was a little girl.

Her father, William Clement Butler (1856-1933), was born in Lawrence County and was a physician, having studied at the Kentucky School of Medicine in Louisville. He and Linda Florence Yates were married in 1883 in Levenworth, Crawford County. Frank Wever's father, Jacob William Wever (1820-1898), was born in Kentucky and died in Lawrence County. He was a farmer and owned one hundred sixty acres of land.

Mrs. Wever's granddaughter is a librarian and genealogist and, wherever possible, has traced the roots of the family. The Wevers (sometimes spelled Weaver or Weber) were Protestants who left Austria to avoid religious persecution. They moved to Holland, then to England, and finally to Georgia in the colonies. The Yates and Butlers (originally Botler, an individual who bottles spirits and wines) came to North Carolina from England, but the latter were apparently Scottish in origin. The earliest records of Yates in America were the births of three brothers in 1782, 1796, and 1800. There is some indication that their father fought in the Revolutionary War and originally came from England.

Nell Wever's maternal grandfather, William Yates, was born in Crawford County in 1812. The lineage of his wife, Nancy Wales, can be traced back to William Wales, firstborn of this family in America in 1762. He also served in the Revolutionary War, and his wife was part Indian. His father had moved to Virginia through the Shenandoah Valley and apparently died around 1812.

Other lineages of the Butler line can be traced back to North Carolina. The members of these families, Crawford, Clayton, Parks, Ray, Crews, and Frazier, were second- and third-generation Americans. In part they originated as indentured servants from Virginia, and the remainder, mostly Crawfords and Morrows, were Scotch-Irish who arrived in Pennsylvania and moved south through the Shenandoah Valley to the Piedmont region of North Carolina. They were primarily devout Presbyterians. When tobacco and cotton became the principal crops in that area, slaves were brought in by several of the ancestral families. Their religious views and the depression of 1819 caused the Crawfords to free their slaves and to move to the Indiana Territory. Many of the Morrow and Parks families had preceded them. It is probable that Nell Wever's mother learned her songs not only from the Yates line but also from relatives in the Butler lineages. These families had lived for long periods in the Southern Uplands.

As seen in Fig. 2 (p. 9), southern Indiana still displays a greater southern cultural influence than the similar regions of its neighboring states. This influence was obviously greater a hundred years ago than it is today, but it is still sufficiently pervasive to produce the so-called "Hoosier Apex." Whether the ballads, the lyric songs, or the humorous songs of the Southern Uplands were preserved until recently in southern Indiana is to a certain extent, of course, dependent upon pure accident. One can, however, conclude on the basis of available evidence that when both the paternal and maternal lines of a family have resided for several generations in the uplands area, the retention of at least part of this repertory is more likely.

The Bryant family is a case in point. Both ancestral lines follow the well-worn path of settling first in Pennsylvania, then moving south through the Appalachians, passing through the Cumberland Gap into Kentucky, and then north into Indiana. Of the thirty-one songs that Lomax recorded from Dora Bryant and her three daughters, fourteen were old English and Scottish ballads and at least four were well known American ballads. On the other hand, Abraham Lincoln Gary, whose English ancestors first settled in Virginia, then moved north into Pennsylvania, and thence directly to Rush County, sang only a play-party song in his interview with Herbert Halpert. Later he sent the texts of two other songs to Halpert, but neither, as far as I can determine, was part of the Appalachian repertory.[12]

Contrast Gary's repertory with that of Albert J. Fields, also a lawyer as well as a mayor of a city. At an age equally advanced as that of Gary, he was recorded singing old British ballads and an American ballad which had commonly been heard in the Appalachians. Fields came from a wealthy and highly educated family, but again both paternal and maternal lines led back to the Southern Uplands. Although his daughter, Nancy Fields Fadum, had never heard him sing a ballad before she left home at age seventeen, this Southern Uplands inheritance was apparently strong enough to maintain itself through the years and find its final outlet in the 1950s through her father.

Where the lineage led back primarily to Germany, and the internal migration had been directly from Pennsylvania to Indiana, as in the case of the Schreibers--a singing family if ever there was one--items from the Southern Uplands are almost entirely absent. In the case of the Dixons, whose German ancestors came directly from Pennsylvania, but those Scottish and English ancestors followed the route north from Virginia or North Carolina, one finds less of the upland tradition than might be expected. Possibly this is because so many of the girls learned to play the piano, and Clay Dixon, himself, became a schoolteacher. In any case, his repertory included only one song descended from British ballads, the ever-present midwestern and southern lullaby, "Two Babes in the Woods" (TR 2). He knew one or two traditional American ballads, a children's game song, a second omnipresent lullaby, "Go Tell Aunt Rhody" (TR 1), and many sentimental and popular songs, including some from the minstrel repertory. The Dixon family, of course, is not the only one represented whose repertory included nineteenth-century popular songs such as "She's Only a Bird in a Gilded Cage" and "After the Ball." The Bryant family also sang these songs.

Oscar "Doc" Parks also had a strong southern heritage. He knew only two of the old British ballads but did know many American ballads, some of local origin. He and his wife, Sudie, also sang a number of the Appalachian lyric and humorous songs. Marion Stogdill of the Brown County hills, on the other hand, knew mostly old British ballads. He and "Doc" Parks were the only singers who retained the old Appalachian ornamented singing style. Parks learned it from his father, and it obviously must have been a tradition among Stogdill's ancestors who, like those of the Parks, came from Virginia and Kentucky.

Dora Ward is a special case. She claimed to be fully Irish and sang Irish songs to her children, but Lomax recorded none of these. Of the nine songs she did record, five were old British or Scottish ballads and one a widely diffused American ballad. In his notes Lomax lamented the fact that he could spend so little time with her, believing that she probably had the greatest repertory of old ballads of any singer he had contacted in Indiana. Most of her immediate ancestors were born in Warrick County, and no information could be secured concerning earlier lineage. Did she perhaps learn her repertory in Indiana from neighbors as she grew up?

The Souths, Garland, Lula, and Roxie South King of Monroe and Spencer counties, and Anna Underhill and Virgil Sandage of Perry County present a somewhat different picture. Their repertory, like that of Parks, includes only a few of the traditional British ballads, many more American ballads, and a large percentage of the sentimental songs of the nineteenth century. The Souths' background, if we are to credit the assertions of Lula's daughter, Dorothea, is commensurate with that of the Bryant family, while the Sandage/Underhill family had never inquired concerning its ancestral heritage. Lula wrote me that both her mother and Roxie King, as was the fashion in their day, collected ballads, and both, it seems, played the piano. In her later days Anna Underhill learned to play the pump organ by ear. This reminds us that the two most common methods described of learning songs were by listening to someone singing from the porch swing or clustering around a mother or sister accompanying herself with the pump organ.

The two singers from the Paoli region are of a different order. Vern Smelser was primarily an entertainer, though an unpaid one, while Lotus Dickey in his later years became a semiprofessional folksinger. Smelser's ancestry is primarily German, but the family moved to Kentucky from Pennsylvania before settling in Indiana. He learned many of his songs from a grandmother who came from Kansas. He had a large repertory and was very catholic in his taste, picking up songs wherever he could. A number were from the upland repertory but probably were not inherited family traditions. For example, he learned "Barbara Allan" from a book and a reworked variant of "Our Goodman" from a record. I know Lotus Dickey's repertory primarily from what others have told me and from the recording he made of songs he learned from his father. He had a strong German ancestry which never moved south, or did his Irish or Scottish ancestors. Only the English Dickey came from the South, and he apparently began his American experience in Florida.

In Lotus Dickey's repertory there are English and Scottish ballads, although ones not very well known. There are some lyric songs from the South, one concerning an old dying black who wishes to be awakened when the Jubilee arrives, and two American ballads, one the popular "Bury Me Not on the Lone Prairie." The most interesting items are two ballads whose origins I have not traced. One concerns a Hussar dying of his battle wounds on the banks of the Danube who is found among the dead and wounded by his sweetheart. The second is in a medieval setting. A page boy who is enamored of his

49

mistress (who is about to be married) vows to fight to the death in Palestine.

"Pretty Sarry," sung by "Aunt" Phoebe Elliott, came from Virginia and has been collected primarily in the Appalachians. The one traditional song sung by John Collier, "John Roger, the Miller," came with his family from Scotland to Virginia and thence to Kentucky and Indiana. Of the others who sang only one song each, Dodson, Kirk, Lindsey, and Wever, only the item sung by the last seems to be part of a family tradition and possibly came from the South.

Ancestors who lived in New England or even New York are conspicuously absent. There was a ballad-singing tradition in both of these areas, but it apparently was not transferred to southern Indiana. Pennsylvania or the Atlantic states south of Maryland seem to be the first points of settlement. Then two principal routes were followed: the first westward from Pennsylvania through Ohio to Indiana; the second movement from the southern states through the Cumberland Gap from Virginia into Kentucky and then north. Only one ancestor hailed from Tennessee, and less than half a dozen came to Indiana from further west, three or four from Kansas, and one from Missouri.

From this mixed bag of evidence certain cautious conclusions can be derived. The great majority of the singers were involved at one time in farming or the cutting of timber or came from parents who followed these occupations. Although some of the British ballads sung may have originated as broadsides published in London, in the United States they formed part of the rural repertory. The upland ornamented style of singing was maintained only by two men who had little education and who lived in the poorest and hilliest counties in southern Indiana, Brown and Crawford. In the 1930s the sentimental popular songs of the late nineteenth century had entered the repertory of most of the families. Finally, the musical evidence matches the linguistic and cultural evidence offered by Craig Carver. Southern Indiana is indeed part of the North, but until the middle of this century, at least, it preserved a good part of the song tradition characteristic of the Upland South.

All the singers are white. Nevertheless, the black musical tradition had its effect upon their repertories. Clay Dixon and the Schreibers sang minstrel songs imitative of that tradition, and the Schreiber male quartet sang black spirituals. The Bryant children sang blues from the black repertory. Although black elements entered into the mainstream of American song, the blacks themselves

50

received no credit. During the first half of this century there were almost no blacks living in rural areas of southern Indiana. Small towns in the region had signs posted warning blacks not to remain in the precincts overnight. Songs pejorative of their race were taught in public schools.

Most of this is now altered, but Dale Schreiber is not happy in his recollection of his participation in it. Much of what he sang, to quote him from taped interview, "is in bad reputation now because it was unfortunately at the expense of the colored people. We had to learn to show them the kind of respect they deserve and desire."

Thomas M. Bryant and Mary Vandora McNeely Bryant, n.d.

L to R: Ethel Bryant Niemeyer (Daganhard); Esther Bryant Frazier (Scales); Kathleen Bryant (Clemens), n.d.

Samuel Clay Dixon, c. 1938

"Aunt" Phoebe Stoker Elliott, n.d.

Abraham Lincoln Gary, 1955

Albert Jeremiah Fields, n.d.

Oscar "Doc" Parks and Sudie Summers Parks, 1968

L to R: Anna Sandage Underhill; Sigler Underhill; Virgil Sandage, 1969

Walter Schreiber, 1967

Virgil Sandage and Ida Sandage, n.d.

Dale Schreiber, 1982

Paul Emmet Schreiber and Clara Belle Smith Schreiber

Courtesy of Nellie Smelser

Vern Smelser, c. 1957

Courtesy of Lula Beard South

Garland "Jack" South and Lula Beard South, 1952

Courtesy of Carmen Ritter

Roxie South King, n.d.

Courtesy of William P. Ward

Isie Dora McMurtry Ward, 1944

CHAPTER 2 CHILDHOOD

The first song a child usually hears is a lullaby. As can be gathered from the bio-histories offered in the previous chapter, it may be the father singing as often as the mother. In most cases it does not seem to matter what words are sung. Apparently almost any song can be used as a lullaby, no matter how much it may be concerned with violence or even death. In fact, some type of violence, if not death, seems to be found in the texts of most lullabies. Take, for example, the one that almost every-one knew when I was a child:

> Rockabye, baby, upon the tree top.
> When the wind blows the cradle will rock.
> When the bough breaks the cradle will fall;
> Down comes the cradle, baby, and all.

In the following lullaby, although it deals with the death of an animal, there is a certain degree of humor.

TR 1 Go Tell Aunt Rhody

Sung by Samuel Clay Dixon, Mount Vernon, 10 April 1938.

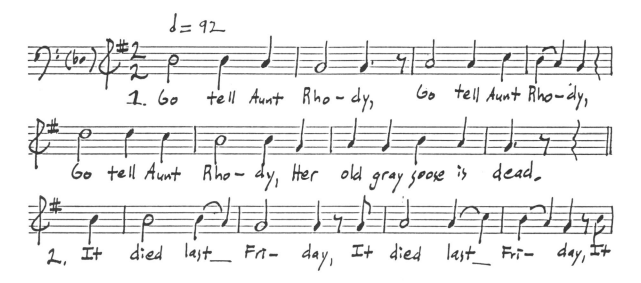

56

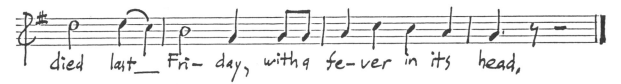

died last___ Fri- day, with a fe- ver in its head,

1. Go tell Aunt Rhody,
   Go tell Aunt Rhody,
   Go tell Aunt Rhody,
   Her old grey goose is dead.

2. It died last Friday,
   It died last Friday,
   It died last Friday,
   With a fever in its head.

3. The one she was saving,
   The one she was saving,
   The one she was saving,
   To make her feather bed.

This is one of the lullabies which Sue Becknell, Samuel Clay Dixon's daughter, remembers his singing to her when she was a child. This song is so well known in the Midwest and South that many collectors have not bothered to record it. The unfortunate loss of the makings of a feather bed may also be brought to the attention of Aunt Tabby, Aunt Nancy, or Aunt Phoebe. Usually, but not always, the last line of each stanza rhymes. No other variants of this little lullaby seem to be published in Indiana, but the following rhyming final lines can be found elsewhere:

She died in the manger (etc.)
With a toothache in her head.

She died with the slow fever (etc.)
Out behind the shed.

No more little goslin's (etc.)
To make a feather bed.[1]

And one I remember:

She died in the mill-pond, (etc.)
A-standing on her head.

In the last century this simple tune was frequently employed by the compilers of southern hymnals. The tune can be seen in the middle voice of "Sweet Affliction," which is reproduced from *The Sacred Harp* by B. F. White and E. J. King, the most popular of these nineteenth-century hymnals. Their compilers, to facilitate sight-singing, used notes of different shapes, not only oval but also triangular, square, and diamond-shaped. These "shape notes" or "buckwheat notes" came from

SWEET AFFLICTION. 8, 7. Rippon's Hymns, p. 541.

B. F. White and E. J. King, *The Sacred Harp* (Facsimile of 3d ed., 1859. Reprint. Nashville: Broadman Press, 1968), 145

the southern singing-school movement beginning earlier in the century.

The fasola compilers attributed the melody to Jean-Jacques Rousseau, the author of *The Social Contract* and the creator of Emile, the natural man. The tune is traditionally known as "Rousseau's Dream."[2] James T. Lightwood writes that the melody was employed by the composer, J. B. Cramer, as the basis for a set of variations for piano published in 1818.[3] From a different source we learn that the melody was used "in an opera written by Jean-Jacques Rousseau in 1750."[4]

Unfortunately, none of these statements concerning the use or origin of the melody can be verified utilizing the best available present sources. Rousseau wrote a variety of music: some has been lost, some remains in manuscript, and only part is published. There is no record of his writing an opera in 1750. J. B. Cramer, who lived most of his life in England, composed some thirty sets of piano variations which are not cataloged.

TR 2 Two Babes in the Woods

(Child ESB, The Children in the Wood)

Sung by Samuel Clay Dixon, Mount Vernon, 10 April 1938.

58

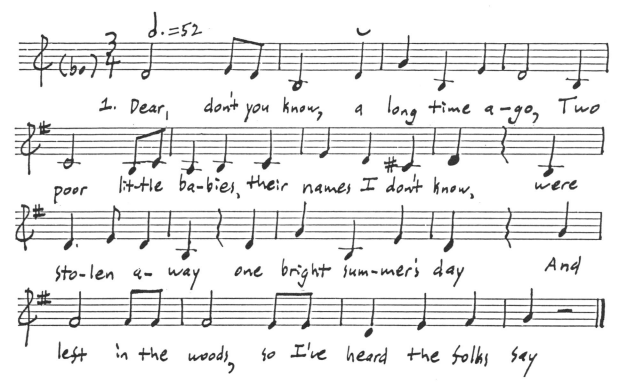

1. Dear, don't you know, a long time ago,
   Two poor little babies, their names I don't know,
   Were stolen away one bright summer's day,
   And left in the woods, so I've heard the folks say.

2. And when it was night, so sad was their plight,
   The sun went down, the stars gave no light;
   They sobbed and they sighed, they bitterly cried;
   Poor babes in the woods, they laid down and died.

3. And when they were dead, the robins so red
   Brought strawberry leaves and over them spread,
   And all day long they sang their sad song:
   "Poor babes in the woods, poor babes in the woods."

TR 3 Two Babes in the Woods

Sung by Orpha Mae Curry, Bloomington, 29 August 1955.

1. Oh, don't you remember a long time ago
   These poor little babes, whose names I don't know,
   Were stolen 'way one dark summer's day
   And lost in the woods I've heard people say.

60

2. And when they were dead the robins so red
   Brought strawberry leaves and over them spread
   And all the day long they sang them this song:
   "Poor babes in the woods, poor babes in the woods."

After singing this song Mrs. Curry said, "This is a song my dad used to sing to me. It's real sad and I used to enjoy it and cry."

This is a very old ballad which has often been issued as a broadside, a copy of a poem printed on one side of a sheet of paper designed to be hawked through the streets or sold in shops. The broadside might include the name of a tune to which it should be sung and possibly the name of the printer but never that of an author. For its first printing this ballad was registered at Stationers' Hall in London on 15 October 1595 "under the hands of both of the wardens" by Thomas Millington. It was entitled "The Norfolk gent, his will and testament, how he committed the keeping of his children to his own brother who dealt most wickedly with them and how God plagued him for it."

Samuel Pepys, from whose famous diary we have learned much of what we know concerning life and manners in seventeenth-century London, made a collection of these broadsides. Bishop Thomas Percy in his *Reliques* of 1886 publishes a variant based on "two ancient copies, one of them . . . in the Pepys Collection. Its title at large is, *The Children in the Wood; or, The Norfolk Gentleman's Last Will and Testament: To the Tune of Rogero, &c.*"[5]

In the ballad, when a mother and father find they are dying they decide to give over the care of their two children to their uncle. Breaking his promise to take care of them, he pays two ruffians to dispatch them. Before the deed is accomplished, one of the ruffians becomes "repentant," and a fight ensues in which the "unrepentant one" is killed. The surviving ruffian leaves, saying that he will return with food. He does not, and the children wander forlornly through the forest.

The ballad has twenty stanzas of eight lines each. The following, the latter half of the fifteenth and the entire sixteenth, parallel the abbreviated form sung in this country:

Their prettye lippes with black-berries,
Were all besmear'd and dyed,
And when they sawe the darksome night,
They sat them downe and cryed.

The Children in the Wood.

Thus wandered these poor innocents,
    Till death did end their grief;
In one anothers armes they dyed,
    As wanting due relief:
No burial this pretty pair
    Of any man receives,
Till Robin Red-breast piously
    Did cover them with leaves.

And now the heavy wrathe of God
    Upon their uncle fell;
Yea, fearfull fiends did haunt his house,
    His conscience felt an hell:
His barnes were fir'd, his goodes consum'd,
    His landes were barren made,
His cattle dyed within the field,
    And nothing with him stay'd.

And in a voyage to Portugall
    Two of his sonnes did dye;
And to conclude, himself was brought
    To want and miserỳe:
He pawn'd and mortgaged all his land
    Ere seven yeares came about.
And now at length this wicked act
    Did by this meanes come out:

" AND WHEN THEY SAW THE DARKSOME NIGHT,
THEY SAT THEM DOWNE AND CRYED."

131

Illustration by C. Gregory. George Barnett Smith (ed.), *Illustrated British Ballads, Old and New*, 2 vols. (London: Cassell, Petter, Galpin and Co., 1881), 1:131

Thus wandered these poor innocents,
Till death did end their grief,
In one anothers armes they dyed,
As wanting due relief:
No burial 'this' pretty 'pair'
Of any man receives,
Till Robin-red-breast piously
Did cover them with leaves.

God's heavy wrath now falls upon the uncle whose barns are fired, his goods consumed, and his sons killed. He pawns and mortgages all his lands and eventually dies in a debtors' prison. The ballad ends with the following homily:

You that executors be made,
And overseers eke
Of children that be fatherless,
And infants mild and meek;
Take you example by this thing,
And yield to each his right,
Lest God with such like miserye
Your wicked minds requite.[6]

This was one of the most popular of English ballads. Joseph Addison in the *Spectator*, no. 85, writes, "One of the darling songs of the common people, [which] has been the delight of most Englishmen in some part of their age." The long form was frequently reprinted during the eighteenth and nineteenth centuries. One reprint in Massachusetts carries this intriguing legend:

Sold by the Thousand, Groce, Hundred, Dozen, or Single, at the Bookstore and Printing-office of W. and J. GILMAN, Middle-street, Newburyport: Where may be had, wholesale or retail, a variety of Ancient and Modern Popular Songs and Ballads.--Price 3 cts.

The ballad was also included in a songbook, *The Warbler*, published in Augusta, Maine, in 1805. The ballad is frequently found in volumes of nursery rhymes and was also printed in a tiny book entitled *A Song Book for Little Children* in Newburyport in 1818.[7]

Paul Brewster published one text of this lullaby from Tell City, Perry County, which I give below. It is very much like the variant sung by Samuel Clay Dixon.

1. O don't you remember a long time ago,
   Three little babes whose names I don't know
   Were stolen away one bright summer day
   And lost in the woods, I've heard people say.

2. And when they were gone, so sad was their plight;
   The moon shone bright, the stars gave good light.
   They sighed; they sighed and bitterly cried,
   And those three little babes all lay down and died.

3. And when they were dead, the robins so red
   Scattered strawberry leaves all over their bed;
   They sang sweet songs and mourned along
   For those three little babes who are now dead and
       gone.[8]

And now a fourth stanza as sung in Missouri:

And after a while their mama came by.
She saw the poor babes and how she did cry!
She fainted and fell and by them she lay;
"God bless that robin!" was all she could say.[9]

The belief that the robin covers dead human bodies with moss or leaves is very old. It appears in a passage from Shakespeare's *Cymbeline*, Act 4, Scene 2:

the ruddock would,
With charitable bill . . .
bring thee all this,
Yea and furr'd moss besides, when flowers are none,
To winter-ground thy corse

We find it also in an old tome with the following long-winded title: *Cornucopiae, or, divers Secrets; Wherein is contained the rare secrets of man, beasts, fowles, fishes, trees, plants, stones, and such like, most pleasant and profitable, and not before committed to be printed in English. Newlie drawn out of divers Latine Authors into English by Thomas Johnson. 4to. London, 1596*:

The robin red-breast if he find a man or woman dead will
cover all his face with mosse, and some thinke that if the
body should remaine unburied that hee woulde cover the whole
body also.[10]

64

The remaining songs in this chapter are those sung by children, rather than to them. In many cases, however, they are sung by adults who remember them from childhood.

TR 4 Ransum, Tansum

Sung by "Aunt" Phoebe Stoker Elliott, New Harmony, 10 March 1938.

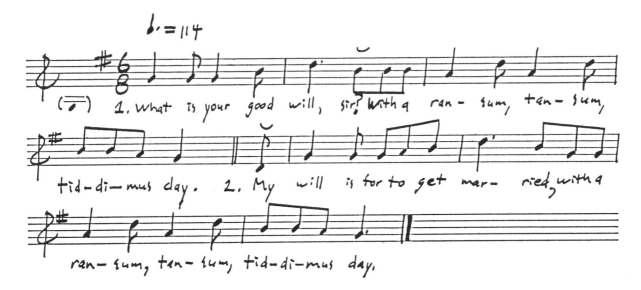

1. What is your good will, Sir?
    With a ransum, tansum, tiddimus day.

2. My will is for to get married.
    With a ransum, tansum, tiddimus day.

3. You're all too ragged and dirty.
    With a ransum, tansum, tiddimus day.

4. We're good enough for you, Sir.
    With a ransum, tansum, tiddimus day.

Mrs. Elliott, who was better known as "Aunt" Phoebe, said this was the song to a game she had played in 1865. She was ten years old at the time. This is a very old and widely distributed singing game, which was probably brought to this country from the British Isles. Alice Gomme transcribes and describes a number of variants of this game played around the turn of the century in England and Ireland.[11] "Aunt" Phoebe does not sing the usual first and last stanzas, and her stanzas are shorter than those commonly heard. Here is a text collected by Gomme in 1891:

1. Here come three dukes a-riding,
   A-riding, a-riding;
   Here come three dukes a-riding,
   With a rancy, tancy, tay!

2. What is your good will, sirs?
   Will, sirs? will, sirs?
   What is your good will, sirs?
   With a rancy, tancy, tay!

3. Our good will is to marry,
   To marry, to marry; (etc.)

4. Marry one of us, sirs,
   Us, sirs, us, sirs; (etc.)

5. You're all too black and greasy [or dirty],
   Greasy, greasy; (etc.)

6. We're good enough for you, sirs,
   You, sirs, you, sirs; (etc.)

7. You're all as stiff as pokers,
   Poker, pokers; (etc.)

8. We can bend as much as you, sirs,
   You, sirs, you, sirs; (etc.)

9. Through the kitchen and down the hall,
   I choose the fairest of you all;
   The fairest one that I can see
   Is pretty Miss -----, walk with me.[12]

Note the two extra stanzas of repartee.

The game could be played with one duke or several; in the latter case it was usually three or four. "Aunt" Phoebe describes the game as she played it as follows:

There was a crowd of girls in a row and they would all march forward to meet this young man, this boy, and we'd say, "What is your good will, sir?" etc.

"Aunt" Phoebe's further description of the game was sketchy. Brewster describes the way the game was played in Indiana with one duke. The game begins with a row of girls hand in hand and one person, the duke, coming forward singing the first stanza. As the duke moves backward the line of girls moves forward and sings the second stanza.

66

The first stanza sung by the duke is:

Here comes one duke
a-roving, a-roving, a-roving;
Here comes one duke a-roving
for the ranzy, tanzy, tee.

As he sings the last stanza the duke selects a partner from the line. The girl selected then becomes a duke, and the two advance singing, "Here comes two dukes a-roving," etc. The game continues until all have changed places.[13]

The English variant from Gomme given above contains the words "Three Dukes" in the first line, as does another variant from Indiana published by Brewster.[14] The first lines of the variants published by Mabel Evangeline Neal[15] and Leah Jackson Wolford[16] refer to "Four Dukes." Although Wolford's variant is published in her *The Play-Party in Indiana*, she writes that in her area at the time she collected her material this game was played only by children, not by the young people in the play-party (see Chapter 3).

Since it was a popular play-party singing game elsewhere, she has included it. I give below the music and the transcription of the first two and the last stanzas of the text.

TR 5 Here Come Four Dukes A-Riding

Name of informant and place of collection not given, prior to 1916.

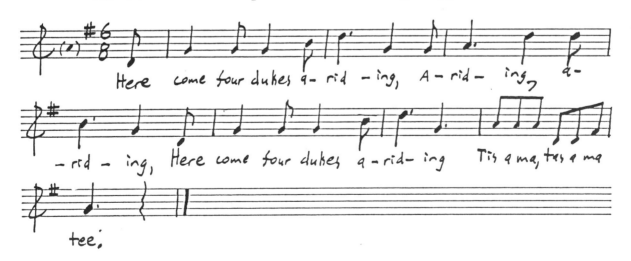

St. 1. Boys: 1. Here come four dukes a-riding,
                        2. A-riding, a-riding.
                        3. Here come four dukes a-riding,
                        4. Tis a ma, tas a ma tee.

St. 2. Girls: 1. What are you riding here for?
                        2. Here for, here for?
                        3. What are you riding here for?
                        4. Tis a ma, tas a ma tee.

St. 7. Boys: 1. I think then I'll take you, Miss,
                        2. You, Miss, you, Miss.
                        3. I think then I'll take you, Miss,
                        4. Tis a ma, tas a ma tee.

Wolford describes two ways in which the game is played. In the first, the boys form a line and lock arms. The girls do the same, facing the line of the boys about six steps from them. At 1 the boys advance with prancing gait toward the girls. At 2 they recede and at 3 advance again. At 4 they recede to their former positions. The girls then advance and recede from the boys keeping the same time. During the second line of the last stanza each boy takes the arm of one of the girls and skips away with her.

In the second way of playing the game, after choosing a girl the boy takes her back with him. Then they all advance again, and another boy chooses a girl and returns with her. This occurs with a third boy and girl. Finally, all four boys and the three girls advance, and this time the fourth boy chooses the last girl.[17] Gomme describes the prancing gait used by the boys as an imitation of riding.[18]

The earliest known reference to the playing of this game comes from Lancashire, England, between 1820 and 1830. It begins:

Here comes Three Dukes a-riding
With a rancy tancy terry boy's horn!
Here comes Three Dukes a-riding
With a rancy tancy tee!

The game was "acted with much energy and gestures and tones of servility, scorn, etc."[19] In 1816 the game appears in a book addressed to the English gentility, *Merrie Games in Rhyme*, by E. M. Plunket, who was of the opinion that by playing such games "children of the well-to-do . . . might

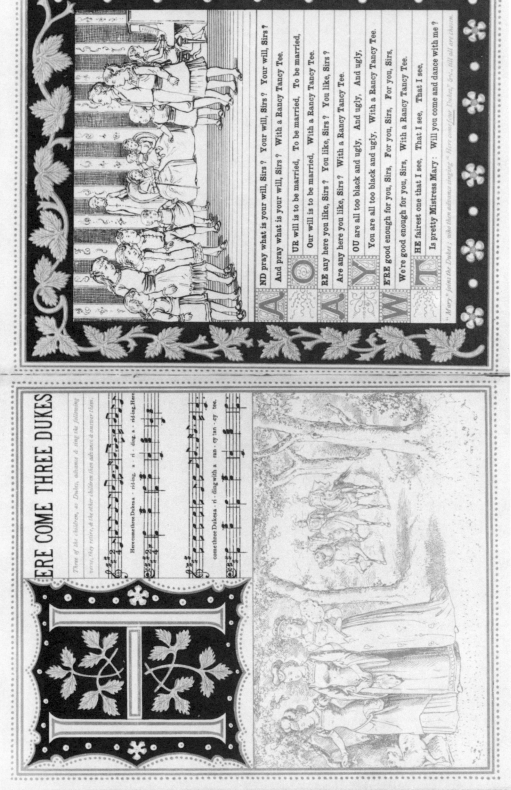

E. M. Plunket, *Merrie Games in Rhyme* (London: W. Garner, Darton and Co., 1886)

69

find pleasure for themselves and their elders," as seen in the accompanying illustration.[20]

William Wells Newell quotes a variant of the game in which the word "ducks" is substituted for "dukes." He found this variant to be "common through the Middle states" in the middle part of the last century.[21] Gomme also encountered children singing "ducks" instead of "dukes" in London's Regent's Park.[22]

Newell believes the game to be a descendant of an older European game known as "Three Kings," in which suitors address mothers negotiating a marriage.[23] No reference to a game called "Three Kings" was found, but the following variant of "Three Dukes A-Riding" published in *Shropshire Folk-lore* in 1883 fits this description:

1st Party.	'Here comes Three Dukes a-riding, a-riding, With a ransome dansome day!
2nd Party.	Pray what is your intent, sirs, intent, sirs? With a ransome dansome day!
1st.	My intent is to marry, to marry!
2nd.	Will you marry one of my daughters, my daughters?
1st.	You are as stiff as pokers, as pokers!
2nd.	We can bend like you, sir, like you, sir!
1st.	You're all too black and too blowsy, too blowsy, For a dilly-dally officer!
2nd.	Good enough for *you*, sir! for *you*, sir!
1st.	If I must have any, I will have this, So come along, my pretty miss![24]

Alternatively, Newell suggested that the game, also known as "The Knights of Spain," may represent the action of an intermediary arranging marriage for other parties.[25] Perhaps he was referring to "The Knights Out of Spain," described in the same volume as the variant of "Three Dukes A-Riding" given above. "The Knights Out of Spain" is played as follows:

> The girl at each end of the long row goes over to the Knights, and the game is repeated with five, seven, etc. Knights. The last who is left takes the Knight's part in the next game. Thus [it was played] at Edgemond: but in other places the Knights call one girl only by name each time.[26]

In a similar game played in Italy it is an ambassador who makes the marital arrangements. It begins:

70

È rivato l'ambasciatore,
Olì olì olela;
È rivato l'ambasciatore,
Olì olì ola.

The ambassador is asked what he wants, and he replies that he wants one of their daughters. When queried as to his purpose, he says that he wishes to give her away in marriage. To whom does he wish to give her? To a knight of the king. And what gift will he give her? A basket of flowers. The gift is declared insufficient. He offers a palace of gold, which is readily accepted.[27]

Newell believes the American game, "Three Ducks A-Riding," as played in his day, to be a vulgarized version of the earlier game, which subsequently lost the aspect of mercenary negotiation. It now represents coquetry and bargaining by the suitors directly with the young unmarried women, rather than with their mothers or through an intermediary.[28]

Gomme is of the opinion that the game as played in her time was a reflection of a children's tradition of a thousand years before. She believes it to be a survival of a group marriage custom, of exogamous marriage in which young men of one clan go to the abode of another where there are women waiting who are willing to be married. The boys' deprecation of the girls and the latter's rejoinder is a display of wit which enhances the value of the brides. Gomme points out that there is no indication of love, individual courtship, no marriage rite of any kind, nor even kissing.[29]

Singing games involving kissing were commonly played by children in the last century.

TR 6 Sister Phoebe

Sung by "Aunt" Phoebe Stoker Elliott, New Harmony, 10 April 1938.

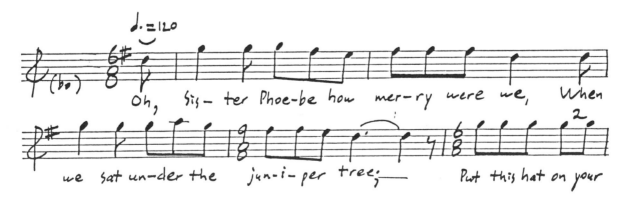

71

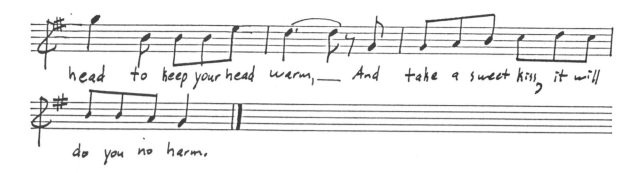

head to keep your head warm,___ And take a sweet kiss, it will
do you no harm.

> Oh, Sister Phoebe, how merry were we,
> When we sat under the Juniper tree;
> Put this hat on your head to keep your head warm,
> And take a sweet kiss, it will do you no harm.

"Aunt" Phoebe commented, "Then the hat was placed on our head and we got a sweet kiss. Of course, it didn't do us any harm at all." This children's game, also known as "The Juniper Tree," like "Four Dukes A-Riding," was incorporated into the play-party (see Chapter 3). In playing the game the children form a ring, the girl in the center holding a hat. She chooses a boy from the ring, draws him into the circle, places the hat upon his head, and kisses him. She then returns to the circle. The boy in his turn selects a girl, places the hat upon her head, kisses her, and then returns to the ring. The game continues, boys and girls alternately in the circle, each choosing a partner of the opposite sex.

There are no analogues in the English repertory as far as the words of the song are concerned nor the placing of a hat upon the head of the individual to be kissed. However, Gomme describes a number of games in which one individual stands within a ring and chooses another from it to come within and be kissed. The first individual then returns to the ring, and the second chooses a third to enter the ring and be kissed, etc. This is the action carried out in "Here Stands a Young Man,"[30] "Lady on the Mountain,"[31] "Sally Water,"[32] and "The Silly Old Man."[33] However, no marriage formula is found in "Sister Phoebe," as it is in most of these English ring-kissing games as, for example, in "Lady on the Mountain."

> Now you're married I wish you joy,
> First a girl and then a boy;

Seven years after a son and a daughter,
Kiss your bride and come out of the ring.[34]

TR 7 Soldier, Soldier, Won't You Marry Me?

Sung by Vern Smelser, Paoli, 1963.

1. "Soldier, soldier, won't you marry me?"
   Fife, fiddle, and a drum.
   "How could I marry such a pretty little miss
   When I got no socks to put on?"
   Away she ran to the socker-ocker shop
   Just as fast as she could run.
   There she got the finest, finest socks
   And the soldier put 'em on.

2. "Soldier, soldier, won't you marry me?"
   Fife, fiddle, and a drum.
   "How could I marry such a pretty little miss
   When I got no shoes to put on?"
   Away she ran to the shoeterooter shop
   Just as fast as she could run.
   There she got the finest, finest shoes
   And the soldier put 'em on.

3. "Soldier, soldier, won't you marry me?"
   Fife, fiddle, and a drum.
   "How could I marry such a pretty little miss
   When I got no pants to put on?"
   Away she ran to the pantserantser shop
   Just as fast as she could run.
   There she got the finest, finest pants
   And the soldier put 'em on.

4. "Soldier, soldier, won't you marry me?"
   Fife, fiddle, and a drum.
   "How could I marry such a pretty little miss
   When I got no shirt to put on?"
   Away she ran to the shirterirter shop
   Just as fast as she could run.
   There she got the finest, finest shirt
   And the soldier put it on.

5. "Soldier, soldier, won't you marry me?"
   Fife, fiddle, and a drum.
   "How could I marry such a pretty little miss
   When I got no hat to put on?"
   Away she ran to the hatteratter shop
   Just as fast as she could run.
   There she got the finest, finest hat
   And the soldier put it on.

6. "Soldier, soldier, won't you marry me?"
   Fife, fiddle, and a drum.
   "How could I marry such a pretty little miss
   When I got a wife at home?"

Newell records that this dialogue was being sung by American children over a hundred years ago.

Our version was sung by children of from five to eight years of age, and made a favorite amusement at the afternoon gatherings. When one couple had finished, another pair would begin, and so on for hours at a time. The object was to provide for the soldier the most varied wardrobe possible; while the maiden put the question with spirit, laying her hand upon her heart, respecting which the prevailing opinion was that it was under the left arm.[35]

This children's song was recorded by a country group, Gid Tanner and His Skillet Lickers, in 1930.[36]

TR 8 Green Gravel

Sung by Samuel Clay Dixon, Mount Vernon, 10 April 1938.

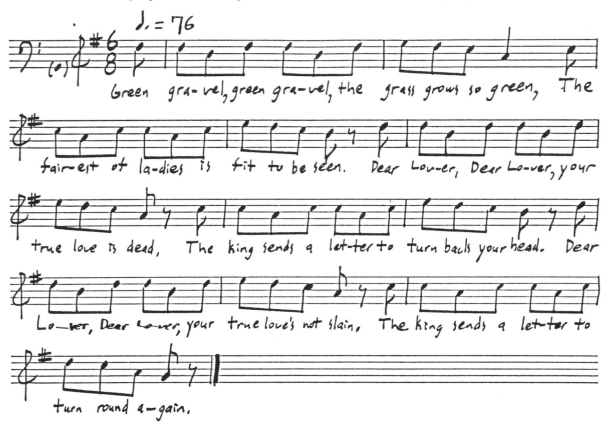

Green gravel, green gravel, the grass grows so green.
The fairest of ladies is fit to be seen.
Dear lover, dear lover, your true love is dead.
The King sends a letter to turn back your head.
Dear lover, dear lover, your true love's not slain.
The King sends a letter to turn round again.

Here a song usually sung only by girls is sung by a man. This game has intrigued all who have known it. The English novelist, Thomas Hardy, remembering it from his youth, speculated that "green

75

gravel" meant "green grave-O." There have been many other interpretations of these mysterious words. Could "green gravel" come from "green graff," meaning "green grave?"[37] Or might "green" as applied to "gravel" mean freshly disturbed earth as "green grave" refers to a freshly made grave?[38]

I find no information as to how the game was played in Indiana. Newell prints only the first four lines of the song, but in the third line "lover" is replaced with a blank space where the name of one of the participants in the game is to be mentioned. He reports that in Washington the game is played in a ring with the girls clasping each other's hands. As they dance around singing, the girl whose name is mentioned turns her head over her shoulder. The stanza is repeated with a different name sung in each until each girl has turned her head over her shoulder. According to Newell the turning of the head is a sign of sorrow.[39]

Gomme reproduces seventeen variants of the text of this singing game. The first, collected in Belfast, reads:

> Green gravel, green gravel, your grass is so green,
> The fairest young damsel that ever was seen;
> We washed her, we dried her, we rolled her in silk,
> And wrote down her name with a glass pen and ink.
> Dear Annie, dear Annie, your true love is dead,
> And we send you a letter to turn round your head.[40]

This variant is played by a ring of children who walk around singing the words. When the last line is sung, the child whose name has been mentioned turns to face the outside of the circle with her back to the center. She continues to dance with the others in that position. This is repeated until all the children's names have been mentioned and all have turned. The game commonly ends at this point in most variants. But in other variants, such as the following collected in Lincoln, Winterton, and Wakefield, it continues:

> 1. Green gravel, green gravel,
>   The grass is so green,
>   The fairest young damsels
>   As ever were seen.
>   O ___, O ___, your true love is dead;
>   He sent you a letter to turn round your head.

2. Green gravel, green gravel,
   The grass is so green,
   The dismalest damsels
   As ever were seen.
   O ___, O ___, your true love's not dead;
   He sends you a letter to turn back your head.

As the second stanza is sung, each girl, as her name is called, reverses position until all are facing inward again.[41]

Gomme compares the seventeen variants of the text and extracts the elements most frequently heard to make the following composite poem.

Green gravel,
Your grass is so green.
Fairest damsel ever seen
Washed her, dried her, rolled her in silk.
Wrote name in glass pen and ink
Your true love is dead
He sent you a letter to turn your head.[42]

Note that "washed her, dried her, and rolled her in silk" and "wrote name in glass pen and ink" do not appear in the American variants.

Gomme writes that this is evidently a funeral game and that these two lines represent the preparation for burial of the corpse of a well-loved lady and the placing of an inscription upon the place where she is laid.

Gomme believes that the turning of the back by the children is a sign of grief, possibly derived from an old funerary custom in Derbyshire and the Isle of Man in which those watching with the corpse go out of the room and return walking backward while repeating a verbal formula known as "saining."[43]

Newell's interpretation is necessarily different since his variant has a happy ending. "In this case the absent lover has gone to war, and the letter announcing his death in battle comes, I should think, from his officer (the King)."[44]

An interesting aspect of the American variants is the expression of prejudice against freemasonry not manifest in the English variants. "Aunt" Phoebe only remembers the first two lines which are:

>Green gravel, green gravel, how green the grass doth
>>grow.
>Freemason, Freemason, it is a shame to show.[45]

A variant reproduced by Newell begins:

>Green gravel, green gravel, the grass is so green,
>And all the free masons are ashamed to be seen.[46]

Song is often used as a mnemonic device. It seems easier to remember a series of numbers or words if they are sung or chanted rather than spoken. Thus the skills learned in school are often incorporated into song either by the children themselves or by their teachers. As "Aunt" Phoebe relates:

>When I was a little girl, about five years old, I went to school with an old lady who taught school here for a number of years. Her name was Mrs. Craddock, Elizabeth Craddock. We learned the multiplication table by singing it to a singsong tune which always remained in my memory and also the multiplication table.

TR 9 The Multiplication Table Song

Sung by "Aunt" Phoebe Stoker Elliott, New Harmony, 10 April 1938.

twice eight are six-teen

Twice one are two and twice two are four,
Twice three are six and twice four are eight.
Twice five are ten and twice six are twelve.
Twice seven are fourteen, twice eight are sixteen.
Twice nine are eighteen and twice ten are twenty.
Twice eleven are twenty-two, twice twelve are
      twenty-four.

And then "Aunt" Phoebe said, "And when we sang the fives we just added an extra touch to the tune of 'Yankee Doodle Dandy.'"

TR 10 Multiplication Table Song Continued

Sung by "Aunt" Phoebe Stoker Elliott, New Harmony, 10 April 1938.

Five times five are twenty-five
And five times six are thirty.
Five times seven are thirty-five;
And five times eight are forty.
Five times nine are forty-five;
Five times ten are fifty.
Five times 'leven are fifty-five;
And five times twelve are sixty.

"Aunt" Phoebe was also taught the capitals of the states in the same manner.

TR 11 Capitals of the States

Sung by "Aunt" Phoebe Stoker Elliott, New Harmony, 10 April 1938.

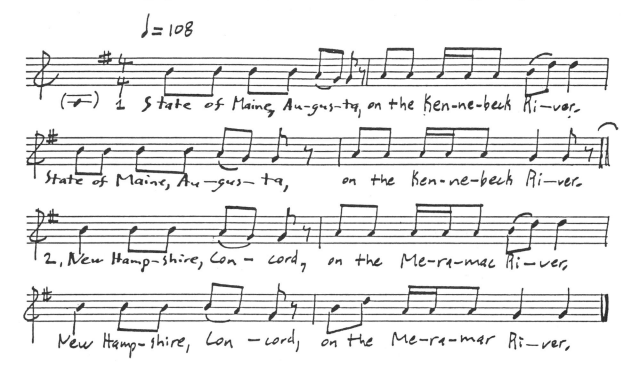

1. State of Maine, Augusta, on the Kennebeck River.
   State of Maine, Augusta, on the Kennebeck River.

2. New Hampshire, Concord, on the Meramec River.
   New Hampshire, Concord, on the Meramec River.

3. Vermont, Montpelier, on the Onion River.
   Vermont, Montpelier, on the Onion River.

"Aunt" Phoebe was a native of New Harmony, a community with a fascinating history. It was

named Harmony by its founder, Father George Rapp, leader of the Harmony Society, a band of German peasants who were dedicated to perfect Christian communal living. They had migrated from the province of Württemberg in 1803 and had first settled in Pennsylvania. In 1813 they moved to Indiana. In 1824 the Harmonists moved again, and the land and buildings were acquired by Robert Owen, a Scots manufacturer and philanthropist. He used the site for an experiment in secular communal living, in which a number of leading scientists, educators, and artists from both Europe and America participated. Although the experiment did not last long, it was the birthplace of many things now considered commonplace, such as free public schools and free libraries.[47]

"Aunt" Phoebe Elliott was a descendant of Benjamin Stoker, who settled in the area in 1804 before the Rappites arrived. At the time that "Aunt" Phoebe went to school in New Harmony, the school was located in the old Harmonist church, which had been erected in 1822. The accompanying photograph of the church-schoolhouse was made in 1870.

Courtesy of Josephine Elliott
School in New Harmony attended by "Aunt" Phoebe Stoker Elliott

The singer of the following song learned it in school in the period following the Civil War. The song reflects an optimistic view of education that was probably shared by many at the time. The song was taught to her by an elderly man, a veteran of the Civil War who was her teacher from the second through the seventh grades at a little rural school at Gordon Hill, near Patoka.

TR 12 Uncle Sam

Sung by Mary Vandora McNeely Bryant, Evansville, 11 April 1938.

broad Saint Lau-rence flow, Come from Flor-i-dy and Texas, come from

Maine and Mex-i-co, Come and wel-come to our school-room from the

broad At-lan-tic shore, To the gol-den re-gions

where they hear the old Pa-cif-ic roar.

1. Of all the institutions in the East or in the West,
    The glorious institution of the schoolroom is the best.
    We have room for ev'ry scholar and our banner is
        unfurled,
    With a gen'ral invitation to the people of the World.

CHORUS:

    Then come along, come along, make no delay,
    Come from ev'ry dwelling, come from ev'ry way.
    Bring your slates and books along and don't be a fool.
    For Uncle Sam is rich enough to send us all to school.

2. Come from where the mighty waters of the broad St.
        Lawrence flow,
    Come from Floridy and Texas, come from Maine and Mexico.
    Come and welcome to our schoolroom from the broad
        Atlantic shore,
    To the golden regions where they hear the old Pacific
        roar.

CHORUS

3. While Europe's in commotion and her people in a fret,
    We are teaching them a lesson that they never can
        forget;
    And there, they're fast a-learning Uncle Sam is not a
        fool,
    For the people do the voting while the children go to
        school.

CHORUS

Uncle Sam.

1. Of all the institutions in the east or in the west,
The glorious institution of the schoolroom is the best,
We have room for every scholar, and our banner is unfurled,
With a general invitation to the people of the world.

Chorus:

Then come along, come along, make no delay,
Come from every dwelling, come from every way;
Bring your slates and books along and don't be a fool,
For Uncle Sam is rich enough to give us all a ~~school~~

2. Come from where the mighty waters of the broad St. Lawrence flow,
Come from Florida and Texas, come from Maine and Mexico;
Come and welcome to our schoolroom from the broad Atlantic shore,
To the golden regions where they hear the old Pacific roar.

3. We will spell and read and cipher, write and think when thoughts are free,
And in study with attention carve a noble destiny;
Our motto is "Excelsior" and with our watchword true,
We will leave the world the wiser when we've passed our lifetime through.

4. While Europe's in commotion and her people in a fret,
We are teaching them a lesson that which they never can forget;
And then they fast are learning Uncle Sam is not a fool,
For the people do the voting while the children go to school.

5. Our fathers gave us liberty, but little did they dream
Of the grand results that follow in the wondrous age of steam;
With the march of education all the world is set on fire,
And we send our thoughts by lightning on the telegraphic wire.

Gordon Hills Sept. 26, 1887.

Your Friend J. P. S.

Handwritten text of "Uncle Sam"

84

The reproduced text of the song was a gift to Dora from her seventh-grade teacher. The hand-written script is incredibly fine. She was obviously singing from memory for the Lomaxes since she sings only three stanzas of the song.

Most of us, being human, occasionally find a reason to be angry at another person. Adults have learned to repress or to disguise hostility, or to express it in socially acceptable ways. Small children commonly express hostility to each other quite overtly, often singing taunts or jeers. Here is a classic which I remember singing as a small child.

TR 13 Crybaby, Crybaby (No. 1)

Sung by Larry, Bloomington, 27 August 1955.

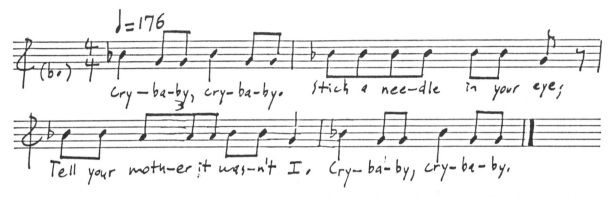

Since the taunts are so short the words are given only under the music. Larry (his surname was unfortunately not secured) was eight years of age at the time he was recorded, as were Patty Curry and Linda Crow, who also sang taunts recorded on the same date in Bloomington. The last taunt is sung by Mandie List on 7 October 1986, also in Bloomington. She was twelve years of age when she was recorded singing the taunt, but had made use of it at a much earlier age.

Here is an extended version of TR 13 above as sung by Patty.

TR 14 Crybaby, Crybaby (No. 2)

Sung by Patty Curry, Bloomington, 27 August 1955.

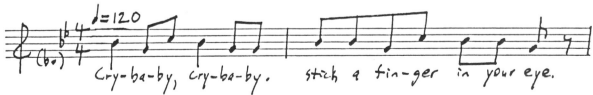

85

haw, haw, haw, haw, haw, I have some-thing that you don't have and I will squash it in your face.

Of the following two jeers or taunts, the first is directed to a boy, the second to a girl.

TR 15 "Crazyhead, Michael" and "I Know a Little Girl"

Sung by Patty Curry, Bloomington, 27 August 1955.

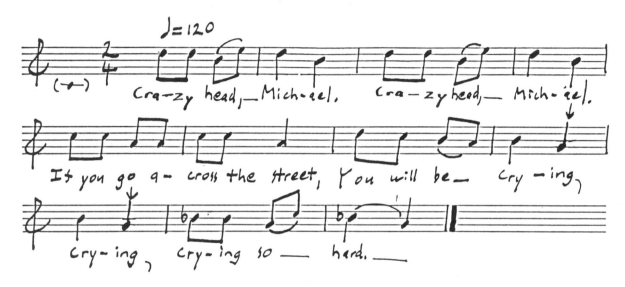

Cra-zy head,— Mich-ael. Cra-zy head,— Mich-ael. If you go a-cross the street, You will be— cry-ing, cry-ing, cry-ing so— hard.—

I know a lit-tle girl, and she is-n't verry nice. Haw, haw, haw, haw, haw.

Of the next three, the first is self-explanatory; the second is sung to dogs; and the third is sung to make people angry.

TR 16 "Shut Up, Brenda," "Doggie Woggie Woo Woo," and "Gabby Fabbly"

Sung by Linda Crow, Bloomington, 27 August 1955.

And finally:

TR 17 Ugly and Rotten

Sung by Mandie List, Bloomington, 7 October 1986.

After singing this, Mandie would stick out her tongue and say, "Nyaaaa!"

Most of these jeers or taunts are sung to a melodic formula that consists of only three pitches. (The remaining two are sung to ones that are quite similar.) This little tune is employed by children for other purposes as well. The following is used in playing "Hide and Go Seek":

TR 18 Ready or Not

Sung by Patty Curry, Bloomington, 27 August 1955.

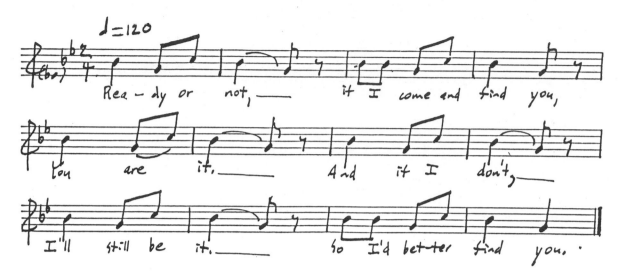

Ready or not, if I come and find you,
You are it.
And if I don't I'll still be it.
So I'd better find you.

The next two impolite ditties obviously were not learned in school. The first is sung when it rains. I asked Patty where she learned the second. She replied, "After school."

TR 19 "It's Raining" and "School's Out"

Sung by Patty Curry, Bloomington, 27 August 1955.

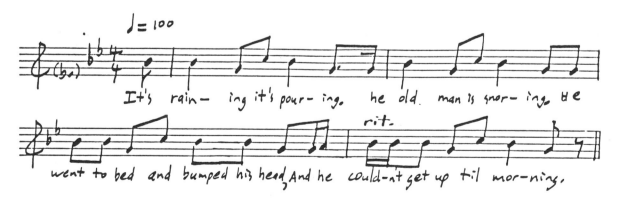

It's raining, it's pouring.
The old man is snoring.
He went to bed and bumped his head,
And he couldn't get up until morning.

School's out, school's out,
The teacher let the news out.
No more pencils, no more books,
No more teacher's dirty looks.
Kick the table, kick the chairs,
Kick the teacher down the stairs.

The following singing game was recorded on the playground of the Rogers School in Bloomington, as sung by a group of girls who informed me that they had learned it at Girl Scout meetings. They were referring to a cadet troop which contains girls from the sixth through the eighth grades. The photograph was made simultaneously. In its own way this children's game reflects the sexual revolution characteristic of the second half of the present century. No group of girls would have played such a game on a playground in "Aunt" Phoebe's day.

TR 20 Here Comes Susie

Sung by a group of sixth-grade girls, Bloomington, Spring 1959.

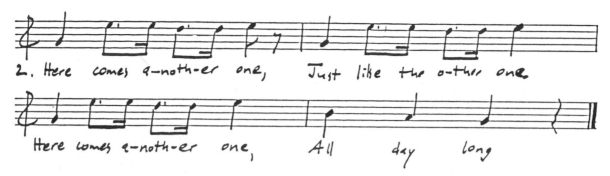

2. Here comes a-noth-er one, Just like the o-ther one
Here comes a-noth-er one, All day long

1. Here comes Susie,
   Strutting like a floozie.
   Here comes Susie,
   All day long.

2. Here comes another one,
   Just like the other one,
   Here comes another one,
   All day long.

3. This way Valerie,
   That way Valerie,
   This way Valerie,
   All day long.

In playing the game the girls form two rows or lines facing each other a few steps apart. The girl at the top of one line slowly and diagonally struts across the intervening space and takes her

Courtesy of Indiana University Radio and TV Department
Group of girls playing "Here Comes Susie"

90

place at the bottom of the opposite line. The girl at the top of that line then struts diagonally down and takes her place at the bottom of the first line. This continues until every girl has had her opportunity to strut. They walk swinging their hips with either one hand on a hip and the other on the head, both hands on hips, or one hand on a hip and the other swinging the girl's skirt. The latter is demonstrated in the accompanying photograph.

This game may have as an antecedent one played by black girls in Chicago in 1956, of which only the words are available:

Strut, Miss Susie!
Strut, Miss Susie!
Here comes another one,
Just like the other one.
Strut, Miss Susie!
All day long![48]

The fact that the white girls' words are sung to the melody of a black folk song, "Shortnin' Bread," further indicates its possible derivation from a black source. However, girls in St. John's Woods in London in 1973 sang as follows:

This way, Valerie,
That way, Valerie,
This way, Valerie,
All day long.

Here comes Valerie,
Here comes the other one,
Here comes Valerie,
All day long.

Here, again, neither the action of the game nor the tune to which it was sung are given. Iona and Peter Opie find a number of girls' games with similar lines being played contemporaneously in England. They believe the games to be constructed partially from lines or verses which are migrants from the United States plus others derived from eighteenth-century English clapping chants as, for example:

Where have you been all day long?
Up the alley, courting Sally,
Picking up cinders,

91

Breaking winders,
All-day-long.[49]

Which way "All day long" traversed the Atlantic seems moot.

Here are two related songs, again sung by adults who remembered them from their childhood.

TR 21 I Don't Want to Play in Your Yard

Sung by Dale Schreiber, Bloomington, 20 February 1988.

92

"You can't play in my yard," But the o-ther saids
Chorus "I don't went to play in your yard; I don't like you a-ny
more. You'll be sor-ry when you see me
Sli-ding down my cel-lor door. You can't hol-ler down our
rain bar-rel; Can't climb up our ap-ple tree.
I don't want to play in your yard ___ If you
won't be good to me."

1. Once there lived side by side
   Two little girls.
   Used to dress just alike,
   Hair down in curls.
   Blue gingham cute pinafores,
   Stockings of red.
   Little sunbonnets tied
   On each pretty head.
   When school was over
   Secrets they'd tell,
   Whispering arm in arm
   Down by the well.
   One day a quarrel came,
   Hot tears were shed
   "You can't play in my yard,"
   But the other said:

93

CHORUS:

"I don't want to play in your yard;
I don't like you any more.
You'll be sorry when you see me
Sliding down the cellar door.
You can't holler down my rainbarrel
Can't climb up our apple tree.
I don't want to play in your yard
If you won't be good to me."

TR 22 Come Over, Playmate

Self-recorded by Isabel Saulman Hoskinson, St. Louis, Missouri, 1 April 1988.

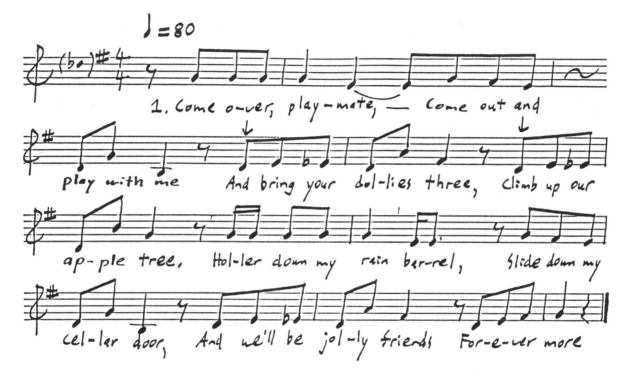

1. Come over, playmate,
   Come out and play with me
   And bring your dollies three,
   Climb up our apple tree.
   Holler down my rain barrel,
   Slide down my cellar door,
   And we'll be jolly friends
   Forever more.

2. I'm sorry, playmate,
   I cannot play with you.
   My dolly has the flu,
   Boo hoo hoo hoo hoo hoo.
   Ain't got no rain barrel,

94

Ain't got no cellar door,
But we'll be jolly friends
Forever more.

Dale Schreiber learned "I Don't Want to Play in Your Yard" from his sister, Hazel, who was ten years his senior. Like other inhabitants of the region, she had the habit of sitting on the porch swing in the evenings and singing to the younger children. Hazel, in turn, had learned the song from her parents. It was a very popular and widely sung song in its day. Like the remainder of their repertory, her parents had probably learned it from a phonograph record, possibly one in the form of a wax cylinder.

Mrs. Hoskinson learned "Come Over, Playmate" while a child living in Wadesville, Indiana. She had learned the song from her mother, Eva Saulman, and in turn had taught it to her daughter, Sara. Mrs. Hoskinson remembers singing the song when she was seven because there was a great snow that year, 1918, which permitted her to slide down their steep outside cellar door in a dishpan.

"I Don't Want to Play in Your Yard" was published in 1894 by the Petrie Music Company of Chicago. The words are by Philip Wingate, the music by H. W. Petrie, and it bears the dedication: "To the Ladies of the Charity Circle, La Porte, Ind." The words of the first verse and chorus are given below, and the cover and chorus of the sheet music are reproduced separately:

Once there lived side by side, two little maids,
Used to dress just alike, Hair down in braids,
Blue ging'am pinafores, stockings of red,
Little sunbonnets tied on each pretty head.
When school was over secrets they'd tell,
Whispering arm in arm, down by the well,
One day a quarrel came, hot tears were shed:--
"You can't play in our yard," But the other said:

CHORUS:

I don't want to play in your yard,
I don't like you any more,
You'll be sorry when you see me,
Sliding down our cellar door,
You can't holler down our rainbarrel,
You can't climb our apple tree,
I don't want to play in your yard
If you won't be good to me.

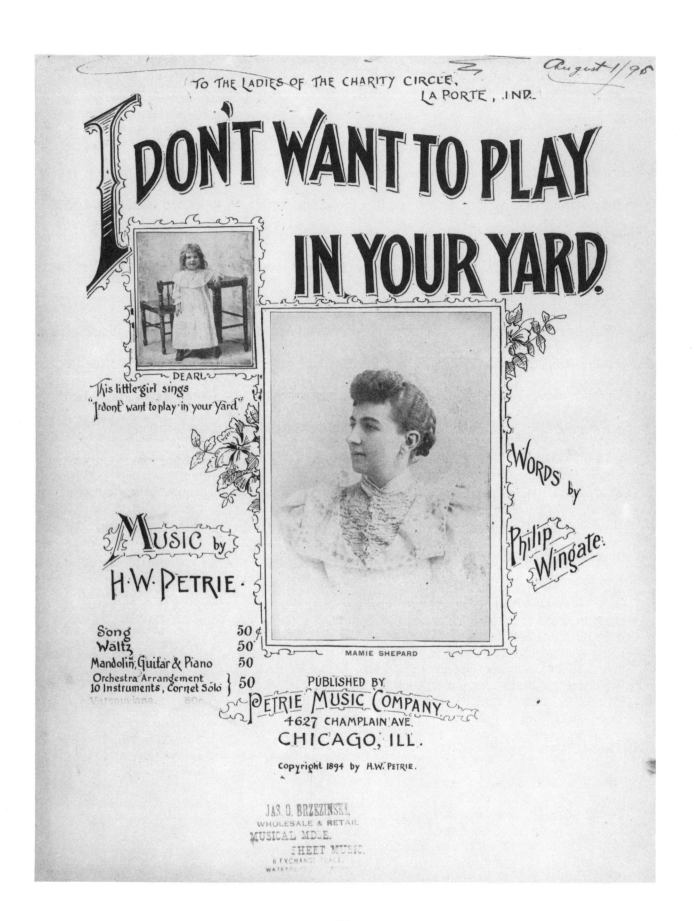

I DON'T WANT TO PLAY IN YOUR YARD.

Words by PHILIP WINGATE.

Music by H. W. PETRIE.

97

CHORUS.

I don't want to play in your yard, I don't like you a - ny more, You'll be sor-ry when you see me,

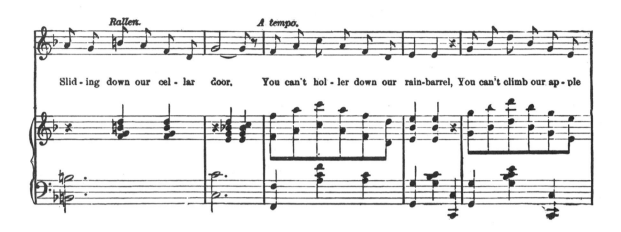

Slid - ing down our cel - lar door, You can't hol - ler down our rain-barrel, You can't climb our ap - ple

tree,...... I don't want to play in your yard If you wont be good to me....

I don't want to play in your yard. 3.

"WILL YOU LOVE ME, SWEETHEART, WHEN I'M OLD?"

WALTZ SONG.

By H. W. PETRIE.

The words are unusually good, and the melody as simple and pretty as can be. It is easy to sing and suits all voices. It is said to be the best composition of this favorite composer. Send for it. You will be well pleased and will recommend it to your friends.

PRICE 50c.

98

A song entitled "Playmates" was published in 1940 by Santly-Joy-Select, Inc., of New York. Words and music are by Saxie Dowell.

The choruses of both published songs contain three phrases alluding to some then-common activities of childhood: hollering or looking down a rain barrel or pipe, sliding down a cellar or kitchen door, and climbing an apple tree. On the basis of these three phrases the Opies came to the conclusion that the text of the chorus of the 1940 "Playmates" is based on the chorus of the 1894 "I Don't Want to Play in Your Yard." They note, however, that the melodies of the two songs are quite different.[50] The melody of TR 22, as sung by Mrs. Hoskinson, is almost identical to that of the chorus of the published "Playmates."

That the three phrases in question are alike is evident, but it would seem that both published songs have a common origin rather than one being derived from the other. The chorus of "Playmates" must be a children's traditional song which existed before either song was published. The verse of the 1940 "Playmates" strongly implies that the chorus which follows it is a previously existing song. Further, Isabel Hoskinson learned "Come Over, Playmate" from her mother, Eva Saulman, who was born in 1883. If she had known the song at age seven, as did her daughter, this would have antedated the publication of the 1894 song by four years. The three phrases concerning the rain barrel, the cellar door, and the apple tree must therefore have been lifted by the author of "I Don't Want to Play in Your Yard" from the existent children's song, "Come Over, Playmate," "My Jolly Playmate," or whatever beginning line may have been used by the many children who have sung it.

The school has adopted some of the traditional children's games but, as far as I can determine, the greater number of them are no longer sung. An exception to this are the girls' singing games in which clapping, gestures, or both form an integral part. They continue to flourish where young girls congregate, on the playground, at camp, or at Cadet Girl Scout meetings. The claps heard or the motions made in the following songs are represented in rhythm notation on a line above the staff. The capital letters placed below the rhythm notation have the following meanings:

F   Partners face each other, hands perpendicular to floor or ground. Each claps both hands against those of partner.

R   Same position. Clap right hand against right hand of partner.

L   Same position. Clap left hand against left hand of partner.

H   Same position. Girl claps own two hands together.

P   Partners face each other, hands held parallel to floor or ground. One hand is held above that of partner with palm facing down and the other hand below that of partner with palm facing up. Partners clap hands together.

T   Girl claps both hands on thighs or lap.

B   Bang. Imitation of shooting a pistol. Forefinger is pointed forward, thumb held upward, and the other fingers curled.

One other special notation is used:

   Rapid alternation of clapping hands on thighs, like a drum roll.

TR 23 My Jolly Playmate

Sung and clapped by the Binford School Cadet Troop No. 5,

Bloomington, 12 November 1975.

rain barrel, Into my cellar door, And we'll be jol-ly friends for-e-ver more; jol-ly friends for-e-ver more

O jolly playmate,
Come out and play with me,
And bring your dollies three,
Climb up my apple tree.
Slide down my rain barrel,
Into my cellar door,
And we'll be jolly friends,
Forever more; forever more.

This is a variant of the song as sung by Isabel Hoskinson. Rain barrels have gone out of style, but one still slides down a cellar door. Not, one opines, because the houses in which the girls lived in 1975 were equipped with outside cellar doors, but rather for need of a rhyme. The next clapping song is an exercise in memory and articulation.

TR 24 Flea

Sung and clapped by the Unionville Cadet Troop No. 273,

Unionville, 10 August 1975.

102

103

1. Leader: Flea.
   Group: Flea.

2. L: Flea fly.
   G: Flea fly.

3. L: Flea fly flo.
   G: Flea fly flo.

4. L: Vista.
   G: Vista.

5. L: Kuma la ta, kuma la ta, kuma la ta vista.
   G: Kuma la ta, kuma la ta, kuma la ta vista.

6. L: Oh, no, no, no not the vista.
   G. Oh, no, no, no not the vista.

7. L: Eeny, meeny, des a meeny, oo wa da wa da meeny.
   G: Eeny, meeny, des a meeny, oo wa da wa da meeny.

8. L: Ex a meeny, sola meeny, oo wa da wa.
   G: Ex a meeny, sola meeny, oo wa da wa.

9. L: Beat billy oaten doten, bo bo bu deat-en dotten,
      sssshhhh . . .
   G: Beat billy oaten doten, bo bo bu deat-en dotten,
      sssshhhh . . .

The next game is one in which words are spelled out rather than spoken as a whole.

TR 25 Ford

Sung and clapped by the Dyer Middle School Cadet Troop No. 197,

Bloomington, 24 November 1975.

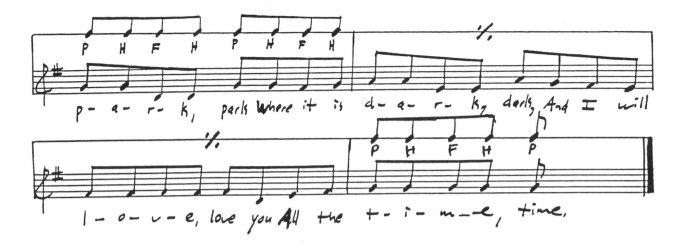

I have an F-o-r-d, Ford,
Made out of c-a-r-d board.
And I will t-a-k-e, take you
For a r-i-d-e, ride
Into the p-a-r-k, park,
Where it is d-a-r-k, dark.
And I will l-o-v-e, love you
All the t-i-m-e, time.
You are the b-e-s-t, best
Of all the r-e-s-t, rest.
And I will k-i-s-s, kiss you
All the t-i-m-e, time.

The singer of the following three songs was twelve years of age when she was recorded, but informed me that she had commonly sung the songs at ages eight through ten. Although not given here, she did sing and clap for me a variant of TR 23 above, "My Jolly Playmate." Except for minor changes in the first and last lines, her variant is the same as TR 23. TR 26 is what she describes as a "mean" version of the song.

TR 26 My Enemy

Sung and clapped by Mandie List, Bloomington, 7 October 1986.

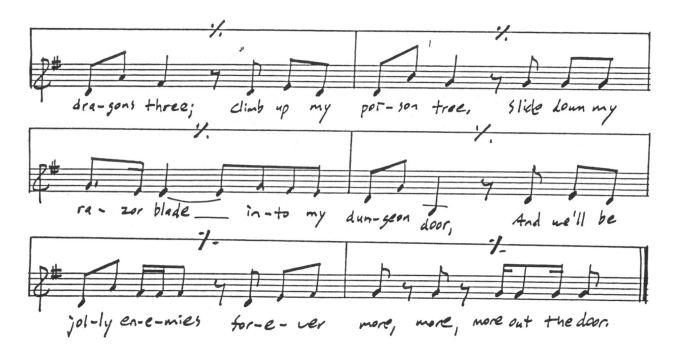

dra-gons three; climb up my poi-son tree, slide down my

ra - zor blade___ in-to my dun-geon door, And we'll be

jol-ly en-e-mies for-e-ver more, more, more out the door.

1. My enemy, come out and fight with me,
   And bring your dragons three;
   Climb up my poison tree.
   Slide down my razor blade into my dungeon door,
   And we'll be jolly enemies forever more,
   More, more out the door.

2. Oh, enemy, I cannot fight with you,
   My dragon's got the flu, boo hoo hoo hoo hoo hoo,
   Ain't got no razor blade, ain't got no dungeon door,
   But we'll be jolly enemies forever more,
   More, more out the door.

The repeated pattern of four claps was known in Mandie's circle as the "reverse clap." She and her friends enjoyed singing and clapping these songs as rapidly as they could while taking as few breaths as possible.

In the following song each participant claps her own hands. There is no hand contact between players. Thus, this singing game can be performed by one individual alone or by any number of individuals simultaneously. In spelling out the name of the dog, Bingo, a decreasing number of claps is substituted for its last four letters. When the name is finally spelled out in full, there is a clap accompanying each letter.

106

TR 27 Bingo

Sung and clapped by Mandie List, Bloomington, 7 October 1986.

1. There was a farmer had a dog,
    And Bingo was his name-o!
    B (clap, clap, clap, clap)
    B (clap, clap, clap, clap)
    B (clap, clap, clap, clap)
    And Bingo was his name-o!

2. There was a farmer had a dog,
    And Bingo was his name-o!
    B-I (clap, clap, clap)
    B-I (clap, clap, clap)
    B-I (clap, clap, clap)
    And Bingo was his name-o!

3. There was a farmer had a dog,
    And Bingo was his name-o!
    B-I-N (clap, clap) (etc.)

4. There was a farmer had a dog,
    And Bingo was his name-o!
    B-I-N-G (clap) (etc.)

5. There was a farmer had a dog,
    And Bingo was his name-o!
    B-I-N-G-O (clap on all letters) (etc.)

According to history this item began as a comic song which was sung at the Theatre Royal, Haymarket, London, by a Mr. Swords, ca. 1780. The song became very popular and was still being sung by adults in England at the end of the nineteenth century, for example, at harvest suppers.[51] By that date it had also been adapted by children as a game, and some of the variant stanzas which were sung in England follow:

A farmer's dog lay on the floor,
And Bingo was his name O!
B, i, n, g, o, B, i, n, g, o,
And Bingo was his name O!
The miller's mill-dog lay at the mill-door,
And his name was Little Bingo.
B with an I, I with an N, N with a G, G with an O,
And his name was Little Bingo.

The text of the miller's variant was also expanded as, for example:

The miller he bought a cask of ale,
And he called it right good Stingo.

S with a T, T with an I, I with an N, N with a G,
G with an O,
And he called it right good Stingo.

There were a number of ways in which the game was played. In each there is one child in the center, and the remainder of the children dance around her while singing the verses. When it comes to the part of the game where the name of the dog has to be spelled, the girl in the center points to one child after another, each having to say the appropriate letter immediately. If anyone fails, she takes the place of the child in the center. In another variant, when they reach the spelling part of the game the girl in the center cries "B" and then points to a child in the ring who immediately has to say "I." The child to the left or right of the one pointed to (as agreed upon in advance) has to say "N," the next in that direction "G," and the last, "O, his name was Bobby Bingo." In another variant, the letters are said as rapidly as possible, each child clapping as he says the letter. In most variants if no errors are made the first time around, the word "Bingo" might be spelled backward the second time.[52]

Children's games seem susceptible to indefinite variation. Although as sung and clapped by Mandie TR 27 is obviously related to the English game, it does not exactly duplicate any of the English variants.

The last song is of the cumulative type and, like TR 27, can be played by one individual alone or by several simultaneously. It is accompanied by gestures rather than clapping. At A a new element is introduced in each stanza, a thing, an animal, or a person. At B the singer states what this thing, animal, or person is called and illustrates with a gesture. It is this half-phrase and the accompanying gesture that are cumulative. As the song progresses, half-phrases B from previous stanzas with their accompanying gestures are added in reverse order.

TR 28 When I First Came to This Land

Sung with gestures by Mandie List, Bloomington, 7 October 1986.

109

1. When I first came to this land,
   I was not a wealthy man,
A   So I got myself a shack,
   And I did what I could.

B¹ CHORUS: And I called my shack, "Ooh," breaking my back,
   And the land was sweet and good,
   And I did what I could.

110

2. When I first came to this land,
   I was not a wealthy man,
A So I bought myself a farm,
   And I did what I could.

B^2
B^1 CHORUS: And I called my farm, "Muscle in the arm,"
         And I called my shack, "Ooh," breaking my back,
         And the land was sweet and good,
         And I did what I could.

3. When I first came to this land,
   I was not a wealthy man,
A So I got myself a cow,
   And I did what I could.

B^3
B^2
B^1 CHORUS: And I called my cow, "No milk now,"
         And I called my farm, "Muscle in the arm,"
         And I called my shack, "Ooh," breaking my back,
         And the land was sweet and good,
         And I did what I could.

4. When I first came to this land,
   I was not a wealthy man,
A So I got myself a pig,
   And I did what I could.

B^4
B^3
B^2
B^1 CHORUS: And I called my pig, "Doing the jig,"
         And I called my cow, "No milk now,"
         And I called my farm, "Muscle in the arm,"
         And I called my shack, "Ooh," breaking my back,
         And the land was sweet and good,
         And I did what I could.

5. When I first came to this land,
   I was not a wealthy man,
A So I got myself a horse,
   And I did what I could.

B^5
B^4
B^3
B^2
B^1 CHORUS: And I called my horse, "Trigger, of course,"
         And I called my pig, "Doing the jig,"
         And I called my cow, "No milk now,"
         And I called my farm, "Muscle in the arm,"
         And I called my shack, "Ooh," breaking my back,
         And the land was sweet and good,
         And I did what I could.

6. When I first came to this land,
   I was not a wealthy man,
A So I got myself a duck,
   And I did what I could.

B^6 CHORUS: And I called my duck, "Out of luck,"
B^5 And I called my horse, "Trigger, of course,"
B^4 And I called my pig, "Doing the jig,"
B^3 And I called my cow, "No milk now,"
B^2 And I called my farm, "Muscle in the arm,"
B^1 And I called my shack, "Ooh," breaking my back,
         And the land was sweet and good,
         And I did what I could.

      7. When I first came to this land,
         I was not a wealthy man,
A   So I got myself a wife,
         And I did what I could.

B^7 CHORUS: And I called my wife, "Ooh, love of my life,"
B^6 And I called my duck, "Out of luck,"
B^5 And I called my horse, "Trigger, of course,"
B^4 And I called my pig, "Doing the jig,"
B^3 And I called my cow, "No milk now,"
B^2 And I called my farm, "Muscle in the arm,"
B^1 And I called my shack, "Ooh," breaking my back,
         And the land was sweet and good,
         And I did what I could.

      8. When I first came to this land,
         I was not a wealthy man,
A   I got myself a son,
         And I did what I could.

B^8 CHORUS: And I called my son, "Work to be done,"
B^7 And I called my wife, "Ooh, love of my life,"
B^6 And I called my duck, "Out of luck,"
B^5 And I called my horse, "Trigger, of course,"
B^4 And I called my pig, "Doing the jig,"
B^3 And I called my cow, "No milk now,"
B^2 And I called my farm, "Muscle in the arm,"
B^1 And I called my shack, "Ooh," breaking my back,
         And the land was sweet and good,
         And I did what I could.

      9. When I first came to this land,
         I was not a wealthy man,
A   I got myself a daughter,
         And I did what I could.

B^9 CHORUS: And I called my daughter, "Yat 'n yater,"
B^8 And I called my son, "Work to be done,"
B^7 And I called my wife, "Ooh, love of my life,"
B^6 And I called my duck, "Out of luck,"
B^5 And I called my horse, "Trigger, of course,"

B^4 And I called my pig, "Doing the jig,"
B^3 And I called my cow, "No milk now,"
B^2 And I called my farm, "Muscle in the arm,"
B^1 And I called my shack, "Ooh," breaking my back,
        And the land was sweet and good,
        And I did what I could.

The following gestures accompany the half-phrases marked B.

B1   Both hands are placed on the back as though it hurts.

B2   Making a fist, the right arm is held up and the muscle felt with the left hand.

B3   Both hands are held out in front of the player with the palms facing down. In rapid motion the right hand is passed over the left while simultaneously the left hand passes under the right. This motion is then reversed, the left hand passing over the right and the right under the left. According to Mandie this means "No, I don't need any."

B4   The index fingers of both hands are pointed straight up, the thumb is extended backward at right angles, the remaining fingers curl. The arms are moved rapidly up and down in alternative motion.

B5   In rapid motion the thighs above the knees are slapped, the fingers snapped, and the index fingers are extended forward like six-shooters, the thumb up and the fingers curled.

B6   The head is hit with the palms of the hands.

B7   Both hands are placed over the heart, the eyes are rolled up, and the singer looks dreamily at the ceiling.

B8   The index finger of the right hand is shaken as though at the sun.

B9   The hands are held up with the palms forward and slowly moved back and forth, one behind the other.

Mandie thought that "yat n yater" meant "You oughten and you oughter," or spelled out, "You ought to and you ought not to." In the cumulative singing of the half-phrases, where there is an initial "ooh" it is usually omitted.

Mandie believed that she had learned "My Enemy" and "Bingo" from other girls on the playground. She had learned "When I First Came to This Land" on a field trip with other children from her school. To while the time away on the bus, a boy had begun to sing this song, and she had learned it from him. She did not know how or from whom he had learned it.

Commentary

Writers concerning children's singing games have at times been indefinite in assigning gender to the participants. In describing games of courtship and marriage, of which "Here Come Three Dukes A-Riding" and "The Knights Out of Spain" are examples, Charlotte Sophia Burne in *Shropshire Folk-Lore: A Sheaf of Gleanings* (1883) writes of "players" and "parties" rather than of "boys" and "girls."[53] On the other hand, she clearly labels the participants in "Bobby Bingo," which is not concerned with courtship, "girls."[54] Gomme is a little more explicit. Writing in 1898 concerning "Three Dukes," she seems to indicate that the game might be played by girls only. "Three children, generally boys, are chosen to represent the three dukes. The rest of the players represent maidens."[55] Should we interpret this to mean that the boys may also represent maidens? She shows greater clarity in describing a variation of the game in which "one boy stands facing the girls, and sings the first verse advancing and retiring with a dancing step."[56] On the other hand, in her discussion of "Three Knights from Spain" she is fully explicit. "The players stand in two lines, facing one another, three boys on one side and the girls (any number) on the other."[57]

Neither "Aunt" Phoebe Elliott nor Wolford leaves any doubt as to the sex of the participants. "Aunt" Phoebe, describing her playing of the game in 1866, says, "There was a crowd of girls in a row and we would all march forward to meet this young man, this boy." Wolford, writing in 1916, heads her alternate stanzas "Boys" and "Girls," thus indicating the gender of those who sing a particular stanza.[58] According to Newell, the stanzas of "Soldier, Soldier, Will You Marry Me" are sung alternately by a girl and a boy. This is the only case in which the age of the children is specified, from five to eight years.[59]

Describing her playing "Sister Phoebe" in 1866, "Aunt" Phoebe Elliott says, "Then the hat was placed on our head and we got a sweet kiss. And of course it didn't do us any harm at all." It can be assumed that if she had received a kiss from a girl the question of "harm" would not even be considered. In any case, the game was adapted into the play-party repertory. In this a lone girl or boy in the ring selects a member of the opposite sex, places the hat upon his or her head, kisses the individual selected, and retires to the ring. The individual now within the ring selects a member of the opposite sex who is treated in the same manner.

Gomme describes several English ring kissing games which follow procedures similar to the American except that no hat is employed. Here Gomme is again somewhat less than specific in assigning gender. In "Lady on the Mountain" the noun used to describe the individual in the center is "child" and the pronoun "she." At the end of the description of "Here Stands a Young Man" she merely writes, it is "played by both girls and boys." There is greater clarity as to what happens in "Silly Old Man." "A child, usually a boy, stands in the middle. . . . The boy in the centre chooses a girl when bidden by the ring," and they then kiss.[60]

Both Newell and the Opies describe the game, "The Miller Boy," as having been played by pairs or couples of boys and girls. The Opies lament the fact that the game is only played contemporaneously under the supervision of a teacher, never spontaneously on the playground. They also comment that the boys and girls may feel embarrassed about having to walk around linked arm in arm.[61]

These last statements by the Opies point to the tremendous change which has taken place in the relationships of boys and girls of grade-school age since the First World War, a cultural as well as a political watershed. Despite lack of clarity in the descriptions, there is ample evidence that from the 1860s to the First World War girls and boys spontaneously played together in singing games involving courtship, marriage, and kissing. This is no longer the case. Except under special circumstances, girls and boys no longer join together for games. And as for courtship or kissing games, as one public teacher I talked to put it, "They wouldn't be caught dead doing them on the playground."

As sociologist Barrie Thorne has stated, "Sex segregation is so common in elementary schools that it is meaningful to speak of separate girls' and boys' worlds."[62] The segregation is apparently enforced by the risk of being teased if choosing to be with the other sex. "'Jimmy likes Beth' or 'Beth likes Jimmy' is a major form of teasing, which a child risks in choosing to sit by or walk with one of the other sex."[63] Only the presence of the teacher, indicating that the choice was not their own, justifies their proximity to the other sex.

The structure of teasing, and children's sparse vocabulary for relationships between girls and boys, are evident in the following conversation which I had with a group of third-grade girls in the lunch room:

Susan asked me what I was doing, and I said I was observing the things that children do and play. Nicole volunteered, "I like running. Boys chase all the girls. See Tim over there? Judy chases him all around the school. She likes him." Judy, sitting across the table, quickly responded, "I hate him. I like him for a friend." "Tim loves Judy," Nicole said in a loud sing-song voice.[64]

The singsong was probably:

There are, of course, exceptional circumstances. When I look back at my own childhood--I was seven at the end of the First World War--I remember occasionally playing a game of "Hop-Scotch" with a girl in my neighborhood. There was also a large Mexican family who lived in a house in our alley. I knew them very well, and although my mother looked askance at my playing with Mexicans, at dusk I often engaged in a game of "Cops and Robbers" with both girls and boys of the family. But on the playground at school I never played with girls. My son, Michael, who was born in 1948, had similar experiences. He might play "Hop-Scotch" with a girl living nearby, but he never played with girls on the school playground. My research assistant, Marc Satterwhite, born in 1954, tells me that in his neighborhood there were about three other boys and three girls of his age. They all played together amicably in the neighborhood, but at school, although they remained reasonably friendly, the boys and girls did not play together. I have talked with teachers who taught in one- and two-room schoolhouses. They tell me that in these situations boys and girls often play together on the playground, even those of different ages.

Barrie Thorne offers the following explanation:

Girls and boys may interact more readily in less public and crowded settings. Neighborhood play, depending upon demography, is more often sex and race integrated than play at school, partly because with fewer numbers, one may have to resort to an array of social categories to find play partners or to constitute a game. And in a less crowded environment there are fewer potential witnesses to "make something of it" if girls and boys play together.[65]

Songs which are to accompany physical movement, such as games or dancing, are constructed over a regular, equidistant, underlying pulse, which may be realized in the music or represented by a rest or silence rather than a sung pitch. These pulses are divided into groups of two or three, the first of the group receiving greater stress than the other(s). The first is called "duple meter" and consists of a series of strong-weak, strong-weak, etc. The second is known as "triple meter" and consists of strong-weak-weak, strong-weak-weak, etc.

In music these groups are indicated by measures, the vertical lines setting off the measures appearing before the stressed pulses. Duple meter is much more frequent in Anglo-American singing games than is triple meter. The usual phrase is four pulses in length, thus:

<u>1</u> 2 <u>1</u> 2

However, phrases do not necessarily begin with the first pulse of a measure. They may, for example, begin with a weak pulse, thus:

2 <u>1</u> 2 <u>1</u>

In Anglo-American song the musical and the verbal stresses almost always coincide. In the majority of cases in the song poem, the musical pulses are matched by verbally stressed vowels or diphthongs:

H<u>e</u>re comes S<u>u</u>sie str<u>u</u>tting like a fl<u>oo</u>zie.

       1   2   1   2

Less frequently those vowels or diphthongs which are matched with the pulses are not those which are stressed in speech:

G<u>o</u> t<u>e</u>ll Aunt Rh<u>o</u>d<u>y</u>.

   1 2   1 2

The last vowel, the "y" of "Rhody," is not stressed in speech but here is accented because it matches a musical pulse. Or there may be more than one unaccented syllable between two accented ones:

Of all the institutions in the East or in the West.

    1   2   1   2

("Here Comes Susie . . ." above also illustrates this.)

"I Don't Want to Play in Your Yard" (TR 21) and the sheet music arrangement of "Playmates" (TR 22-23) are popular songs not necessarily composed to accompany action. The former is a song of the 1890s, when songs were commonly composed in triple meter or waltz time. Thus there are three pulses to a measure in:

I don't want to play in your yard.

1   2   3   1   2   (3)

By far, the most common poetic form of Anglo-American folk song is a quatrain in which the lines will display three or four verbal stresses. There is usually a consonantal rhyme at the end of the second and fourth lines. Not as common are the eight-line stanza and the couplet.

The popular song of the 1890s had a different form. It contains two or more verses consisting of a double quatrain (or octet, as it is also called) and a chorus consisting of a single quatrain. The chorus is usually in waltz time, and the verses often are, as well. The most common rhyming scheme remains the matching of the second and fourth lines. "Playmates," in its sheet music form, is a later popular song and has a rather unusual form. There is only one verse, and the chorus is repeated after a musical and textual interlude, called a "bridge" in popular music terminology. It is also in duple meter.

The term "chorus" is usually applied to a quatrain which is repeated after each stanza or verse. The term "refrain" is applied to a line or lines appearing regularly within a stanza, although the remainder of the stanza may change. The second nonsense line seen in "Aunt" Phoebe's variant of "Ransum, Tansum" (TR 4) is an example of a refrain.

Finally, it should be pointed out that on occasion in Anglo-American folk poetry one finds assonant rhyme, that is the rhyme of an accented vowel or diphthong only, not of the following con-sonants or vowels as well:

They telephoned for miles around
At last an answer came
Saying, "Helen, that woman's body
It must have been Pearl was slain." (TR 97)

CHAPTER 3   THE PLAY-PARTY

We have turned the clock back a hundred years or more. We are in a typical farmhouse of the second half of the last century, a farmhouse located in Ripley County, Brown County, Vanderburgh County, or in any rural area in southern Indiana. We are in the largest room in the house, but the room is nearly empty. The furniture has been removed and the rug lifted from the floor. The room is ringed with improvised benches made by placing planks on chairs or on sawed-off sections of tree trunks.

Dusk is falling, and the woman of the house bustles in and lights the candles. A roaring fire is burning in the fireplace of the adjoining kitchen, its light flickering in through the open doorway. It is winter, and the room is cold. There is only the heat of the fire in the kitchen to warm the large, bare room.

The guests are now beginning to arrive. Everyone from ten miles around is coming, young people and old. Some bump along in jolt-wagons, some come on horseback. Others straggle through the cornfields on foot. Many a boy has brought a girl. They come two on a horse, the girl riding sideways behind the saddle.

The boys and girls quickly climb the stairs to the bedrooms, the boys to remove their heavy wraps, the girls to slip off their long calico riding skirts and to hurriedly put their muslin dresses in order. The older folks repair to the kitchen where the men discuss crops and politics while the women pop corn, wash the shining red apples, cut the cakes, and watch the babies. The smaller children huddle into the corners of the big room to watch the fun.

The young folks quickly gather in the party room. There is very little gossip; everyone is anxious to begin. The first game is chosen. All the young people stand around the outside of the room, but not in a circle. One boy begins to skip to the right and the more forward of the others begin to sing, the remainder joining in little by little.

TR 29 Coffee Grows in a White Oak Tree

Contributed by Mrs. Leslie Beall, Versailles, prior to 1916.

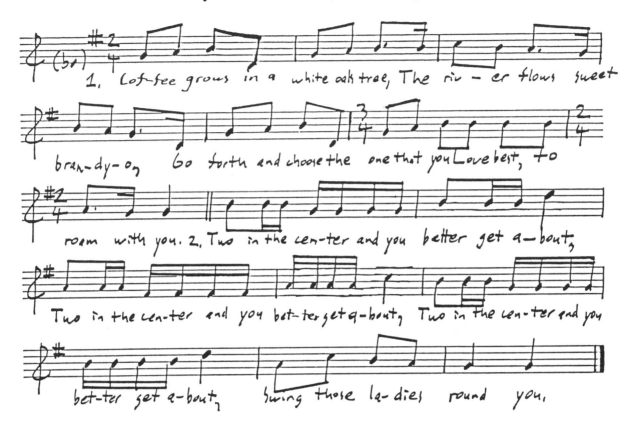

1. Coffee grows in a white oak tree,
   The river flows sweet brandy-o,
   Go forth and choose the one that you
   Love best, to roam with you.

2. Two in the center and you better get about,
   Two in the center and you better get about,
   Two in the center and you better get about,
   Swing those ladies round you.

3. Four in the center and you better get about,
   Four in the center and you better get about,
   Four in the center and you better get about,
   Swing those ladies round you.

4. Six in the center and you better get about, (etc.)
   Swing those ladies round you.

5. Eight in the center and you better get about, (etc.)
   Swing those ladies round you.

6. Ten in the center and you better get about, (etc.)
   Swing those ladies round you.

7. Eight in the center and two step out, (etc.)
   Swing those ladies round you.

8. Six in the center and two step out, (etc.)
   Swing those ladies round you.

9. Four in the center and two step out, (etc.)
   Swing those ladies round you.

10. Two in the center and two step out, (etc.)
    Swing those ladies round you.

At 1 the skipping boy completes a circle in the middle of the room. At 2 he chooses a girl as a partner, and together they promenade, making a complete circle to the right.

In promenading the couple faces the same direction with the girl at the boy's right. The boy's left hand and the girl's right hand are joined in front of them, the boy's right hand resting on the girl's waist and her left hand resting on his right arm.

At 3 the couple chooses a second couple who then enters the circle with them, and the four make a figure eight. Boy 1 is in the center facing down and Girl 1 is in the center facing up. Boy 1 takes his partner's right hand and passes her by the right. He proceeds to trace the lower half of the figure eight while she traces the upper half of it. They walk, rather than skip. At the start Boy 2 is at the top following Boy 1, and Girl 2 is at the bottom following Girl 1. All simultaneously make a complete figure eight, boy following boy and girl following girl, the boys and girls going in opposite directions.

Partners always meet at the center. There the boy takes the right hand of the girl and passes her by the right. When he meets the girl who is not his partner he takes her left hand and passes her by the left.

At 4 all are in the same position as at the beginning of the figure. The couple who entered the circle last chooses from the crowd a third couple. Repeat the figure with six. Each boy always takes the right hand of his partner and passes her by the right and takes the left hand of each other girl and passes her by the left.

122

At 5 another couple is chosen. Repeat the figure with eight. At 6 a last couple is chosen. Repeat the figure with ten.

At 7 the first couple drops out of the center, and the boy and girl return to their original positions in the crowd. Repeat the figure with eight. Likewise at 8, repeat with six players, at 9 with four. Finally, at 10, the last two promenade in a circle to the right and take their original places.[1]

This complex game is not considered a dance, and the occasion on which it is played is known by the participants as a party, a game party, doings, a bounce around, or frolic, although the latter term was often applied to a dance. None of the participants had ever heard of a play-party, a term invented later by folklorists as a general description of this type of entertainment.

Most of the players were youths of courting age, although some might be as young as thirteen, and young married couples also often participated. The play-party was the principal form of recreation for rural youth from New England to Texas from approximately the Civil War until the First World War. It was a pretty informal affair. Anyone in the neighborhood who wished to come did so. It might follow a spelling bee, a cornhusking, or a church supper. Or it might be organized on the spur of the moment, "jumped up," as they called it. It consisted almost entirely of singing games. These games and songs came from many sources, children's singing games, folk songs and ballads, minstrel songs, and songs from the popular stage.

The origin of the text of "Coffee Grows in a White Oak Tree" is obscure. It is believed to have grown out of the war with Mexico. As happened to many texts of songs incorporated into the play-party, dance directions have been substituted for most of the original words. Compare Leah Jackson Wolford's version given above with the following from B. A. Botkin.

Pretty Little Pink

1. My pretty little pink, I once did think
   That you and I would marry,
   But now I've lost all hope of that,
   And I have no time to tarry.

2. I'll take my knapsack on my back,

123

My rifle on my shoulder,
And I'll march away to the old Rio Grande
And there I'll be a soldier.

3. There coffee grows on tall oak trees
   And the rivers flow with brandy,
   The rocks and hills are covered with gold,
   And the girls are sweeter than candy.

4. Now the war's all over and we'll turn back
   To the place where we first started,
   So open the ring and choose another
   To relieve the broken hearted.[2]

William Wells Newell indicates that this song text was also employed in a children's singing game.

Where coffee grows on a white-oak-tree,
And rivers flow with brandy,
Where the boys are like a lump of gold,
And the girls as sweet as candy.

However, Newell did not secure information concerning how the game was played.[3]

The young people now start a different game which requires an uneven number of players. A lone boy or girl stands in the middle while the others form couples and circle around him or her.

TR 30 The Miller Boy

Contributed by Mrs. Leslie Beall, Versailles, prior to 1916.

Oh,___ hap-py is the mil-ler boy That lives by the mill, He___ takes his toll with a free good-will, One hand in the hop-per and the oth-er in the sack, The ladies step for-ward and the gents step back.

124

1. Oh, happy is the miller boy that lives by the mill,
   He takes his toll with a free good will,
   One hand in the hopper and the other in the sack,
2. The ladies step forward and the gents step back.

During 1 the couples promenade around the person, boy or girl, who stands in the center of the circle. The movement is regular and rather quick to imitate the turning of a wheel. At 2 each boy drops his partner's arm and tries to get the arm of the girl behind him and at his right. While the change is being made the one in the center, the miller, tries to get a partner. If he or she succeeds, the person without a partner is the one in the center for the next game. If this individual fails to get a partner, he or she must be in the center a second or even third time.[4]

"The Miller Boy" is based on an American children's game which Newell entitled "Happy Is the Miller" or "The Jolly Miller Boy." The action in the children's game is almost identical to that of the play-party:

> An odd number of players, of whom the one not paired stands in the centre of the ring. The others march in couples, each consisting of a girl and a boy, till the sudden end of the song, when each boy grasps the girl in front of him.

This differs from the play-party game in that the boy grasps the arm of the girl in front rather than that of the girl behind. Newell offers two texts, the first from western New York, and the second from Cincinnati:

> Happy is the miller, who lives by himself,
> All the bread and cheese he piles upon the shelf,
> One hand in the hopper, and the other in the bag,
> The wheel turns around, and he cries out, Grab!
>
> Happy is the miller that lives in the mill;
> For the mill goes around, he works with a will;
> One hand in the hopper, and one in the bag,
> The mill goes around, and he cries out, Grab![5]

One assumes that Newell has forgotten to mention that the miller is also attempting to "grasp" a girl.

This was one of the most popular singing games in England during the end of the last century.

125

In 1894 Alice Gomme possessed so many recordings and found the words so stereotyped that for once she found it unnecessary to set out all, or even the majority of, her texts.[6]

In all of Gomme's variants, as well as in the play-party game described by Wolford, the miller attempts to secure a partner.

There seems to have been a general feeling among the farming population that the share of grain taken by millers as their fee for grinding was excessive, a feeling which might have been underlaid by envy. This attitude is more obvious in the words of the children's game from western New York and Cincinnati than in the play-party text given by Wolford. In the former case "grab" has a double meaning since it figures in the action. The term "grab" can also be found in variants of the game played in Indiana:

How happy is the miller that lives by himself;
The turning of the wheel is the making of his pelf.
One hand in the hopper, the other in the sack,
When the wheel goes round he cries out "Grab!"[7]

The earliest printing of a poem related to this singing game is in *Pills to Purge Melancholy* (1707), of which the first stanza reads:

How happy is the mortal that lives by his mill!
That depends on his own, not on Fortune's wheel;
By the sleight of his hand, and the strength of his
   back,
How merrily his mill goes, clack, clack, clack![8]

The words of the Wolford variant (TR 30 above) are sung to the well-known tune, "Turkey in de Straw," which is frequently heard as a fiddle tune. This melody has a paradoxical history. "Turkey in de Straw" is originally the tune of a comedy song called "Zip Coon," the words of which have no relation to a miller. It was printed in the United States in five different editions in 1834. Authorship was claimed by George Washington Dixon, on one hand, and Bob Farrel and George Nichols on the other. The authorship is still in dispute. I reproduce the title page from one of these anomalous editions. In 1861 a song entitled "Turkey in de Straw" was copyrighted by Dan Bryant. Neither the words nor the

126

ZIP COON.

BALTIMORE Published and Sold by GEO. WILLIG Jr.

I went down to San—dy hook, toder arter _ noon; I went down to

Sandy hook, toder arter _ noon; I went down to Sandy hook,

toder arter _ noon; And de fust man I met dere was old Zip Coon.

Courtesy of Library of Congress

music of the song are like those of "Zip Coon," as can be seen by comparing the title pages of the two songs. However, on the last page of the sheet music of "Turkey in de Straw" there is added what is called the "Old Melody." This is a slightly ornamented version of the melody of "Zip Coon." No words are given. I have also reproduced this page. For some reason the title "Turkey in de Straw" has become attached to the melody of "Zip Coon," and it is much better known by that name.[9]

Composed by

DAN.¹ BRYANT.

De col_or'd man is ber_ry good, Way down in de
Ar_kan saw, To brack_de boots an saw de wood, Den hide dat tur_key's
paw. He's good to dance an good to sing Tom turkey in de buck_wheat straw, An

The fact that a tune is copyrighted as part of a popular song does not necessarily mean that the person listed as such was actually its composer. In the last chapter we saw an example of this in "Playmates" (TR 22-23), and in subsequent chapters we shall encounter more. In most of these, there will not even be the hint given by Saxie Dowell in "Playmates" that the chorus comes from traditional sources rather than the author's own composition. In the case of "Zip Coon," which became known as

gib de straw a twist a bout to hide de tur_key's paw, An I   play'd up a chune call'd

Tur_key in de straw.   Old melody.

"Turkey in de Straw" (Old Melody)

"Turkey in de Straw," several individuals claimed copyright. It is therefore not surprising that a number of attempts have been made to trace the melody to certain English, Scottish, and Irish sources.[10]

Mabel Evangeline Neal publishes the singing game, "The Miller Boy," under the title "The Jolly Miller." She writes that the tune was harmonized in 1624 [*sic*] by Beethoven for George Thomson.[11] A Scottish song, "The Jolly Miller of the Dee," was indeed arranged by Beethoven,[12] but the melody bears no relationship to "Turkey in de Straw," nor are the words of the song like those

129

employed in either the play-party or the children's game.

This melody is so well known that it is included in *Twice 55 Plus Community Songs*, published by C. C. Birchard in 1919, a songbook commonly used for high school assembly singing in the United States. It was, as a matter of fact, employed for this purpose when I was in high school.

Gomme's transcription of the melody from Doncaster is somewhat similar:

The Jolly Miller

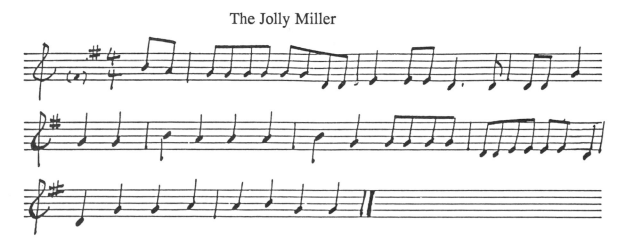

There was a jolly miller, and he lived by himself,
As the wheel went round he made his pelf;
One hand in the hopper, and the other in the bag,
As the wheel went round he took his grab.[13]

As can be seen in the change in the name of the American tune from "Zip Coon" to "Turkey in the Straw," titles can shift from tune to tune as well as from text to text. It requires more than a title to establish a likeness.

The boys and girls at this party are promenading, an activity often associated with dances. They are also singing a tune which was a favorite among fiddlers. Nevertheless, as far as they and the community are concerned they are not dancing. All those present, whether Quakers, Methodists, Disciples, or Campbellites, know very well that dancing is a sin. Playing games, even kissing games, is a different matter. That is harmless, innocent diversion. All the old folks played these games when they were children, and they see no objections to them, no objections whatsoever.

And so the party continues with the next game.

TR 31 The Needle's Eye

Contributed by Mrs. Allie B. Jackson, Versailles, prior to 1916.

St. 1   The needle's eye, that doth supply,
         The thread that runs so true,
         And many a girl have I let go,
         But now I have caught you.

131

St. 2 1. The needle's eye, that doth supply,
           The thread that runs so true,
           Many a beau have I let go
       2. Because I wanted you.

St. 3   I won't have you,
           Because I can't get you,
           Many a lass have I let pass,
           Because I wanted you.

One couple joins hands high over their heads and forms an arch. All the other players form a line, each girl behind her partner and each person having both hands on the hips of the person in front of him. The long line then passes through the arch as the arch makers sing 1.

As soon as possible the ones who have passed under the arch circle around one of the arch makers without breaking line and join with those who have not been under the arch. All the time the persons who have gone through or are under the arch keep pulling forward while those behind, fearful of being caught, pull backwards. "The arch-makers secretly choose their symbols, silver or gold, ring or bracelet, cake or pie, apple or pear. Whenever they sing 2, the arch falls and encloses one of the players." The person caught under the arch must choose between the symbols whispered to him and then kiss the arch maker whose symbol he or she has chosen. He then changes places with him or her, the former becoming arch maker and the latter filling the gap in the line. Repeat from the beginning and continue repeating until each singer has been caught at least once.[14]

This, again, is an old children's game incorporated into the play-party. In a variant played in the United States during the Civil War, a couple, a boy and a girl, rather than an individual, is caught by the arch makers.

Threading the Needle

The needle's eye
None can surpass
But those who travel through;
It hath caught many a smiling lass,
But now it hath caught you.

132

There's none so sweet
That is dressed so neat;
I do intend,
Before I end,
To make this couple meet.

The couple then kisses, and the game proceeds as in "London Bridge," ending with a tug-of-war.[15]

The game as played by English children was very much like "London Bridge" with a somewhat different text.

Through the Needle Eye, Boys

Clink, clink, through the needle ee, boys,
One, two, three,
If you want a bonnie lassie,
Just tak me.

In this case the two arch makers have secretly adopted the symbols, golden apple or golden pear, and the detained child lines up behind the arch maker whose symbol he chooses. When all the children have been caught, a line is drawn on the ground between the arch makers who hold each other's hands, stand with the others behind them, and pull like a tug-of-war. Whichever side pulls the other over the line wins the game and shouts at the other, "Rotten eggs, rotten eggs."[16]

For the next game of the play-party the young people select "Captain Jinks." This can be played by two or more couples.

TR 32A Captain Jinks

Contributed by Mrs. Leslie Beall, Versailles, prior to 1916.

1. Cap-tain Jinks came home last night, Gentle-men pass-es to the right,

1. Captain Jinks came home last night,
    Gentleman passes to the right,
    Swing your lady very polite,
    For that's the style in the army.

2. Go to your partner and promenade,
    Promenade, promenade,
    Go to your partner and promenade,
    For that's the style in the army.

The following is the refrain as Wolford knew it in 1905 when she was thirteen years of age.

TR 32B Captain Jinks

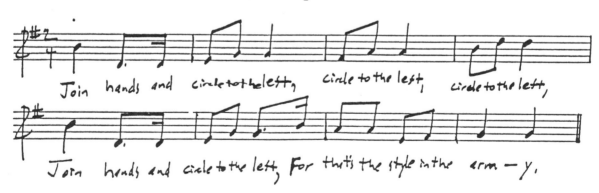

Join hands and circle to the left,
Circle to the left, circle to the left,
Join hands and circle to the left,
For that's the style in the army.

Wolford then gives the following textual variant, contributed by Miss Fannie A. Steward of Shelby Township, which she uses to illustrate the game:

1. Captain Jinks came home last night,
2. Pass the lady to the right.
3. Promenade with all your might,
   For that's the style in the army.
4. All join hands and circle to the left (thrice)
   For that's the style in the army.

The manner of playing this game necessarily varies with the words. All join hands and form a circle, each girl being two places to the right of her partner. At 1 circle left. At 2 all drop hands, the boys face to the right, the girls to the left. Each boy with his left hand takes the left hand of the girl to his right, passes her, and at 3 reaches his partner with whom he promenades. At 4 all return to their original positions.[17]

"Captain Jinks of the Horse Marines" was an English "hit" of the 1860s written by T. Maclagan. It achieved popularity in the United States in the late 1860s through performances by William Horace Lingard, a British actor who specialized in comic monologues and songs.[18]

This was a period when it was considered appropriate to publish parodies of songs which had achieved popularity. There soon appeared a song entitled "Lady Jinks of the Foot Dragoons," whose title character made little secret of her adoration of the dashing captain.[19]

The song achieved even wider popularity in 1901 when a play, *Captain Jinks of the Horse Marines*, appeared on Broadway, one of the main characters being the gay blade of a captain. The play also featured Ethel Barrymore of the famous acting family in her first leading role.

CAPTAIN JINKS.

OF THE HORSE MARINES.

LYRIC LYRE.

Arr: for Guitar, by

SEP. WINNER.

I'm Cap-tain Jinks of the

Horse Ma-rines, I oft-en live be-yond my means, I sport young la-dies

in their teens.To cut a swell in the ar-my. I teach the la-dies how to dance,

10,208.3.

how to dance, how to dance, I teach the la_dies how to dance, For

SPOKEN. Ha!ha! ha!
CHORUS.

I'm their pet in the ar_my. I'm Cap_tain Jinks of the Horse Marines, I give my horse good

colla voce.

corn and beans; Of course its quite be_yond my means,Tho'a Cap_tain in the ar_my.

10,208.3.

137

Now it is time for another kissing game.

TR 33 Old Sister Phoebe

Contributed by Mrs. William Hunter, Versailles, prior to 1916.

St. 1 1. High-O Sister Phoebe, how merry were we,
The night we sat under the juniper tree,
The juniper tree, high-o, high-o,
The juniper tree, high-o.

St. 2 2. Take this hat on your head, keep your head warm,
       3. And take a sweet kiss, it will do you no harm,
But a great deal of good, I know, I know.
       4. But a great deal of good, I know.

"All join hands and circle left around one girl who stands in the center holding a hat in her hand. At 2, she chooses a partner from those in the ring, draws him into the center, places the hat on his head and at 3 gives him a kiss." For the last two lines the following were often substituted:

It will do you no harm, but a great deal of good,
And so take another while kissing goes good.

She then at 4 joins the players in the ring. Repeat from the beginning with the boy in the center.[20]

It was usually the boy who took the extra kiss, but only if he was bold enough to claim it and if the girl was willing. These kissing games may not have been quite as innocent as the parents imag-

138

ined. In Rushville, for example, they were known to the participants as "gumsucks" (see first part of interview following TR 38, "Weevily Wheat," pp. 153-54).

"Old Sister Phoebe" is, of course, adapted from the children's game of the same name (see TR 6 in the previous chapter). The commonly held belief that when a woman puts on a man's hat she is inviting a kiss from its owner may have originated from this game.[21]

Now it is time to play the most popular game of all.

TR 34 Skip to My Lou

Name of informant and place of collection not given, prior to 1936.

Pretty as a red bird, prettier too;
Pretty as a red bird, prettier too;
Pretty as a red bird, prettier too;
Skip to my Lou, my darling.

The following three stanzas are from Wolford:

The cat's in the buttermilk, skip-to-my-Lou, (etc.)
Skip-to-my-Lou, my darling.

Little red wagon painted blue, (etc.)
Skip-to-my-Lou, my darling.

Mule's in the cellar, kicking up through, (etc.)
Skip-to-my-Lou, my darling.[22]

Or innumerable other stanzas either known or invented and sung in any order.

In playing the game all stand around in a circle, the girls to the left of their partners. A lone boy skips around to the right inside the ring. He slyly takes the arm of one girl whose partner is not watching and skips around the circle with her. Her partner then skips after them in hot pursuit while singing, perhaps, "I'll get her back in spite of you." If he can catch the couple before the girl gets back to her former position he gets back his partner. If he does not overtake her, he must skip around the circle and continue as the former boy has done. Much of the singing is in character, and each boy tries to get words that will fit the situation including the name of the girl he chooses.[23]

Here are some of the stanzas a skipping boy, whether chasing after his partner or looking for a new one, might sing:

> I'll get another one, Skip to my Lou, (etc.)
> Skip to my Lou, my darling.
>
> If I can't get her back another one'll do, (etc.)
> Skip to my Lou, my darling.
>
> Gone again, what shall I do? (etc.)
> Skip to my Lou, my darling.
>
> I'll get another one sweeter than you, (etc.)
> Skip to my Lou, my darling.

If the boy is clumsy he may be admonished:

> Hurry up slow poke, do oh do, (etc.)
> Skip to my Lou, my darling.

This game is described as one in which one boy steals another boy's partner. However, no boy ever attempts to keep his partner from being taken away from him, and only rarely does a girl refuse to be stolen. On occasion, she may refuse in order to tease a boy who is awkward in playing the game. Then he may be taunted by the remainder of the players:

> Stand there, bigfoot, what'll you do? (etc.)
> Skip to my Lou, my darling.

According to Wolford, "this of all the games, is the most indicative of the country life and of the things which are considered comic."[24] It is the typical form of dance song developed by the play-party. It eliminates the complications of the square dance and develops to the utmost the opportunity for humorous and dramatic byplay.[25]

The "Lou" of the song probably derives from the Scottish word "Loo," meaning love.[26] Both the Scotch-Irish and the highlanders themselves carried it into the South.[27]

The tune used in "Skip to My Lou" is the same as that employed in the chorus of "Coffee Grows in a White Oak Tree." The tunes, the words, and the figures of the play-party are not static, they are not fixed forms. The play-party was a folk tradition, and the songs and games were continually in process of change.

The young people have played a number of games without halting between them. It is now time for a breather.

TR 35 Billy Boy

Contributed by Mrs. Allie B. Jackson, Versailles, prior to 1916.

1. "Oh where have you been, Billy Boy, Billy Boy,
    Oh where have you been, charming Billy?"

141

"I have been to see my wife, she's the darling
   of my life,
She's a young thing and can not leave her mommy."

2. "How old is she, Billy Boy, Billy Boy,
   How old is she, charming Billy?"
   "Twice six, twice seven, twice forty and eleven,
   She's a young thing and can not leave her mommy."

3. "Can she bake a cherry pie, Billy Boy, Billy Boy,
   Can she bake a cherry pie, charming Billy?"
   "She can bake a cherry pie quick as a cat can wink
      its eye,
   She's a young thing and can not leave her mommy."

4. "Can she make a feather bed, Billy Boy, Billy Boy,
   Can she make a feather bed, charming Billy?"
   "She can make a feather bed, with the pillows at the
      head,
   She's a young thing and can not leave her mommy."

5. "Did you ask her to wed, Billy Boy, Billy Boy,
   Did you ask her to wed, charming Billy?"
   "I did ask her to wed, and this is what she said,
   'I'm a young thing and can not leave my mommy!'"

There is no formal game for this song. It is sung as a dialogue, a girl singing the questions and a boy the answers. Each is done with dramatic effect when possible and, depending upon the capability of the singers, new questions and answers may be improvised. The text given above is short, so I append two more stanzas from another Indiana source.

3. "Can she make a loaf of bread, Billy Boy, Billy Boy,
   Can she make a loaf of bread, charming Billy?"
   "She can make a loaf of bread with a night cap on her
      head,
   But she's a young thing, and cannot leave her mamma."

4. "Can she milk a mulie cow, Billy Boy, Billy Boy,
   Can she milk a mulie cow, charming Billy?"
   "She can milk a mulie cow if her mamma shows her how,
   But she's a young thing, that cannot leave her mamma."[28]

"Billy Boy" is generally believed to be an English nursery song, and variants can be found in nineteenth-century collections. I give below a portion of a variant of the text as published in 1842.

Willy Boy

"Where have you been all the day,
My boy Willy?"

"I've been all the day
Courting of a lady gay:
But oh! she's too young
To be taken from her mammy."

"What work can she do,
My boy Willy?
Can she bake and can she brew,
My boy Willy?"

"She can brew and she can bake,
And she can make our wedding cake:
But oh! she's too young
To be taken from her mammy."

"What age may she be? What age may she be?
My boy Willy?"

"Twice two, twice seven,
Twice ten, twice eleven:
But oh! she's too young
To be taken from her mammy."[29]

There is now a pause for refreshments. Youths and children crowd into the kitchen and emerge

with plates of cake and mugs of cider. For those who are still hungry there are apples and popcorn,

but most of the players are anxious to continue. Soon the munching of apples is heard only in the

corners where the sleepy children are still watching the game.

TR 36 Marching to Quebec

Name of informant and place of collection not given, prior to 1916.

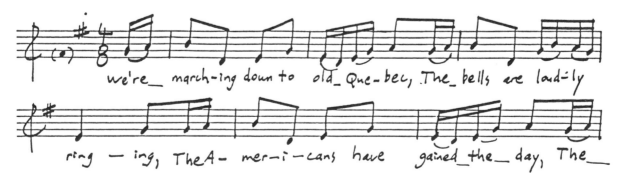

St. 1   We're marching down to Old Quebec,
The bells are loudly ringing,
The Americans have gained the day,
And the British are retreating.

St. 2 1. We're marching down to Old Quebec,
The drums are loudly beating.
America has gained the day,
And the British are retreating.

St. 3 2. The war is over and we'll turn back
To the place where we first started,
3. We'll open a ring and choose a couple in
4. To release the broken-hearted.

According to Wolford: "Partners take promenade positions and march forward in a straight line during the singing of 1. At 2 the line makes a double turn to the left and marches back in a line parallel to that made first. At 3 all join hands and form a circle, circle left, and choose a couple to enter center. Repeat from the beginning with the last center couple heading the line. This couple chooses the next to enter center."[30]

This is an old song. Since a similar game was played by children in Philadelphia around 1800 and the first stanza mentions Quebec,[31] the reference is obviously to the American attempt to capture that city during the projected takeover of Canada from the British during the Revolutionary War.

In September of 1775 Benedict Arnold with a force of eleven hundred men moved up the Kennebec River with the intention of launching a surprise attack against Quebec. It was an arduous trip. It was unseasonably cold, and the boats used were poorly constructed for their purpose. Many turned back, and Arnold arrived at the St. Lawrence River opposite Quebec with only five hundred men, most of whom were in very poor condition.

They were prevented from crossing the river immediately by a snowstorm and lack of boats. The Quebec garrison, which had been engaged in fighting American forces under Richard Montgomery, who had captured Montreal, returned to the fortified city before Arnold and his men could cross the river. Montgomery and Arnold joined forces and laid siege to the city. In the attempt to storm its walls at the end of December, Montgomery was killed and Arnold badly wounded. Some American reinforcements arrived and other generals took over, but they were unable to take the city.

In May a fleet carrying a large body of British regulars arrived, and the Americans, outnumbered and weakened by an epidemic of smallpox, were forced to retire to Montreal and eventually had to retreat south from Montreal as well.[32]

The words of "Marching to Quebec" have often been changed to fit contemporary conditions. During the Civil War it was "The Yankee boys have gained the day, and the Rebels are retreating."[33] On the other hand, for Southern sympathizers it was "The Rebels brave have won the fight the Yankees are retreating."[34] Later it was adapted for the First World War.

> We're marching down to Old Berlin,
> Where the drums are loudly beating.
> The American boys have gained the day
> And the Germans are retreating.[35]

The kitchen has now been put in order, and the older generation is ready to leave. The men must get up early to take care of the unending chores of the farm, and the women look forward to equally arduous tasks. Since the young people have very little chance for social contact in the isolated countryside, they are usually permitted to remain on for a little longer period of merriment. However, they will be expected to be up the next morning and working at the same time as their elders.

145

The master of the house and his spouse retire to bed, where they supposedly keep one ear open as a means of long distance chaperonage. The other parents, with their sleeping children in their arms, make their way home.

This is the time to play the more daring games.

TR 37 We'll All Go Down to Rowsers

Sung by Samuel Clay Dixon, Mount Vernon, 10 April 1938.

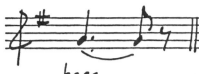

beer.____

St. 1   1. We'll all go down to Rowsers,
            To Rowsers, to Rowsers;
            We'll all go down to Rowsers,
            And get some lager beer.

CHORUS 1:
        2. Sweet lager beer,
        3. Sweet lager beer,
        4. Curtsey to your partner,
        5. Swing around your lady;
        6. Go back and get your partner,
            And swing around again.

        2. We'll step lively to the music,
            The music, the music;
            We'll step lively to the music,
            When we get lager beer.

CHORUS 2:
        Sweet lager beer,
        Sour lager beer,
            (rest as Chorus 1)

        3. Oh, never mind the old folks,
            Oh, never mind the old folks;
            Never mind the old folks,
            They're in bed asleep.

CHORUS 2

        4. So we went home til morning,
            Til morning, til morning;
            We'll go home til morning,
            For music will not stop.

CHORUS 2

Except for one word, the first stanza and chorus as sung by Dixon are identical to Wolford's text.[36]   The Dixon text is therefore numbered like the Wolford text to assist in understanding how the game is played. Two couples play the game. They join hands to form a circle, partners facing each other. At 1 they circle around to the left. At 2 partners cross their right hands making a "star." Each boy raises his partner's hand to his lips as though it were a beer glass. Repeat,

147

forming the "star" with the left hands. At 4 the boys bow, the girls curtsey. At 5 each boy swings the girl next to him, and then at 6 swings his own partner. If a second stanza is desired, the last four lines remain the same, but the first four are changed as in the second stanza given above. (The third stanza sung by Dixon is not present in the Wolford variant.)

This is also a game for eight and as such is a dance with rather complex figures.[37]

This game, like "Weevily Wheat," is not considered proper for church members who are supposed to neither drink nor dance. This was in contrast with rural practice between the Revolutionary and Civil wars when "pleasurin'" was common with fiddle and liquor and the dancing of the Virginia Reel and the Kentucky Big Circle. These were high-spirited and boisterous affairs. Whiskey was more common than water and certainly was thought to be more healthful. The bottle passed from hand to hand, and all, no matter what sex or age, partook. The fiddler often expected no extra pay other than an additional swig at the bottle as it passed his way. Hence, the saying, "as drunk as a fiddler."

During the first half of the nineteenth century a strong evangelical movement developed in the United States, which resulted in certain restrictions being placed upon social behavior. The consumption of liquor, for example, was frowned upon. Temperance societies sprang up; crusading ladies sang hymns in front of saloons, and the movement which produced Carrie Nation and Prohibition had begun. The boisterous conduct displayed at most dances led people on the frontier to condemn social dancing entirely, as well as the fiddle, which in their eyes symbolized the dance. Although there was some ebb and flow in the force of this religious movement, it became even stronger after the Civil War, and these restrictions were still in place in most rural communities until the First World War. The play-party was, at least in part, the answer to the ban on dancing and the use of instrumental music.

"Down to Rowsers" was out of favor with the church not only because of its mention of drinking but also because it included the frowned-upon "waist swing." Those young people attending who were most scrupulous of their reputation quietly dropped out when the game included the waist swing. Wolford describes the waist swing as follows:

Partners take ball-room position, (i.e., the boy's right hand at his partner's waist, his left hand holding his partner's right hand, and the girl's left hand on his right arm) and turn on spot, usually taking eight steps.[38]

The objection to the waist swing is obviously that the partners face each other and that torso as well as hand contact may take place. No objection seems to have been raised to promenading in which arms and hands are held in the same position but the partners are side by side and move forward.

At the turn of the century, "Down to Rowsers" was also a popular children's game. According to Wolford, it was played by the children at her school during the noon hour and at recess, when there was little danger of discovery.[39]

The history of the melody to which "Down to Rowsers" is sung is even more complex and confusing, if that is possible, than that of "Turkey in the Straw." The melody of "Down to Rowsers" can be traced back to early eighteenth-century France as the melody of "The Ballad of Marlborough." John Churchill, the Duke of Marlborough and an ancestor of the Sir Winston Churchill of this century, was successful in defeating French armies during the War of Spanish Succession. Legend has it that the French, after their defeat in the Battle of Malplaquet in 1709, spread the rumor that Marlborough had been killed. An anonymous French camp minstrel immediately composed the ballad, which apparently remained in the oral tradition for decades, there being no printing of text and melody in association until 1783.[40]

When Marie Antoinette of France was delivered of a child in 1781, her physician brought in a nurse from the north of France, who sang the "Ballad of Marlborough" every evening to the infant dauphin as a lullaby. The queen was much taken with the song, and thus some ten versions of it appeared in print in 1783 and 1784.[41] From the song also rose a Malbrouk or Marlbourouck (the French equivalent of Marlborough) fashion, the wearing of indigo coats with black facing, white breeches with black stockings, and shoes with mourning buckles. The ladies dressed in black and red, the court's own mourning colors, and the gentlemen wore patches on the right side to mark the wound Marlborough suffered at Malplaquet.

The song became extremely popular throughout Europe in part due to the use of the tune in Pierre-Augustin Beaumarchais's celebrated comedy, *The Marriage of Figaro*. Johann Wolfgang von

Goethe is said to have complained that he heard it wherever he went, including in Italy.[42] Fernando Sor composed a set of variations on the melody for guitar.

A rough paraphrase into English of a portion of one version of the popular ballad follows. It roughly parallels the French text of the accompanying "Couplets, Sur la morte de Mr. Malbrourk."

Courtesy of British Library, London

Marlborough, prince of commanders,
Has gone to war in Flanders;
His fame like Alexander's;
But when will he come home?

He won't come home until morning,
Till daylight doth appear.

The English, not caring for the uncomplimentary words of the French, replied with a version of their own:

> Marlborough, prince of commanders,
> Has conquered the French in Flanders,
> His fame is like Alexander's,
> And he's the best of all.
>
> For he's a jolly good fellow,
> And so say all of us.[43]

From the French and English versions, two common texts sung to this melody apparently developed. The first, "We Won't Go Home Till Morning," was first printed in both England and the United States in the 1840s. A portion of this text is incorporated in the variant of "Down to Rowsers" given above (TR 37). "For He's a Jolly Good Fellow," the best-known text sung to this tune, is obviously

61. For He's a Jolly Good Fellow!

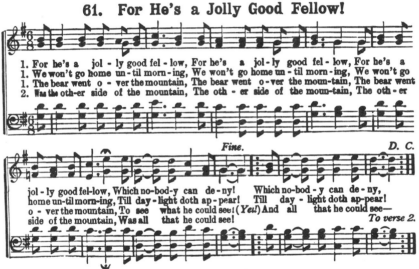

Twice 55 Plus Community Songs. Copyright 1929. Used by permission of Warner/ Chappell Music, Inc., Los Angeles, California.

English in origin, but its first printing seems to be in an American songster in 1870. A further text to which the tune is sung, "The Bear Went Over the Mountain," is apparently both recent and American in origin. As James J. Fuld points out, "there are no bears in England!"[44] The tune was in use in the play-party in Michigan, but not sung to the same words.[45] The earliest known printing of "The Bear Went Over the Mountain" in association with the Marlborough tune is found in *Twice 55 Community Songs,* published by Birchard in 1919.

The French composer of the Duke of Marlborough tune, which over the years has been sung to at least four English texts as well as the French, is also unknown. There have been a number of attempts to trace the tune to origins earlier than the Battle of Malplaquet in 1709. Wilhelm Tappert couples it with two Mideast tunes, one Egyptian and one Arabic, stating that the three are similar.[46] I find the supposed resemblance doubtful. Others have noted its resemblance to the melody of "Calino Casturame," included in the eighteenth-century manuscript of the *Fitzwilliam Virginal Book*.[47] This melody is referred to by Shakespeare in *Henry V*, Act IV, Scene 4. I find the first phrase of this to be quite similar to that of the Marlborough tune, but little resemblance in the subsequent phrases.

And, finally, there were always some who would play "Weevily Wheat," much disapproved by the church since it was more or less the Virginia Reel without the fiddle.

TR 38 Weevily Wheat

Sung by Abraham Lincoln Gary of Rushville, in Bloomington, 1941.

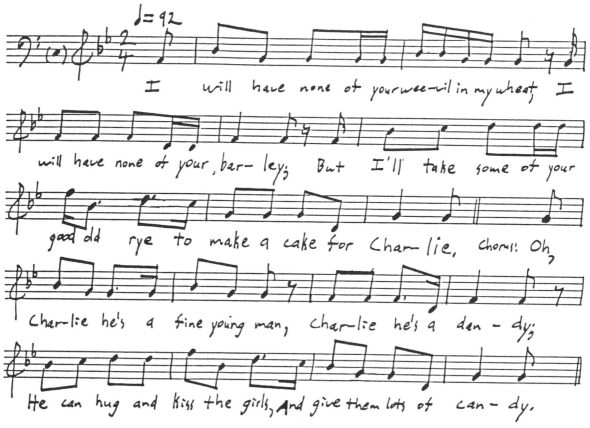

1. I will have none of your weevil in my wheat,
   I will have none of your barley;
   But I'll take some of your good old rye
   To make a cake for Charlie.

CHORUS:

   Oh, Charlie he's a fine young man,
   Charlie he's a dandy;
   He can hug and kiss the girls,
   And give them lots of candy.

2. Oh, Dear, d'you love me as I love you?
   We won't have long to tarry.
   We'll keep the older folks hustling about
   To fix for us to marry.

Mr. Gary sang "Weevily Wheat" during a fairly long interview conducted by Herbert Halpert, then a graduate student at Indiana University and later a distinguished folklorist. Several other unidentified individuals were present. Mr. Gary was seventy-four years of age at the time, and his descriptions of the singing and playing of "Weevily Wheat" in his youth and of the religious restrictions in place at the time are interesting. I am therefore reproducing much of this interview below.

Halpert: What was the name of this?

Gary: "Weevily Wheat."

H: And what is it or what is it like?

G: Well, it's something like . . . it's a game, a young people's game and it was played something like they did the square dance.

H: What did they call games of that sort, did they have any kind of a name?

G: Well, they . . .

H: Did you ever hear a name like "play-party?"

G: Well, they were played at parties. . . . At times they said they were "gum sucks."

153

H: They were what?

G: Gum sucks. (Laughter.)

H: What does that mean?

G: A kissing party. (Laughter.)

H: And did "Weevily Wheat" have kissing in it?

G: No, it doesn't, but it was played at those parties.

H: Well, suppose you sing it and then we'll talk about it.

(Mr. Gary sings.)

G: That's about all.

H: You just repeat that?

G: Just repeating.

(He sings first stanza again.)

G: Just repeating, just repeating, it's a round like . . . while the couples were dancing across the floor a good deal the same as the old square dance.

H: How was it? In two lines?

G: Two lines with the boys on one side and the girls on the other. Then they would skip across and take their girl and waltz up and down the floor with her.

H: Now, did they have any music with it?

G: Only the singing, everybody singing.

H: Everybody singing together?

G: Singing together and it was astonishing sometimes. Some in monotone and some singing all bass but it was entertaining. They kept the time.

H: Well, why did they sing? Why not a fiddle or banjo?

G: Well, we had no musical instruments in the neighborhood and the singing was to keep step to the music, to keep time to the music as they sang it. They furnished it themselves.

H: If you had had a fiddler, let's say, would people have not objected to your playing, having a fiddle at your parties?

G: Usually. It was the devil that was in the fiddle. In our community there were Methodists and Campbellites. The Methodists were all sure the devil was in the fiddle. The Campbellites didn't object so much, but if the Methodist preacher, if he found anyone had a fiddle in his house or had been playing it, why that person was called before the Church.

H: What happened to him when he was called before the Church?

G: Well they'd remonstrate. If he wouldn't agree not to commit that sin again why he would be put out or put on probation again. You see the Methodists had six months' probation for anyone who joined the Church. He wasn't taken into full membership for six months. After he had behaved himself for six months he was taken into full membership. But after that if he committed a sin like playing a fiddle, going to the circus, or racing horses, he was brought before the Church. He had to apologize and promise not to do it again or he would be put out. They took their religion very seriously in those days.

"Campbellite" was another name given to the Protestant religious body, the Disciples of Christ. It arose on the basis of a desire to develop unity among all Christians and the belief that all should be allowed to worship together as they wished. Its founders were two Presbyterian ministers,

155

Martin W. Stone of Kentucky and Thomas Campbell, who came from Ireland seeking a better home for his family. The latter's writings became the basis for the new movement, the leadership of which was passed on to his son, Alexander Campbell.

As could be expected, the younger generation resented the restrictions imposed on their activities. The only play-party songs remembered by Lomax's three informants in 1938 (TR 37-39) were precisely those frowned upon by the church. This resentment was rarely shown openly, but it often appeared in the songs sung at the play-party, as in the third stanza of "Down to Rowsers."

> Oh, never mind the old folks,
> Oh, never mind the old folks;
> Never mind the old folks,
> They're in bed asleep.

Here, in addition, is a satirical stanza sung to the playing of "Weevily Wheat."

> Take a lady by her hand,
> Lead her like a pigeon,
> Make her dance the Weevily Wheat,
> She loses her religion.[48]

Wolford observes that the game is the Virginia Reel figure for figure. Here is her text and description of how the game is played.

Weevily Wheat

> Charley, he's a nice young man,
> Charley, he's a dandy.
> Charley hugs and kisses the girls,
> And feeds them all on candy.
>
> Come down this way with your weevily wheat,
> Come down this way with your barley,
> Come down this way with your weevily wheat,
> To bake a cake for Charley.

Longways dance for an even number of players, preferably six couples.

The player[s] stand in two lines, the boys facing the girls and partners opposite each other.

First - The boy at the top and the girl at the bottom of the dance advance to the center, the boy bows, the girl curtsies and each dances backwards to position.

Second - The same couple advance to center, cross right hands, turn around to the left and retire as in former figure.

Third - The same figure is repeated with the left hand, and turning around to the right.

Fourth - Repeat the third figure with both left and right hands crossed, circling to the right.

Fifth - The same couple advance to the center, dance around each other (i.e., first face, then left shoulders almost together, next backs turned to each other, then right shoulders almost together and back to facing position) and retire.

Sixth - The same couple advance to the center and swing turning to the right. Each of the two then swings his (and her) partner.

Seventh - The same couple again meet in the center, and each then swings the person at the left of his (or her) partner.

Repeat this last figure until the first couple have swung every person in the line. This couple then swings in the center and retires to position.

The couple at the top promenade down the center and take position at the bottom of their respective lines.

Repeat from the beginning, the boy who is now at the head of his line advancing to meet the girl at the foot of her line. Continue repeating until all the players are in their original position.[49]

Newell claims that the game is an imitation of weaving, the first movement representing the shooting of the shuttle from side to side, the passage of the woof over and under the thread to the warp. The last movements indicate the tightening of the thread and the bringing together of the cloth.[50]

Mari Ruef Hofer theorizes that the game is related to the ancient Scottish weaving game from which the Virginia Reel developed.[51]

Further evidence indicating a Scottish origin for the song is found in the text, as in this variant.

157

TR 39 Over the River to Charlie's

Sung by Oscar "Doc" Parks, Deuchars, 6 or 8 April 1938.

1. Over the river to feed my sheep,
   Over the river to Charlie's;
   Over the river to feed my sheep
   On buckwheat dough and barley.

2. Give me some of the best you've got,
   Give me some of your barley;
   Give me some of your buckwheat dough
   For to bake a cake for Charlie.

3. Charlie he's a handsome boy,
   Charlie he's a dandy;
   Charlie he's a handsome boy,
   He feeds the girls on candy.

Emma Bell Miles suggests that "the 'Charlie' of these songs is the Prince Charlie of Jacobite ballads."

> "Over the River, Charlie" may or may not be an echo of "Over the Waters to Charlie," for a large proportion of the mountain people are descended from Scotch Highlanders who left their homes on account of the persecution which harassed them during Prince Charlie's time, and began life anew in the wilderness of the Alleghenies.[52]

The Jacobites were Catholics who continued to consider James II, who was deposed by the Protestants in 1688, and his successors in the House of Stuart to be the legitimate heirs to the throne of England. For a period of years there were uprisings in favor of the Stuarts in Catholic Scotland and Ireland, all of which failed (see pp. 304-5). The last attempt was made in 1745 by the grandson of James II, Charles III, known as "Bonnie Prince Charlie," who had been living in France. He rallied many Highlanders to his cause, which was initially successful in Scotland, but he was finally defeated in the succeeding year, and the Jacobites were severely punished.

Many scholars have followed Miles's suggestion, usually linking the line of the play-party song, "Over the River to Charlie" with the following Jacobite ballad:

O'er the Water to Charlie

Come boat me o'er, come row me o'er,
Come boat me o'er to Charlie;
I'll gie John Ross anither bawbee
To ferry me o'er to Charlie.
We'll o'er the water, we'll o'er the sea,
We'll o'er the water to Charlie;
Come weel, come wo, we'll gather and go,
And live and die wi' Charlie.[53]

W. Edson Richmond and William Tillson, editors of the revised edition of Wolford's *The Play-Party in Indiana*, feel that it is quite unjustified to conclude that the words of the play-party song are based upon those of the Jacobite ballad. "The verbal parallels are hardly greater than those found in 'Charley Is My Darling.'"[54] Parenthetically, when some fifty years ago I first learned a song titled "Charlie Is My Darling," I was under the impression that the "gay cavalier" referred to was Bonnie Prince Charlie, and there are, incidentally, Jacobite ballads with that particular title.[55]   What Richmond and Tillson seem to have missed is a variant of the play-party song published by Paul Brewster in his "Game-Songs from Southern Indiana."

Bonnie Prince Charlie

1. I won't have none of your weevily wheat,
   Neither rye nor barley;
   I want some of your good old wheat
   To bake a cake for Charlie.

2. Over the river to feed my sheep,
   Over the sea to Charlie;
   Come weal, come woe, I'll gath'r and go
   And live or die for Charlie.[56]

That the game or dance of "Weevily Wheat" developed from the Virginia Reel there can be little doubt. Whether, in turn, the Virginia Reel developed from a Scottish weaving game is a point concerning which I, for one, do not care to argue. However, it would seem to me that the above is sufficient evidence to trace at least part of the text of "Weevily Wheat" to Jacobite ballads concerning Bonnie Prince Charlie.

Like all young folks since time immemorial, the participants in the play-party had their own peculiar customs and picturesque jargon. Girls were always referred to in complimentary terms. They were pretty little pinks, redbirds or bluebirds, sweethearts, darlings, or, at least, fair ladies. As pointed out previously (p. 141), "Lou," as in "Skip to My Lou," is a synonym for love. In Eastern Tennessee, "Lou" meant sweetheart.[57]   Girls were sweet as sugar, sweet as molasses candy, or scented like cinnamon.

Boys, on the other hand, were usually referred to in derogatory terms, if not merely as "gents." Boys were bums, old bums, or at least, old bachelors. If they danced badly they were bigfoot or clubfoot.[58]

One had to be "hep" or, in more contemporary parlance, "cool" to understand the meaning of some of their expressions. Take, for example, the following couplet:

Swing them around, pat them on the head.
If you can't get biscuit, take cornbread.

Deciphered, the second cryptic line, "If you can't get biscuit, take cornbread," carries the following meaning: If the girl won't let you swing her by the waist--the waist swing is biscuit--then take corn bread, swing her by her hands.

The party we left to make the above comments is now beginning to wind down, but it will continue until every boy who came without a girl musters up enough courage to ask his partner if he can "see her home safely." Or perhaps the master of the house stops the party with, "One o'clock! Time to go home." The departure of the guests is hasty. While the girls slip on their long riding skirts the boys go for the horses. Very soon each girl is mounted behind her partner, and the scene is suddenly quiet except for a fragment of song floating back:

Little red wagon painted blue,
Skip to my Lou, my darling.

Commentary

In this chapter I set the play-party in the 1880s, and all the songs with music were recorded in southern Indiana. However, some of the comments made refer to the play-party in general. I have, for example, insufficient information to assert that all the jargon reproduced above was in use in southern Indiana. The play-party was a widespread and constantly changing phenomenon, in efflorescence approximately between the Civil War and the First World War, a period of about half a century. Practice differed from place to place and from time period to time period. The informant who sang "The Needle's Eye" for Wolford reported that in the 1880s most games were kissing games, but they were considered even then as undignified.[59]

161

Wolford first describes how "The Needle's Eye" was played in her day with the "London Bridge" type of ending, and then the manner in which it was played in the 1880s when kissing was part of the game. Concerning the latter she writes, "The person caught under the arch had to kiss the arch-maker whose symbol he had chosen and then exchange places with him." In describing the first part of the game she writes, "One couple join hands high over the heads and form an arch. All the other players form a line, each girl behind her partner."[60] The possibility therefore exists that a boy caught by the arch makers could select a symbol of the male member of the arch-making couple and thus a boy be required to kiss a boy, a situation unlikely to be relished by the participants. Although Wolford is more precise and explicit than most writers concerning the play-party, there are occasional anomalies of this sort.

Oddly enough, Altha Lea McLendon reports that "before 1890 kissing was proper, waist swinging never--after that the custom gradually reversed itself."[61] Wolford, who originally presented her material as a master's thesis at the University of Chicago in 1915, describes only one kind of swing, the waist swing. In the couplet taken from B. A. Botkin's *The American Play-Party Song*, which covers a wider time period, a distinction is made between "biscuit," the waist swing, and "cornbread," the swing with the hands.

There is controversy among folklorists as to whether the get-togethers they have termed the play-party evolved into that particular form because of church proscription or in the attempt to make do. Was there no instrumental accompaniment, no fiddle, because the church opposed it, or because no fiddler was available? Wolford is of the opinion that the play-party developed primarily as a means of circumventing the restrictions of the church against dancing and the performance of instrumental music. Most of those who have written concerning the play-party have taken the same line. However, Richmond and Tillson express doubt that the church played such a strong role in the matter. They point out that the play-party was open to anyone who wished to come, that those who also attended public dances were welcome as long as they did not drink.[62]

Probably the best summation of the situation was made by McClendon:

[The play-party games] are American in form though sometimes adapted from European songs and games, especially from England. Everyone in the communities where they are played, chiefly in the Southern, the Middle Atlantic, and Middle Western states, was welcome. The church gave the form impetus through its ban on instruments; though the play-party was just a camouflaged dance, the word *dance* was never mentioned. The entire evening of play was informal, no class was excluded though such actions as drinking were not sanctioned.[63]

The same comments concerning the association of verbal and musical phrases and their underlying pulses discussed in the commentary of the previous chapter are equally applicable to the play-party songs. Many of the melodies were originally employed in children's singing games. The remainder are dance tunes which follow the same patterns. All are in duple meter, and all display a steady pulse with one exception, TR 39, "Over the River to Charlie's." If "Doc" Parks had been singing the song while playing the game, he undoubtedly would have kept a steady pulse. Since he is not, the upland singing style, with its very free rhythm, has had some slight influence on his performance.

It is amazing how much repetition of words we will accept when they are sung rather than spoken. The same words are sung over and over again in a chorus or a refrain. In actual casual speech no one would say three times in a row "Flies in the buttermilk, shoo, flies, shoo." Rather, there would have to be some variation, "Shoo, flies, get out of the buttermilk" or "Get away, you flies, shoo, shoo." I realize, of course, that the singing is accompanied by rhythmic action (I dare not say dancing).

Rhyme is another factor which keeps our interest. It can be handled in many ways. In "Skip to My Lou" it is the first three repeated lines which rhyme from stanza to stanza; in "Go Tell Aunt Rhody," which is not a singing game, it is the fourth lines which rhyme from stanza to stanza. Some say the melody of a song is merely a vehicle which carries along the words; others that the melody, itself, has a direct, abstract emotional appeal. Perhaps it is because we receive so many signals simultaneously that we can bear the repetition of the words without becoming bored.

It has been established how one melody can be employed in the singing of four or five completely different texts, from "Couplets, Sur la morte de Mr. Malbrourk" to "The Bear Went Over the Mountain." In "Zip Coon" and "Turkey in de Straw" it is demonstrated that not only a text of a song may change titles, but also a tune. In addition a relatively simple melody can be made more complex in order to change it into a suitable fiddle tune, as in "Turkey in de Straw." In folk song and folk music, change and variation are the rules, not the exceptions.

CHAPTER 4 LOVE, COURTSHIP, SEX, AND MARRIAGE

Fulfilled, happy, and long-lasting love is as rare a subject in folk song as it is in other literature and probably for the same reason: it does not hold our interest. What attracts our attention is conflict, the emotional interaction of man and woman, or even the lone expression of the reaction of one to the other. This last is best expressed in song, for example, the following concerning unrequited love.

TR 40 I Don't Know Why I Love Him

Sung by Lula Beard South, Bloomington, May 1956.

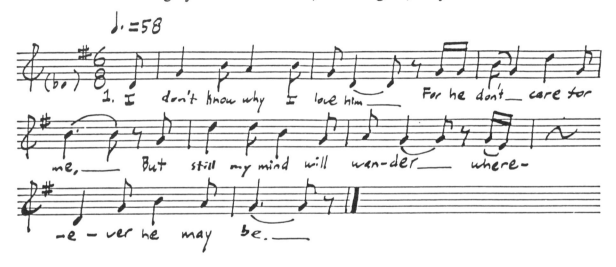

1. I don't know why I love him
   For he don't care for me.
   But still my mind will wander
   Wherever he may be.

2. He may sail across the ocean;
   He may sail across the sea.
   He will travel the wide world over
   But he'll never find one like me.

3. There's gold and silver plenty
   But that will melt like snow
   And when poverty and death o'ertakes him
   He will think of me, I know.

4. I don't know why I love him

165

For he don't care for me.
But still my mind will wander
Wherever he may be.

When I interviewed Mrs. South at her farmhouse west of Ellettsville in February 1986, she sang an additional stanza preceding the above:

Why can't I take love easy
Like leaves upon the tree?
They always die and wither
And that's the love for me.

The text is similar in many respects to songs like "Some Say Love Is a Blessing" or "True Love." Below are some stanzas from a variant from the Ozarks:

Dark and Dreary Weather

1. It's dark an' dreary weather,
   Almost inclined to rain,
   My heart is almost broken,
   My beau has went off on the train!

2. I don't see why I love him,
   He does not care for me,
   But my pore heart will wander
   Wherever he may be.

3. Oh how can he forget me,
   An' go so far away?
   I wisht I had never met him
   On that bright an' golden day.

4. Some say that love is a pleasure,
   What pleasure do I see?
   For the one I love so dearly
   Has gone square back on me.

5. Some say that silver melts like snow,
   An' gold will turn to tin,
   If poverty overtakes him
   I reckon he'll think of me then.[1]

There is considerable speculation concerning the origin of this song, which has never been determined. According to one source, it is originally a Cockney song by a London housemaid.[2] It

166

has been recorded as "They Tell Me Love's a Pleasure" by Grover Rann and Harry Ayers in 1930.[3]

In the next song a woman worries about the possible loss of the affection of her lover while he is absent.

TR 41 I Worry My Heart Away for You

Sung by Clara Belle Smith Schreiber, Bloomington, 1959.

day. I wor-ry my heart__ a-way for you.

1. I wonder where you are tonight, my love,
   As all alone I sit and dream.
   I wonder if your heart's with me tonight
   And if the same stars o'er you gleam?
   I sometimes fear there is another love,
   Some fairer face has won your heart.
   But, oh, I hope the day will never come,
   The day when we must live apart.

CHORUS:
   I worry my heart away for you,
   It cries aloud, "My love be true!"
   I dream of you by night;
   I long for you by day.
   I worry my heart away for you.

2. The bees are droning in the wildwood, love;
   The flowers their tiny heads bowed low.
   The birds are singing soft and plain of late;
   They miss your dear, kind face, I know.
   From o'er the meadow comes a faint perfume,
   It whispers gently, "Love, you're true."
   But, oh, my darling if you only knew
   I worry my heart away for you.

CHORUS

The words and music of this song were copyrighted in 1902 under the title "I'm Wearing My Heart Away for You" by Charles K. Harris, a prolific composer of popular songs best known for "After the Ball" (1892) and "Break the News to Mother" (1897).[4] A bellhop, pawnbroker, and banjo picker, his first song was published on Tin Pan Alley in 1891.[5]

Dale Schreiber, the son of the singer, believes his mother learned the song from a cylinder phonograph record played for her by Paul Emmet Schreiber, his father, when the two were courting.

Economics has always played a large part in marriage, but here class allegiance overrides it.

TR 42 Pretty Sarry

Sung by "Aunt" Phoebe Stoker Elliott, New Harmony, 10 April 1938.

168

1. Way down in some lone valley or in some other place,
    Where the small birds do whistle, and their notes do
        increase,
    I'll think of Pretty Sarry, her ways so complete;
    I love her, my Sarry, from her head to her feet.

2. My love she won't have me, as I understand

She wants a freeholder and I have no land.
Yet I could maintain her on silver and gold
And as many other fine things as my love's house could
    hold.

3. I went to my Sarry, my love to unfold,
   To tell her my passion so brave and so bold.
   I said to her, "Sarry, will you be my bride,
   And walk with me ever, right here by my side?"

4. "I love you, my Sarry, as you can well see.
   I will take you a-traveling o'er land and o'er sea.
   . . . some jewels I will buy you to wear,
   For there's no one, my true love, to me is more fair."

5. Then Sarry held out her sweet little hand,
   And said, "I can't love you for you have no land.
   I have promised another to be his dear wife,
   And walk with him ever, all the days of my life."

6. "You have broken my heart strings, Pretty Sarry," I
    said.
   "I will go from your presence. I wish I was dead.
   Some other lover will kneel at your feet
   And take the dear kisses that I once thought so sweet."

"Aunt" Phoebe explains how and when she learned this song at the beginning of Chapter 1. She had learned it from a great aunt who, in turn, had learned it in Virginia before 1800. George Malcolm Laws considers this a lyric song rather than a ballad.[6] The song seems to be associated with the Appalachian region, there being only one non-Appalachian text printed, from the Ozarks.[7] However, the song obviously refers to the colonial plantation life of the coastal plain, to a period when the English semifeudal aristocratic view still prevailed. The ownership of land was not only the mark of a family of good breeding but also the source of political power. A merchant, a nonfreeholder, no matter how successful, was to be rejected.

The next song is concerned not with colonial class distinctions but with the everyday economic needs of the thousands who worked small farms to earn their corn bread.

TR 43 The Young Man Who Wouldn't Hoe Corn

Sung by Vern Smelser, Paoli, 16 February 1964.

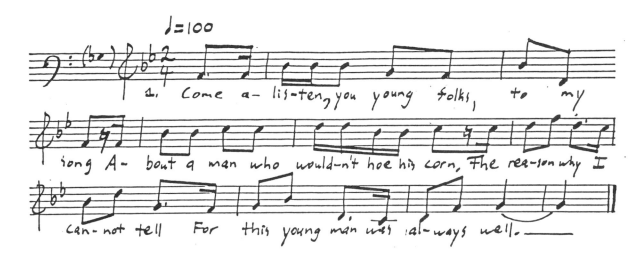

1. Come a-listen, you young folks, to my song
    About a man who wouldn't hoe his corn.
    The reason why I cannot tell
    For this young man was always well.

2. He had planted his corn in the month of June
    And in July it a-wasn't knee-high.
    In the fall it came up frost
    And all this young man's corn was lost.

3. So he went around to his sweetheart's door
    Where he had often gone before,
    But ere this courting they began
    She asked him if he'd hoed his corn.

4. He hung his head and began to sigh
    Saying, "Lady, lady, I'll tell you why.
    I tried and tried and all in vain.
    I don't believe I'll raise a grain."

5. "Then why do you ask a girl to wed
    If a man can't earn his own cornbread?
    Single I am and I'll remain:
    For a lazy man I won't maintain."

6. At this the young man turned away
    Saying, "Lady, lady, you'll rue the day.
    You'll rue it, madam, just as sure as you're born
    For giving me the shivers 'cause I didn't hoe my corn.

No clearer statement could be made concerning the economic position of women in American rural society in the past. This song is also known as "The Lazy Young Man" and "Hiram Slick." It is widely diffused in the United States, variants having been collected in Arkansas, Indiana, Iowa, Mississippi,

Missouri, North Carolina, Tennessee, and West Virginia. Since there are no reports of its collection in Canada or England, it is apparently a purely American product.[8]

The variant printed by Paul Brewster is shorter but similar in most other respects.[9]

A phonograph recording of the song, under the title "A Lazy Farmer Boy," was made by Buster Carter and Preston Young as a vocal duet with violin, guitar, and banjo in 1931.[10]

Songs concerning a May-December courtship are common in the Appalachians[11] and are very old.

TR 44 His Old Gray Beard Needs Shaving

Sung by Sudie Summers Parks, Deuchars, 6 April 1938.

1. Once an old man come over the sea.
    Oh, but I won't have him.
    Come over the sea and he courted me
    And his old gray beard needs shaving.

2. My mama told me to give him a chair.
   Oh, but I won't have him.
   I give him a chair with the rings in the ears
   And his old gray beard needs shaving.

3. My mama told me to fix him a bed.
   Oh, but I won't have him.
   I fixed him a bed with a pillow under his head
   And his old gray beard needs shaving.

When Lomax asked Mrs. Parks where she had learned the song she replied that she had known it as long as she could remember. There are many songs on this topic with titles such as "Maids When You're Young Never Wed an Old Man," "Get Away, Old Man, Get Away," "An Old Man Courted Me," "Boots and Leggings," and "My Mother Bid Me." In many of them, as above, the mother commands the daughter to wait on the old man. The old man's interest is understandable, but why should a mother be interested in such a marriage? Is her daughter already eighteen, almost an old maid in those times? Is the old man simply rich? The situation must have occurred with some frequency or such songs would not be so widespread. At times the mother does not appear. Here is a variant of that character collected in Warren, Indiana:

An Old Man Came to See Me

1. An old man came to see me, and his name I will not
      tell;
   An old man came to see me, and I liked him very well.

CHORUS:
   An old man, an old man, an old man soon turns gray;
   But a young man comes so full of love. Stand back
      old man, get away.

2. An old man came to see me, a-sitting on a stool,
   An old man came to see me, the blamed old sleepy fool.

CHORUS

3. I do not like an old man, I'll tell you the reason why:
   He always [is] so slobbery; his chin is never dry.

CHORUS

4. I'd rather have a young man with an apple in his hand,

173

Than to have a old man, his house and his land.

CHORUS

5. I'd rather have a young man with his jacket made of
      silk,
   Than to have an old man with forty cows to milk.

CHORUS[12]

In England the song is commonly known as "The Old Man Who Came Over the Moor.[13]

The following is a combination of the above song complex and a minstrel show song of the 1860s.

TR 45 Shoo Flies, Don't Bother Me

Sung by Dale Schreiber, Bloomington, 20 February 1988.

~way,

CHORUS 1:
    Shoo flies, don't bother me.
    Shoo flies, don't bother me.
    Shoo flies, don't bother me.
    Get away, old man, get away.

1. I'll never marry an old man.
    I'll tell you the reason why.
    His lips are all terbakker juice
    And his chin is never dry.

CHORUS 2:
    For an old man he is old,
    And an old man he is gray,
    But a young man's heart is full of love.
    Get away, old man, get away.

CHORUS 1
2. I'd rather marry a young man
    With an apple in his hand,
    Than to marry an old man
    With a thousand acres of land.

CHORUS 2

Dale learned this song from his older sister, Hazel Schreiber Merry, who in turn had learned
it from a phonograph record. She could not remember who recorded the song.

The first lines come from a nonsense song published in 1869 which became extremely popular.
The words are by Billy Reeves, and the music is by Frank Campbell. The chorus runs:

Shoo fly, don't bother me!
Shoo fly, don't bother me!
Shoo fly, don't bother me!
I belong to Company G!

I feel, I feel, I feel,
I feel like a morning star,
I feel, I feel, I feel,
I feel like a morning star.

"There were serious discussions at the time as to whether or not one could feel like a morning star." This song was also sung in the 1901 play *Captain Jinks of the Horse Marines*[14] (see TR 32). I remember from my childhood that "I belong to somebody" was frequently substituted for the fourth line given above.

The two songs were apparently first combined in a phonograph recording by Frank Crumit in 1926 under the title "Get Away, Old Man, Get Away."[15] It was copyrighted the following year, "revised and arranged from an old folksong" by Oliver E. Story under the same title. Numerous other recordings of the song in this form were issued, six alone by Vernon Dalhart, one of the earliest of the "singing cowboys," through various recording companies.

A battle of wits between a man and a woman concerning love and marriage is a common theme in folklore. Here it is couched in ballad form.

TR 46 The Two Lovers

(Child 2, The Elfin Knight)

Sung by Anna Sandage Underhill, Uniontown, 30 December 1963.

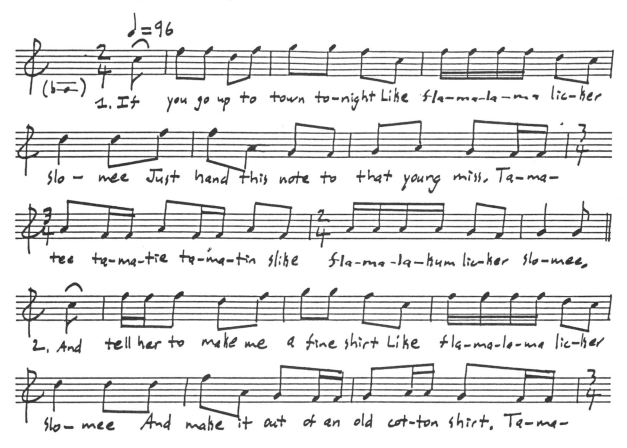

tee ta-ma-tie ta-ma-tin slike fla-ma-la-ma lic-her slo-mee.

1. If you go up to town tonight
   Like flamalama licker slomee
   Just hand this note to that young miss.
   Tamatee tamatie tamatin slike flamalakum licker slomee.

2. And tell her to make me a fine shirt
   Like flamalama licker slomee
   And make it out of an old cotton sheet.
   Tamatee tamatie tamatin slike flamalama licker slomee.

3. And tell her to sew it with her gold ring
   Like flamalama licker slomee
   And ev'ry stitch that put between.
   Tamatee tamatie tamatin slike flamalama licker slomee.

4. And tell her to wash it in yonder well (etc.)
   Where never a drop of water fell. (etc.)

5. And tell her to hang it on yonder thorn (etc.)
   That never grew there since Adam was born. (etc.)

6. If you go down to town tonight (etc.)
   Just hand this note to that young gent. (etc.)

7. And tell him to buy me an acre of ground (etc.)
   Between salt water and sea sand. (etc.)

8. And tell him to plow it with tare and corn (etc.)
   And feed it down with one grain of corn. (etc.)

9. Tell him to reap it with his penknife (etc.)
   And haul it in with two yoke of mice. (etc.)

10. And tell him to haul it to yonder barn (etc.)
    That's never been built since Adam was born. (etc.)

11. Just tell that gent if he's done his work (etc.)
    He can call tonight and get his shirt. (etc.)

This ballad is also frequently known as "The Cambric Shirt" since this is the material of
which the man's shirt is usually to be made. The Elfin Knight, the supernatural being after whom Francis James Child names the ballad, appears only in some early variants. He is of little relevance to

the ballad, and Child believes that the stanzas concerning this figure were added from some lost ballad.[16]

In this duel of wits one lover, usually but not always the man, requires the other to perform a difficult or impossible task. The other lover is acquitted of this responsibility if an equally unattainable task is imposed in return. In folktales it is usually a king who poses the initial challenge. In an Italian story a king sends a woman a few strands of flax with instructions to quickly make enough shirts for an entire regiment of his soldiers. She returns the scalings from the flax with the message that she has no loom, but if he will have one made from the scalings she will carry out his orders immediately. In a Russian tale a somewhat similar task is imposed by the czar. He sends a girl a silken thread and desires that she weave an embroidered towel for him by the next morning. She returns a twig broken from a broom with the request that the czar find a master who can make a loom from the twig upon which she can weave the towel. The czar sends back 150 eggs requiring the same number of chicks be hatched by the morrow. She asks for one-day grain for the chicks since they will peck no other kind: a field must be plowed, sown, and the grain harvested and threshed in one day.[17]

In these tales the second task or set of tasks are requisite for achieving the first. In ballads in the English language this relationship is not usually present, the only requirement being that the chores assigned be equally difficult or impossible.

An English variant of the ballad published in 1893 is remarkably like the Indiana variant except that the man speaks first rather than the woman, and the motivation for imposing the tasks is more evident:

Scarborough Fair

1. Is any of you going to Scarborough Fair?
   Remember me to a lad as lives there,
   Remember me to a lad as lives there;
   For once he was a true lover of mine.

2. Tell him to bring me an acre of land
   Betwixt the wild ocean and yonder sea sand,
   Betwixt the wild ocean and yonder sea sand;
   And then he shall be a true lover of mine.

3. Tell him to plough it with one ram's horn,
   And sow it all over with one peppercorn; (etc.)

4. Tell him to reap it with sickle of leather,
   And bind it together with one peacock feather; (etc.)

5. And now I have answered your questions three,
   I hope you'll answer as many for me; (etc.)

6. Is any of you going to Scarborough Fair?
   Remember me to a lass as lives there; (etc.)

7. Tell her to make me a cambric shirt,
   Without any needles or thread or owt through't; (etc.)

8. Tell her to wash it by yonder wall
   Where water ne'er sprung, nor a drop o' rain
       fall; (etc.)

9. Tell her to dry it on yonder thorn,
   Where blossoms ne'er grew sin' Adam was born; (etc.)

10. And now I have answered your questions three,
    And I hope you'll answer as many for me, (etc.)[18]

A variant of the above was made extremely popular by the singing duo Simon and Garfunkel in the 1960s.[19] Their version was prominently featured in the sound track of the 1967 movie, *The Graduate*.

TR 47 My Heart's Tonight in Texas

(Laws AM B 23)

Sung by Vern Smelser, Paoli, 6 June 1966.

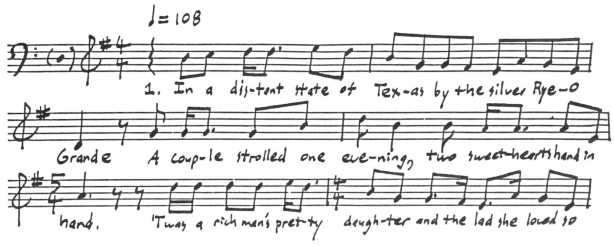

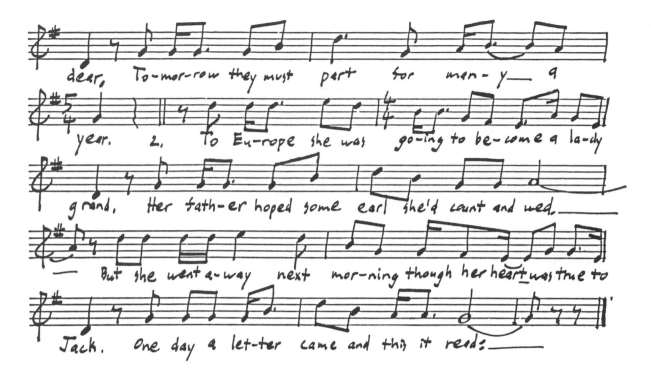

1. In a distant state of Texas by the silver Rye-o Grande
   A couple strolled one evening, two sweethearts hand
      in hand.
   'Twas a rich man's pretty daughter and the lad she
      loved so dear.
   Tomorrow they must part for many a year.

2. To Europe she was going to become a lady grand.
   Her father hoped some earl she'd court and wed.
   But she went away next morning though her heart was
      true to Jack.
   One day a letter came and this it read:

3. "My heart's tonight in Texas by the silver Rye-o
      Grande.
   The band is playing 'Dixie' and it's there I long
      to be.
   Dad says some earl I'll marry, Jack, but you shall have
      my hand,
   For my heart's tonight in Texas by the silver Rye-o
      Grande."

4. In a stately ball in England stood a Texas lad [sic]
      one night
   Though the air was one of splendor and the lights were
      dazzling bright.
   An earl knelt there beside her, begging her to take
      his hand.
   But she says, "My thoughts tonight are by the silver
      Rye-o Grande."

180

5. "I cannot take your title; I'd rather have my Jack.
   It was only yesterday that I wrote and said,
   'My heart's tonight in Texas by the silver Rye-o
       Grande.
   And the band is playing "Dixie" and it's there I
       long to be.
   Dad says some earl I'll marry, Jack, but you shall have
       my hand,
   For my heart's tonight in Texas by the silver Rye-o
       Grande.'"

This ballad seems to antedate the rise of the Texas oil millionaires since the father's ambitions reach only to an earl, a title about halfway down the British noble hierarchy. Above earls are marquesses and dukes and below are viscounts and barons (not to mention the Royal Family at the very top and plain peers at the bottom). In the early colonial period the daughters of the landed aristocracy were usually educated in England and on occasion married a titled Briton. With the advent of Jacksonian democracy and, to some extent, the separation of political power from wealth, such liaisons became rare. They returned to fashion with the marriage of Jennie Jerome, daughter of a wealthy banker, to Lord Randolph Churchill, the youngest son of the seventh Duke of Marlborough and the father of Winston Churchill, a descendant of the first Duke of Marlborough (see p. 149). As the century progressed, such alliances became more frequent, and for good reason. In English noble families, with their rule of primogeniture, younger sons had no hope of inheriting the father's estate. These younger sons had to live on allowances, as snobbery kept them from pursuing any occupation but those in the army, navy, and civil service. None of these, of course, provided great incomes. The way out for younger sons and tax-impoverished peers was to marry an heiress. In fact, in a letter to her mother, Lady Randolph wrote that unless an upper-class English girl was an heiress it was very difficult for her to marry at all.

There were now more men of great wealth in America than in Great Britain, and Americans were quite willing to pass on their wealth to their daughters, as well as to their sons. Thus a brilliant marriage could be achieved by combining American dollars with an English title. No American heiress could secure equal prestige or position by marrying an American husband. She was unfortunately cut off from the possibility of a title by our Revolution and Constitution.

ENGLAND'S POOREST DUKE AFTER OUR RICHEST HEIRESS

The Young Duke of Manchester, Who Couldn't Pay His Livery Bill, Coming to America to Win Miss May Goelet.

A Romance of the Duke and the Dollars.

She Owns an Enormous Slice of New York, and He Is One of the Only Two Marriageable Dukes Now in the Market.

MISS MAY GOELET

THE DUKE OF MANCHESTER

In the search for titles Consuelo Vanderbilt surpassed most of her competitors by marrying the Duke of Marlborough.[20] Such marriages, of course, were a made-to-order sensation for the press. The accompanying reproduction from a newspaper of the time is ample evidence of this.

The girl in the ballad was probably right in refusing her earl. Such marriages, as demonstrated fictionally by Henry James in his novel, *The Golden Bowl*, and by the eventual legal separation of the Duke and Duchess of Marlborough, did not necessarily produce the anticipated happiness. Of course, one cannot be sure how the rich girl of the ballad will get along with her Texas Jack, either.

Through oral tradition this song has acquired at least two alternative titles, "By the Silvery Rio Grande" and "Texas Jack." However, as composed by R. Roden and Max S. Witt and copyrighted in 1900, the title is "My Heart's Tonight in Texas." The song was recorded by the Carter Family in 1934.[21]

TR 48 The Farmer and the Damsel

(Laws BR N 20, The Golden Glove)

Sung by Albert Jeremiah Fields, Bedford, 7 August 1954.

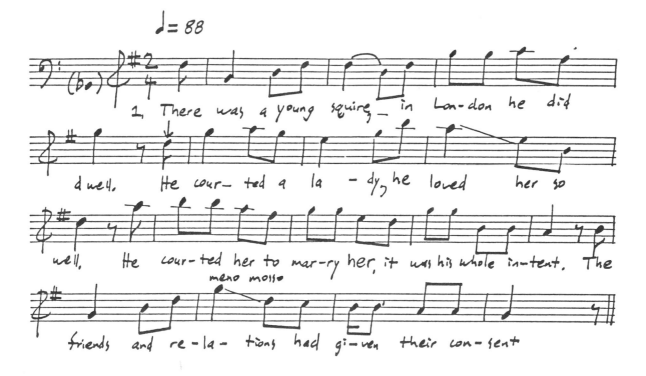

1. There was a young squire, in London he did dwell.
   He courted a lady, he loved her so well.
   He courted her to marry her, it was his whole intent.
   The friends and relations had given their consent.

2. The day was appointed all for the wedding day.
   The farmer was chosen to give her away.
   But instead of getting married she went to her bed;
   The thought of the farmer ran sole in her head.

3. It ran in her head till it troubled her mind,
   And the way to win the farmer she quickly defined.
   A vest, coat, and pantaloons this damsel she put on
   And she went a-hunting with her dog and her gun.

4. She hunted all around where the farmer he did dwell,
   For she knew in her heart that she loved him so well.
   She oft times would fire but nothing did she kill,
   Till at length the young farmer came into the field.

5. "Why ain't you at the wedding," this damsel she
         inquired,
   "To wait upon the squire and give him his bride?"
   "Oh, no, kind Sir, if the truth I must tell,
   I can't give her away for I love her too well."

6. This pleased the young lady to find him so bold.
   She gave him her glove that was bordered with gold.
   She told him she found it as she was coming along,
   As she was a-hunting with her dog and her gun.

7. She quickly returned with her heart full of love,
   And soon she reported the loss of her glove,
   Saying, "The man that will find it and bring it home
         to me,
   I vow and declare that his bride I will be."

8. This pleased the young farmer to hear of the news.
   Straightway to this honor'ble lady he goes,
   Saying, "Dear Honor'ble Lady, I've brought home your
         glove,
   If you will be pleased for to grant me your love."

9. "It's already granted," this damsel she replied.
   "Oh, how I love the sweet breath of the farmer," she
         cried,
   "While mistress of my dairy and milking of my cow,
   The jolly, brisk young farmer goes whistling at his
         plow."

This British ballad is more frequently known as "The Golden Glove" or "Dog and Gun."[22]

A variant taken from a nineteenth-century chapbook, *Five Favorite Songs*, is reprinted below, as is a reproduction of the title page of the chapbook:

The Golden Glove

1. A wealthy young 'squire of Tamword we hear.
   He courted a nobleman's daughter so fair;
   And for to marry her it was his intent,
   All friends and relations had given their consent.

2. The time was appointed for the wedding-day,
   A young farmer was chosen to father to be;
   As soon as the lady the farmer did spy,
   It flamed her heart, O my heart, she did cry.

3. She turned from the squire, nothing she said,
   Instead of being married she went to her bed,
   The thoughts of the farmer still run in her mind,
   The way for to have him she soon then did find.

4. Coat, waistcoat, and breeches she then did put on,
   And a-hunting she went with her dog and her gun;
   She hunted all round where the farmer did dwell,
   Because in her heart she lov'd him so well.

5. She oftentimes fired, but nothing she killed,
   At length the young farmer came into the field;
   Then for to talk with him it was her intent,
   With her dog and gun to meet him she went.

6. I thought you had been at the wedding, she cry'd
   To wait on the 'squire and to give him his bride:
   No, sir, said the farmer, I'll take sword in hand,
   By honour I'll gain her, or my life's at command.

7. It pleased the lady to hear him so bold,
   And she gave him a glove the was flower'd with gold,
   She told him she found it in coming along,
   As she was a-hunting with her dog and her gun.

8. The lady went home with her heart full of love,
   And she gave out a speech she lost her glove;
   And the man that does find it and bring it to me,
   The man that does find it, his bride I shall be.

9. The farmer was pleased when he heard the news--
   With a heart full of joy to his lady he goes;
   Dear honoured lady, I've pick'd up your glove,
   If you will be pleased to grant me your love.

10. It is already granted, I will be your bride,
    I love the sweet breath of a farmer, she cry'd;
    I'll be the mistress of the dairy and milking the cows,
    While my jolly brisk farmer is whistling at plows.[23]

By permission of the Houghton Library, Harvard University

Poems printed on a single sheet, in chapbooks or songsters, are usually listed under the single rubric, "broadside." The broadside reprinted above contains one more stanza than the variant sung by Fields. The last two lines are also a little clearer.

186

The social relationships in this ballad seem a bit confusing. Perhaps it expresses the decay of the old social order occurring in Victorian England. In the previous century most farmers were tenants of a squire. It would be as unlikely that one would give a bride away to a squire as it would be that he would be able to handle a sword. There is a bit of reverse Cinderella in the desire of this noble lady to marry the follower of a plow.

TR 49 John Riley

(Laws BR N 36)

Sung by Albert Jeremiah Fields, Bedford, 7 August 1954.

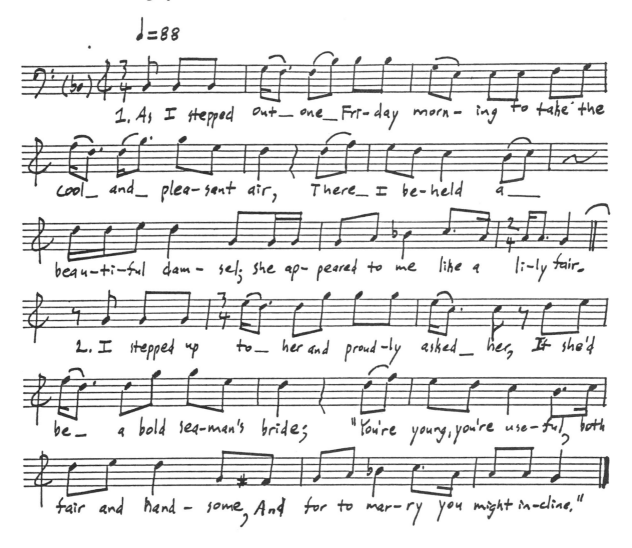

1. As I stepped out one Friday morning
   To take the cool and pleasant air,

187

There I beheld a beautiful damsel;
She appeared to me like a lily fair.

2. I stepped up to her and proudly asked her,
   If she'd be a bold seaman's bride;
   "You're young, you're useful [*sic*], both fair
     and handsome,
   And for to marry you might incline."

3. "Oh, no, kind sir, if truth I must tell you,
   I could have been married ten years ago
   To one John Riley lives in this country,
   Has been the cause of my overthrow.
   To one John Riley lives in this country,
   Has been the cause of my overthrow."

4. "Don't think of Riley but do disclaim him
   And we'll sail over to a distant shore.
   Yes, we'll sail over to Pennsylvania,
   Adieu to Riley forevermore."

5. "I can't sail with you to Pennsylvania,
   I can't sail with you to a distant shore.
   My heart is with him, I can't forget him,
   Although I never shall see him more."

6. And when he found her love was loyal,
   He gave her kisses one, two, and three;
   Saying, "I'm the man whom you do all Riley,
   Has been the cause of your misery."
   Saying, "I'm the man whom you do all Riley,
   Has been the cause of your misery."

7. "I've sailed the ocean in ev'ry motion,
   I have riches laid up in store;
   Now let us marry, no longer tarry,
   I vow I never shall leave thee more.
   Now let us marry, no longer tarry,
   I vow I never shall leave thee more."

One of the nineteenth-century broadsides upon which Laws apparently bases his listing is "Young Riley," which is reproduced here.

The two texts have much in common in addition to the name of the absent lover. A sailor compliments a young woman on her attractiveness and boldly proposes marriage, a proposition she declines because of a previous love. However, in one case it is the absent lover who is speaking. Finding her loyal, he makes himself known and they plan marriage. In the broadside she is already married to the

YOUNG RILEY

(A favourite Song by Richard Newton.)

As I was walking through the county of Cavan,
All for to view the sweet charms of life,
There I beheld a most clever woman,
She appeared to me like an angel bright.

I said fair maiden now could you fancy,
All for to be a young Sailor's bride,
She said, kind sir, I would rather tarry,
For I choose to live a single life.

I said fair maiden what makes you differ,
From all the rest of your female kind,
For you are youthful, both fair and handsome,
All for to wed me pray be inclined.

She says, kind sir, if I must tell you,
I have been married five years ago,
Unto one Riley all in this country,
'Tis he that proved my overthrow.

He was a young man of handsome fortune,
He courted me both night and day,
Until he had my favours gained,
He left the country and fled from me.

I says fair maiden, come let us travel,
Unto some far and distant shore,
Then we'll sail over to Pennsylvania,
And bid adieu to Riley for evermore.

If I should go to Pennsylvania,
Or if I should go to some distant shore,
Why my poor heart would be always aching,
For my young Riley whom I do adore.

It's youthful folly makes young folks marry,
And when we are bound we must obey,
What can't be cured must be endured,
So farewell Riley till a future day.

By permission of the Houghton Library, Harvard University

absent sailor and philosophically rejects the advances of the new suitor. Most would agree that "John Riley" has a happy ending. Whether "Young Riley" does or not is impossible to determine. It cannot be established that this particular broadside is complete. It is found in a volume at the Houghton Library at Harvard University, a volume which once consisted of loose broadsides, now bound together. There is no way of knowing that the broadside did not continue on another page. Assuming there is no second page, the two variants certainly have contrasting conclusions.

The next song concerning a seafarer is considered by many to be the most romantic and poetic of all American ballads.

TR 50 The Isle of Mohea

(Laws AM H 8, The Little Mohea)

Sung by Albert Jeremiah Fields, Bedford, 7 August 1954.

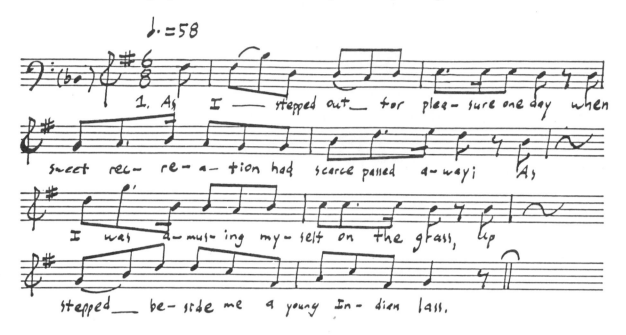

1. As I stepped out for pleasure one day
   When sweet recreation had scarce passed away;
   As I was amusing myself on the grass,
   Up stepped beside me a young Indian lass.

2. She sat down beside me and took up my hand,
   Saying, "I know you're a stranger, not one of our band.
   But if you will come with me it's happy we'll be;
   I'll make you a home on the Isle of Mohea."

3. As the sun was a-setting beside the salt sea
   I rambled along with the lass of Mohea.
   Together we rambled, together we roved,
   Till we came to a hut in the coconut grove.

4. "If you will come saying 'It's married we'll be,'
   I'll teach you the language of the Lass of Mohea.
   I would not desert you for one of our band
   For I think you're as fair as there is in our land."

5. "Oh, no, kind miss, that never can be.
   I have a sweetheart in my own country.
   I would not forsake her for her poverty
   For I think she's as fair as the Lass of Mohea."

190

TR 51 The Little Mohea

Sung by Vern Smelser, Paoli, 6 June 1966.

1. As I was out walking for enjoyment one day
   In sweet recreation to while time away;
   As I sat amusing myself in the shade,
   Oh, who should come nigh me but a fair Indian maid.

2. She sat down beside me and taking my hand
   Says, "You are a stranger and in a strange land.
   But if you will follow, you're welcome to come
   And dwell in the cottage that I call my home."

3. The sun was fast sinking far o'er the blue sea
   When I wandered alone with my Little Mohea.
   Together we wandered, together did roam
   Till we come to the cottage in the coconut grove.

4. And then this fair maiden she said unto me,
   "If you will consent, sir, to stay here with me
   And go no more roving upon the salt sea,
   I'll teach you the language of the lass of Mohea."

5. "Oh, no, my fair maiden, that never can be;
   For I have a true love in my own country.

191

And I'll not forsake her for I know she loves me
And her heart is as true as the Little Mohea."

6. The last time I saw her she stood on the strand,
   And as my boat passed her she waved with her hand,
   Saying, "When you are landed with the girl that you
       love,
   Remember Little Mohee in the coconut grove."

7. And when I had landed on my own native shore
   With friends and relations around me once more,
   I gazed all about me; not one could I see
   Who was fit to compare with the Little Mohea.

8. The girl I had trusted proved untrue to me,
   So I'll turn my course backward far o'er the blue sea.
   I'll turn my course backward; from this land I'll flee.
   I'll go spend my days with my Little Mohea.

Fields performs a rather curtailed variant of the ballad. In the more common form the sailor boards a ship for home, and the Indian lass waves goodbye. Upon arriving home he finds that the girl to whom he has been true has married another, and he wishes he had remained with the Little Mohea. Smelser's variant is unusual in that at its end the sailor vows to retrace his way and return to the Little Mohea.

The incongruity of an Indian lass living in a coconut grove has excited the imagination of many and has led to some interesting speculation concerning the ballad's origin. According to one source Mohee or Mohea is probably Maui of the Sandwich Islands, now the Hawaiian Islands. "To the old explorers and navigators what we call Oahu was Owyhee and Maui was Mohee. This explains the references to the coconut grove."[24] Another explanation derives from the fact that the song is often called "Pretty Maumee." Thus, it is "a song of the frontiersman's Indian sweetheart, [which] probably preserves in its title and refrain the name of the Miami tribe."[25] The Miamis lived in Wisconsin and Michigan and then moved down into Ohio and Indiana. It is a little-known fact that under their great chief, Little Turtle, the Miamis and their Indian allies inflicted great defeats upon American armies in what is now Indiana long before Custer was overwhelmed by the Sioux to the west.[26]

Others have proposed that the ballad is a "chastened American remaking of the favorite English broadside song of 'The Indian Lass.'"[27]

192

Phillips Barry finds variants of this British broadside to mention New Orleans. This proves that the Indian lass must be an American Indian. Originally, therefore, the ballad must have concerned a pioneer and his Indian sweetheart and then have been transformed into the present sea song with its setting in the Hawaiian Islands. He believes that the pioneer song or its transformation was "rewritten and vulgarized for the waterfront trade" in England.[28]

Two variants of "The Indian Lass" have been published on this side of the ocean, one collected in New Jersey and one in Nova Scotia. The Nova Scotian folklorist also prints a variant of "The Lass of Mohee" and concerning the two songs writes as follows:

> There is so close a similarity between this song ["The Indian Lass"] and the one that follows it ["The Lass of Mohee"] that I have hesitated between the alternatives of printing them separately or including them under one title.[29]

The Indian Lass

1. As I went a walking by yon far distant shore
   I went into an ale-house to spend half an hour,
   And as I was musing and taking my glass,
   By chance there came in a fair Indian lass.

2. She sat down beside me, she squeezéd my hand:
   "Kind sir, you're a stranger and not of this land.
   It's I've got good lodgings, so with me you'll stay;
   My portion you'll have then without more delay."

3. With a glass of good liquor she welcomed me in:
   "Kind sir, you are welcome to everything."
   And as I embraced her it was all of her moan:
   "You are a poor sailor and far from your home."

4. We tossed and tumbled in each other's arms;
   All night I enjoyed her sweet lovely charms.
   With love and enjoyment time soon passed away;
   I did not go and leave her till nine the next day.

5. The day was arrived, we were going to sail,
   For to leave this fair maid on the beach to bewail.
   She pulled out her handkerchief and wipéd her eye,
   Saying, "Don't go and leave me, my sailor," she cries.

6. Our anchors being weighed, away then we flew;
   With a sweet pleasant gale parted us from her view.
   And now we are over, and taking our glass,
   And here's a good health to the Indian lass.[30]

193

The Lass of Mohee

1. As I went a walking one evening in June,
   A viewing the roses--they were in full bloom--
   As I was a sitting down on the green grass,
   Who did I happen to spy but a young Hindoo lass.

2. She stepped up towards me, she gave me her hand.
   Said she, "You're a stranger from some foreign land.
   If you will follow, you're welcome to come;
   I live by myself in a snug little home."

3. The sun was a setting all o'er the salt sea
   As I rambled along with the pretty Mohee.
   Together we rambled along, together we roamed,
   Till we came to the cot where the cocoanut grew.

4. With fondest expression she said unto me,
   "If you will consent to live here with me
   And go no more rambling across the salt sea,
   I will teach you the language of the lass of Mohee."

5. "O fairest of creatures, that never could be!
   I have a dear girl in my own counteree.
   I'll never forsake her for her poverty,
   For her heart is as true as the lass of Mohee."

6. 'Twas early the next morning as the sun it arose;
   She seemed much surprised as these words I did say,
   "I'm now going to leave you, so farewell, my dear.
   Our ship hoist her anchor and homeward must steer."[31]

I leave it to the reader to decide if "The Lass of Mohee" is a "chastened remaking" of the British ballad or if "The Indian Lass" is a "vulgarization for the waterfront trade" of "The Lass of Mohee." Nevertheless, it should be noted that it is in "The Lass of Mohee" that it is made clear that she is an East Indian, not an American Indian, and that the seafarer apparently does not mention his true love at home until the morning after. Although some affection is not lacking, both ballads are primarily concerned with sexual gratification, not romantic love.

In the next ballad, to the delight of the seaman, it is again the woman who takes the initiative. He, in turn, is generous with his contribution.

TR 52 Bell Bottom Trousers

(Laws BR K 43, Home, Dearie, Home)

Sung by an anonymous singer with guitar, Bloomington, 1941 or 1942.

1. Now there once lived a pretty maid, down in Drury Lane. Her master he was good to her, her mistress was the same, One day a sailor happy as can be, Coming was the cause of all the misery. Ch. Singing bell bottom trousers, coats of navy blue, He'll climb the rigging like his Daddy used to do. 2. Oh, he asked her for a handkerchief to tie around his head, He asked her for a candle to light his way to bed. She, like a silly ass, Thinking it no harm, Jumped into the sailor's bed to keep the sailor warm.

195

1. Now there once lived a pretty maid down in Drury Lane.
   Her master he was good to her, her mistress was the
       same.
   One day a sailor, happy as can be,
   Coming was the cause of all the misery.

CHORUS:
    Singing bell bottom trousers,
    Coats of navy blue.
    He'll climb the rigging
    Like his daddy used to do.

2. Oh, he asked her for a handkerchief to tie around his
       head.
   He asked her for a candle to light his way to bed.
   She, being a silly ass, thinking it no harm,
   Jumped into the sailor's bed to keep the sailor warm.

CHORUS

3. Early in the morning before the break of day
   He handed her a five-pound note and this to her did
       say,
   "Take this, my darling, for the harm that I have done.
   Maybe you'll have a daughter and maybe you'll have
       a son.
   If you have a daughter, bounce her on your knee.
   If you have a son, send the bastard out to sea."

CHORUS

4. Now the moral of my story is as plain as it can be:
   Never trust a sailor an inch above your knee.

CHORUS

This recording was made by Herbert Halpert, who questioned the singer following his performance:

Halpert: What do you call that song?

Singer: "Bell Bottom Trousers."

H: Where did you get it and when?

S: I heard it about a month ago from an English tar off a destroyer in the drydock in Quantico, Virginia.

H: What were you doing down there?

196

S: On a party.

H: Would you say your name on these records?

S: Uh, thank you, no.

Sanitized versions of this ballad were published in 1907 and 1944. The latter was copyrighted by Moe Jaffe and popularized by Vincent Lopez and Tony Pastor, among others. The song apparently has its origin in the broadside of a sea chantey, "Home, Dearie, Home," listed by Laws, of which the following is the first stanza:

> There came a jolly sailor
> To my house to lodge.
> He called for a candle
> To light him to bed.
> He called for a candle
> To light him to bed,
> And likewise a napkin
> To bind up his head.

The story of "Home, Dearie, Home" differs from that of "Bell Bottom Trousers" primarily in that the sailor invites the girl to join him in bed.

The following variant was popular with both soldiers and sailors during the First World War.

The Waitress and the Sailor

(A solemn warning to working girls)

1. Once there was a waitress in the Prince George Hotel,
    Her master was a fine one and her mistress was a-swell
    Along came a Sailor lad fresh from the sea
    And that was the beginning of all her misery.

2. She gave him a candle to light his way to bed,
    She gave him a pillow to rest his weary head.
    Then she, like a foolish one, seeing no harm,
    Jumped right into bed with him to keep the sailor warm.

3. Early next morning, when he arose,
    Hands in his pockets, shelling out the dough.
    "Take this, my fair one, for the harm that I have done,
    If it be a daughter or if it be a son.

4. "And if it be daughter, just bounce her on your knee,
   And if it be a son, send the blighter out to sea,
   With bell-bottom trousers and a coat of navy blue,
   And let him fool the Navy the way that I fooled you."

5. So gather round, my fair ones, and listen to my plea,
   Never trust a sailor man an inch above your knee.
   For I trusted one once and he put out to sea,
   And left me sitting here with this broken
      family tree.[32]

This little ditty concerns egg production.

TR 53 The Big Fat Rooster and the Little Red Hen

Sung by an anonymous singer, Bloomington, 27 August 1955

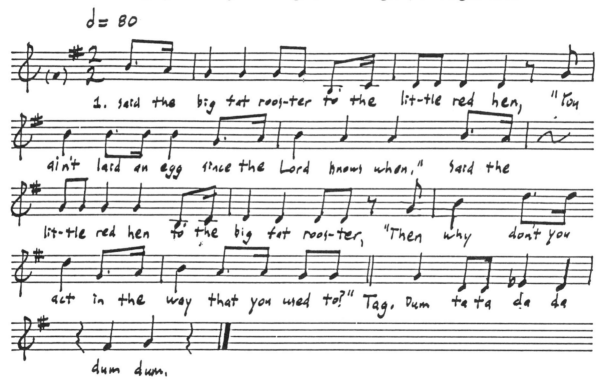

1. Said the big fat rooster to the little red hen,
   "You ain't laid an egg since the Lord knows when."
   Said the little red hen to the big fat rooster,
   "Then why don't you act in the way that you used to?"

2. Said the big fat rooster to the little red hen,
   "I'll meet you in the barn at half past ten."
   So they met in the barn at half past ten
   And they did what they used to till the Lord knows
      when.

198

Like TR 30, "The Miller Boy," in the previous chapter, this little song is sung to the tune known as "Turkey in de Straw," but to the first part only.

The short melodic formula sung at the end of the song was one used by instrumentalists in the 1920s and 1930s to indicate that they had come to the end of what they were doing. It might signal the end of a piece, that they were going to rest for a while, even the end of the evening's performance. It is often sung to the words, "Shave and a haircut, six bits."

The following is a bit of double entendre.

TR 54 The Birthday Cake

Sung by an anonymous singer with guitar, Bloomington, 14 May 1957.

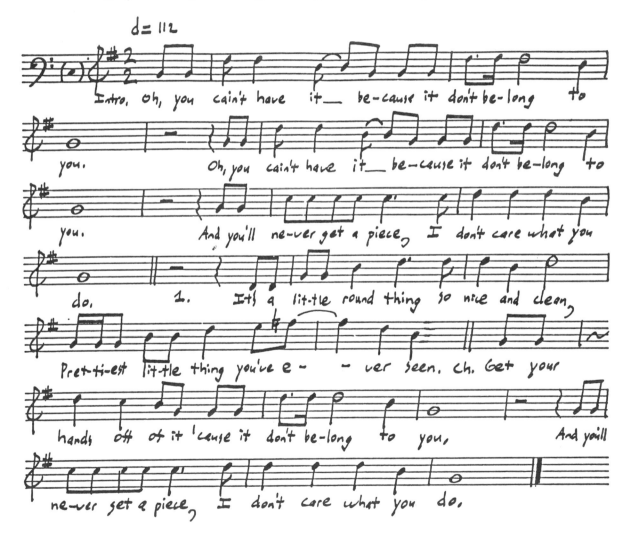

INTRODUCTION:
 Oh, you cain't have it because it don't belong to you.
 Oh, you cain't have it because it don't belong to you.
 And you'll never get a piece, I don't care what you do.

1. It's a little round thing so nice and clean,
 Prettiest little thing you've ever seen.

CHORUS:
 Get your hands off it 'cause it don't belong to you.
 And you'll never get a piece, I don't care what you do.

2. You cut it once, you cut it twice,
 The third time you cut it deep and nice.

CHORUS

3. And folks and gents make no mistake:
 This song here's about a birthday cake.

CHORUS

The singer learned this song in his teens from some "string musicians" in Bullitt County, Kentucky.

And now a song concerning a prostitute.

TR 55 Her Name Was Lil

Transcribed from memory by George List.

1. Her name was Lil and she was a beau-ty; she lived in a house of dis-re-pu-tee, The men they came from far to see,— oh, Lil-lian in her des-ha-billé.— 2. Now you should know her cli-en-tel-lee was sup-por-ted by her bel-ly, she rolled that

thing like the great Pa-ci-fic Oh, it was sim-ply cal³ or-if-ic

1. Her name was Lil and she was a beauty;
   She lived in a house of disrepu-tee.
   The men they came from far to see
   Oh, Lillian in her déshabillé.

2. Oh, you should know her clientel-lee
   Was supported by her belly.
   She rolled that thing like the great Pacific;
   Oh, it was simply calorific.

3. Our Lil was comely; she was fair.
   She had lots of yaller hair.
   But she drank too much of the demon rum
   And she smoked hashish and opy-um.

4. Day by day our Lil grew thinner
   From insufficient proteins in 'er.
   She grew deep hollows in her chest
   And she had to go around completely dressed.

5. Lil took treatments in the sun;
   She drank Scott's Emulshy-un.
   Three times daily she ate yeast,
   But still her clientele decreased.

6. So Lillian underwent baptism.
   She adopted Mister Cism.
   She prayed the Lord her soul to keep
   In a penthouse on Park Avenue.

I learned this song from a young married woman named Shirley in the Bronx in 1933. She was attending college. At the time Scott's Emulsion was a highly advertised patent medicine, and people were eating yeast to improve their health. The latter seems to have come back into style. The ending doesn't make too much sense, but this is the way it was sung for me.

The song was sung for me again by another young woman student while I was teaching at Colorado College in Colorado Springs in 1946. Thus, this student song had a distribution outside of New York City as well.

The following ballad is the only one found in this chapter which is concerned with a married couple. As such it naturally deals with cuckoldry.

TR 56 John Came Home

(Child 274, Our Goodman)

Sung by Vern Smelser with guitar, Paoli, 11 June 1963.

Saw a coat hang on the wall where his coat ought to be;— "Oh, wife-y, dear, come o-ver here, ex-plain this thing to me, whose coat is this up-on the wall where my coat ought to be?" "You sil-ly fool, you drun-ken fool you're drunk and can — — not see, why that is the bath-ing suit my moth-er gave to me," "I've tra-veled east, I've tra-velled west, a mil-lion miles or more,— But a bath-ing suit with a fan-cy vest I ne-ver 'ad seen be-fore

1. John came home the other night just as drunk as he
        could be,
     Saw a hat hang on the wall where his hat ought to be;
     "Oh, wifey dear, come over here, explain this thing to
        me,
     Whose hat is this upon the wall where my hat ought to
        be?"

     "You silly fool, you drunken fool, you're drunk and
        cannot see;
     Why that is the frying pan my mother gave to me."
     "I've travelled east, I've travelled west, a million
        miles or more,
     But a frying pan with a lining I never 'ad seen
        before."

2. John came home the other night just as drunk as he
        could be,
   Saw a coat hang on the wall where his coat ought to be;
   "Oh, wifey dear, come over here, explain this thing to
        me,
   Whose coat is this upon the wall where my coat ought to
        be?"

   "You silly fool, you drunken fool, you're drunk and
        cannot see,
   Why that is the bathing suit my mother gave to me."
   "I've travelled east, I've travelled west, a million
        miles or more,
   But a bathing suit with a fancy vest I never 'ad seen
        before."

3. John came home the other night just as drunk as he
        could be,
   He saw a shoe lay on the floor where his shoe ought to
        be;
   "Oh, wifey dear, come over here, explain this thing to
        me,
   Whose shoe is this upon the floor where my shoe ought
        to be?"

   "You silly fool, you drunken fool, you're drunk and
        cannot see,
   Why that is the cuspidor my mother gave to me."
   "I've travelled east, I've travelled west, a million
        miles or more,
   But a cuspidor with a rubber heel I never 'ad seen
        before."

4. John came home the other night just as drunk as he
        could be,
   Saw a head lay on the bed where his head ought to be;
   "Oh, wifey dear, come over here, explain this thing to
        me,
   Whose head is this upon the bed where my head ought to
        be?"

   "You silly fool, you drunken fool, you're drunk and
        cannot see,
   Why that is the cabbage head my mother gave to me."
   "I've travelled east, I've travelled west, a million
        miles or more,
   But a cabbage head with a mustache I never 'ad seen
        before."

Francis James Child prints two variants of this ballad. The first is reprinted from David

Herd's *Ancient and Modern Scottish Songs*, published in 1776;[33] the second from a broadside

204

"'The Merry Cuckold and Kind Wife,' Printed and Sold at the Printing-Office in Bow Church-Yard, London" (no date given).[34]

The items viewed by John, their transformations by his wife, and his comments thereon reflect the vintage of the variants. In Child's variant A, John sees a saddle horse which his wife declares to be a broad sow. He replies, "A saddle on a sow's back I never saw nane." A pair of jackboots becomes a pair of water-stoups. To this he complains, "Siller spurs on water stoups I saw never nane." He spies a powdered wig. "'Tis naething but a clocken-hen," retorts the wife. "But powder on a clocken-hen I saw never nane."

In variant B the wife takes a wholesale approach, all items being tripled: three horses become three milking cows; the same number of swords become roasting spits; cloaks become mantuas; breeches become petticoats; hats become skimming dishes; and three men in bed are transformed into milking maids. "Heyday! Godzounds! Milking-maids with beards on! The like was never known!" In both variants all transformed objects were given to the wife by her mother.

When the Indiana singer was asked where he had learned the song he replied, "That's one I learned off a record in the place I used to work." This is obviously an adaptation of the earliest variants since it retains the same basic form. But the objects spied by the husband and transformed by the ingenious wife are consonant with a later period: a frying pan, a swimming suit, a fancy vest, and a cuspidor.

Commentary

The compendium title of this chapter reflects the fact that the relationships described between male and female may occur in combinations, as well as individually. Of the four words in the title, the term "love" receives the longest list of definitions in the dictionary. It may be concerned entirely with sexual intercourse, as with the legend of Venus and Adonis, or be purely chaste as in the case of the nun who has dedicated her life to being a bride of Christ. It can, in fact, as in tennis, have nothing whatsoever to do with male-female relationships. But within such a relationship, love is normally thought to consist of affection and caring for an individual of the opposite sex.

Courtship can lead to love, merely to sexual gratification, or to marriage. Marriage, in itself, is often only a matter of convenience, offering regular access to a sexual partner in return for wealth and/or social advancement. In this chapter I have endeavored to select celebrations in song of as wide a variety of relationships as possible, differing not only in the era in which they occur but also in the social classes involved.

The forms of the song texts display an almost equal variety. Although the quatrain is still the most common form, there are some couplets as well as stanzas formed of three, five, and six lines. Two rhyming schemes predominate, *a b c b* and *a a b b*, but there may be an occasional *a a a a* or no rhyme at all. The lines, as usual, have either three or four verbal stresses, but in some lines of TR 54, "The Birthday Cake," there are five stresses. Some poems have three stresses to a line throughout, some four, and some a mixture of the two. The folksinger is conservative, he or she falls easily into conventional patterns, but consistency should not be expected. Consistency is not a virtue as far as the folksinger is concerned.

"The Birthday Cake," subtle in more ways than one, breaks the mold with its three-line stanzas and lines with five stresses. It demonstrates that patterns may be altered when it seems useful.

TR 41, "I Worry My Heart Away for You," follows the form of the popular song of the 1890s discussed in the previous chapter. While most of the singers keep a reasonably steady pulse here, the song is broken up into small, discrete phrases, probably because the singer lacks sufficient breath control to carry the pulse forward.

As far as repetition is concerned, in TR 45, "Shoo Flies, Don't Bother Me," we again have a stanza made up of three lines repeated and a fourth differing line, an easy and efficient way to construct a quatrain. TR 46, "The Two Lovers," is an example of a couplet expanded into a quatrain by the repetition of the second and fourth lines of nonsense syllables, a pattern often followed.

In TR 49, "John Riley," the singer thrice repeats the last two lines of a quatrain. It is thought that the repetition of a line or two of a stanza is a means by which the singer gains time to remember the following stanza.

I have written TR 56, "John Came Home," in quatrains with lines of seven verbal stresses so that they will match the musical phrases. This is a very old ballad to which someone has written a newly composed melody, a melody which is not the same for each quatrain. The original undoubtedly consisted of quatrains with the shorter pattern of 4, 3, 4, and 3 verbal stresses. Some two-thirds of the older ballads follow this particular form.

"John Came Home," with the possible exception of TR 7, "Soldier, Soldier, Won't You Marry Me," is our first good example of what has been termed "incremental repetition." This consists of repetitions of a previous phrase, or part thereof, with changes to adapt it to the situation.[35] Thus:

> "You silly fool, you drunken fool, you're drunk and
>   cannot see,
> Why that is the bathing suit my mother gave to me."
> "I've travelled east, I've travelled west, a million
>   miles or more,
> But a bathing suit with a fancy vest I never 'ad seen
>   before."
>
> "You silly fool, you drunken fool, you're drunk and
>   cannot see,
> Why that is the cuspidor my mother gave to me."
> "I've travelled east, I've travelled west, a million
>   miles or more,
> But a cuspidor with a rubber heel I never 'ad seen
>   before."
>
> "You silly fool, you drunken fool, you're drunk and
>   cannot see,
> Why that is the cabbage head my mother gave to me."
> "I've travelled east, I've travelled west, a million
>   miles or more,
> But a cabbage head with a mustache I never 'ad seen
>   before."

CHAPTER 5 HUMOR AND PATHOS

Exaggeration is a common aspect of folk humor.

TR 57 The Derby Ram

Sung by Guthrie T. Meade with guitar, Bloomington, 14 June 1956.

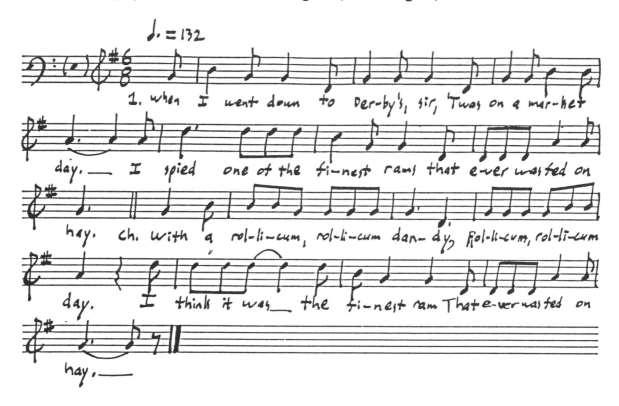

1. When I went down to Derby's, sir,
   'Twas on a market day.
   I spied one of the finest rams
   That ever was fed on hay.

CHORUS:
   With a rollicum, rollicum dandy,
   Rollicum, rollicum day.
   I think it was the finest ram
   That ever was fed on hay.

2. The wool upon this ram, sir,
   It reached into the sky.
   The eagles built their nest in it;

I heard their young ones cry.

CHORUS

3. Now the horns upon this ram, sir,
   They reached up to the moon.
   The possum went up in November;
   He didn't come back until June.

CHORUS

4. The man who cut his throat, sir,
   Was drowndéd in the blood.
   And forty thousand . . .
   Were washed away in the flood.

CHORUS

5. Now the man who sold this ram, sir,
   He got awful rich.
   The man who told the story, sir,
   Is a lying son of a _____.

CHORUS

Gus Meade learned this ballad while growing up in Louisville, from a neighbor, Mrs. Alice Tucker. She had been reared in Nelson County, Virginia, and had learned the song there from an old black woman. Gus secured the last stanza elsewhere, but does not remember from whom.

The oldest printed variants of this "lying song" come from Scotland and England, each with a title tying it to a different locality.

> Here it is "The Ram o' Bervie," there "The Ram o' Derby," in another place "The Ram o' Diram," again "The Ram o' Doram," and so on.[1]

Whatever its origin, the song seems to have become centered in the English county of Derbyshire (Derby is pronounced and often spelled Darby), where the first reference to it can be read in a letter written in 1739 by a minister to his son.[2] Other evidence of the popularity of the ballad in Derbyshire includes the establishment of a periodical by the name of *The Derby Ram*, the adoption of a ram as a mascot by the First Regiment of Derbyshire Militia, and the arrangement of the song as a glee by a Dr. Calcott for entertainment at public dinners.[3]

However, the first printing of the song with a title linking it to Derbyshire, "The Ram of

Darby," occurred in Manchester in 1833. Of its thirteen stanzas four are like those sung by Meade:

> As I was going to Darby,
> All on a market day,
> I met the finest ram Sir,
> That ever was fed on hay.
>
> The wool upon his back Sir,
> Reach'd up unto the sky,
> The eagles built there nest there,
> For I heard the young ones cry.
>
> The space between the horns Sir,
> Was far as a man could reach,
> And there they built a pulpit,
> But no one in it preach'd.
>
> The butcher that kill'd this ram Sir,
> Was drowned in the blood,
> And all the people of Darby,
> Were carried away in the flood.

It has, however, a different chorus:

> Indeed Sir, it's a truth Sir,
> For I was never taught to lie,
> And if you'll go to Darby Sir,
> You may see it was well as I.[4]

Choruses to this song in which nonsense syllables are heard, as in the variant sung by Meade, are common. The following chorus appears in a variant titled "The Ram o' Bervie," published in 1899:

> Singing hey dingle derby,
> Hey dingle day;
> This was the greatest ram, sir,
> That ever was fed on hay.

Note that the word "Derby" occurs in the chorus. The last stanza of this variant is also related to that performed by Meade:

> Oh, the man that owned the ram, sir,
> He must have been very rich;
> And the man that sings the song, sir,
> Must be the son of a witch.[5]

There is much speculation among folklorists as to the origin of this ballad. One theory relates it to the sacrificial rites of the ancient British priests. In such a rite the animal would be glorified to impress the god, and from such glorification may have come the exaggerations which characterize the ballad. It has also been associated with long-standing practices in Derbyshire, which include mumming and luck visits of animal maskers.[6] The "lying" motif is contained in

> a story about it to the effect that a prisoner had been condemned to death, in the time of the feudal laws, and was promised free pardon should he succeed in composing a song without a grain of truth in it, and that this was the song he produced.[7]

The song spread through the British Isles and parts of Europe, as well as to the United States. It must have come to our shore early. George Washington is reputed to have recited the ballad of "The Darby Ram" to the children of Chief Justice Oliver Ellsworth. This anecdote, as well as the first printing of the ballad in the United States, is found in the *American Monthly Magazine* of October 1897.[8]

Most variants contain the elements found in Meade's: the description of a ram of great size, its wool, its horns, and its slaughter. Some blacks in the South sang similar variants, as is attested by the fact that the woman who taught Meade the song learned it from a black in Virginia. Other blacks adopted only parts of the ballad, inventing many new stanzas and a new chorus in which the noun, "ram," was transmuted to the verb, "ramble." The earliest published variant sung by blacks containing the "ramble chorus" was collected in Texas in 1888, but not published until 1926. I quote some of the stanzas which were taken from the old ballad, some probably composed by blacks, and the "Didn't He Ramble?" chorus:

> The man who butchered the ram,
> He butchered him for his life;
> He sent to Cincinnati for
> A four-foot butcher knife.
>
> CHORUS:
>
> Didn't he ramble! Didn't he ramble!
> Oh, he rambled till the butcher cut him down!

211

The habits of that ram
They hung upon the wall;
A couple o' gals came into the shop,
Says, "We never eats mutton a-tall!"

Of all the animals in this world
I'd ruther be a bull;
I'd curl my tail upon my back
And graze* my belly full.

Of all the animals in this world
I'd ruther be a boar;
I'd twist my tail into a knot
And eat* forever more.

Oh, the man that owned the ram,
Well, he must-a been turribly rich;
But the man that made the song up,
Wuz a lying son of a _____.[9]

Two of the stanzas are related to those sung by Meade, the remainder are not. Gates Thomas, the author of the article in which these stanzas were published, writes that some are suggestive, and where there are asterisks he has substituted other words for the originals which he thought were obscene. Variants with bawdy verses sung by white singers have also been reported. I reproduce two such stanzas taken down from a Cape Cod sailor during the War of 1812 when it was commonly sung:

Now this old ram's pizzle, sir, measured forty yards
    and an ell,
That was sent to Ireland to ring St. Patrick's bell.

There was forty gentlemen of honor, sir, come to see
    this old ram's bones.
And forty ladies of honor went to see this old ram's
    stones.[10]

A bawdy version was also sung with gusto by freshmen at Harvard College in the early 1860s. The writer quotes only the chorus, indicating that the stanzas are "decidedly coarse":

O! a hunkey, dunkey Derby Ram,
A hunkey, dunkey day.[11]

A sheet music version of "Didn't He Ramble?," with words and music by Will Handy (nom de plume of the black songwriting team of Robert "Bob" Cole and J. Rosamond Johnson), was published by Joseph W. Stern and Company in New York in 1902. The tune to which the song was commonly sung by blacks in the South was retained, as well as the words of the "Didn't He Ramble?" chorus:

> Oh! Didn't he ramble, ramble?
> He rambled all around in and out the town.
> Oh! Didn't he ramble, ramble?
> He rambled till the butchers cut him down.[12]

But the words of the stanzas were newly written. The song was popular among college students, especially on the football field. The sheet music had influence in the cities, but in the rural South the earlier oral tradition persisted among the blacks.[13] Several folklorists, including Newman Ivey White, published variants secured from the latter group in which stanzas of "The Derby Ram" were combined with the chorus, "Didn't He Ramble?"[14]

Finally, elements of "The Derby Ram--Didn't He Ramble" combination were adopted by black brass bands in New Orleans for use at funeral processions. These bands began to be active in the 1880s in imitation of white military bands which served similar functions. It was from the improvisation of such black bands that New Orleans jazz is traditionally believed to have developed. Singing formed part of the funeral ceremony and often included a performance of "Didn't He Ramble?" Of the five recordings made by New Orleans jazz bands of the traditional funeral ceremony, only one, that made by Celestin's Tuxedo Jass [sic] Band[15] included a full stanza related to the ballad, "The Derby Ram."

> The ram's horns were so long,
> Till they never touched the sky,
> An eagle went up to build a nest,
> And the young ones they did cry.[16]

In another recording only the first two lines of a stanza from the ballad are heard:

> The wool upon this ram's back,
> It grew so might high.[17]

The remaining two lines bear no relationship.

The tunes and texts of ballads and other folk songs do not necessarily remain in association. Any relationship between what was performed at the New Orleans black funeral procession and the old English ballad must be determined by the words sung. They are only distantly related, but related they obviously are. "The Derby Ram" had

> undergone many variations since some gifted balladeer created a "lying song" about a ram some several hundred years ago. One of the strangest--yet seemingly natural--modifications in its long history must certainly be its metamorphosis from a medieval ritual ballad into a brass band funeral piece.[18]

The animal celebrated in the following short saga is notable for his handling of a crisis, rather than for his size.

TR 58 Thorne's Goat

Sung by Dale Schreiber, Bloomington, 20 February 1988.

1. There was a man whose name was Thorne.
   He had a goat that had a horn.
   He loved that goat, indeed, he did;
   He loved that goat just like a kid.

2. One day that goat, so fat and fine,
   Ate three red shirts right off the line.
   He grabbed that goat right by the neck
   And tied it to the railroad track.

3. The whistle blew, the train grew near;
   The goat grew white and shook with fear.

214

He wiggled and squirmed as if in pain,
Coughed up those shirts and flagged that train.

This is another of the songs that Dale's older sister, Hazel, sang to the younger children of the Schreiber family from the porch swing. She had learned it from other children on the playground when she attended school at Loogootee.

It is known by various names, all establishing different ownership of the goat: "Riley's Goat," "Rosenthal's Goat," and "Bill Grogan's Goat," besides "Thorne's Goat." It was published in 1904 under a further title, "A Tale of a Shirt," with words by William W. Bracket and music by Lottie L. Meda. However, as in the case of many songs of this type, it was probably adapted from the oral tradition. In the earliest country music recording of the song made in 1923 by Fiddlin' John Carson, "Papa's Billy Goat," the owner of the goat is anonymous.[19] There were many other such recordings of the song in the 1920s by singers such as Vernon Dalhart and Uncle Dave Macon.

TR 59 The Frog Went A-Courting

Sung by Ethel Bryant Niemeyer, Evansville, 8 or 9 April 1938.

215

1. Frog went a-courting, he did ride. Ah hum.
   Frog went a-courting, he did ride.
   Sword and pistol by his side. Ah hum.

2. He rode into Miss Mousie's hall. Ah hum.
   He rode into Miss Mousie's hall.
   Found Miss Mousie upon the wall. Ah hum.

3. He asked Miss Mousie to be his bride. Ah hum. (etc.)
   She opened her eyes so big and wide. Ah hum.

4. He asked Uncle Rat for his consent. Ah hum. (etc.)
   He came downstairs with his back half bent. Ah hum.

5. Uncle Rat he went to town. Ah hum. (etc.)
   To buy his niece a wedding gown. Ah hum.

6. Where shall the wedding supper be? Ah hum. (etc.)
   Way down yonder in the hollow tree. Ah hum.

7. What shall the wedding supper be? Ah hum. (etc.)
   Catnip broth and dogwood tea. Ah hum.

8. First that came was a bumblebee. Ah hum. (etc.)
   With his fiddle upon his knee. Ah hum.

9. Next that came was a big black flea. Ah hum. (etc.)
   To dance a jig with the bumblebee. Ah hum.

10. The bread and cheese all sits on the shelf. Ah hum.
    (etc.)
    If you wish any more you'll sing it for yourself.
    Ah hum.

Ethel learned the song from her mother, Dora, who heard it sung by her mother or aunts. Most think of this well-known song as one sung to children in the Upland South, but it is also a very old ballad. Under the title, "A Moste Strange Weddinge of the ffrogge and the mowse," it was entered into the register of the London Company of Stationers' Register by Edward White on 21 November 1580.[20] The Company of Stationers was a guild of printers established by the Puritan government as a means of controlling what was published. By law all broadsides and books had to be approved before they could be registered. The registration fee for a broadside was fourpence, that for a book, sixpence.

The earliest extant printing of the ballad, "The Marriage of the Frogge and the Mouse," is

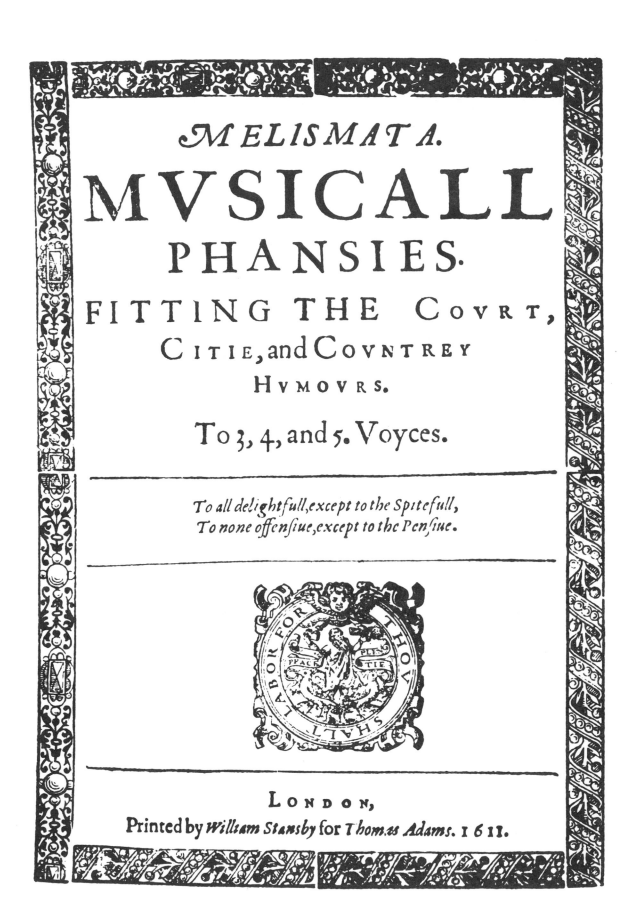

MELISMATA.

MVSICALL

PHANSIES.

FITTING THE COVRT,

CITIE, and COVNTREY

HVMOVRS.

To 3, 4, and 5. Voyces.

To all delightfull, except to the Spitefull,
To none offenſiue, except to the Penſiue.

LONDON,
Printed by *William Stansby* for *Thomas Adams.* 1611.

217

COVNTRY PASTIMES.

¶ The Marriage of the Frogge and the M ovse.

Treble.   21.   4. Voc.

T was the Frogge in the well, Humble-dum, humble-dum. And

the merrie Mouse in the Mill, tweedle, tweedle twino.

2 The Frogge would a woing ride,
        humble dum humble dum
Sword and buckler by his side,
        tweedle, tweedle twino.

3 When he was vpon his high horse set,
        humble dum, humble dum
His loots they shone as blacke as iet,
        tweedle, tweedle twino.

4 When she came to the merry mill pin,
        humble dum, humble dum
Lady Mouse beene you within?
        tweedle, tweedle twino.

5 Then came out the dusty Mouse,
        humble dum, humble dum
I am Lady of this house,
        tweedle, tweedle twino.

6 Hast thou any minde of me?
        humble dum, humble dum
I haue e'ne great minde of thee,
        tweedle, tweedle twino.

7 Who shall this marriage make?
        humble dum, humble dum,
Our Lord which is the rat,
        tweedle, tweedle twino.

8 What shall we haue to our supper?
        humble dum, humble dum,
Three beanes in a pound of butter,
        tweedle tweedle twino.

9 When supper they were at,
        humble dum, humble dum
The Frog, the Mouse, and euen the Rat,
        tweedle, tweedle twino:

10 Then came in gib our cat,
        humble dum, humble dum,
And catcht the mouse euen by the backe,
        tweedle, tweedle twino.

11 Then did they separate,
        humble dum, humble dum,
And the frog leapt on the floore so flat,
        tweedle, tweedle twino.

12 Then came in Dicke our Drake,
        humble dum, humble dum,
And drew the frogge euen to the lake,
        tweedle, tweedle twino.

13 The Rat run vp the wall,
        humble dum, humble dum.
A goodly company, the diuell goe with all,
        tweedle, tweedle twino.

found in the songbook, *Melismata*, of 1611. *Melismata* was compiled by Thomas Ravenscroft, who contributed many of the numbers himself. The ballad is arranged for four voices. In addition to the cover, I reproduce the first page of the song, which contains the melody and the text. I have omitted the subsequent page on which is printed the music for the other three voices. The song has appeared in print many times since. Some of these published texts are based on the earlier publications; others represent the song as heard in the oral tradition in England, Scotland, Ireland, and the United States.

In the first decade of the last century an English traditional form of the ballad was modified for comic use on the stage. To fit the customs of the time, the frog went a-courting in an opera hat. It was sung in this form as "The Frog in the Cock'd Hat" or "The Love-Sick Frog" by a famous comedian of the time, Liston, to an original melody composed by Charles Edward Horn.[21] There were other burlesques of the original text in *The Merry Musician or a Cure for the Spleen* of 1716 and in *Pills to Purge Melancholy* of 1714. In the latter the song begins:

"Great Lord Frog to Lady Mouse"

and is accompanied by its tune.[22]

In Irish and American printings other wedding guests are introduced, the bee with the fiddle, the snail with bagpipes, the pig, the duck, and the hen. The last stanza of TR 57, as sung by Ethel Bryant Niemeyer, is the only closing with which I am familiar. It seems to have superseded in America, at least, the tragic ending seen in *Melismata*, in which the cat catches the mouse and the drake the frog.

Humorous exaggeration is also applied to the actions of humans.

TR 60 Away Out West in Kansas

Sung by Anna Sandage Underhill, Uniontown, 30 December 1963.

han-sas, They take the side-walk in at eight A-way out west in
han-sas. The town's so small that I de-clare You can stand on the
old town square, Knock on ev'ry front door there, A-way out west in
han-sas, 2. The sun's so hot that eggs will hatch A-way out west in
han-sas. It pops the corn in the pop-corn patch A-way out west in
han-sas. An old mule com-ing down the path Saw all the corn and
lost his breath. He thought it was snow and he froze to death A-
-way out west in han-sas.

1. Folks don't stay out very late
   Away out west in Kansas.
   They take the sidewalk in at eight
   Away out west in Kansas.
   The town's so small that I declare
   You can stand on the old town square,
   Knock on every front door there,
   Away out west in Kansas.

2. The sun's so hot that eggs will hatch
   Away out west in Kansas.
   It pops the corn in the popcorn patch
   Away out west in Kansas.
   An old mule coming down the path
   Saw all the corn and lost his breath.
   He thought it was snow and he froze to death
   Away out west in Kansas.

3. There's a man who grew so tall
   Away out west in Kansas.
   That if he ever should fall
   He'd be out of Kansas.
   I'll declare and I'll repeat
   That he's as long as our main street,
   With the lot turned down for feet
   Away out west in Kansas.

4. There's a man named Crosseyed Pat
   Away out west in Kansas.
   You cain't tell who he's looking at
   Away out west in Kansas.
   He cries because he's such a wreck
   And the tears run down his neck.
   (He don't look straight, looks to me) by heck
   Away out west in Kansas.

5. There's a man who loved his wife
   Away out west in Kansas.
   They must have lived a peaceful life
   Away out west in Kansas.
   There's a reason why each night
   They hold each other's hands so tight.
   If one lets loose they start to fight
   Away out west in Kansas.

The compressed "tall tales" of which this song is composed probably were originally heard in minstrel shows or on the liar's bench in small towns in the last century. The song was copyrighted in the 1920s by Carson J. Robison, a professional songwriter known as the Kansas Jayhawk. However, we can assume that he copied it from the oral tradition as he did several other songs he published. This prolific songsmith was also the composer and lyricist of "The Little Green Valley," "The Wreck of the Number Nine," "The West Plains Explosion," and some three hundred other songs. A commercial recording of "Way Out West in Kansas" was made by Vernon Dalhart in 1924.[23]

TR 61 The Cookery Maid

Sung by Dale Schreiber, Bloomington, 20 February 1988.

1. There was a young maiden to cooking school went.

221

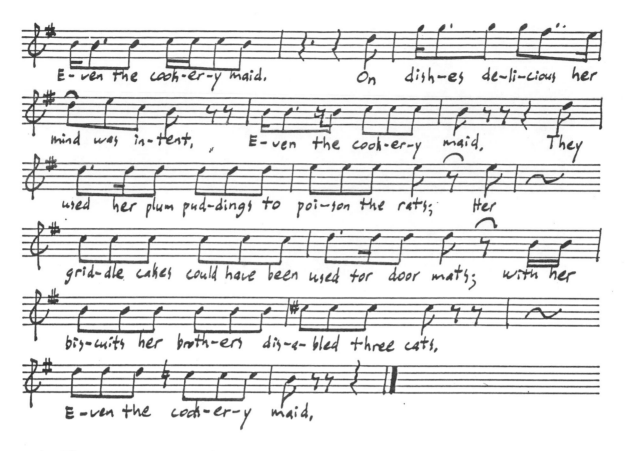

1. There was a young maiden to cooking school went.
   Even the cookery maid.
   On dishes delicious her mind was intent.
   Even the cookery maid.
   They used her plum puddings to poison the rats;
   Her griddle cakes could have been used for door mats;
   With her biscuits her brothers disabled three cats.
   Even the cookery maid.

2. At last she made something, a pie, so she said.
   Even the cookery maid.
   'Twas tough as sole leather and heavy as lead.
   Even the cookery maid.
   She put it away and retired to bed;
   A burglar broke in and upon it he fed.
   Next morning they found the poor burglar dead.
   Even the cookery maid.

Dale also learned this song from his older sister, Hazel. In 1988 I interviewed Hazel by telephone. She was then living in Bedford. She told me that while she was attending school in Loogootee a teacher had taught some boys to sing this song, and she had learned it from their performance of it in assembly. She, of course, had no knowledge of where the teacher had secured the song.

The next two songs demonstrate that the unfortunate are often the butt of folk humor.

TR 62 The Jolly Burglar Boy

(Laws AM H 23, The Old Maid and the Burglar)

Sung by Vern Smelser, Paoli, 6 June 1966.

1. There was a jolly burglar boy, He went to rob a house. He opened the window and then crept in—As quiet as a mouse, Thinking of all of the money he'd get As under the bed he lays, At nine o'clock he saw a sight That made his hair turn gray.

2. At nine o'clock an old maid came in, "Oh, I'm so tired," she said. And thinking everything was all right she forgot to look under the bed. She took out her teeth and her big glass eye And the hair right off of her head, while the burglar rolled in fourteen fits As he

looked from un-der the bed

1. There was a jolly burglar boy,
   He went to rob a house.
   He opened the window and then crept in
   As quiet as a mouse.
   Thinking of all of the money he'd get
   As under the bed he lay,
   At nine o'clock he saw a sight
   That made his hair turn gray.

2. At nine o'clock an old maid came in,
   "Oh, I'm so tired," she said.
   And thinking everything was alright
   She forgot to look under the bed.
   She took out her teeth and her big glass eye
   And the hair right off of her head,
   While the burglar rolled in fourteen fits
   As he looked from under the bed.

3. The burglar came from under the bed;
   He looked a total wreck.
   The old maid, being wide awake,
   She grabbed him around the neck.
   She never screamed nor hollered a bit
   But quiet as a clam
   She says, "Thank God, my prayers are answered;
   At last I've found a man."

4. She then took out a revolver
   And to the burglar said,
   "Young man, if you don't marry me
   I'll blow off the top of your head."
   The burglar, looking all around,
   And seeing no place to scoot,
   He looked at her teeth and her big glass eye
   And said, "For God's sake, shoot!"

This song was copyrighted in 1887 as "The Burglar Man" by E. F. Thilp. As seen by its listing in Laws, it is now widespread in oral tradition. I recorded a variant of it in Bloomington (not reproduced here) from Dale Schreiber.

TR 63 The Old Bachelor's Mourn

Sung by Isie Dora McMurtry Ward, Princeton, 9 April 1938.

1. As I was a-walking all alone
    I met an old bachelor making up his mourn.
    "Of all the girls wherever they may be,
    I can't find a pretty one that will marry me."

2. "I've courted the rich and I have courted the poor,
    And many of the time I was kicked out of doors.
    Of all the girls wherever they may be,
    I can't find a pretty one that will marry me."

3. "I rode three horses out of breath,
    I rode three horses all to death.
    I rode three saddles off to the tree,
    But I can't find a pretty girl that will marry me."

4. He threw himself down on the bed;
   He tore all the hair out of the top of his head.
   There he laid and he screamed and he cried.
   In this condition he kicked and died.

5. Come, young ladies, assemble all around,
   To put the old bachelor under the ground.
   For if he ever comes to life,
   Strive he will for to get him a wife.

The only published variants of this song have been collected in the United States. It is, therefore, probably American in origin. I have discovered little else concerning it.

In Chapter 3 (p. 126), I briefly mentioned how poor a reputation the millers had among the folk. This is confirmed in the following two songs.

TR 64 The Miller's Will

Sung by Vern Smelser, Paoli, 6 June 1966.

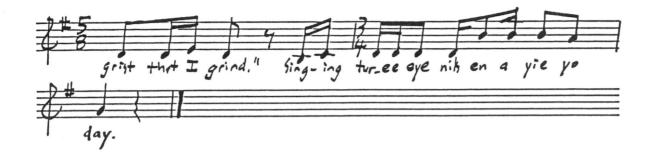

grist that I grind." Sing-ing turee eye nih en a yie yo day.

1. Oh, he called up his eldest son
   Saying, "Son, oh, son, my race is run.
   [I]f I to you the mill do make,
   Pray, what is the toll that you mean for to take?"
   Singing touree eye ni en a yie yo day.

2. "Oh, father, oh, father, my name is Rake.
   Out [of] every bushel I'll take a cake.
   A very fine living I shall find
   If I charge no more for the grist that I grind."
   Singing touree eye ni en a yie yo day.

3. "Oh, the mill ain't yours," the old man cried.
   "The mill ain't yours," the old man cried.
   "By such a law no man could abide." (etc.)

4. So he called up his second son:
   Son, oh, son, my race is run.
   [I]f I to you the mill do make,
   Pray, what is the toll that you mean for to take?"
       (etc.)

5. "Oh, father, oh, father, my name is Heck.
   Out of every bushel I'll take a peck.
   A very fine living I shall find
   If I charge no more for the grist that I grind."
       (etc.)

6. "Oh, the mill ain't yours," the old man cried.
   "The mill ain't yours," the old man cried.
   "By such a law no man could abide." (etc.)

7. So he called up his eldest son
   Saying, "Son, oh, son, my race is run.
   [I]f I to you the mill do make,
   Pray, what is the toll that you mean for to take?"
       (etc.)

8. "Oh, father, oh, father, my name is Raff.
   Out of every bushel I'll take a half.
   If that ain't enough I'll take a whole sack
   And beat the miller's boy when he gets back." (etc.)

227

9. "Oh, the mill is yours," the old man cried.
   "The mill is yours," the old man cried.
   He rolled up his eyes and the old devil died. (etc.)

Vern got this song from his grandfather, "who learned that there in Kansas while he was running a mill."

There is a whole group of ballads concerning "The Rogueries of Millers" in a large collection, *The Roxburghe Ballads*, first published in England in 1869. This group of ballads

> records each stage in the miller's "Decline and Fall". . . . Beginning with fibbing, but coming speedily to downright lying and peculation, stealing corn from sacks and yielding short weight of adulterated flour, the millers in all ages were accused of licentious freedom or betrayal towards the superabundant sex, and too frequently resorted finally to murder.

The editor of the collection then mentions a murder of a woman by a miller which occurred in Shrewsbury.[24] Concerning the ballad in question the editor writes:

> This class of rustics, formerly prosperous, had been addicted to amorous intrigue and breaches of promise, no less than to peculation by "excessive taking of toll."[25]

The popular opinion of such gentry is recorded in this Roxburghe ditty, which still holds favor (the variant above having been sung nearly a century later).

I am printing the entire Roxburghe variant so that the reader may see how little the ballad has changed over the years, and also to correct the order in which the miller approaches his sons. In all variants I have examined, he begins with the eldest son and wills the mill to his youngest.

The Miller's Advice to His Three Sons

On Taking of Toll.

1. There was a Miller who had three sons;
   And knowing his life was almost run,
   He call'd them all, and ask'd their will,
   If that to them he left his mill.

2. He called first for his Eldest Son,

228

Saying: "My life is almost run:
If I to you this Mill do make,
What toll do you intend to take?"

3. "Father," said he, "My name is *Jack*;
Out of a bushel I'll take a peck,
From every bushel that I grind;
That I may a good living find."

4. "Thou art a fool!" the old man said;
"Thou hast not learned well thy trade:
This Mill to thee I ne'er will give,
For by such toll no man can live."

5. He call'd [next] for his Middlemost Son,
Saying: "My life is almost run:
If I to you this Mill do make,
What toll do you intend to take?"

6. "Father," said he, "my name is *Ralph*;
Out of a bushel I'll take it half,
From every bushel that I grind;
That I may a good living find."

7. "Thou art a fool!" the old man said;
"Thou hast not learned well thy trade:
This Mill to thee I ne'er will give,
For by such toll no man [can] live."

8. He called for his Youngest Son,
Saying: "My life is almost run:
If I to you this Mill do make,
What toll do you intend to take?"

9. "Father," said he, "I'm your only Boy,
For taking toll is all my joy:
Before I will a good living lack,
I'll take all, and forswear the sack."

10. "Thou art my boy!" the old man said,
"For thou has well learn'd thy trade;
This mill to thee I'll give!" he cry'd:
And then he clos'd up his eyes, and dy'd.

This version was originally printed in Aldermary Churchyard, London, ca. 1730. The broadside indicates that the ballad is to be sung to the tune of "The Oxfordshire Tragedy."

There are two further stanzas collected in Perrysville, Ohio, prior to 1922, which condemn the miller to perdition:

"O, son, O, son! if this you do,
'Tis you will do as I have done,
The mill is thine," the old man cried,
And shut his d ____ old eyes and died.
With a foll, loll, lolli doll day.

But now he is dead and in his grave,
And the greedy worms his body do crave;
But where he is gone I cannot tell,
But I rather suppose it is down to hell.
With a foll, loll, lolli doll day.[26]

TR 65 John Roger, the Miller

(Laws BR P 8, The Gray Mare)

Sung by John William Collier, Bloomington, 4 April 1938.

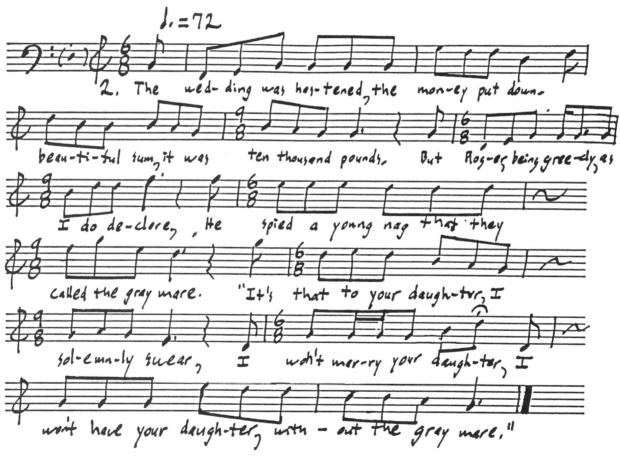

1. [John Roger], the miller, went courting of late
   A farmer's fair daughter called Beautiful Kate.
   Which had to her portion fine jewels and rings,
   Likewise to her fortune it is a fine thing.
   Her eyes is as bright as the stars . . .
   Her cheeks like vermillion all painted in love.

230

2. The wedding was hastened, the money put down.
   A beautiful sum, it was ten thousand pounds.
   But Roger, being greedy, as I do declare,
   He spied a young nag that they called the gray mare.
   "It's that to your daughter, I'll solemnly swear,
   I won't marry your daughter, I won't have your
       daughter,
   Without the gray mare."

3. The old man he jumped up through anger and pique.
   "You thought you would marry my daughter, indeed.
   But if it's no better, thank God it's no worse;
   I'll put up my money once more in my purse.
   As that's to my daughter I'll solemnly swear,
   You shan't have daughter, you shan't have my daughter,
   Nor no the gray mare."

4. The money was hastened quick out of his sight
   And so was Miss Katie, his own heart's delight.
   And Roger was kicked out of doors
   And ordered straightway not to come there no more.
   Which caused him to pull down his long yellow hair
   And wish he had never, and wish he had never
   Stood for the gray mare.

5. Six months or over or something above
   He chanced to meet with Miss Katie, his love.
   He says to Miss Katie, "Don't you know me?"
   If I ain't mistaken, I've seen you," said she.
   "A man of your likeness with long yellow hair
   That used to come courting, that used to come courting
   My father's gray mare."

John Collier learned this song from his father, who was born in Kentucky. His father's family had moved from Scotland to Virginia, and Collier believed that the song had come with them. Variants have been collected in Kansas, Michigan, Nebraska, Massachusetts, and Ohio.[27]

The following ballad offers an excellent description of the division of labor between husband and wife on the old farmstead.

TR 66 Mr. Grumble

(Child ESB, The Wyf of Auchtirmuchty)

Sung by Isie Dora McMurtry Ward, Princeton, 9 April 1938.

1. Mister Grumble he did vow By the green leaves on the tree, tree, That he could do more work in a day Then his wife could do in three, three; That he could do more work in a day Then his wife could do in three,___

1. Mr. Grumble he did vow
   By the green leaves on the tree, tree,
   That he could do more work in a day
   Than his wife could do in three, three;
   That he could do more work in a day
   Than his wife could do in three.

2. Mrs. Grumble she did say,
   "It's you can do so now, now;
   And you may do the work in the house,
   And I will follow the plow, plow;
   You may do the work in the house,
   And I will follow the plow."

3. "You must milk the muley cow
   For fear that she goes dry, dry,
   And you must feed those little pigs
   That lay within the sty, sty;" (etc.)

4. "You must watch the speckled hen
   For fear she lays astray, stray;
   And you must spin the spool of yarn
   That I spin every day, day;" (etc.)

5. "You must churn the cream in the crock
   That stands within the frame, frame;
   You must watch the fat in the pot, or it
   Will all go up in a flame, flame;" (etc.)

6. Mrs. Grumble took the whip

232

To go and follow the plow, plow;
Mr. Grumble took the pail
To milk the muley cow, cow; (etc.)

7. She rared, she pitched, she hit him a biff;
   She sniffled up her nose, nose;
   She hit him a biff in under the chin,
   And the blood streamed down to his toes, toes; (etc.)

8. He went to feed those little pigs
   That lay within the sty, sty;
   He hit his head against a rail,
   And how the blood did fly, fly; (etc.)

9. He went to watch the speckled hen
   For fear she'd lay astray, stray;
   He forgot the spool of yarn
   His wife spun every day, day; (etc.)

10. He went to churn the cream in the crock
    That stood within the frame, frame;
    He forgot the fat in the pot,
    And it all went into a flame, flame; (etc.)

11. He looked to the east; he looked to the west;
    He lookéd toward the sun, sun;
    He swore the day was six weeks long
    And his wife would never come, come; (etc.)

12. Mrs. Grumble she came in;
    He was looking very sad, sad;
    She whirled around and clapped her hands,
    A-saying, "I am glad, glad." (etc.)

The above is a variant of what is probably the oldest ballad offered in this volume. The first known poem on this subject is "The Ballad of the Tyrannical Husband," a fragment of which is preserved in manuscript form from the time of King Henry VII (1488-1509) in the Chetham Library, Manchester. This is printed in *Reliquiae Antiquae* by Thomas Wright and James Orchard Halliwell-Phillipps.[28]

The first full variant, "The wyf of auchtirmuchty," is found in the Bannatyne Manuscript, a large compilation of fifteenth- and sixteenth-century Scottish poetry, both composed and anonymous. The collection was made by George Bannatyne (1545?-1608), a successful merchant of Edinburgh, in 1568 "in tyme of pest." The collection has been printed in four volumes between 1928 and 1934 by the Scottish Text Society as edited by W. Tod Ritchie. In the manuscript the inscription "ffinis q Mofat" appears after the poem. It has therefore been ascribed to Sir John Moffatt who is supposed to have lived in the first half of the sixteenth century. A stanza of the ballad as taken from this source is given later.

Two early eighteenth-century scholars, David Laing and Joseph Ritson, have pointed out that the incidents in the ballad are very much like the first part of the story in *Silva Sermonum Jocundissimorum*, published in Basil in 1568. However, both scholars believe this work and the ballad are both based on earlier models.[29]

In 1629 a ballad, "The Woman to the Plow, and the Man to the Hen-Roost; or, a Fine Way to Cure a Cot-Queen," was registered at the Hall of Stationers. This ballad has been reprinted in several collections, such as those made by Roxburghe and Pepys. A stanza from the Roxburghe collection is also given later.

The first printing of a ballad with a comparable title to that of Mrs. Ward's, although the text is in Scottish dialect, is "John Grumlie," published in 1825 by Allan Cunningham in his *The Songs of Scotland, Ancient and Modern*. According to Cunningham it was an old song and

> a favourite among the peasantry of Nithsdale, where it was formerly sung at weddings, househeatings, prentice-bindings, and other times of fixed or casual conviviality.[30]

Cunningham secured it from the recitation of a George Duff of Dumfries, who learned it from his father. Recitation, rather than the singing of ballads, was common in Scotland. Cunningham points out that it was once the custom to convey the nature of a character, as in morality plays, by the name assigned to it, thus the appellation "Grumlie."

Moving into the eighteenth century one finds an English variant published without title in *Nursery Rhymes of England* by James Orchard Halliwell-Phillipps in 1842. There are also two nineteenth-century broadsides in the Harvard University Houghton Library printed by C. Croshaw, Coppergate, York. These are titled "The Churlish Husband Turn'd Nurse."[31]

234

In addition to TR 64 above, I will list three variants printed in Indiana from Warren and Terre Haute, outside the Hoosier Apex. The first two were contributed by Mrs. Pearl H. Bartholomew of Warren. Of these, the first is titled "Old Father Grumble," and the second, "Old Grumbly."[32] From Terre Haute comes "John Grumlie," as contributed by William Jardine, who learned it from the singing of his father in Scotland.[33]

In order that the reader may observe the variation which occurs as a song is transmitted through the centuries by oral tradition, I give below one stanza each from most of the variants discussed. As the first variant given contains two introductory stanzas, I quote its third stanza, where the story proper begins.

The wyf of auchtirmuchty
(early 1500s)

3. Quho^t he quhair is my horssis corne
   My ox hes nathir hay nor stray
   Dame the mon to the pluche to morne
   I salbe hussy gif I may
   husband q scho content am I
   To tak the pluche my day abowt
   sa the will rowll baith kavis & ky
   And all the houss baith in and owt.[34]

The Woman to the Plow,
And the Man to the Hen-Roost;
Or, a Fine Way to Cure a Cot-Queen
(1629)

1. Both Men and Women, listen well,
   A merry Jest I will you tell,
   Betwixt a Good-man and his Wife,
   Who fell the other day at strife:
   He chid her for her Huswivery,
   And she found fault as well as he
   With him for's work without the doors,
   Quoth he, "A pox on all such whores!
   Sith you and I cannot agree,
   Let's change our work!" "Content!" quoth she,
   "My Wheel and Distaffe here take thou,
   And I will drive the Cart and Plow."[35]

John Grumlie
(1825)

1. John Grumlie swore by the light o' the moon,
   And the green leafs on the tree,
   That he could do more work in a day
   Than his wife could do in three.
   His wife rose up in the morning
   Wi' cares and trouble enow--
   John Grumlie bide at home, John,
   And I'll go haud the plow.[36]

The Churlish Husband Turn'd Nurse
(nineteenth century)

1. Tis of an ancient farmer you'll hear without delay,
   And he went out unto his plough upon a stormy day
   The wind & rain did beat so hard he could no longer
      stay
   But home he came like one stark mad and to his wife
      did say.[37]

Old Father Grumble
(prior to 1916)

1. Old Father Grumble he did say,
   And said it to be true,
   That he could do more work in a day
   Than his wife could do in two.[38]

Old Grumbly
(prior to 1916)

1. Old Grumbly he came in,
   As mad as he could be,
   Saying he, "I can do more work in a day
   Than my wife can do in three, three."
   Saying he, "I can do more work in a day
   Than my wife can do in three, three."[39]

John Grumlie
(1935)

1. John Grumlie he swore by the light o' the moon
   And the green leaves on the tree

236

That he could do more work in a day
Than his wife could do in three.
His wife rose up in the morning
Wi' cares and troubles eneugh:
"John Grumlie, bide at hame, John,
And I'll gae haud the pleugh."[40]

TR 67 My Wandering Boy

Sung by Garland "Jack" South, Bloomington, 15 April 1960.

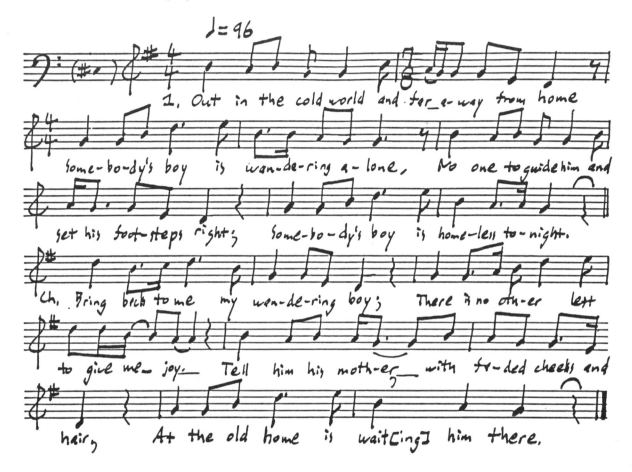

1. Out in the cold world and far away from home
    Somebody's boy is wandering alone.
    No one to guide him and set his footsteps right;
    Somebody's boy is homeless tonight.

CHORUS:
    Bring back to me my wandering boy;
    There is no other left to give me joy.
    Tell him his mother, with faded cheeks and hair,
    At the old home is wait[ing] him there.

2. Out in the hall way there sits a vacant chair;

237

Yonder the shoes that once he used to wear,
And the empty cradle the he used to love so well
At the old home is waiting him still.

CHORUS

This theme is common to a number of songs with differing titles, which are probably related. Their retention in the oral tradition is probably due, to some extent at least, to the commercial country music or hillbilly records issued of them. One is "Somebody's Boy Is Homeless Tonight," words and music composed by R. S. Hanna in 1894. This is also known as "Bring Back My Boy." "My Wandering Boy" was copyrighted by A. P. Carter who, like other country and hillbilly performers of his time, was known to have traditional songs copyrighted in his name. "Wandering Boy" was recorded by Frank Jenkins, vocal with violin, in 1927.[41] Recordings of songs on the same theme were also made by the Carter Family and the Stanley Brothers. A recording of "The Wandering Boy" by the latter was made for Columbia in 1949 or 1950 and has been reissued by Rounder Records.[42]

TR 68 The Orphan Girl

Sung by Roxie South King, Bloomington, 15 April 1960.

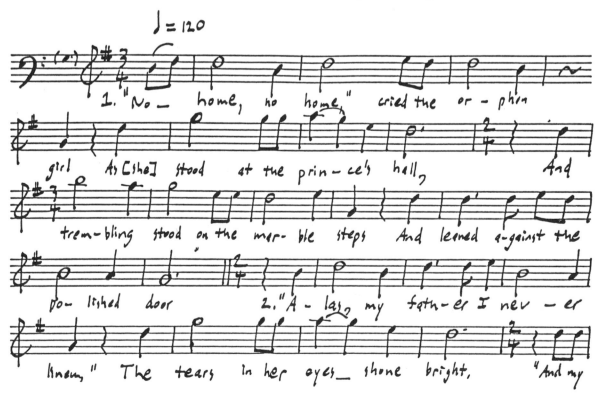

238

1. "No home, no home," cried the orphan girl
   As [she] stood at the prince's hall.
   And trembling stood on the marble steps
   And leaned against the polished door.

2. "Alas, my father I never knew,"
   The tears in her eyes shone bright.
   "And my mother sleeps in her newly made grave;
   It's an orphan that begs tonight."

3. The hours rolled on and the midnight came
   And the rich man shut his door.
   And his proud lips curled as he scornfully a-said,
   "No home, no bread for the poor."

4. The morning dawned and the little girl lay,
   Still lay at the rich man's door.
   But her soul had fled to Heaven above
   Where there is a home for the poor.

TR 69 The Orphan Girl

Sung by Anna Sandage Underhill, Uniontown, 12 June 1963.

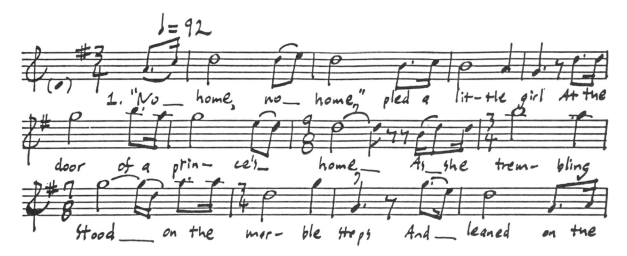

239

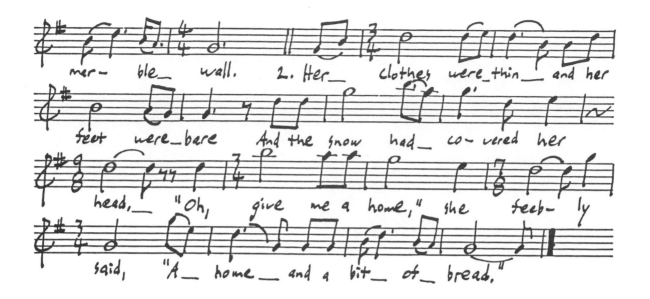

mer-ble_ wall. 2. Her_ clothes were_thin_ and her
feet were_bare And the snow had_ co-vered her
head,_ "Oh, give me a home," she feeb-ly
said, "A_ home_ and a bit_ of_ bread."

1. "No home, no home," pled a little girl
   At the door of a prince's home,
   As she trembling stood on the marble steps
   And leaned on the marble wall.

2. Her clothes were thin and her feet were bare
   And the snow had covered her head.
   "Oh, give me a home," she feebly said,
   "A home and a bit of bread."

3. "My father, alas, I never knew."
   And the tears dimmed her eyes so bright.
   "My mother sleeps in a newly made grave;
   T'is an orphan that begs tonight."

4. It was cold and dark and the snow fell fast
   As the rich man closed his door.
   His proud lip curled as he scornfully said,
   "No room, no bread for the poor."

5. "I must freeze," she said as she sank on the steps
   And sought to cover her feet
   With her tattered dress, all covered with snow,
   All covered with snow and sleet.

6. The rich man slept on his velvet couch
   And dreamed of his silver and gold,
   While the poor little girl on a bed of snow,
   She murmured, "So cold, so cold!"

7. The hours passed on and the midnight chimes
   Rolled out like a funeral knell.
   The world seemed wrapped in a winding sheet
   And the drifting snow still fell.

8. The morning dawned and the little girl
Still lay at the rich man's door,
But her soul had fled to that home above
Where there's room and bread for the poor.

This American ballad, not listed by Laws, can be traced back at least as far as the latter part of the nineteenth century. It was reportedly printed in the Cooper edition of *The Sacred Harp* in 1906 with the tune credited to Elder C. G. Smith, but this is probably an indication of the source of the copy rather than of composition.[43] It has also been published in *Glory Songs* in 1909, the music credited to T. B. Mosley. Carl Sandburg printed a text of the ballad in his *American Song-bag* of 1927, but does not indicate its source.[44]

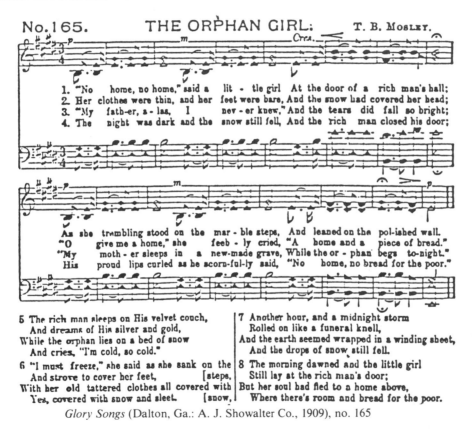

No. 165. THE ORPHAN GIRL. T. B. MOSLEY.

1. "No home, no home," said a lit-tle girl At the door of a rich man's hall;
2. Her clothes were thin, and her feet were bare, And the snow had covered her head;
3. "My fath-er, a-las, I nev-er knew," And the tears did fall so bright;
4. The night was dark and the snow still fell, And the rich man closed his door;

As she trembling stood on the mar-ble steps, And leaned on the pol-ished wall.
"O give me a home," she feeb-ly cried, "A home and a piece of bread."
"My moth-er sleeps in a new-made grave, While the or-phan begs to-night."
His proud lips curled as he scorn-ful-ly said, "No home, no bread for the poor."

5 The rich man sleeps on His velvet couch,
And dreams of His silver and gold,
While the orphan lies on a bed of snow
And cries, "I'm cold, so cold."
6 "I must freeze," she said as she sank on the
And strove to cover her feet,   [steps,
With her old tattered clothes all covered with
Yes, covered with snow and sleet.   [snow,

7 Another hour, and a midnight storm
Rolled on like a funeral knell,
And the earth seemed wrapped in a winding sheet,
And the drops of snow still fell.
8 The morning dawned and the little girl
Still lay at the rich man's door;
But her soul had fled to a home above,
Where there's room and bread for the poor.

Glory Songs (Dalton, Ga.: A. J. Showalter Co., 1909), no. 165

Numerous recordings were made of the song by country musicians, the earliest by Riley Puckett in 1925.[45] Others were made by Fiddlin' John Carson, Buell Kazee, Ernest Stoneman, and the Delmore Brothers.

The melody and words of both renditions are very much alike, except that the first text is

241

shorter. The printings and recordings seem not only to have kept the song alive in the oral tradition but also to have inhibited the development of variation.

TR 70 The Drunkard's Dream

Self-recorded by Quentin Lotus Dickey, Paoli, February 1988.

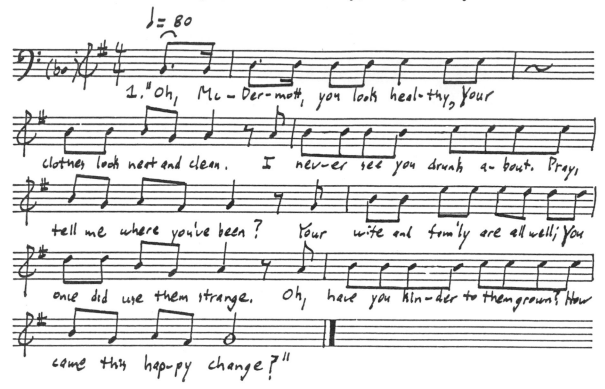

1. "Oh, McDermott, you look healthy,
   Your clothes look neat and clean.
   I never see you drunk about.
   Pray, tell me where you've been?
   Your wife and family are all well;
   You once did use them strange.
   Oh, have you kinder to them grown?
   How came this happy change?"

2. "It was a dream, a warning voice,
   That Heaven sent to me,
   To snatch me from a drunkard's curse,
   Grief, want, and misery.
   My money was all spent for drink.
   Oh, what a wretched view!
   I almost broke my Mary's heart
   And starved my children, too."

3. "What was my home or wife to me?

I heeded not their sighs.
Her pleasant smile had welcomed me
While tears bedewed her eyes.
My children they had oft awoke
And 'Father, dear,' had said,
'Mother has been weeping so
Because we have no bread.'"

4. "My Mary's form did waste away;
I saw her sunken eye,
My babes oft saw in sickness lay
And heard their wailing cry.
Yes, I laughed and sang in drunkard's joy
While Mary's tears did stream.
Then like a beast I fell asleep
And had this warning dream."

5. "I dreamt once more I staggered home.
There seemed a solemn gloom.
I missed my wife, where can she be?
And strangers in the room.
'Poor thing, she's dead,' the people said,
'She led a wretched life.
For grief and want have broken her heart.
Who would be a drunkard's wife?'"

6. "I saw my children gathering round,
They scarcely drew their breath,
Cling and kiss her lifeless form,
Forever cold in death.
'Oh, father dear, come wake her up,
The people say she's dead.
Oh, make her speak and smile once more;
We will never cry for bread.'"

7. "'She is not dead,' I frantic cried;
Then rushed to where she lay,
Fondly kissed those once-warm lips
Forever cold as clay.
'Oh, Mary, speak once more to me,
I will never cause you pain,
Nor ever break your loving heart
Nor ever drink again.'"

8. "'Oh, Mary, speak,' McDermott calls.
'Why, so I do,' she cried.
I woke and there my Mary dear
Was kneeling by my side.
I pressed her to my throbbing heart
While joyous tears did stream.
And ever since I have Heaven blessed
For sending me that dream."

TR 71 The Drunkard's Dream

Self-recorded by Quentin Lotus Dickey, Paoli, March 1988.

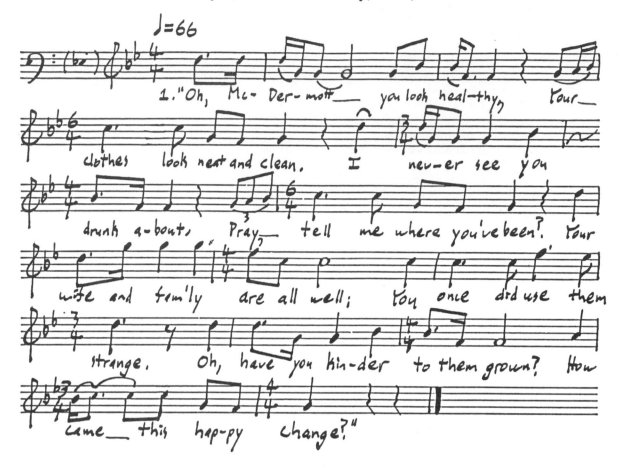

The text sung in the second rendition is the same as that sung in the first. Lotus Dickey learned this song from his father, who sang it to three different melodies. Two of those have been given above; the third is akin to the sheet music reproduced.

Dickey remembered only the tune and one stanza of the text. The remaining stanzas he secured from a clipping from an old farm magazine, the preface of which reads:

An English song, as sung by Fred Hill, an English sailor and ordinary seaman on board the United States sloop-of-war, Portsmouth, West Coast of Africa, 1850.

The clipping is quoted by Vance Randolph in his *Ozark Folksongs*, who also states that "the English version of this piece is known as 'The Husband's Dream.'"[46]

In other American variants the drunkard is addressed as "Dermont" and "Mate." Otherwise the

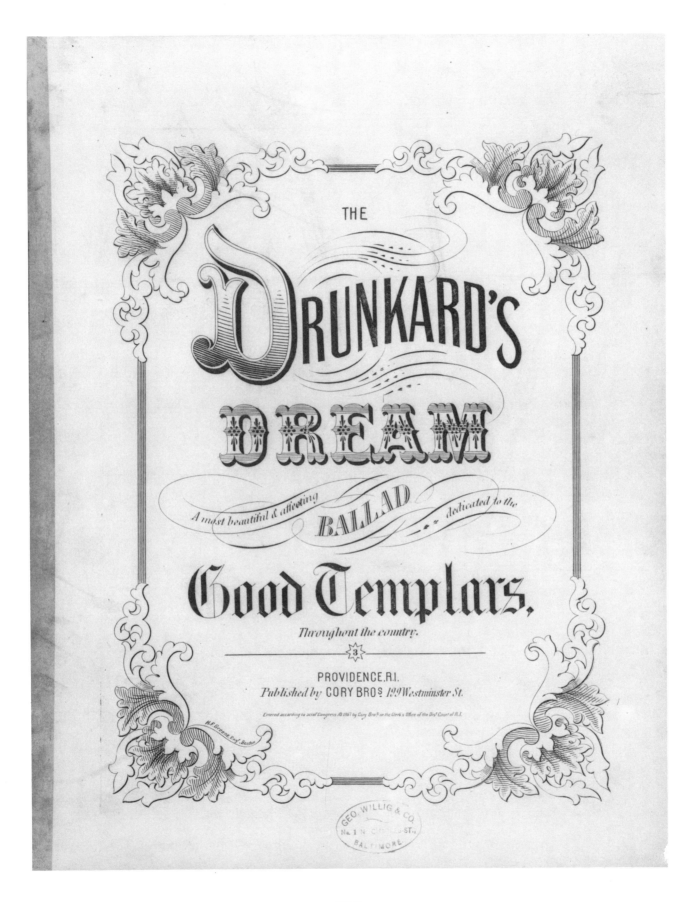

THE

Drunkard's Dream

A most beautiful & affecting *BALLAD* dedicated to the

Good Templars,

Throughout the country.

3

PROVIDENCE.R.I.
Published by CORY BROS 199 Westminster St.

Entered according to act of Congress A.D.1867 by Cory Bros in the Clerk's Office of the Dis.t Court of R.I.

THE DRUNKARD'S DREAM.

Courtesy of Indiana University Lilly Library

texts are almost identical. The farm journal from which the clipping was taken was apparently widely read, and the clipping was preserved by a number of traditional singers.

Many other songs concerning drunkards, "The Drunkard's Doom," "The Drunkard's Life," etc., were composed during the last century against overindulgence in alcoholic beverages. In the factory towns and cities there were saloons and pubs on almost every corner, whose "free lunch" and conviviality tempted workmen, tired by long hours at monotonous work, to squander their wages. Temperance dramas such as "Ten Nights in a Barroom," as well as songs, were employed in this movement in the United States by the Women's Christian Temperance Union. David Lindsey (see TR 74) told me that as a child he

246

had acted the part of a little girl in the above-mentioned play. In attempting to lure the father home, he sang:

Father, dear Father, come home with me now.
The clock in the steeple strikes one.

As a lasting memorial to this movement, which unfortunately led to Prohibition and its attendant evils, there is a street in Ellettsville named Temperance.

In the 1950s I searched the Indiana University Library in a futile attempt to find the author of the text of "The Drunkard's Dream." I unearthed a half dozen nineteenth-century poems with this title, all by different authors and none matching the song text.

The next three are popular songs from the Gay 90s.

TR 72 We All Grow Old in Time

Sung by Paul Emmet Schreiber and Walter Schreiber, Bloomington, 1959.

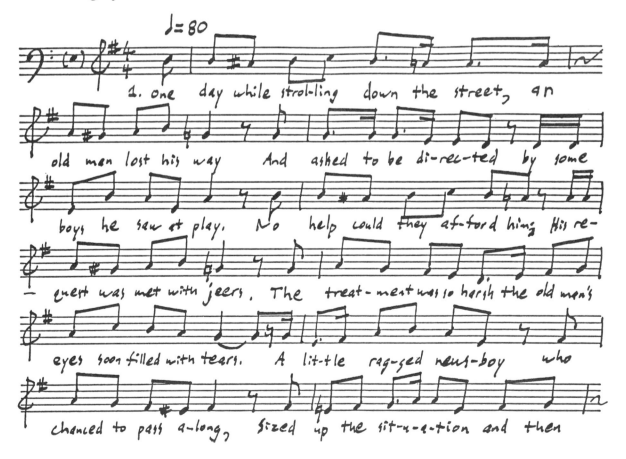

1. One day while strolling down the street, an old man lost his way And asked to be directed by some boys he saw at play. No help could they afford him His request was met with jeers. The treatment was so harsh the old men's eyes soon filled with tears. A little ragged news-boy who chanced to pass along, Sized up the situation and then

el-bowed through the throng. "Don't mind these fel-lows, mis-ter," The
lit-tle ur-chin said. And as he spoke these words each guil-ty
boy there hung his head. Ch. "Don't tease the old man,
boys, be-cause he's old and gray, But speak a
kind-ly word in-stead to help him on life's way. Your
moth-ers taught you to re-spect old age the same as
mine, And you may be like him some-day ____
____ we all grow old in time."____

1. One day while strolling down the street, an old man
      lost his way
   And asked to be directed by some boys he saw at play.
   No help could they afford him; his request was met
      with jeers.
   The treatment was so harsh the old man's eyes soon
      filled with tears.

   A little ragged newsboy, who chanced to pass along,
   Sized up the situation and then elbowed through
      the throng.
   "Don't mind these fellows, mister," the little
      urchin said.
   And as he spoke these words each guilty boy there
      hung his head.

248

CHORUS:
> "Don't tease the old man, boys, because he's old
>   and gray,
> But speak a kindly word instead to help him on
>   life's way.
> Your mothers taught you to respect old age the same
>   as mine,
> And you may be like him some day; we all grow old
>   in time."

2. "God bless you for those kind words, lad," the old man
>   to him said.
> "You have a dear, good mother," but the newsboy shook
>   his head.
> "No mother have I now, sir, in this world I'm all
>   alone,
> But come if you'll allow me and I'll see you safely
>   home."

> They walked along in silence till the old man said,
>   "My son,
> I am immensely wealthy but relations I have none.
> Now if you'll come and live with me, your kindness
>   I'll repay.
> My heart went out to you the moment that I heard
>   you say:"

CHORUS

Dale Schreiber's father, Paul Emmet, and his uncle, Walter, were both elderly when he recorded them singing this song. It was copyrighted in 1899 with music by J. Fred Helf and words by E. P. Moran. J. Fred Helf had his own publishing house and in 1900 collaborated with Will A. Heelan in producing "The House of Too Much Trouble." Among his other songs was one concerning a drunkard, "He Is a Jolly Good Fellow Every Place But at Home Sweet Home," as well as "Make a Noise Like a Hoop and Roll Away," which carried on its cover the legend, "Longfellowed by Ren Shields; Beethovenized by J. Fred Helf." "We All Grow Old in Time" was recorded by Arkansas Charlie in 1929.[47]

TR 73 The Fatal Wedding

Sung by Roxie South King, Bloomington, 15 April 1960.

1. The wedding bells were ringing on a moonlit winter
   night.
   The church was decorated; all within was gay and
   bright.

A mother with her baby came and saw the light aglow.
She thought of how those same bells chimed for her
     three years ago.

2. "I'd like to be admitted, sir," she spoke to the
     sexton old.
"Just for the sake of baby to protect him from the
     cold."
He told her that the wedding there was for the rich
     and grand,
And with the eager watching crowd outside she'd have
     to stand.

3. While the wedding bells were ringing and the bride and
     groom were there,
Marching up the aisle together while the organ pealed
     an air;
Telling tales of fond affection and vowing never
     more to part.
Just another fatal wedding, just another broken heart.

4. She begged the sexton once again to let her pass
     inside.
"For baby's sake you may pass in," the gray-haired
     man replied.
"If anyone knows the reason why this couple should
     not be wed,
Speak now or hold your peace forever," soon
     the preacher said.

5. "I must object," a woman cried in voice so meek and
     mild.
"The bridegroom is my husband, sir, and this our
     little child."
"What proof have you?" the sexton asked. "My infant,"
     she replied,
Then raised her baby [and] knelt to pray. The little
     one had died.

6. The parents of the bride then took the outcast by the
     arm.
"We'll care for you through life," they said. "You've
     saved our child from harm."
The parents, bride, and outcast turned and quickly
     drove away.
And the bridegroom died by his own hand before the
     break of day.

7. No wedding feast was spread that night, two graves
     were made next day,
One for the little baby, and in one the father lay.
This story has been ofttimes told by fireside warm
     and bright

> Of the outcast and the baby and the fatal wedding
> night.

The above song was published in 1893 with words by a popular singer of the time, W. H. Windom, who for some reason dedicated his lyrics to the *Utica* (N.Y.) *Tribune*, and music by Gussie L. Davis, a black songwriter. In entering the oral tradition the song has changed both its form and its tune. I discuss the Victorian fascination with death in the Commentary to Chapter 7 (p. 367).

Davis had worked as a janitor at the Cincinnati Conservatory, and it is assumed that it was there that he somehow learned to write songs. He was the most creative black songwriter of his period, and his melodies, in particular, are on par, when not superior, to those composed by his white contemporaries. In Cincinnati he published two rather successful songs, "Lighthouse by the Sea," in 1886, and "Wait Till the Tide Comes In," in 1887. He later moved to New York City where he first sold his songs for a few dollars and continued to work as a Pullman porter and at other nonmusical tasks.

The original sheet-music edition of "The Fatal Wedding," of which the cover and the first page are reproduced here, is quite an elaborate composition. The Maestoso introduction contains a quote from Mendelssohn's "Wedding March" and the simulation of chimes or wedding bells. There are also instructions to the pianist as to what he can repeat and suggestions for possible ornamentations of the chorus. The composition displays a typical form of the popular song of the day, three eight-line verses alternating with a four-line chorus. In the variant sung by Roxie King, the song is now in quatrain form. Her variant includes all of the original text including the chorus which is sung only once, but each quatrain (including what was once the chorus) is sung to the same melody. This melody resembles that of the first half of the original verse.

This was Davis's first big "hit." Concerning it Sigmund Spaeth, the first serious student of American popular music, writes:

> He allowed a popular singer . . . to write the words, and even their monumental silliness could not destroy the song's appeal to a public that doted on vicarious infidelity, sudden death and artificial melodrama in general.[48]

"The wedding bells were ringing,
On a moonlight winter's night;
The church was decorated,
All within was gay and bright."

... Sung by
WM. H. WINDOM

With Primrose and West's Minstrels.

THE FATAL WEDDING

Dedicated to The Utica Tribune

Words by
WM. H. WINDOM

Music by **GUSSIE L. DAVIS**

WALTZ.
SONG.

④

NEW YORK

Published by **SPAULDING & GRAY.** 16 West 27th St.

THE FATAL WEDDING.

Descriptive Waltz Song.

Words by W. H. WINDOM.

Music by GUSSIE L. DAVIS.

Courtesy of Indiana University Lilly Library

TR 74 In the Baggage Coach Ahead

Sung by David Lindsey, Bloomington, November 1956.

one dark, stor-my night as the train rat-tled on, The pas-sen-gers all gone to bed, Ex-cept one young man with a babe in his arms, sit-ting with bowed — down head. The in-no-cent one be-gan cry-ing just then As though its poor heart would break. An an-gry man said, "Make that child stop its noise, For it's keep-ing all of us a — wake." "Put it out," said a-noth-er. "Don't leave it in here; — We've paid for our bearth and want rest," But nev-er a word said the man with the child As he fon-dled it close to his breast. "Oh, where is its moth-er? Go

take it to her," A la-dy then soft-ly said,
"I wish that I could," was the man's sad re-ply
"But she's dead in the coach a-head."
Oh, while the train rolled on-ward The hus-band
sat in tears, Think-ing of the hap-pi-ness
of just a few short years. Ba-by's
face brings pic-tures of a cher-ished hope that's
dead. But ba-by's cries can't wa-ken
her In the bag-gage coach a-head.

1. One dark, stormy night as the train rattled on,
    The passengers all gone to bed,
    Except one young man with a babe in his arms,
    Sitting with bowed-down head.
    The innocent one began crying just then
    As though its poor heart would break.
    An angry man said, "Make that child stop its noise,
    For it's keeping all of us awake."
    "Put it out," said another. "Don't leave it in here.
    We've paid for our berths and want rest."
    But never a word said the man with the child
    As he fondled it close to his breast.
    "Oh, where is its mother? Go take it to her,"

A lady then softly said.
"I wish that I could," was the man's sad reply.
"But she's dead in the coach ahead."

CHORUS:
 While the train rolled onward
 The husband sat in tears,
 Thinking of the happiness
 Of just a few short years.
 Baby's face brings pictures
 Of a cherished hope that's dead.
 But baby's cries can't awaken her
 In the baggage coach ahead.

2. As he told them the story
 With each eye filled with tears,
 Of a wife that was faithful and true.
 How he'd saved up his earnings for many a year
 Just to build up a home for the two.
 How heaven had sent them this sweet little babe,
 Their two happy lives to bless.
 Just then he broke down when he mentioned her name
 And in tears tried to tell them the rest.
 Ev'ry woman arose to assist with the child;
 There were mothers and wives on the train.
 And soon was the little one sleeping in peace
 With no thought of sorrow or pain.
 Next morn at the station he bade all goodbye.
 "God bless you," he softly said.
 Each one had a story to tell in their home
 Of the baggage coach ahead.

CHORUS

This was Gussie Davis's most successful song and one of the best written in the Gay 90s. In this case Davis wrote both the words and music. It was copyrighted by Howley and Haviland of New York City in 1896.

 Pat Howley placed it with Imogene Comer, a vaudevillian billed as "the queen of song." She introduced it at Howard's Athenaeum Theater in Boston where it stopped the show. She kept it in her act for the next three years. [49]

The song was later sold to Edward B. Marks Music Company, which found it still in demand more than a half century later and reissued it.

 "In the Baggage Coach Ahead" is based on an actual incident, but how Davis developed the text

257

IN THE BAGGAGE-COACH AHEAD

SONG AND REFRAIN

Sweet Voiced Contralto,
IMOGENE COMER,
Queen of Descriptive Vocalists.

THE EMPIRE STATE EXPRESS OF THE NEW YORK CENTRAL.----FASTEST TRAIN IN THE WORLD.

WRITTEN & COMPOSED BY

GUSSIE L. DAVIS.

COMPOSER OF "IF THEY WRITE THAT I'M FORGIVEN, I'LL GO HOME." "THE FATAL WEDDING." ETC. ETC. ETC.

Published by

HOWLEY, HAVILAND & CO.
4 East 20th Street,
NEW YORK.

5

258

In The Baggage Coach Ahead.

SONG and REFRAIN.

Words & Music by GUSSIE L. DAVIS.

Moderato espressivo.

1. On a dark storm-y night as a train rat-tled on, all the pas-sen-gers had gone to bed, _____ Ex-cept one young man with a babe on his arm, who sat there with a bowed-down head, _____ The in-no-cent

2. Ev-'ry eye filled with tears when his sto-ry he told, of a wife who was faith-ful and true, _____ He told how he'd saved up his earn-ings for years, just to build up a home for two, _____ How, when Heaven had

Copyright MDCCCXCVI by HOWLEY HAVILAND & Cº

English Copyright secured.

Courtesy of Library of Congress

259

cannot be clearly defined. Apparently, both Davis and another Pullman porter, Frank Archer of Hector, New York, worked on the same train and observed the occurrence in question. Archer wrote a poem, "Mother," which tells a similar story in which the troubled father is trying to manage three children, and he tells the passengers that the mother "is in a casket in the baggage coach ahead."[50] Whether Davis based his song text on Archer's poem or his own actual experience is not known.

The Kansas newspapers have printed a story describing what actually occurred. The father was apparently Dr. James B. Watson, a Jackson County, Missouri, physician. The child, Nellie, was born in 1867, and Mrs. Watson died in 1869. The incident described occurred while Dr. Watson was taking his wife's body back to her home in Pennsylvania for burial. Nellie Watson later married a J. M. Klapmeyer and died in 1926.[51]

Mr. Lindsey's performance is reasonably faithful to both the original text and melody, as seen partially reproduced here. The rhythmic distortions seen in the transcription are probably reflections of the sentimental renditions of the period.

In his 1948 *A History of Popular Music*, Spaeth writes:

It is customary to include this song in modern burlesque renditions of those too, too funny sob ballads of the Gay Nineties, yet its lines are full of honest pathos and the text and tune are both well above the average. . . . [Davis] was afflicted with a shyness and modesty that had nothing to do with his color, but his contributions to popular music need have caused him little embarrassment, especially by comparison with the typical inspirations of his white colleagues.[52]

In addition to writing a number of "sad songs" typical of his period, Davis also wrote a few more spirited songs, such as "Get On Your Sneak Shoes, Children," and "My Creole Sue."

Laws places "The Fatal Wedding" and "In the Baggage Coach Ahead" in his appendix of "ballad-like pieces," but does not list them because they are "melodramatic and sentimental pieces . . . of professional origin."[53]

TR 75 The Dying Nun

Sung by Anna Sandage Underhill, Uniontown, 12 June 1963.

Parlando rubato

1. Let the air blow in upon me, Let me see the midnight sky. Stand back, sisters, from around me, God, it is so hard to die! Raise the pillows up, Oh, Marcy, Sister Marcy, you are kind, Come and stand along beside me, Here I leave you all behind. 2. Oh, my hand so cold and frozen, Once it was so soft and white. And the ring that now falls from it clasped my finger round so tight, Little ring they thought so worthless That they let me keep it there. Only a plain golden circle with a braid of Douglas's hair.

1. Let the air blow in upon me,
   Let me see the midnight sky.
   Stand back, sisters, from around me.
   God, it is so hard to die!
   Raise the pillows up, oh, Marcy,
   Sister Marcy, you are kind.
   Come and stand along beside me.
   Here I leave you all behind.

261

2. Oh, my hand so cold and frozen,
    Once it was so soft and white.
    And the ring that now falls from it
    Clasped my finger round so tight.
    Little ring they thought so worthless
    That they let me keep it there:
    Only a plain golden circle
    With a braid of Douglas' hair.

3. Sister Marcy, are you near me?
    You were kinder than the rest.
    Lift my head and let me lean it,
    While I live, upon your breast.
    I was thinking of some music
    That I heard long, long ago.
    Oh, how sweet the nuns are singing
    In the chapel, soft and low.

4. Oh, my father, oh, my mother,
    Will you not forgive the past,
    When you hear a stranger tell you
    How your stray lamb died at last?
    Out of all that used to love me
    Who will weep when I am dead?
    Only you, oh, Sister Marcy,
    Keep the last watch by my bed.

5. But a strain of heavenly music
    Drowns the holy midnight dream.
    Still I hear that wild, wild, feeling
    As I float away with him.
    I am coming Douglas, Douglas.
    Where you are I too am there.
    Freed at last I come, my dearest,
    Death gives back your little Claire.

6. Sister Marcy, Sister Marcy,
    Has the moon gone down so soon?
    Ah, the cell seems cold as winter
    Though I know that it is June.
    Sisters, in your white beds lying,
    Sleeping in the June moonlight,
    Through your dreams there comes no message.
    Clairie dies alone tonight.

This song was composed in 1873 by E. Mack, better known as an indefatigable composer of marches. In 1862 he composed the "Monitor," celebrating the victory of the ironclad ship *Monitor* over the *Merrimac* during the Civil War. Later he composed *General Grant's Grand March* and in 1883 *The Brooklyn Bridge March*.[54]

Commentary

This chapter is dedicated to two contrasting moods or emotions, humor and pathos. Concepts concerning what is humorous and what is pathetic change over the years, although the latter more than the former. I have tried to place the songs within these categories according to what these concepts probably were fifty to a hundred years ago. This is particularly difficult in the case of humor since in many songs the singer laughs at the end. This laugh may indicate a nervous reaction rather than a reflection of a song's humorous content. I therefore have omitted consideration of such final laughs in arriving at a decision concerning a song's placement. Some of the songs would seem unlikely to be humorous to us now, particularly those concerning the troubles of an old maid in finding a husband and a bachelor in finding a wife. Nevertheless, the intent is obviously humorous.

Deciding upon the songs to be placed in the section reserved for pathos presents its own particular problems. Our view of what is pathetic is quite different from that of the Victorian era. At times we are affected merely by the form and type of expressions in which the song is couched. The worry of a mother for her absent son in TR 67, "My Wandering Boy," and the situation illuminated in TR 74, "In the Baggage Coach Ahead," represent genuine pathos if one discounts the form into which they are cast. The present listener or reader, in my opinion, need make no exception for TR 75, "The Dying Nun," which I find the most moving of the songs.

The situations presented in the remainder of the "pathetic" songs seem a bit artificial. In my opinion, TR 72, "We All Grow Old in Time," descends to bathos. What group of obstreperous youngsters could be made to "hang their heads" by a moral speech by one of their contemporaries, accepting that he or she would even make such a speech? And what wealthy stranger adopts a stray ragamuffin on the basis of such a slender service rendered? In this day and age the plot is as suspect as those found in the Horatio Alger stories. Have you read one lately?

This chapter also contains a great variety of verse forms. TR 57, "The Derby Ram," as well as several other songs are cast in the most frequently employed of all meters. This is at times called "ballad meter" and at other times "common meter," the latter also being used to describe hymn texts.

In ballad or common meter the quatrain contains the following number of stresses per line: 4 3 4 3. TR 58, "Thorne's Goat," is in long meter, the term for this quatrain meter again being taken from those used in hymnals. In long meter each line has four stresses.

These are the two most often used quatrain forms in folk poetry. Holger Olof Nygard estimates that half of ballad texts are cast in common meter and at least a quarter in long meter. The remaining quarter have lines of three, six, seven, and eight stresses. Five stresses to a line, as seen in TR 54, "The Birthday Cake," in the previous chapter, is quite infrequent.

Since we are concerned with song rather than spoken poetry, the texts are organized on the page according to melodic, rather than verbal, stanzas. A melodic stanza may encompass two quatrains, or, in one extreme case, TR 74, "In the Baggage Coach Ahead," four quatrains. Individual quatrains so combined are almost always in common meter but occasionally in long meter.

As indicated in the commentary of the previous chapter the most frequent rhyming schemes are *a b c b* and *a a b b*. To judge from the songs offered in this volume the first rhyming scheme is most frequently associated with the ballad or common meter and the second with long meter. In some stanzas, of course, there may be no real rhyme, not even assonance.

There are other interesting verse forms in the chapter that are produced by various types of repetition and the use of nonsense syllables. The refrain plays an important part in, for example, TR 60, "Away Out West in Kansas," and in TR 61, "The Cookery Maid." Using "r" to represent "refrain," both can be expressed as *a r a r b b b r*. Short types of repetitions can be seen in TR 65, "John Roger, the Miller," and in TR 66, "Mr. Grumble." The former has six-line stanzas rhyming *a a b b c c* with the first half of line 5 repeated. "Mr. Grumble" is cast in common meter with the last two lines of the quatrain repeated in each stanza. In addition, the last syllable is repeated at the ends of lines 2 and 4.

Nonsense syllables are used in two songs of rather unique form. TR 59, "The Frog Went A-Courting," is a rare example of a three-line stanza. It is a couplet in which the first line is repeated. The nonsense syllables, "Ah, hum," are added to the first and third lines. TR 64, "The Miller's Will," is by far the most complex verse form found in this chapter. It consists of three sets of three stanzas each, each set having two five-line stanzas and one four-line stanza. In every case the last line consists of the same series of nonsense syllables. The rhyming scheme in the longer stanzas is *a a b a*, in the shorter *a a a*. This is the only example in this chapter in which incremental repetition, as defined in the commentary of Chapter 4 (p. 207), is employed. The first stanza of each set of three makes regular use of incremental repetition, while the third stanza makes only partial use of it. There is a change of content in the last stanza, the ninth.

CHAPTER 6 THE TRAGIC TRADITION: THE BRITISH BALLAD

The folk ballad has been defined as a poem that tells a story, and many examples of this type of song have been offered in previous chapters. A few of these have what may be described as happy endings, some have even been comic. However, the great bulk of traditional folk ballads are tragic. This chapter contains ballads of this class which the evidence indicates were brought to this country from England and Scotland. However, their narrative elements and specific plots form elements of ballads in other parts of Europe, particularly Scandinavia. Chapter 7 will be concerned with the tragic ballads which as far as can be determined originated in the United States.

The characteristic themes of the tragic tradition are violence, disaster, and love, the latter in most cases ending in death. The "and they lived happily ever after" ending of the fairy tale seldom occurs in the ballad. Although most ballads are full of tragic events and sad endings, traditional performances are completely devoid of emotion. The approach is purely impersonal. In the following ballad the stanza in which the villain announces his evil intentions is sung in the same manner as that in which the two ride off on their horses.

TR 76 Six Kings' Daughters

(Child 4, Lady Isabel and the Elf Knight)

Sung by Mary Vandora McNeely Bryant, Evansville, 8 or 9 April 1938.

266

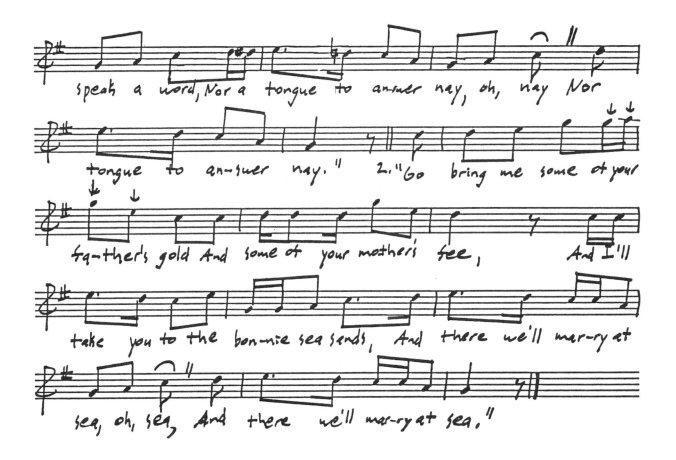

1. "He followed me up and he followed me around
   And he followed me around all day.
   I had not power to speak a word,
   Nor a tongue to answer nay, oh, nay,
   Nor tongue to answer nay."

2. "Go bring me some of your father's gold
   And some of your mother's fee,
   And I'll take you to the bonnie sea sands
   And there we'll marry at sea, oh, sea,
   And there we'll marry at sea."

3. She mounted upon a milk white steed
   And he the iron gray,
   And they rode till they came to the salt sands,
   Three long hours before 'twas day, oh, day, (etc.)

4. "Alight, alight, my pretty Polly Ann,
   Alight, alight," said he,
   "For six kings' daughters have I drownded here
   And the seventh one you shall be, oh, be," (etc.)

5. "Take off, take off those fine, fine clothes
   And lay them on this rock,
   For they are too fine and costelly

To lie in the sea and rot, oh, rot,
To lay in the sea and rot."

6. "It's turn your face three times around,
Your back to the leavcs on the tree."
Then she picked him up most manfully
And plunged him into the sea, oh, sea," (etc.)

7. "Help me out, help me out, my pretty Polly Ann,
Help me out, help me out," said he,
"And we will go to the next sea sands
And there we'll marry at sea, oh, sea," (etc.)

8. "Lie there, lie there, you false-hearted one,
Lie there instead of me.
If six kings' daughters you have drownded here
The seventh one you shall be, oh, be," (etc.)

9. She mounted up on her milk-white steed,
And led the iron gray,
And she rode till she came to her own father's door,
Three long hours before it was day, oh, day,
Two long hours before it was day.

10. "Hush up, hush up, my pretty parrot,
Don't tell no tales on me.
Your cage shall be lined with beads of gold
And hung on a willow tree, oh, tree," (etc.)

TR 77 Six Kings' Daughters

Sung by Francis Marion Stogdill, Elkinsville, 1 April 1938.

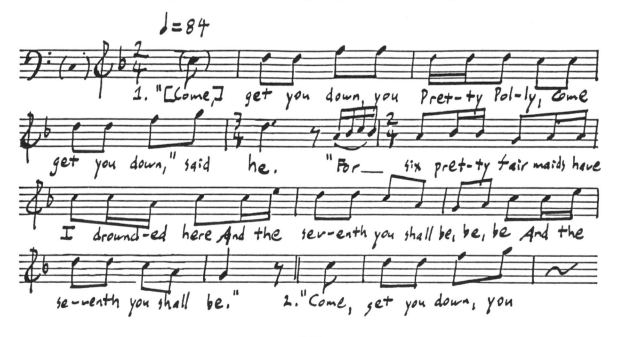

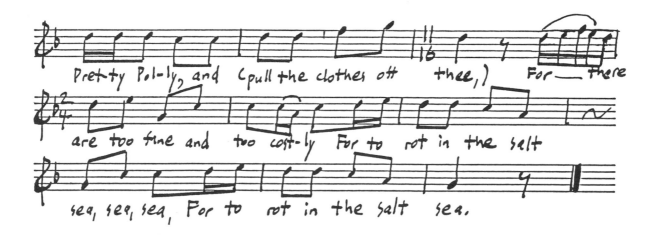

Pretty Pol-ly, and (pull the clothes off thee,) For— there
are too fine and too cost-ly For to rot in the salt
sea, sea, sea, For to rot in the salt sea.

1. ["Come,] get you down, you Pretty Polly,
   Come, get you down," said he.
   "For six pretty fair maids have I drownded here
   And the seventh you shall be, be, be,
   And the seventh you shall be."

2. "Come, get you down, you Pretty Polly,
   And (pull the clothes off thee),
   For there [*sic*] are too fine and too costly
   For to rot in the salt sea, sea, sea,
   For to rot in the salt sea."

3. "Then turn your back all unto me
   And view the leaves upon the tree,
   For it don't . . . such a villain as you
   A naked woman to see, see, see," (etc.)

4. He turned his back all unto her
   And viewed the leaves upon the tree.
   Then she picked him most manfully-like
   And she threwed him into the sea, sea, sea, (etc.)

5. "Come, pull me out, you Pretty Polly,
   Come pull me out," said he.
   "And all the promises I made you
   I'll double them over three, three, three," (etc.)

6. "Yet lay here, lay there, you false-hearted William
   In the stead of me.
   For six pretty fair maids have you drownded here
   And the seventh you shall be, be, be," (etc.)

That this ballad is an importation from the British Isles is clearly shown by the reference to

kings' daughters and lords. Such individuals have been in short supply in the United States, and it is

interesting to find the citizenry of democratic southern Indiana still singing of kings and nobles in the twentieth century. Oral tradition is, indeed, persistent. It is additionally interesting that it is conventional in ballads that no one is able to swim.

As most frequently sung, the maid is ordered to remove her fine clothes since they are too precious to rot in the salt sea. She begs the murderer to turn away so as not to gaze upon her nakedness. Once his back is turned she shoves or throws him into the sea. The ruse of the maid is clearly described in TR 77, the variant sung by Stogdill. In the 6th stanza of TR 76, Mrs. Bryant's variant, and in other published variants from southern Indiana, the ruse of the maid is not made clear. There remains only the formula:

6. "It's turn your face three times around,
   Your back to the leaves on the tree."
   Then she picked him up most manfully
   And plunged him into the sea, oh, sea, (etc.)

Of all ballads, this one probably has the greatest circulation and certainly has been the most studied.[1] Variants are found not only in English but also in French, Flemish, German, Dutch, Danish, Swedish, Icelandic, and Norwegian. Like other ballads it is known under various titles. It is No. 4, "Lady Isabel and the Elf Knight," in Francis James Child's second and greater collection. This is the first variant published by Child, and he gives that generic title to all ballads published under number four. Ballad scholars have accepted this nomenclature, although neither Lady Isabel nor the murderously inclined Elf Knight appears in the overwhelming majority of the ballads displaying a similar narrative. Ironically, the evidence suggests that Child's variant A was never actually found in the oral tradition.[2] The folk know it by other titles: "Six Kings' Daughters," "The False Knight," "Pretty Polly," etc.

The characters also change. Instead of Lady Isabel and the Elf Knight, one has May Collins or Pretty Polly and False Sir John or the Outlandish Knight. In Indiana the heroine becomes Pretty Polly Ann; the villain, if named at all, is False-hearted William. Variants of this ballad have been collected that have as many as thirty stanzas and as few as seven.

The plot of the ballad may be described pithily as "maid outwits murderer." A man lures a young woman from her home by the promise of marriage or wealth. When they reach a lonely spot he informs her that he has murdered six other women at this place and that she shall be his seventh victim. She distracts him by a ruse, and he suffers the death he had planned for her. In Child's variant A, Lady Isabel lulls the Elf Knight to sleep with a magic charm and then slays him with his own dagger. In all other American, English, and Scottish variants of Child 4, death is effected by drowning.

Other ruses than the one described in TR 77 are employed. In one the villain is asked to remove nettles or briers from the brink so these will not entangle the maid's hair. While he is thus distracted she pushes him into the sea. In Child's variant B the maid is to be drowned by being gradually forced to wade into water over her head. She asks for a last kiss, and the villain leans down from his horse. She drags him in and drowns him and escapes by hanging on to the horse's tail. Holger Olof Nygard believes this variant may have been composed by David Buchan, but possibly entered oral tradition in England.[3]

As sung in the Low Countries, the maid is given her choice as to the means of her death, and she chooses the sword. She suggests that the villain remove his cloak since a maid's blood spurts far. As he does so, she gains his sword and cuts off his head. Child's variant A, the only variant with the dramatis personae of the original title, "Lady Isabel and the Elf Knight," is closely related in method of murder to this tradition.

In the Danish tradition the maid is to be buried in a grave that the villain digs. She asks the villain to lay his head upon her lap so she may delouse him. She puts him to sleep, binds him, wakes him, and dispatches him. In the High German tradition she is to be hanged. She asks for three cries that are granted. She directs one to Jesus, one to Mary, and the third to her brother who hears her and saves her, killing the villain. Thus she outwits the villain through the agency of her brother.

In the East German tradition the maid fails to outwit the murderer. The villain accomplishes his purpose by hanging the maid, and the crime is then avenged by her brother.[4]

The stanza concerning the parrot is found in some variants and not in others. It has no direct bearing on the plot.

TR 78 is sung by Mrs. Bryant's daughter, Esther, who learned it from her. The collector did not start his recording apparatus in time, and the first part of the first phrase is missing. An examination of other variants of the ballad indicates that the phrase should begin "Lord Thomas."

TR 78 Fair Eleanor

(Child 73, Lord Thomas and Fair Annet)

Sung by Esther Bryant Frazier, Evansville, 8 or 9 April 1938.

1. [Lord Thomas] he was a bold for'ster,
   A treasur' of the King's deer.
   Fair Eleanor was a fine young lady,

272

Lord Thomas he loved her dear, oh, dear,
Lord Thomas he loved her dear.

2. "Oh, mother, dear mother, come read my riddle,
   And riddle it all in one,
   Whether I shall marry fair Eleanor,
   Or bring the brown girl home, oh, home,
   Or bring the brown girl home."

3. "The brown girl she has money plenty,
   Fair Eleanor has none.
   Therefore I charge thee with my blessing,
   To bring the brown girl home, oh, home," (etc.)

4. He rode till he came to Fair Eleanor's bower,
   And rattled at the ring,
   And who was there so ready as she,
   To rise and let him in, oh, in, (etc.)

5. "What news, what news, Lord Thomas," she said,
   "What news have you brung to me?"
   "Sad news, for I've come to invite you to
   My wedding dinner this day, oh, day," (etc.)

6. "O God forbid, Lord Thomas," she said,
   "That any such thing should be.
   I'd hoped on being the bride myself,
   And thou too the bridegroom might be, might be," (etc.)

7. "Oh, mother, dear mother, come riddle my riddle,
   And riddle it all in one,
   Whether I shall go to Lord Thomas's wedding,
   Or whether I'll tarry at home, oh, home," (etc.)

8. "My daughter, we have many friends,
   And we have many foes,
   Therefore I charge thee with my blessing,
   To Lord Thomas's wedding don't go, don't go," (etc.)

9. "I know that we have many friends,
   And we have many foes,
   But death betide me or life betide,
   T' Lord Thomas's wedding I'll go, I'll go," (etc.)

10. She dressed herself in scarlet red,
    Put on the robes of green,
    And ev'ry city that she passed through,
    She was taken to be some queen, oh, queen, (etc.)

11. She rode till she came to Lord Thomas's bower
    And rattled at the ring,
    And none was there so ready as he,
    To rise and let her in, oh, in, (etc.)

12. He took her by the lily-white hand
    And led her through the hall,
    And seated her at the head of the table
    Among the ladies all, oh, all, (etc.)

13. "Is this your bride, Lord Thomas?" she said,
    "Me thinks she looks wondrous brown,
    When once you could marry as fair young lady
    As ever the sun shone round, oh, round," (etc.)

14. The brown girl she had a little pen knife,
    The blade both keen and sharp.
    Betwixt the long ribs and the short
    She pierced Fair Eleanor's heart, oh, heart, (etc.)

15. "Oh, art thou blind, Lord Thomas?" she said,
    "Or cans't thou very well see,
    Oh, don't you see my own heart's blood
    Go crisping down my knee, oh, knee," (etc.)

16. He took the brown girl by the hand
    And led her through the hall.
    He took his sword, he cut off her head,
    And flung it against the wall, the wall, (etc.)

17. He put the blade against the ground,
    The point against his breast,
    Saying, "This is the death of three true lovers,
    God send their souls to rest, oh, rest," (etc.)

18. "Oh, mother, dear mother, go dig my grave,
    And dig it both wide and deep,
    And place Fair Eleanor in my arms,
    The brown girl at my feet, oh, feet," (etc.)

TR 79 Fair Ellender

Sung by Anna Sandage Underhill, Uniontown, 12 June 1963.

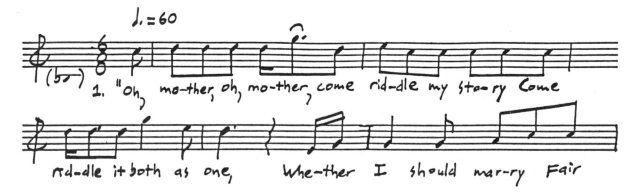

1. "Oh, mother, oh, mother, come riddle my story,
   Come riddle it both as one,
   Whether I should marry Fair Ellender
   Or bring the brown girl home?
   Whether I should marry Fair Ellender
   Or bring the brown girl home?"

2. "The brown girl she has a house and land;
   Fair Ellender she has none.
   Therefore I charge you with my best presence,
   Go bring the brown girl home.
   Therefore I charge you with my best presence,
   Go bring the brown girl home."

3. He dressed his waiters in highland so white,

275

Himself in the tercel green.
And ev'ry bar that he rode through
They took him to be some king. (etc.)

4. He rode till he came to Fair Ellender's gate.
   He jingled at the ring,
   And who was so ready as Fair Ellender, herself,
   To rise and let him in? (etc.)

5. "What news, what news, Lord Thomas," she cried,
   "What news have you brought to me?"
   "I have come to invite you to my wedding.
   Bad news it will be to thee." (etc.)

6. "Oh, mother, oh, mother, come riddle my story,
   Come riddle it both as one,
   Whether I should go to Lord Thomas's wedding
   Or stay and tarry at home?" (etc.)

7. "You may have friends, you may have none;
   You have foes where'er you go.
   Therefore I charge you with my best presence
   Lord Thomas's wedding don't go." (etc.)

8. She dressed her waiters in highland so white,
   Herself in the tercel green.
   And ev'ry bar that she rode through
   They took her to be some queen. (etc.)

9. She rode till she came to Lord Thomas's gate.
   She jingled at the ring,
   And who was so ready as Lord Thomas, himself,
   To rise and let her in? (etc.)

10. He took her by the lily-white hand
    And led her through the hall.
    He placed her at the head of the table
    Among the ladies all. (etc.)

11. "Is this your bride, Lord Thomas?" she cried,
    "I think she look [sic] wonderful brown.
    You once could have wed as fair a lady
    As ever the sun shone on." (etc.)

12. The brown girl she had a knife in her hand,
    It was both keen and sharp.
    She pierced Fair Ellender in the side
    Intending for her heart. (etc.)

13. "Oh, what's the matter, Fair Ellender?" he said,
    I think you look wonderful pale.
    You once't had two as rosy, red cheeks
    As ever my eyes beheld." (etc.)

14. "Oh, are you blind, Lord Thomas?" she said,
    "Or can't you very well see?
    For now I feel my own heart's blood
    Come tinkling over my knee." (etc.)

15. Lord Thomas he had a long broadsword,
    It was both keen and sharp.
    He cut off his own bride's head
    And throwed it against the wall. (etc.)

16. "Dear mother, dear mother, go dig my grave;
    Go dig it both wide and deep,
    And bury Fair Ellender in my arms,
    The brown girl at my feet." (etc.)

17. He turned the heel into the wall,
    The point unto his breast,
    Saying, "Here is the end of three true lovers.
    Lord, take us home to rest."
    (Last two lines not repeated)

As in other ballads, various titles are applied to the variants sung. The heroine may be named Anne or Annie as well as Annett or Eleanor, and the hero may be Sweet Willie as well as Lord Thomas. The bride is known as "the brown girl," "the brown bride," or "the nut-brown bride." Beauty in a woman is culturally relative. The Chinese found feminine beauty in small feet, the Eskimos in

"SHE SAT HER BY THE NUT-BROWNE BRIDE."
Illustration by H. M. Paget. George Barnett Smith (ed.), *Illustrated British Ballads, Old and New*, 2 vols. (London: Cassell, Petter, Galpin and Co., 1881), 2:21

strong teeth. In the Scottish-English ballad tradition a fair complexion is the primary requisite. Our present beauties with their tanned faces would not qualify. Alas, they have forgotten their sunbonnets.

The unfolding of the plot differs considerably from variant to variant. The two given above represent the classic gory plot in which the brown girl is the victim of Lord Thomas's revenge. In other variants she gets off scot-free. In Child's variant G the nut-brown bride stabs Annie at the bridal reception, but the latter rides off without Sweet Willie being cognizant of this fact. In his bridal bed he dreams of his beloved and immediately leaves his bride to ride off and find her. He arrives at her home to find her sisters preparing her for burial. He dies the next day of heartbreak. In another variant, Child 73F, the two women do not even meet. Annie appears at the bridal bed--one assumes it is her spirit--and Willie, as before, rides off to her house to find that she is dead and is being made ready for burial. She has died of unrequited love, and he dies of sorrow on the morrow.

The ballad is found in Samuel Pepys's collection of broadsides. It was printed during the reign of Charles II and licensed by L'Estrange, who was censor from 1663 to 1685 (the Hall of Stationers was abolished in 1641). The broadside from Pepys's collection is reprinted in Child as variant D. TR 78 above, recorded in the twentieth century, and the broadside, published in the seventeenth century, are remarkably alike. If we assume TR 78 to be a descendant of the broadside, three centuries have produced surprisingly little change. Below, the first few stanzas of TR 78 and the broadside are given alternately for purposes of comparison. Note that the fourth stanza of the broadside is omitted in TR 78. The broadside has nineteen stanzas, the sung variant, eighteen. For convenience in reading, the repetition of words and lines has been omitted.

TR 78

1. [Lord Thomas] he was a bold for'ster,
    A treasur' of the King's deer.
    Fair Eleanor was a fine young lady,
    Lord Thomas he loved her dear.

Child 73D

278

1. Lord Thomas he was a bold forrester,
   And a chaser of the king's deer;
   Faire Ellinor was a fair woman,
   And Lord Thomas he loved her dear.

2. "Oh, mother, dear mother, come read my riddle,
   And riddle it all in one,
   Whether I shall marry fair Eleanor,
   Or bring the brown girl home."

> 2. "Come riddle my riddle, dear mother,"
>   he said,
>   "And riddle us both as one,
>   Whether I shall marry Fair Ellinor,
>   And let the brown girl alone."

3. "The brown girl she has money plenty,
   Fair Eleanor has none.
   Therefore I charge thee with my blessing,
   To bring the brown girl home."

> 3. "The brown girl she has got houses
>   and lands,
>   And Fair Ellinor she has got none;
>   Therefore I charge you on my blessing
>   To bring me the brown girl home."

> 4. And as it befell on a high holidaye,
>   As many did more beside,
>   Lord Thomas he went to Fair Ellinor,
>   That should have been his bride.

4. He rode till he came to fair Eleanor's bower,
   And rattled at the ring,
   And who was there so ready as she,
   To rise and let him in.

> 5. But when he came to Fair Ellinor's bower,
>   He knocked there at the ring;
>   But who was so ready as Fair Ellinor
>   For to let Lord Thomas in.

5. "What news, what news, Lord Thomas," she said,
   "What news have you brung to me?"
   "Sad news, for I've come to invite you to
   My wedding dinner this day."

> 6. "What news, what news, Lord Thomas," she
>   said,
>   "What news hast thou brought unto me?"
>   "I am come to bid thee to my wedding,
>   And that is bad news to thee."

6. "O God forbid, Lord Thomas," she said,
   "That any such thing should be.
   I'd hoped on being the bride myself
   And thou too the bridegroom might be."

7. "Oh, God forbid, Lord Thomas," she said,
   "That such a thing should be done;
   I thought to have been thy bride my own
           self,
   And you to have been the brid's-groom."

7. "Oh, mother, dear mother, come riddle my riddle,
   And riddle it all in one,
   Whether I should go to Lord Thomas's wedding,
   Or whether I'll tarry at home."

8. "Come riddle my riddle, dear mother," she
           sayd,
   "And riddle it all in one;
   Whether I shall go to Lord Thomas's
           wedding,
   Or whether I shall tarry at home."

The text of Mrs. Underhill's variant, TR 79, contains some expressions which are archaic and others which are difficult to interpret. "Waiter" is an old term for manservant or waiting maid. "Highland white" is probably a corruption of "Holland white," a linen shirting made in former times in the Netherlands. "Presence," as in "my best presence," might possibly be a corruption of "prescience," foreknowledge or foreboding of what is to come, although it seems unlikely that such a term would be employed in a ballad. No information could be secured as to the meaning of "bar" in these circumstances or concerning the color specified by "tercel green."

Although word by word the text of this variant is not as close to its original broadside as is TR 78, the plot remains reasonably constant. Mrs. Underhill's variant, TR 79, does not contain three stanzas which are found in TR 78, nos. 1, 6, and 9. On the other hand, two stanzas are sung in this variant which are not found in Mrs. Frazier's, stanzas 3 and 13. The last two stanzas are sung in reverse order in the two performances. The sequence as sung by Mrs. Underhill, TR 79, seems more logical since it would be difficult for Lord Thomas to ask his mother to dig his grave after he commits suicide.

The texts and tunes of composed songs, that is, popular or art songs which have not entered

280

the oral tradition, usually remain in association. This is not commonly the case in folk songs. If a particular ballad text does not remain in association with a particular melody, it follows that two different ballad texts can be sung to the same melody. This is what occurs in TR 76 and TR 78. TR 79 also employs the same melody, thus indicating that two variants of a ballad can be sung to the same tune. However, the melody of TR 79 differs in some particulars from that employed in TR 76 and 78.

While Child 4, "Lady Isabel and the Elf Knight," has been the most widely diffused ballad in Europe, Child 84, "Bonny Barbara Allan," has been the favorite of ballad singers in the United States and English-speaking Canada. Child reproduces only three variants from Britain. However, Bertrand Bronson in his four-volume work, *The Traditional Tunes of the Child Ballads*, which contains the text of all Child ballads for which tunes have also been published, reproduces 126 variants from the United States and Canada and only 53 from Britain. (In 19 cases it cannot be established whether the ballad was sung in Europe or America.)[5]

Paul Brewster, who was active in collecting ballads in Indiana in the 1930s, found it to rank first among traditional British ballads sung in this state, publishing fourteen variants.[6]

TR 80 Barb'ry Allan

(Child 84, Bonny Barbara Allan)

Sung by Oscar "Doc" Parks, Deuchars, 6 April 1938.

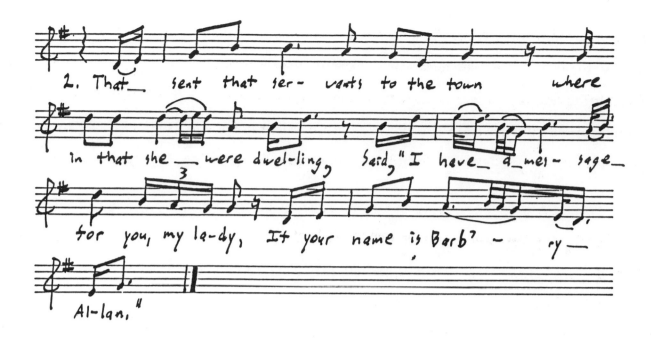

2. That____ sent that ser-vants to the town where
in that she____ were dwel-ling, Said, "I have____ a____mes-sage____
for you, my la-dy, It your name is Barb'____ ry____
Al-lan,"

1. [When I first] came to this country,
   The redbuds they were swelling.
   Sweet William was upon his death bed a-lie[ing]
   For the sake of Barb'ry Allan.

2. That [sic] sent that servants to the town
   Wherein that she were dwelling,
   Said, "I have a message for you, my lady,
   If your name is Barb'ry Allan."

3. Slowlye, slowlye she got up.
   Slowlye she went to him,
   And all she said when she got there,
   "Young man, I think you're a-dying."

4. He says, "I'm sick and I'm a-mighty sick;
   Death is on me dwelling.
   And I don't think that I'll never see ano[ther]
      sunrise
   If I don't get Barb'ry Allan."

5. She said, "Do you remember last Friday night
   When [we] were drinking at the tavern?
   You give the drinks to the ladies all around
   But you slighted Barb'ry Allan."

6. He said, "I remember last Friday night
   Drinking at the tavern.
   I give the drinks to the ladies all around
   And my heart to Barb'ry Allan."

7. He turned his pale face to the wall,

282

Turned his back upon her.
Said, "Ladies, ladies, do you all
Be kind to Barb'ry Allan."

8. Well, the young man died on Thursday's Even,
The young lady died on Friday,
And the old woman died for the sake of both,
And were buried on Easter Sunday.

9. Up out of his grave sprung a red, red rose;
Up out of her grave sprung a briar.
They growed so high and they growed so tall
That love could grow no higher.
And a-left them tied in the true love's knot,
And the rose wrapped around the briar.

TR 81 Barb'ry Allan

Sung by Oscar "Doc" Parks, Alton, 30 December 1963.

283

la-dy, If your name is Barb'—ry—Al-lan."

1. When I first came to this country,
   The redbuds they were swelling.
   Sweet William was upon his death bed a-lying
   For the sake of Barb'ry Allan.

2. They sent that servants to the town
   Wherein that she were dwelling,
   Saying, "I have a message for you, my lady,
   If your name is Barb'ry Allan."

3. Slowlye, slowlye she got up,
   Slowlye she went to him
   And bold she said when she got there,
   "This young man, I think you're a-dying."

4. He says, "I'm sick, I'm a-mighty sick;
   Death is on me dwelling,
   And I think I'll never see another sunrise
   If I don't get Barb'ry Allan."

5. She said, "You're sick and you're mighty sick;
   Death is on you dwelling.
   But I guess that you'll never see another sunrise
   For you'll never get Barb'ry Allan."

6. She said, "Do you remember last Friday night
   When we was drinking at the tavern?
   You give the drinks to the ladies all around
   But you slighted Barb'ry Allan."

7. He says, "I remember last Friday night
   Drinking at the tavern.
   I give the drinks to the ladies all around
   And my heart to Barb'ry Allan."

8. And when she had turned to go home
   She saw the corpse coming.
   She said, "Take him down, oh, take him down,
   And let me look upon him."

9. Tha [*sic*] more she looked, the more she weeped.
   She bursted out to crying,
   Saying, "Take Sweet William to the cold graveyard
   For I believe I'm now a-dying."

10. She said, "Mother, mother, go make my bed

And make it long and nigher.
Sweet William has died for me today
And I'll die for him tomorrow."

11. They buried Sweet William in the old churchyard
    And they buried Barb'ry by him.
    Above his grave sprung a red, red rose,
    Up out of her grave sprung a briar.

12. They growed so high and they growed so tall
    That love could grow no higher.
    And they left them to tie in a true love's knot
    And the rose wrapped round the briar.

TR 82 Barb'ry Allan

Sung by Mary Vandora McNeely Bryant, Evansville, 11 April 1938.

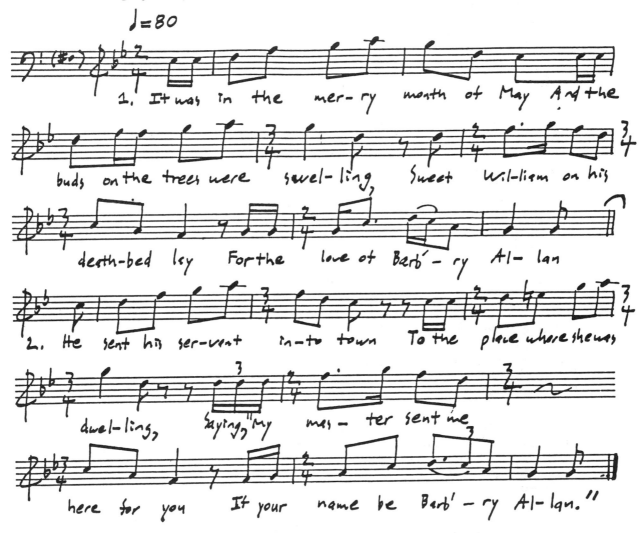

1. It was in the merry month of May
   And the buds from the trees were swelling,
   Sweet William on his death bed lay
   For the love of Barb'ry Allan.

2. He sent his servant into town
   To the place where she was dwelling,
   Saying, "My master sent me here for you
   If your name be Barb'ry Allan."

3. She mounted up on her milk white steed
   And went through the town a-sailing
   And all he [sic] said when she got there
   Was, "Young man, you are a-dying."

4. "Oh, yes, I'm sick and very sick,
   And death's within me dwelling.
   I'll never see my time again
   If I don't get Barb'ry Allan."

5. "I know you're sick and very sick,
   And death is within your dwelling.
   But none the better you will be
   For you can't have Barb'ry Allan."

6. "Oh, don't you remember the other day
   When we were in the tavern drinking?
   You drank your health to the ladies all around
   And you slighted Barb'ry Allan."

7. She looked to the east and she looked to the west
   And she saw his coffin coming.
   "Go bring him here and lay him down
   Let me take my last look upon him."

8. Sweet William died on Saturday night
   And Barb'ry died on Sunday.
   Their mother she died for the love of them both
   And she died on Easter Monday.

9. They buried her in the churchyard grave,
   Sweet William was lain beside her.
   On William's grave there sprang a sweet rose,
   On Barb'ry's sprang a briar.

10. They grew in length and they grew in breadth
    Until they could grow no higher.
    They linked, they tied in a true lover's knot,
    The rosy 'round the briar.

Here we have the unusual opportunity of examining two performances of a song by the same singer after an intervening period of twenty-five years. Although the stanzas that he does sing in both performances are very much alike, there are a different number of stanzas in the two renditions, and some of the stanzas differ.

Further, the performance by Mrs. Bryant (TR 82) does not exactly duplicate either performance by Mr. Parks. His initial line, "When I first came to this country," is not conventional. Reference to "The merry month of May," as seen in the first stanza of Mrs. Bryant's variant, is more common. By changing names or adding references, ballad singers occasionally have added local color to their performances. Here the "buds" are "redbuds," tree blossoms characteristically seen in the spring in southern Indiana. Thus, different variants of the same ballad can be carried successfully forward, not only with differences in wording but also with the omission or addition of whole stanzas.

In all variants of this ballad the heroine remains Barbara Allan, Barbary Allan, or, as heard in these recordings, Barb'ry Allan. The names of the hero are legion. In the Indiana ballads alone he may be Sweet William, Young William, Jemmy Groves, Johnnie Green, and Willie Green.[7]

Mr. Parks's southern dialect produces some interesting effects. "Tha" at the beginning of stanza 9 in the 1963 variant is probably a mispronunciation of "the," and "nigher" in the second line of stanza 10 of "narrow" (or "narrer" as it is sometimes pronounced in colloquial speech). It is "narrow" in Brewster's variants in which this stanza appears.[8]

The final stanzas of each of these variants use a motif known in other folk traditions. In the legend of Tristan and Isolde a rosebush and a vine are planted by King Mark over the lovers' graves, and these grow together "so that they could in no wise be sundered."[9] This legend goes back at least to the twelfth century. Much the same occurs in the Greek myth of Philomen and Baucis in which an elderly couple extends hospitality to Zeus and Mercury without knowing who they are. In return they are granted one boon and ask that they meet death simultaneously. At death they are transformed into trees with intertwining branches, offering cool shade to passersby for many years after.

"Bonny Barbara Allan" and "Lord Thomas and Fair Annett" are the quintessence of romantic love in the grand tradition of the ballad in which unrequited love, jealously, remorse, and sorrow lead to almost immediate death. It would appear that ballad characters are not very hardy. Our planet would be somewhat depopulated if we all reacted to the vicissitudes of personal relationships in this manner.

The return of a mariner to the woman he left behind and the sinking of a ship are common ballad themes, as in the following.

TR 83 The House Carpenter

(Child 243, James Harris [The Daemon Lover])

Sung by Albert Jeremiah Fields, Bedford, 7 August 1954.

1. "It was late when I crossed the salt, salt sea And 'twas all for the love of thee, For I could have mar-ried the king's daugh-ter dear And she would have mar-ried me, But the col-or of her gold I did re-fuse And 'twas all for the love of thee." 2. "If you could have mar-ried the king's daugh-ter dear, I'm sure you are to blame, For I have mar-ried a house

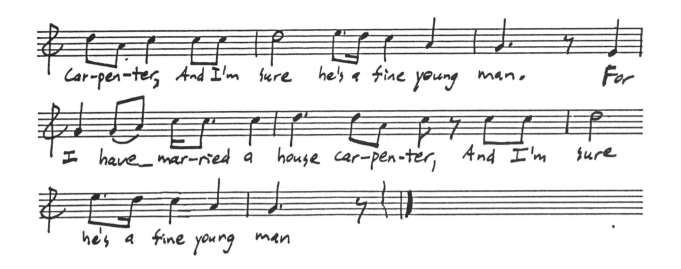

Car-pen-ter, And I'm sure he's a fine young man. For I have married a house car-pen-ter, And I'm sure he's a fine young man

1. "It was late when I crossed the salt, salt sea
   And 'twas all for the love of thee.
   For I could have married the King's daughter dear
   And she would have married me,
   But the color of her gold I did refuse
   And 'twas all for the love of thee."

2. "If you could have married the King's daughter dear,
   I'm sure you are to blame,
   For I have married a house carpenter,
   And I'm sure he's a fine young man.
   For I have married a house carpenter,
   And I'm sure he's a fine young man."

3. "If you leave your house carpenter
   And go along with me,
   I'll set you down on yon green grass.
   On the banks of sweet Lily.
   I'll set you down on yon green grass,
   On the banks of sweet Lily."

4. "If I should leave my house carpenter,
   And go along with thee,
   It's what have you got to support me on,
   An keep me from slav'ry?" (etc.)

5. "I have seven ships on shore
   And seven more at sea,
   One hundred and ten all fine young men
   All ready for to wait on thee." (etc.)

6. She dressed herself in scarlet red
   And no one looked so gay.
   She shined like a glittering star of the West
   And no one else so gay. (etc.)

7. She picked up her little babe
    And gave it kisses three,
    Saying, "Lie here, lie here, my dearest little babe
    In your father's company." (etc.)

8. She hadn't been gone more than two weeks,
    I'm sure it wasn't three,
    Till this young lady was known to weep
    And she wept most bitterly. (etc.)

9. "Is it my gold that makes you weep,
    Or is it my store?
    Or is it for that house carpenter
    That you left on yonder shore?" (etc.)

10. "It's not your gold that makes me weep
    Nor neither your store.
    It's all for the love of my dearest little babe
    That I left on yonder shore." (etc.)

11. She hadn't been gone more than three weeks,
    I'm sure it wasn't four,
    Till under the deck the ship spring a leak
    And she sunk for to rise no more. (etc.)

12. "A curse, a curse, a curse," cried she,
    "A curse to all seamen.
    They robbed me of my dearest little babe
    And stolen my life away." (etc.)

This ballad is most commonly known as "The House Carpenter." The name, James Harris, given to the seaman in Child's variant A, rarely appears in later variants. The Daemon Lover, however, appears with some frequency.

It is the function of the ballad, unlike that of the tale, not only to expose and resolve a conflict in poetic form but also to do so with the greatest economy of means. It is for this reason, perhaps, that as ballads are transmitted from singer to singer they tend to lose much of their initial expository material. Since the subsequent stanzas make the situation quite clear, we could easily dispense with the first stanza of TR 78, "Fair Eleanor:"

[Lord] Thomas he was a bold for'ster,
A treasur' of the King's deer.
Fair Eleanor was a fine young lady,
Lord Thomas he loved her dear.

290

In "The House Carpenter" this process seems to have gone too far. One wonders why this wealthy mariner, who could have married a king's daughter, returns across the sea to lure away a married woman who has a child. In the earlier variants reproduced in Child, the woman had been engaged to the mariner and while he was away had broken her vows and married the carpenter. The mariner is no longer alive. It is not he who returns for her but his vengeful spirit. In some variants, once on the ship the woman sees that her lover has a cloven hoof. The devil has taken on the seaman's form. There is mention of a bright hill, which is Heaven, and of a dark hill, which is Hell. When the woman inquires as to their destination she is told that they will dwell in the dark hill.

In the Indiana variants there is no mention of the past relationship between the mariner and the woman. It is he, himself, who returns, not his spirit or the devil in his guise. The earlier ballads end with the distraught husband cursing all seamen:

> Oh cursed be those mariners!
> For they do lead a wicked life;
> They ruind me, a ship-carpenter,
> By deluding away my wife.[10]

In the later variants, as TR 83 above, it is the woman who curses seamen. Occasionally a warning to other women is substituted, as the following from Virginia:

> Come all of you now, nice young girls,
> Take warning now from me
> And never leave your house carpenter
> To go with a man on sea.[11]

TR 84 The Lowland Sea

(Child 286, The Sweet Trinity [The Golden Vanity])

Sung by Mary Vandora McNeely Bryant, Evansville, 11 April 1938.

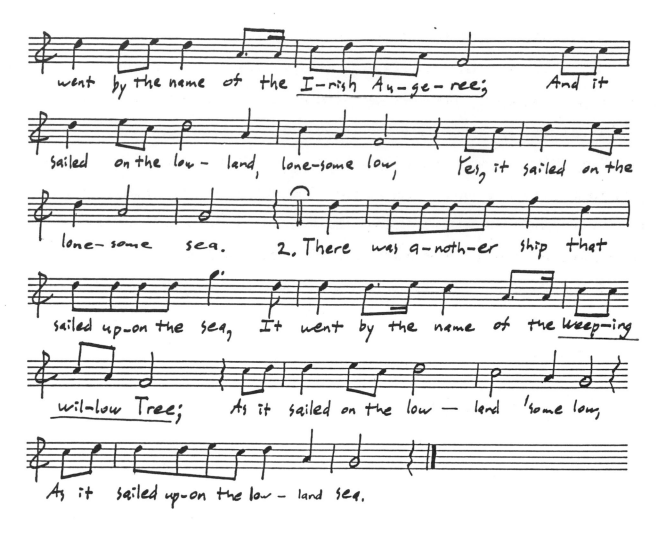

went by the name of the I-rish Au-ge-ree; And it
sailed on the low - land, lone-some low, Yes, it sailed on the
lone-some sea. 2. There was a-noth-er ship that
sailed up-on the sea, It went by the name of the weep-ing
wil-low Tree; As it sailed on the low - land 'some low,
As it sailed up-on the low - land sea.

1. There was a jolly ship that sailed upon the sea,
   It went by the name of the *Irish Augeree*;
   And it sailed on the lowland, lonesome low
   Yes, it sailed on the lonesome sea.

2. There was another ship that sailed upon the sea,
   It went by the name of the *Weeping Willow Tree*;
   As it sailed on the low, land 'some low,
   As it sailed upon the lowland sea.

3. Up stepped a sailor boy saying, "What will you give me,
   If I will sink the old *Irish Augeree*?
   I can sink her in the lowland, lonesome low,
   I can sink her in the lonesome sea."

4. "I will give you gold and I will give you fee,
   Besides my eldest daughter your wedded bride shall be;
   If you'll sink her in the lowland, lonesome low,
   If you'll sink her in the lonesome sea."

5. He started with his instruments all fitted for his use,

He cut nine gashes and let in sluice;
As she sailed on the lowland, lonesome low,
As she sailed on the lonesome sea.

6. Some were playing cards and some were throwing dice;
   Some were standing by (her) and giving good advice,
   As she sailed on the lowland, lonesome low,
   As she sailed upon the lonesome sea.

7. Some with their hats and some with their caps,
   Trying to stop those salt water gaps;
   As she sank in the lowland, lonesome low,
   As she sank in the lonesome sea.

8. He turned on his back and away swam he,
   Until he came to the *Weeping Willow Tree*;
   As she sailed on the lowland, lonesome low,
   As she sailed on the lonesome sea.

9. "Captain, oh, Captain, be as good as your word,
   And will you not take me up on board?
   For I sunk her in the lowland, lonesome low,
   I sank her in the lonesome sea."

10. "No, I won't be as good as my word,
    Neither will I take you up on board.
    You can sink in the lowland, lonesome low,
    You can sink in the lonesome sea."

11. "If it wasn't for the love I have for your men,
    I'd serve you a trick that I just served them;
    I would sink you in the lowland, lonesome low,
    I'd sink you in the lonesome sea."

12. He turned on his back and away swam he,
    And he bid adieu to the *Weeping Willow Tree*;
    As he sank in the lowland, lonesome low,
    He sank in the lonesome sea.

Child's variant A is a broadside issued in the second half of the seventeenth century. Sir Walter Raleigh builds a ship in the Netherlands which is then captured at sea by a false galley. The remainder of the plot is similar to that of TR 84 above, except that the captain does take the cabin boy on board and gives him his gold, but refuses to give him his daughter. The ship's boy then says farewell to the captain since he is not as good as his word. There is no indication as to the former's fate. In other variants the boy secures what he was promised by threatening to sink his own ship. Child's variant C is similar to TR 84 and other later variants in that the ship's boy or cabin boy is not taken aboard and drowns.

In most variants, other than the broadside, there is no mention of capture of the ship. It is merely held at bay by another ship, usually Turkish or French. The ships are given numerous names.

Spelling was rather informal in the seventeenth century, as can be seen in the following first stanza from the broadside:

> Sir Walter Rawleigh has built a ship,
> In the Neather-lands . . . .
> And it is called The Sweet Trinity,
> And it was taken by the false gallaly.
> Sailing in the lowlands

Raleigh might be spelled Rawleigh, Ralai, Rawlei, or Rawlay. The ship is captured by a galley (gallaly), a fighting ship propelled by ranks of oarsmen as well as sails.

The most interesting development of the ballad as it passed through oral tradition, and one which adds considerably to its poetic impact, is the dropping of "Neatherlands" and "lowlands." "Lowlands" (or "lowland sea," as it appears in other Child variants) refers to the seas around Holland. This has been transmuted to "lonesome seas," which refers more generally to the vast and dangerous deep sea. Residents of southern Indiana are naturally unlikely to know that "lowlands" or "lowland sea" refers to the seas around the Netherlands. Thus one finds that a variant found in Indiana begins:

> All on the Spanish Main the Turkish Shiveree
> Was trying for to stop the Golden Willow Tree
> As she sailed on the Lowland, lonesome, low,
> As she sailed on the Lowland Sea.[12]

The Spanish Main, of course, is the Caribbean Sea.

The highwayman is a natural figure around which to weave a ballad. There are many English ballads concerning Robin Hood, but apparently none have reached Indiana. Here is one concerning an Irish latter-day Robin Hood.

TR 85 Brennan on the Moor

(Laws BR L 7)

Sung by Garland "Jack" South, Elkinsville, May 1956.

295

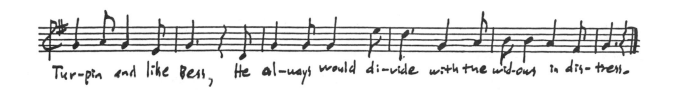

Tur-pin and like Bess, He al-ways would di-vide with the wid-ows in dis-tress.

1. 'Tis of a fearful Irishman this story I will tell,
   His name was Willie Brennan; in Ireland he did dwell.
   'Twas on the top of Cal'vry Mount he commenced his wild
     career,
   And many a wealthy gentleman before him shook with
     fear.

CHORUS:
   Brennan on the moor, Brennan on the moor,
   Bold, gay, and daring stood young Brennan on the moor.

2. A brace of loaded pistols he carried with him each day.
   He never robbed the poor man upon the Queen's highway,
   But what he took from rich men, like Turpin and
     like Bess,
   He always would divide with the widows in distress.

3. One night he met a packsman by the name of Jerry Brown.
   They walked along together till day began to dawn.
   The packsman found his pack was gone, likewise his
     watch and chain.
   He then encountered Willie and robbed them back again.

4. When Brennan found the packsman as good a man as he,
   He took him for a partner upon the Queen's highway.
   The packsman threw his pack away, no moments to delay
   And proved to be a faithful friend until his dying day.

5. When they arrested Willie in irons he was bound,
   They took him to a jail house; stone walls they did
     surround.
   The jury found him guilty; the judge made this reply,
   "For robbery upon the Queen's highway you are condemned
     to die."

6. "Farewell to you, my loving wife and you, my children
     three.
   Farewell to you, my father, who will shed tears for me.
   Farewell to you, my mother, who'll tear your locks and
     cry,
   You'd better, Willie Brennan, while in the cradle die."

CHORUS

This ballad also exists as a broadside and is based on a historical character. Brennan was a

PIRATE CREW.

BRENNAN ON THE
MOOR.

J. Bebbington, Printer, 31, Oldham Road, Manchester,
and sold by H. Andrews, and J. Beaumont, Leeds.

It's of a fearless highwayman a story I will tell,
His name was Willy Brennan, in Ireland did dwell,
And on the Lilvart mountains, he commenced his wild career,
Where many a wealthy gentleman before him shook with fear.
Brennan on the Moor.

A brace of loaded pistols he carried night and day,
He never robbed a poor man upon the king's highway ;
But what he'd taken from the poor, like Turpin and Black Bess,
He always did divide it with the widow in distress.

One night he robbed a pack man, the name of Pedlar Bawn,
They travelled on together, till the day began to dawn,
The pedlar seeing his money gone, likewise his watch and chain,
He at once encountered Brennan, and robbed him back again.

When Brennan, seeing the pedlar was as good a man as he,
He took him on the highway his companion for to be ;
The pedlar threw away his pack without any more delay,
And proved a faithful comrade until his dying day.

One day upon the highway, as Willie he sat down,
He met the Mayor of Cashel, a mile outside the town,
The Mayor he knew his feature, I think young man said he,
Your name is Willie Brennan, you must come along with me.

As Brennan's wife had gone to town, provisions for to buy,
When she saw her Willie she began to weep and cry,
He says give me that tenpenny, as soon as Willie spoke,
She handed him a blunderbuss from underneath her cloak.

Then with the loaded blunderbuss, the truth I will unfold,
He made the Mayor to tremble and robbed him of his gold ;
One hundred pounds was offered for his apprehension,
And he with his horse and saddle to the mountains did repair.

Then Brennan being an outlaw. upon the mountains high,
Where cavalry and infantry to take him they did try ;
He laughed at them with scorn, until at length, its said,
By a false-hearted young man he was betrayed.

In the county of Tipperary, in a place they called Clonmore,
Willie Brennan and his comrade, that day did suffer sore,
He lay amongst the fern which was thick upon the field,
And nine wounds he did receive, before that he did yield.

Then Brennan and his companion knowing they were betrayed,
He with the mounted cavalry a noble battle made,
He lost his foremost finger which was shot off by a ball,
So Brennan and his comrade were taken after all.

So they were taken prisoners, in irons they were bound,
And conveyed to Clonmel gaol, strong walls did them surround ;
They ware tried and found guilty, the judge made this reply,
For robbing on the king's highway, you're both condemned to die.

Farewell unto my wife, and unto my children three,
Likewise to my aged father, he may shed tears for me,
And to my loving mother, who tore her grey locks and cried,
Saying, I wish Willie Brennan in your cradle you had died.

401

Robin & Gran'num.

As Robin and Gran'num were going to town,
Betwixt them both they spent half-a-crown,
Whilst Robin drank one glass old Gran'num drunk two,
Till she was as drunk as my David's old sow.
Tol de rol, &c.

And as they were going old Gran'num did fall,
Into a deep ditch and to Robin did call,
Eh ! bless thee Robin ; eh ! bless thee, said hoo,
Eh ! bless thee Robin, come hither and poo !

Then Robin he laid fast hold of her foot,
To poo her out of the ditch he thought he could do't,
He poo'd and he poo'd till he made his arm sore,
O, dang it, says he, I can poo thee no more.

Old Gran'num, she did'nt much like such a fall,
And to Robin once more she louder did call,
Eh ! bless thee, Robin ; eh ! bless thee, said hoo,
Eh ! bless thee, Robin, come try 'tother poo.

Then Robin he poo'd with his might and his main,
Till he brought old Gran'num to the bank once again
Eh ! bless thee Robin, eh ! bless thee said hoo,
Eh ! bless thee Robin, thou's poo'd a rare poo.

And as they were going old Gran'num did say,
Thee deserves a new jacket for pooing to-day ;
There's an owd 'un o' Grandad's I wish it were new,
For, bless thee Robin, thou's poo'd a rare poo.

PIRATE CREW.

O'er the wide world of waters we roam ever free,
Sea kings and rovers, bold pirates are we ;
We own no dominion—what matter ! we sail
Light-hearted and free, in the loud roaring gale.
We love the black storm, as we ride o'er the billows,
The strong timbers creak, & the masts shake like willows,
But fearless in danger, we brave the mad foam,
Ever free on the deep, the wide ocean our home.

Then hurra ! hurra ! hurra !
Merry is the life of the bold pirate crew.
Dauntless and daring are the deeds that we do ;
Hurrah ! the black banner is nailed to the mast,
Death to the foe as it waves in the blast. As it, &c

"Crowd sail—a strange vessel is heaving in sight,"
Shouts the pirate aloft, "she's our's to-night ;"
Now we dash thro' the spray, bearing down on the prize.
No quarter we give to the stranger that flies.
Clear the decks—ever brave are the pirates in battle,
The strong timbers creak,, and the loud cannons rattle !
Now we board her in triumph and bear her away,
Three cheers for the prize, as we bound o'er the spray.
Then hurra ! hurrah ! &c.

noted seventeenth-century highwayman, who carried on his trade in the area of the Kilworth Mountains near Fermoy in Cork.[13] This is a short variant of the ballad which omits many of Brennan's adventures. A fuller version can be read in the accompanying reproduction of a nineteenth-century broadside. The blunderbuss was a gun with a very wide bore from which a number of balls could be shot simultaneously.

The reference in stanza 2 is to Dick Turpin and his horse, Black Bess. Turpin, whose real name was Richard Palmer, was a highwayman who was hanged in 1739 at York at the age of thirty-three. He was the hero of several broadside ballads (Laws BR L 8-10).[14]

TR 86 The Hangman Song

(Child 95, The Maid Freed from the Gallows)

Sung by Garland "Jack" South, Bloomington, 1960.

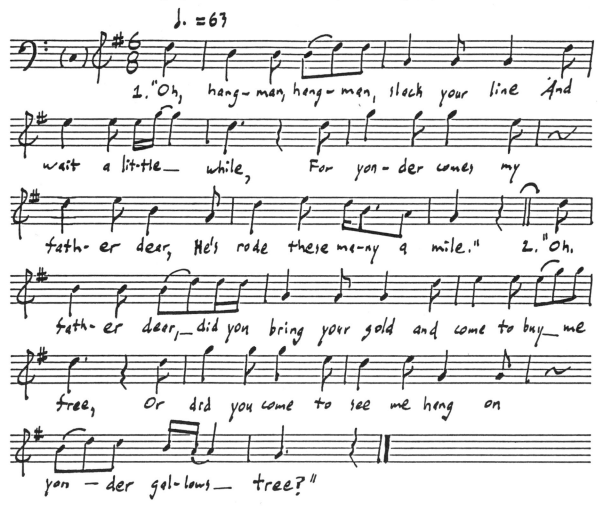

1. "Oh, hang-man, hang-men, slack your line And wait a lit-tle while, For yon-der comes my fath-er dear, He's rode these ma-ny a mile."

2. "Oh, fath-er dear, did you bring your gold and come to buy me free, Or did you come to see me hang on yon-der gal-lows tree?"

1. "Oh, hangman, hangman, slack your line
   And wait a little while,
   For yonder comes my father dear,
   He's rode these many a mile."

2. "Oh, father dear, did you bring your gold
   And come to buy me free,
   Or did you come to see me hang
   On yonder gallows tree?"

3. "No, daughter dear, I didn't bring your gold
   Or come to buy you free.
   I only came to see you hang
   On yonder gallows tree."

4. "Oh, hangman, hangman, slack your line
   And wait a little while,
   For yonder comes my mother dear,
   She's rode these many a mile."

5. "Oh, mother dear, did you bring your gold
   And come to buy me free,
   Or did you come to see me hang
   On yonder gallows tree?"

6. "No, daughter dear, I didn't bring your gold
   Or come to buy you free.
   I only came to see you hang
   On yonder gallows tree."

7. "Oh, hangman, hangman, slack your line
   And wait a little while,
   For yonder comes my brother dear,
   He's rode these many a mile."

8. "Oh, brother dear, did you bring your gold
   And come to buy me free,
   Or did you come to see me hang
   On yonder gallows tree?"

9. "No, sister dear, I didn't bring your gold
   Or come to buy you free.
   I only came to see you hang
   On yonder gallows tree."

10. "Oh, hangman, hangman, slack your line
    And wait a little while,
    For yonder comes my lover dear,
    He's rode these many a mile."

11. "Oh, lover dear, did you bring your gold
    And come to buy me free,
    Or did you come to see me hang
    On yonder gallows tree?"

12. "Yes, lover dear, I brought my gold
    And came to buy you free.
    I did not come to see you hang
    On yonder gallows tree."

This is a ballad in which all semblance of motivation seems to have been dropped. Why was the young woman to be hanged, and why was her family so dead set against her? These questions have been debated at great length for years, and the ballad has been the subject of numerous articles, the most recent being by Ingelburg Urcia in 1966 and Tristram P. Coffin in 1967, and a book by Eleanor Long in 1971. The ballad formed part of a *cante fable* (a story including song), published by Baring-Gould in 1866.[15] A little man dressed all in gold presents two girls with golden balls and warns that they will be hanged if they lose them. One of the girls loses her ball, and her sweetheart goes in search of it. The lass is taken to York to be hanged, and this tale is then concluded with the ballad stanzas which form variant H in Child.

"Stop, stop, I think I see my mother coming.
Oh, mother, has thou my golden ball and come to set me
    free?
I've neither brought thy golden ball nor come to set
    thee free."

Later Lucy Broadwood and Anne Gilchrist provide an allegorical explanation of the story and ballad.[16] The golden ball signifies the maiden's honor, which when lost can only be restored by her lover. In earlier days, as now, gold was a symbol of purity. In Danish ballads a circlet of gold is the insignia of a virgin. This is thought to be based upon a Swedish custom of the Middle Ages in which unmarried women of noble rank wore such ornaments on all festive occasions.[17]

Other scholars have moved from the consideration of the golden ball as a symbol of the maid's virginity to the belief that she is being hanged because of the actual loss of that commodity. Thus in Child's variant E the maid speaks of "Warrenston, the father of my chile." Many variants include the "prickly bush" motif:

"If I could get out of this prickly bush
I'd never get in no more."

300

This motif is an old symbol for a fatal love entanglement. Obviously this is a crime of much greater severity than the loss of a golden ball.

The golden ball may not only be a symbol of virginity but also the cause of preventing pregnancy, and in this sense its loss is perhaps the cause of the maid's predicament. In his *Memoirs*, Casanova tells of fashioning small gold balls about two ounces in weight which he gave to courtesans he patronized both as payment and as a means of contraception. According to the evidence of a medical doctor, who came to the United States as a refugee from Central Europe, small golden balls had been used for centuries by the wealthy in Europe as an intrauterine contraceptive device. To be placed in the uterus it had to be of pure gold so as not to irritate its tissues or cause cancer. The IUD may have a longer history than is generally supposed.

Thus golden balls were probably in use as contraceptives in the past in areas where the *cante fable* and the ballad concerning the gallows tree were heard. While in the *cante fable* the loss of the golden ball may not have symbolized the actual loss of virginity, it may have so appeared in truncated ballads.

> The rationalization which opened the way for the "prickly bush" refrain was caused by the habit of thinking of golden balls as protectors of virginity as the circlet of gold in the hair was the symbol of purity itself.[18]

Unfortunately, most later variants of the ballad have lost any reference to the golden ball and any motivation which might explain the maid's situation. There remains only the scene under the gallows, the faithful lover, and the sense that love conquers all. It seems that the singers of ballads are interested only in a crisis and its resolution. As to how the crisis came about, they can do quite well without this knowledge.

Strangely absent in the above discussion is the consideration of two variants of the ballad collected by Cecil J. Sharp in the Appalachians, the second stanzas of which explain quite simply why the maid is in danger of being hanged.

301

Variant A

2. "O father, O father, have you got any gold for me?
Or silver to pay my fee?
They say I've stoled a silver cup
And hanged I must be."

Variant B

2. "O father, have you any gold for me?
Any silver to pay my fee?
For I have stoled a golden cup
And hanging it will be."[19]

At least one battle ballad must be included. In the following, a singer in southern Indiana

celebrates a battle which occurred in Ireland three hundred years ago.

TR 87 The Battle of the Boyne

Sung by Jacob Oatman Forester Kirk, Oakland City, 7 April 1938.

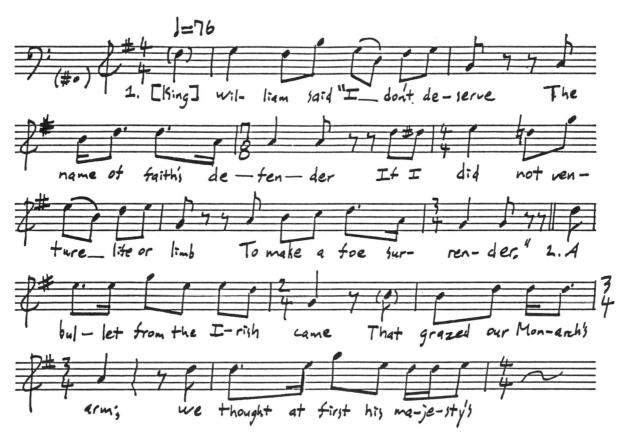

Slain, But it did him little harm.

1. [King] William said, "I don't deserve
   The name of faith's defender
   If I did not venture life or limb
   To make a foe surrender."

2. A bullet from the Irish came
   That grazed our monarch's arm;
   We thought at first his majesty's slain,
   But it did him little harm.

3. "Brave boys," he said, "be not dismayed
   At the losing of one commander,
   For God will be our king this day
   And I'll be general under."

4. Then let us all with heart and hand
   Unite forever after,
   And bless this noble memoral [sic] day
   Of King William that crossed the water.

Compare these four stanzas with the song text entitled "Boyne Water," published in the *American Songster*. This variant has ten stanzas of eight lines each. Longer variants are also known. The original is obviously a composed piece. Only part of the text is reproduced below.

Boyne Water

1. July the first, in Oldbridge town,
   There was a grievous battle,
   Where many a man lay on the ground,
   By cannons that did rattle.
   King James he pitched his tents between
   The lines for to retire;
   But King William threw his bomb-balls in
   And set them all on fire.

2. Thereat enraged they vowed revenge
   Upon King William's forces,
   And oft did cry vehemently,
   That they would stop his courses.
   A bullet from the Irish came,
   And grazed King William's arm,
   They thought his majesty was slain,

303

Yet it did him little harm.

3. Duke Schomberg then in friendly care,
   His King would often caution,
   To shun the spot where bullets hot
   Retained their rapid motion;
   But William said, he don't deserve
   The name of Faith's Defender,
   Who would not venture life and limb
   To make a foe surrender.

6. When valiant Schomberg he was slain,
   King William he accosted
   His warlike men for to march on,
   And he would be the foremost;
   "Brave boys," he said, "be not dismayed
   For the loss of one commander,
   For God will be our Guide this day,
   And I'll be general under."

7. Then stoutly we the Boyne did cross,
   To give our enemies battle;
   Our cannon, to our foes great cost,
   Like thund'ring claps did rattle.
   In majestic mien our Prince rode o'er;
   His men soon followed after,
   With blows and shouts put our foes to rout
   The day we crossed the water.

10. Come, let us all with heart and voice
    Applaud our lives' defender,
    Who at the Boyne his valour showed
    And made his foe surrender.
    To God above the praise we'll give,
    Both now and ever after;
    And bless the glorious memory
    Of William, who crossed the Water.[20]

This ballad refers to the victory of the army led by King William III of England over the forces of the former King, James II, on the banks of the River Boyne in Ireland 1 July 1690 (11 July in the later Gregorian calendar). The Roman Catholic, James, had been forced to abdicate in 1688 and was still recognized as King of England by France and Spain. He was attempting, with the aid of the Catholic Irish and regular French forces, to regain his throne. William, formerly the Dutch Prince of Orange, had the larger force, which included Dutch guards and French Huguenots as well as English and some mercenaries. William's cavalry crossed the Boyne to the left and right of James's army, and fear-ing encirclement James left the field and fled to France. Although deserted by the French, the Irish army retired in good order and fought on until defeated a year and a day later.

The Battle of the Boyne is still celebrated as a victory for the Protestant cause by the Orangemen of Northern Ireland with a procession on 12 July, usually through Catholic districts. (12 July is actually the date of the defeat of the Irish army by William's generals at Aughrim in 1691.)

The introduction into Ulster in the seventeenth century of Presbyterian settlers from Lowland Scotland increased the enmity that had existed between Protestants and Catholics. Such sectarian feelings ran especially high at the end of the eighteenth century. Following a major confrontation between the two sides in 1795, the Ulstermen formed a secret society called the Orange Society or Order. Named in honor of William of Orange, its purpose was the protection of Protestants from Catholics, support for the Protestant religion, and the maintenance of a Protestant monarchy. The early Orangemen initiated a campaign of violence against Catholic peasants, driving thousands of them from Ulster. The Society is still a potent political and religious force in Northern Ireland, where the dominant Protestant community opposes union with the Irish Free State. Strife still continues between militant Protestants and the illegal Irish Republican Army. In an attempt to avoid conflict there has been an official prohibition of the provocative 12 July procession celebrating the Battle of the Boyne. The early settlers of southern Indiana were primarily Protestants.

It is interesting to note that the patronymic of the singer, Kirk, is the Scottish term for "church." He said that he learned the song from an Irishman in Somerville. It can be assumed that this Irishman came from Ulster.

Commentary

The British ballad is primarily a sung tradition. Although the words may exist in print or may have been written down by the singer, the performance is normally in the form of a song. In the past in Scotland, however, the ballad has been treated purely as poetry and in many cases has been recited rather than sung.[21]

The ballad usually consists of a number of stanzas of the same form and length, which in most cases are sung to the same melodic stanza throughout. The texts of the ballads have been more widely studied than any other form of folk song, but much less attention has been paid to the melodies to which they are sung. In fact, Francis J. Child in his famous collection, *The English and Scottish Popular Ballads*, includes only a few tunes which are added in an appendix. It is probably safe to assume that the bulk of the texts of the ballads transcribed were sung by memory without reference to a printed or written text. When the contrary is known to be true, it has been indicated. Probably few, if any, of the ballads were sung from musical notation, since the ability to read music is much less widespread than that of reading words.

The quatrains of all but two of the ballads offered in this chapter are in ballad, or common, meter, the stress pattern being 4 3 4 3. Occasionally the first line of the first stanza will contain only three stresses. The rhyming scheme in all is *a b c b*, although it must be admitted that many quatrains are characterized by faulty rhymes or contain no rhyme at all. One of the two ballads not in quatrain form, TR 85, "Brennan on the Moor," consists of eight-line stanzas to accommodate the musical stanza. Each half of the musical stanza is a quatrain in common meter with the rhyming scheme *a a b b* rather than *a b c b*. The stress pattern in the chorus is 4 4 4 3. The only other exception, TR 84, "The Lowland Sea," is a couplet to which a two-line refrain has been added to make it a quatrain. It is the first two lines of the couplet which rhyme.

Many of the quatrains are extended by the repetition of their last line or last two lines. In TR 76-78 two syllables are added to the fourth line of the quatrain to accommodate the melodic stanza. These involve the repetition, in some form, of the last syllable of the fourth line. This syllable or word may be preceded by "oh," it may be repeated, or some other combination may be employed. In TR 79, "Fair Ellender," and TR 83, "The House Carpenter," the last two lines of the quatrain are repeated.

Incremental repetition is very common in the British ballad. It can be found in most of the ballads in this chapter. TR 86, "The Hangman Song," is composed almost entirely of incremental repetition. The only change in each set of three stanzas is the name of the relative mentioned or the substitution of "my lover."

Another common form of repetition in the British ballads is what is termed a "commonplace." In some cases these are short phrases such as "lily-white hand," "milk-white steed," or "She dressed herself in scarlet red." They appear in ballad after ballad. Entire stanzas or sets of stanzas may also be commonplaces. The motif concerning the rose and the brier found at the end of the three variants of "Barb'ry Allan" (TR 80-82) is much too expressive a device to be restricted to use in only one ballad. It is employed in "Fair Margaret and Sweet William" (Child 74) and "Lord Lovell" (Child 75), among others.

I have stressed the fact that the folksinger is not consistent in repeating any part of a ballad poem. In TR 85, "Brennan on the Moor," the chorus is sung only after the first and last stanzas. Customarily, it is sung after each stanza of a song. In TR 79, "Fair Ellender," the singer repeats the last two lines of every quatrain but the last. In TR 83, "The House Carpenter," several of the repetitions of the last two lines are not exact but contain new material. In the repetition of the last lines of the stanzas of TR 76, "Six Kings' Daughters," a number of small variations are found.

Some of these variations are, of course, purely accidental. Others are traditional or are due to conscious or unconscious aesthetic responses on the part of the singers to the material being sung. However, since all but one of the singers represented is deceased at this writing (1988), there is no way of validating this assumption. What I can say is that when I have worked with informants in the past they have found it very difficult, indeed, to articulate their reasons for modifying what is usually repeated exactly.

CHAPTER 7   THE TRAGIC TRADITION: THE AMERICAN BALLAD

In the following ballad, as in "Barb'ry Allan," two young people die because they cannot consummate their love.

TR 88 The Golden Dagger

(Laws AM G 21, The Silver Dagger)

Sung by Nellie Rebecca Butler Wever (Weaver), Bloomington, 3 April 1938.

1. Come all young maids and lend attention
   To these few lines I'm going to write.
   'T is of a youth whom I will mention,
   He courted her to be his bride.

2. This maid being young and for want of information,
   Not knowing what she ought to do,
   She rambled forth; she left her station
   Down by a lonesome grove to view.

3. She rambled along by the side of a river
   And sat down by the roots of a tree,
   Saying, "Shall I, shall I, shall I ever,
   Evermore my true love to see?"

4. She picked up a golden dagger
   And pierced it through her snow-white breast.
   These words she spoke although she staggered,
   "Farewell, vain world, I'm going to rest."

5. Her love being near in a lonely thicket
   And hearing of her dismal groan,
   He sprang out like one distracted,
   Crying, "Oh, vain world, I'm left alone."

6. She opened her eyes and gazed upon him.
   Saying, "Oh, my dear, you are come too late.
   Prepare to meet me on Mount Zion
   Where all our joys will be complete."

7. He picked up the bloody weapon;
   He pierced it through his troubled heart,
   Saying, "Warning take from this young couple,
   'T is hard to see two lovers part."

Mrs. Wever had come to Indiana some fifty to sixty years earlier as a child and apparently had learned the song from her mother. She performed from a handwritten copy of the song and said that she played the piano and could write music. Considering the metrical irregularity of the performance, these skills were not very highly developed.

The situation portrayed in the ballad is reminiscent of that found in Shakespeare's *Romeo and Juliet*. However, no motivation for the double suicide is offered. It can be found in other Indiana variants, as for example:

But when his parents came to know it,
They strove to part them both night and day,

To part him from his own dear darling;
"'Tis true she is poor," they oft would say.[1]

The motivation is the same as in "Fair Eleanor," or "Fair Ellender" (TR 78-79). Although in the American version there are no longer lords and ladies, the lack of wealth seems to be as potent a factor in dividing lovers as it was earlier in British ballads.

The English ballads from the late sixteenth through the early nineteenth centuries were characterized by a straightforward and impersonal unfolding of the narrative in which no personal sentiment was expressed by the teller. From 1830 through the remainder of the nineteenth century, the Victorian period, ballads became less impersonal, with the singer often expressing his or her own sentiments. Note the use of the first person singular by the narrator in the following commonplace introduction to the above ballad:

Come all young maids and lend attention
To these few lines I'm going to write.

Commentary or moralizing now often appears at the end of ballads:

Saying, "Warning take from this young couple,
'T is hard to see two lovers part."

TR 89 Florella

(Law AM F 1, The Jealous Lover)

Sung by Samuel Clay Dixon, Mount Vernon, 10 April 1938.

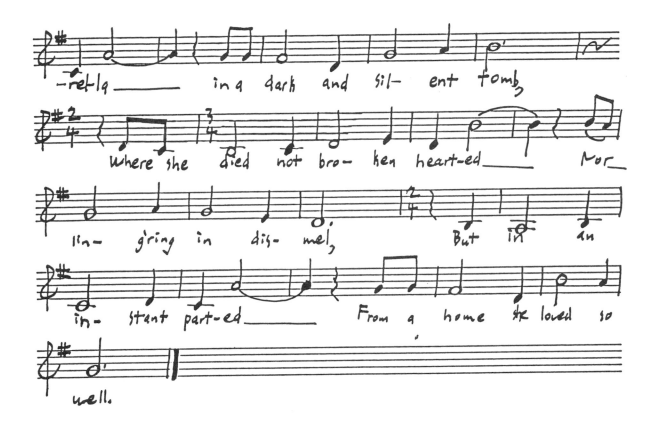

-rel-la_____ in a dark and sil- ent tomb, where she died not bro- ken heart-ed_____ Nor_____ lin- g'ring in dis- mel, But in an in- stant part-ed_____ From a home she loved so well.

1. She came into the meadow where the flowers fade and
      bloom.
   There lies our own Florella in a dark and silent tomb,
   Where she died not brokenhearted nor ling'ring in
      dismel,
   But in an instant parted from a home she loved so well.

2. One night the moon shone brightly, and the stars were
      shining too,
   When to her cottage window her dearest lover drew.
   "Come, Florella, let us ramble the meadows deep and
      gray;
   There's no disturb can ponder, we'll name our wedding
      day."

3. Deep, deep into the meadow he drew his love so near.
   He [sic] said, "It's for you only that I would wander
      here
   These woods seems all so lonely that is afraid to stay,
   Of rambling I grow weary and would retrace our way."

4. "Retrace your way, no never, those woods you'll roam no
      more.
   Long, long they'll wait your coming to the little
      cottage door.
   Down in those woods I have you, from me you cannot fly.
   No human arm can save you. Florella, you must die."

311

5. "What have I done, dear Edward, what you should take my
      life?
   You know I always loved you and would have been your
      wife."
   Down on her knees before him she pleaded for her life.
   Into her snowy bosom he plunged his fatal knife.

6. "Farewell, dear loving parents; you'll never see me
      more.
   Long, long you'll wait my coming to the little cottage
      door.
   But I'll forgive you, Edward, my last and dying
      breath."
   Her heart had ceased its beating; her eyes were closed
      in death.

7. The birds sang in the morning but doleful was the
      sound.
   They found Florella lifeless a-lying on the ground.
   She died not brokenhearted nor ling'ring in dismel,
   Nor in [an instant parted from a home she loved
      so well.]

The text of this ballad contains a number of mispronunciations or corruptions. The third

lines of the first and last stanzas read:

   [Where] she died not broken-hearted nor ling'ring in
      dismel.

This seems to be a corruption of the first and second lines of the second stanza of a mixed version of

"Florella" and "Pearl Bryan," which is given later (p. 351) and reads:

   She died not broken-hearted,
   Nor lingering ill befell,[2]

The fourth line of the second stanza reads:

   There's no disturb can ponder we'll name our wedding
      day.

A couplet from another Indiana variant makes more sense:

   Where we will sit and ponder
   Upon our wedding day.[3]

312

Line 2 of the third stanza should obviously begin, "She said," rather than "He said," and in the next line it should be "that I'm afraid to stay," rather than "is afraid to stay."

Again, no motivation is offered, no explanation is given as to why the lover felt deceived. The same is true for other Indiana variants of this ballad published by Paul Brewster,[4] or in George Malcolm Laws's outline of the ballad story.[5]

TR 90 The Jealous Lover

(Laws AM F 1)

Sung by Roxie South King, Bloomington, 14 April 1960.

1. One eve when the moon shone brightly
There fell a gentle dew,
As to a lonely cottage
A jealous lover drew.

2. Said he to fair young Ellen,
"way down by the sparkling way
we'll wait and watch and wander
Until our wedding day."

313

1. One eve when the moon shone brightly
   There fell a gentle dew,
   As to a lonely cottage
   A jealous lover drew.

2. Said he to fair young Ellen,
   "Way down by the sparkling way
   We'll wait and watch and wander
   Until our wedding day."

3. "Oh, Edward, I am tired
   And I care not far to roam,
   For roaming is so lonely.
   Pray, Edward, take me home."

4. He sighed not when he pressed her
   To his young but cruel heart,
   But she did sigh when he caressed her
   For she knew they soon would part.

5. She knelt down there before him
   And begged him to spare her life.
   But in her fair, young bosom
   He plunged the dagger's knife.

6. "Oh, Edward, I'll forgive you;
   This being my dying breath.
   I never was deceivick
   So I close my eyes in death."

7. Way down in yonder scallick,
   Where the snow white daisies bloom,
   Sleeps the fair young maiden,
   All silent in the tomb.

8. We know not how she suffered;
   We know not what she moaned.
   But we know these words were spoken:
   "Pray, Edward, take me home."

Again there are words which are either mispronunciations, dialect terms, or corruptions. Thus in line 3 of stanza 6 I hear "deceivick" and in line 1 of stanza 7, "scallick." I assume these are corruptions of "deceiver" and "valley."

The variant sung by Mr. Dixon is more developed than that sung by Mrs. King since it has a reprise of the same material at the end. However, in the variant sung by Mrs. King the jealousy of the lover is made more apparent, and there is an effective last stanza. Note that this last stanza makes

314

use of the first person plural, thus not only the narrator, but also the audience, participates in the sentiment expressed. Nevertheless, Mrs. King's variant offers no more information concerning the motivation of the murderer than that of Mr. Dixon. This situation is apparently quite common in murder ballads. In an international congress devoted to the question of developing a type-index for European folk ballads, which was held at the Deutcher Volksliederarchiv in Freiburg in September 1966, an outline of typology was adopted which included the category of "Unmotivated Human Brutality."[6] "Florella" and "The Jealous Lover" certainly fall within this category.

American ballads, like the British, often have their poetic origin in printed sources. The following, which has a rather complex literary history, is based upon a poem printed in a magazine, rather than one found in a broadside, songster, or chapbook.

TR 91 Young Charlotte

(Laws AM G 17)

Sung by Kathleen Bryant, Evansville, 8 or 9 April 1938.

315

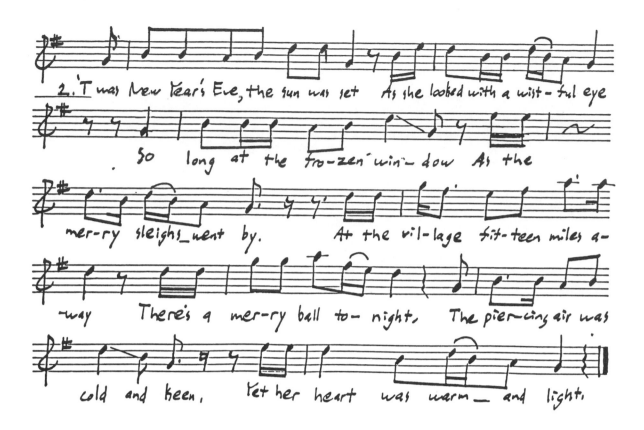

1. Young Charlotte lived on a mountain side
   In a quiet and lonely spot.
   No dwelling is for three miles round
   Except her father's cot.
   Her father loved to see her dressed
   As gay as a city belle,
   For she was all the child he had;
   He loved his daughter well.

2. 'T was New Year's Eve, the sun was set
   As she looked with a wistful eye
   So long at the frozen window
   As the merry sleigh went by.
   At the village fifteen miles away
   There's a merry ball tonight.
   The piercing air was cold and keen,
   Yet her heart was warm and light.

3. How gaily beamed her sparkling eyes
   As a well-known sound she hears,
   When darting up to her father's house
   Young Charles's sleigh appears.
   "My daughter, dear," her mother says,
   "This blanket around you fold,
   For it is a dreadful night abroad.
   You may take a fatal cold."

316

4. "Oh, no, dear mother," Charlotte said,
   As she laughed like a gypsy queen,
   "To ride in a blanket muffled up
   I never can be seen.
   My silken shawl is quite enough,
   You know it's lined throughout.
   Besides I have a silken scarf
   To tie my neck about."

5. Her bonnet and her gloves were on
   As she stepped into the sleigh.
   And off they ride o'er the mountain side
   And o'er the hills away.
   For five dark and lonesome miles
   In silence they passed o'er,
   Till Charlotte in a frozen word
   This silence broke no more.

6. "It's such a night I never seen,
   The reins I scarce can hold."
   And Charlotte replied in a feeble voice,
   "I am extremely cold."
   He cracked his whip and urged his steed
   Much faster than before.
   Till five more dark and lonesome miles
   In silence they passed o'er.

7. He says, "How fast the glittering ice
   Is gathering on my brow."
   And Charlotte replied in a feeble voice,
   "I'm growing warmer now."
   Then on they ride on the mountain side
   As the stars shine on them bright.
   At length they reach the village
   And the ballroom it is in sight.

8. They stopped then and he stepped out
   And offered his hand to her.
   "Why sit you there like a monument
   That has no power to stir?"
   He called her once and he called her twice
   But yet she never stirred.
   He called for her once again
   Yet she answered not a word.

9. He raised the veil from o'er her face
   And the cold stars on her shone.
   He took her hand into his own
   Poor girl's, 'twas cold as stone.
   Then quickly to the lighted hall
   Her lifeless form he bore.
   For Charlotte was a frozen girl
   And there to speak no more.

10. Now ladies think of this fair girl
    And always dress up right
    And never venture thinly-clad
    On a cold and dreary night.

TR 92 Young Charlotte

Sung by Vern Smelser with guitar, Paoli, 16 February 1964.

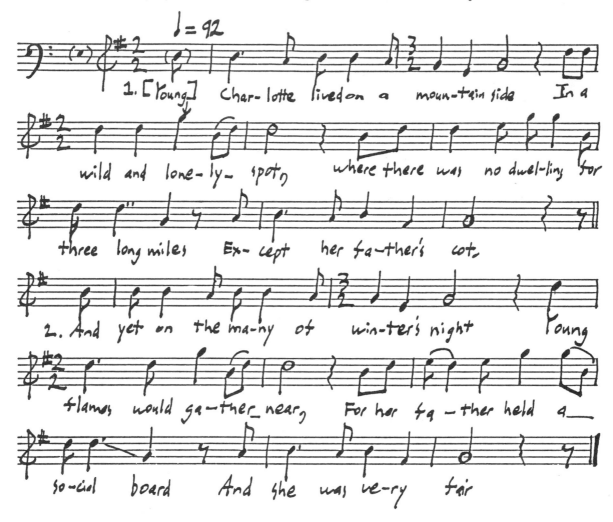

1. [Young] Charlotte lived on a mountain side
   In a wild and lonely spot,
   Where there was no dwelling for three long miles
   Except her father's cot.

2. And yet on the many of winter's night
   Young flames would gather near,
   For her father held a social board
   And she was very fair.

3. One New Year's Eve as the sun went down,

Far looked her questioned eyes
From out the frosty-a window pane
As the merry sleighs dashed by.

4. At the village fifteen miles away
Was to be a ball that night.
Though the air was very piercing cold,
Her heart was warm and light.

5. How lightly beamed her laughing eyes
As a well-known voice she heard,
When dashing up to the cottage door,
Her lover's sleigh appeared.

6. "Oh, daughter dear," her mother cried,
"A blanket around you fold,
For 't is a dreadful night abroad
And you'll take your death of cold."

7. "Oh, nay, oh, nay," young Charlotte cried,
And she laughed like a gypsy queen.
"To ride in blankets a-muffled round
I never could be seen."

8. Her bonnet and her gloves were on,
She sprang into the sleigh;
And down they sped o'er the mountain side
And o'er the hills away.

9. How muffled being so silently
Five miles at length were passed,
When Charles with few and shiv'ring words
The silence broke at last.

10. "Such a dreadful night I never saw:
My reins I scarce can hold."
And Charlotte then faintly replied,
"I am exceedingly cold."

11. He cracked his whip and he urged his steed
Much faster than before,
Until five more weary miles
In silence has passed o'er.

12. Quoth Charles, "How fast this freezing night
Is a-gathering on my brow."
Charlotte still more faintly said,
"I'm getting warmer now."

13. Thus on they rode through the frosty air,
Through the glittering cold starlight.
Until at last the village lamp
And a ballroom came in sight.

319

14. They reached the door and Charles sprang out;
    He held his hand to her.
    "Why sit you there like a monument
    That hath no power to stir?"

15. He called her oncet and he called her twice;
    She answered not a word.
    He asked her for her hand again,
    But still she never stirred.

16. He took her hand in his: 't was cold!
    And as hard as any stone.
    He tore the mantle from her face
    And the cold stars o'er it shone.

17. There he sat down by her side
    And the bitter tears did flow.
    He cried, "My own and charming bride
    You never more shall know."

18. He twined his arms around her neck;
    He kissed her marble brow.
    And his thoughts flew back to where she said,
    "I'm getting warmer now."

19. Quickly to the lighted hall
    Her lifeless form he bore.
    Young Charlotte's eyes had closed for aye
    And her voice was heard no more.

20. They put the corpse into the sleigh
    And with it started home.
    And when they reached the cottage door
    Oh, how her parents mourned!

21. They mourned the loss of their daughter dear;
    Young Charles wept o'er the tomb.
    In after years he died of grief
    And they both lie in one tomb.

In Indiana this ballad is also known as "Fair Charlotte," "Charlotte," "Charlotta," and "The Frozen Girl."[7]

Note the warning given in Kathleen Bryant's last half-stanza. It was not uncommon in the nineteenth century for the endings of traditional English ballads to be modified so that such sage counsel could be offered. In a variant of "Barbara Allan," Phoebe Elliott omits the traditional stanzas concerning the rose and the brier and substitutes the following:

"Farewell," she said, "ye virgins all;
And shun the fault I fell in.
Henceforth take warning of the fall
Of cruel Barbara Allen."[8]

"Young Charlotte" is a very widely distributed ballad. Variants have been collected from California to Maine. Phillips Barry, who was much interested in determining its origin, wrote three articles concerning this. He had initially accepted the common belief that it had been composed by a Mormon, William Lorenzo Carter, in 1833 and was spread by him in his travel across the country to Utah.[9] Mabel Evangeline Neal mentions another tradition in which the "girl was Charlotte Dills of Auburn, Indiana, who was frozen to death in 1862. She had two brothers who were lawyers and another who was a minister." However, Neal believes that this tradition merely represents the localization of the ballad.[10] Change of locale often occurs when ballads are diffused from place to place.

Later Phillips Barry discovered that the poem had been written by Seba Smith (1779-1868), author of "The Snowstorm" and "The Little Graves," often reprinted in school readers.[11]

The poem, under the title "A Corpse Going to a Ball," was published in *The Rover* on 28 December 1843, the front page of which I reproduce here. *The Rover*, a weekly literary magazine containing poems, tales, and engravings, was edited by Seba Smith and Lawrence Labree. John Greenleaf Whittier was an early contributor, and the magazine later published fiction by authors such as Victor Hugo and Washington Irving. In 1845 the periodical's name was changed to the *New York Illustrated Magazine*.

The incident upon which the ballad is based was apparently known to the author only through a story which appeared in the *New-York Observer* on 8 February 1840, which is also reproduced here. The *Observer* was an orthodox Presbyterian weekly begun in 1823 by Sidney E. and Richard Morse, brothers of Samuel Morse, inventor of the Morse code. The newspaper's main focus was religious topics representing the conservative element of the Presbyterian Church.

Most of the details of the ballad were derived from this newspaper story. The poem follows this story quite closely. Other details, including the name, Charlotte, were taken from a chapter entitled "Death at the Toilet" from a book, *Passages from the Diary of a Late Physician*, by Samuel

321

THE ROVER.

REBECCA AND DE BOIS GUILBERT.

The engraving which we had hoped to use in the present number not being ready, we have substituted one illustrating that remarkable and thrilling scene in "Ivanhoe," one of Scott's best novels, where the high souled Rebecca, in defence of her honor and her religion, prepares to throw herself from the battlements of the castle, and the proud and fierce Templar is abashed and subdued by the exhibition of her sublime moral courage. To those who have read Ivanhoe, any description we could give of the scene must be tame and lifeless, and those who have not, should look nowhere else for the description but in the inimitable work itself, as it came from the master hand of Scott.

A CORPSE GOING TO A BALL.
BY SEBA SMITH.

The incident, from which the following ballad is woven, was given in the papers three or four years ago as *a fact*. It was stated, that a young lady in the country, while riding some distance to a ball on New Year's evening, actually froze to death.

Young Charlotte lived by the mountain side,
    A wild and lonely spot;
No dwelling there, for three miles round,
    Except her father's cot;

And yet on many a winter's eve
    Young swains were gather'd there,
For her father kept a social board,
    And she was very fair.

Her father loved to see her dress'd
    As prim as a city belle,
For she was all the child he had,
    And he loved his daughter well.

'Tis New Year's eve—the sun is down—
    Why looks her restless eye
So long from the frosty window forth,
    As the merry sleighs go by?

At the village inn, fifteen miles off,
    Is a merry ball to-night—
The piercing air is cold as death,
    But her heart is warm and light;

And brightly beams her laughing eye,
    As a well-known voice she hears;
And dashing up to the cottage door
    Her Charley's sleigh appears.

"Now daughter dear," her mother cried,
    "This blanket round you fold,
"For 'tis a dreadful night abroad,
    "You'll catch your death a-cold."

"O nay, O nay," fair Charlotte said,
    And she laugh'd like a gipsy queen,
"To ride with blankets muffled up
    "I never could be seen—

"My silken cloak is quite enough;
    "You know 'tis lined throughout;
"And then I have a silken shawl
    "To tie my neck about."

Her bonnet and her gloves are on,
    She jumps into the sleigh;
And swift they ride by the mountain side,
    And over the hills away.

There's life in the sound of the merry bells,
    As over the hills they go;
But a creaking wail the runners make,
    As they bite the frozen snow.

How long the bleak and lonely way!
    How keen the wind does blow!
The stars did never shine so cold—
    How creaks the frozen snow!

With muffled faces, silently,
    Five cold, long miles they've pass'd,
And Charles, with these few frozen words,
    The silence broke at last—

"Such night as this I never saw—
    "The reins I scarce can hold;"
And Charlotte, shivering, faintly said,
    "I am exceeding cold."

He crack'd his whip, and urged his steed
    More swiftly than before,
And now five other dreary miles
    In silence are pass'd o'er—

"How fast," said Charles the freezing ice
    "Is gathering on my brow;"
But Charlotte said, with feebler tone,
    "I'm growing warmer now."

And on they went through the frosty air
    And the glittering, cold star-light;
And now at last the village inn
    And the ball-room are in sight.

They reach the door, and Charles jumps out,
    And holds his hand to her—
Why sits she like a monument,
    That hath no power to stir?

He call'd her once—he call'd her twice—
    She answer'd not a word;
He ask'd her for her hand again,
    But still she never stirr'd—

He took her hand in his—O God!
    'Twas cold and hard as stone;
He tore the mantle from her face,
    The cold stars on her shone—

Then quickly to the lighted hall
    Her voiceless form he bore—
His Charlotte was a stiffen'd corse,
    And word spake never more!

"NEW YEAR'S VISITING IN HADES."
BY C. F. HOFFMAN.

"When we seem particularly dull, the reader may rest assured there is always some deep meaning under it."
                                    BRITISH ESSAYIST.

"Happy new year to you! Paris, my dear fellow, where do you call next?" cried the dashing Castor, reigning up his three-minute trotter in passing the handsome Trojan.

"Why, I've just begun on my list," replied the dandy rival of Menelaus, "it's not a long one however. Society in Hades is becoming so mixed, that one really must be particular; and I visit only the old standbys."

The Rover, *28 December 1843*

NEW-YORK OBSERVER.

NEW-YORK, SATURDAY, FEBRUARY 8, 1840.   SIDNEY E. MORSE & CO. EDITORS AND PROPRIETORS.   VOLUME XVIII. NUMBER 6.—WHOLE NO. 615.

RELIGIOUS.

For the New York Observer.

A CORPSE GOING TO A BALL.

Those who read the thrilling "passages from the diary of a London Physician," that were published a few years since, will remember one tale under the title of "Death at the Toilet." Although it was asserted by the writer that those narratives were the records of facts, few, I presume, were willing to believe that real life could furnish matter of such romantic interest. Especially did the one alluded to strike my own mind as quite unnatural, and I read it, as others, admiring the genius more than the veracity of the writer.

Perhaps some who have seen the words at the head of this article may imagine that they are about to be treated to a passage from the dreams of fancy; but they are mistaken. I have a sad and solemn tale of truth to relate, and when it has been read, there will be no hesitation in believing that "truth is stranger than fiction." No colouring shall be laid on the story; no art of embellishment shall heighten its interest; it shall be told to others as it was told to me, and you shall be convinced that there is nothing more than *truth* in the story of a corpse that went to a ball.

You recollect the first day of January, 1840. It was a bitter cold day. It was cold as far south as the city of New-York, and up here in the country, where I am writing, it was terribly severe. You could not ride far against the wind without being exposed to freezing. I have heard of two cases of death by cold on that day in this region, and of another case in which the sufferer was saved by great exertion, when at the point of perishing.

The night of that day was to be observed, as is usual here, by a New Year's ball. Invitations had been extended for many miles around, and a great gathering of the young, and gay, and thoughtless, was expected. Extensive preparations had been made for an evening of merriment and glee, and merry hearts beat quickly in anticipation of the pleasures of the scene. None was happier in the thought of coming joy than Miss ——, who took her seat in the sleigh, by the side of her partner for the evening, and set out for a ride of some twenty miles, to join the dance. She was young and gay, and her charms of youth and beauty never were lovelier than when too thinly clad for the season, and especially for that dreadful day, she had not gone far before she complained of being cold, very cold; but their anxiety to reach the end of their ride in time to be present at the opening of the dance, induced them to hurry onwards without stopping by the way. Not long after this complaining she said that she felt perfectly comfortable, was now quite warm, and that there was no necessity of delay on her account. They reached, at length, the house where the company were gathering; the young man leaped from the sleigh, and extended his hand to assist her out, but she did not offer hers; he spoke to her, but she answered not; a corpse on the way to a ball.

Is this last statement doubted? I remember reading of a ball in New Hampshire, a few years since, at which four young men retired to play cards, and while at their game, one of the number fell in a fit and expired. The rest rolled his body under the table, and covered it up with cloaks, and said nothing about it till the ball was over.

In the village in which I lived for many years there was a ball but a few steps from my house, and one of the young ladies who was to be there died suddenly on the very day of the ball. It was proposed by one of the managers to postpone the dance, but the others would not consent, and on it went, although the corpse lay in a house directly in front of the ball-room, and the dim light could be seen by every dancer, and the sound of the music and dancing disturbed the melancholy watchers. I have no comments to make.   W

But the most shocking part of the tale is yet to be told; THE BALL WENT ON!!! The dance was as merry, and the music as sweet, as if one of the invited guests had not been called into eternity.

"A Corpse Going to a Ball"

New York Observer, 8 February 1840

Warren, published in Paris in 1838. The chapters which made up the two volumes had appeared initially in *Blackwood's Magazine*.

"Death at the Toilet" concerns an unmarried woman of twenty-six, who insists on gadding about although warned by her physician that she suffers from both liver and heart disease. She dies from the latter while preparing herself in her room to attend a ball. When the physician arrives, he finds Charlotte dead at her dressing table and discovers that:

> various articles of the toilet lay scattered about--pins, brooches, curling-papers, ribands, gloves, etc. . . . Her face was turned toward the glass, which, by the light of the expiring candle, reflected with frightful fidelity the clammy fixed features, daubed over with rouge and carmine. . . . On examining the countenance more narrowly, I thought I detected the traces of a smirk of conceit and self-complacency which not even the palsying touch of Death could wholly obliterate. . . . Poor creature! struck dead in the very act of sacrificing at the shrine of female vanity! . . . . I have seen many hundreds of corpses, as well in the calm composure of natural death, as mangled and distorted by violence; but never have I seen so startling a satire on humanity . . . as a *corpse dressed for a ball!*[12]

Note the similarity between the title, "A Corpse Going to a Ball," and the phrase, "a corpse dressed for a ball."

Barry cites this ballad as conclusive proof that the re-creative efforts of folk poets include the composition of additional stanzas for a ballad in tradition.[13] He refers back to the last two stanzas of a variant of "Young Charlotte" from Maine, which he had published earlier:

323

11. He threw himself down on his knees and the bitter tears
    did flow,
    Saying, "My young and intended bride, no more with me
    you'll go!"
    He threw himself down by her side, and he kissed her
    marble brow,
    And his thoughts ran back to the place she says, "I'm
    growing warmer now."

12. They bore her out into the sleigh, and Charles with her
    rode home.
    And when they reached her cottage door, oh, how her
    parents mourned!
    They mourned the loss of their daughter dear, and
    Charles mourned o'er his bride,
    Until at length his heart did break and they slumber
    side by side.[14]

The two stanzas added to TR 92 above are quite similar and corroborate his conclusion. They incorporate the nineteenth-century emphasis on the mourning of the parents and the earlier theme of dying for love and being buried with or adjacent to the beloved.

Many American ballads relate the story of actual disasters, such as the Johnstown flood, the Santa Barbara earthquake, the Avondale mine catastrophe, the sinking of the *Titanic*, the wreck of the old 97, and other assorted accidents and acts of nature, with the emphasis upon those which took many lives. These songs were widely diffused and sung in areas quite distant from the locales where the actual disasters occurred. The following ballad is based upon a fire which consumed the Conway Theater in Brooklyn, New York, on 5 December 1876, in which 295 lives were lost. Variants of this ballad have been sung in areas as distant from Brooklyn as Wisconsin and New Mexico.[15]

TR 93 The Brooklyn Theater Fire

(Laws AM G 27)

Sung by Viola Dodson, Bloomington, 3 April 1938.

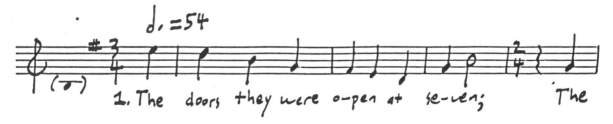

324

cur-tains rolled up at eight, And those who had

seats they were hap-py; Out- side they were mad who were

late. The per- for-mance went on very smooth-ly

Till sparks from the scen'ry did fly. Twas

then that men, wo-men, and chil-dren, "Oh, God, save our

live!" they did cry. 2. But we ne'er shall for-get those Two

Orphans; Bad luck seems to lie in its wake. It

seems that it was sent to our ci-ty The lives of our

dear ones to take. Far out in the ceme-te-ry of

Green-wood, where the winds__ make the wild wil-lows

sigh, 'Twas there__ the fu-ne-ral is go-ing,

The poor, un-known dead there to lie.

1. The doors they were open at seven; the curtains rolled
      up at eight.
   And those who had seats they were happy; outside they
      were mad who were late.
   The performance went on very smoothly till sparks from
      the scen'ry did fly.
   'Twas then that men, women, and children, "Oh, God,
      save our lives!" they did cry.

2. But we ne'er shall forget those *Two Orphans*; bad luck
      seems to lie in its wake.
   It seems that it was sent to our city the lives of
      our dear ones to take.
   Far out in the cemetery of Greenwood, where the winds
      make the wild willows sigh,
   'Twas there the funeral is going, the poor unknown
      dead there to lie.

Mrs. Dodson was quite old at the time she recorded this song and had learned it fifty years earlier from schoolgirls she had taught in Rummersfield, Bradford County, Pennsylvania. She sang from a written copy. A fuller version collected in Missouri is given below:

1. The evening bright stars they were shining,
   The moonbeams shone clear o'er our land,
   The city was quiet and peaceful,
   The hour of midnight close at hand.
   But hark, hear the loud cry of Fire,
   How dismal the fire bells sound,
   The Brooklyn Theater is burning,
   Alas, burning fast to the ground.

CHORUS:
   Who then can forget the *Two Orphans*?
   Bad luck seems to follow in its wake,
   Seems as if they were sent to our city
   The lives of our dear ones to take.

2. The doors they were open at seven,
   The curtains were rolled up at eight,
   And those that had seats they was happy,
   And mad were the crowd that were late.
   The play it went on very quietly,
   Till sparks from the scenery did fly,

326

'Twas then that men, women and children
Oh God save our lives, they did cry.

CHORUS

3. Next morn all among the black ruins
    Oh God, what a sight met our eyes!
    The dead they was lying in all shapes,
    There was some that none could recognize.
    Poor mothers was weeping and crying
    For sons that were out all that night,
    Oh God, let their souls rest in heaven
    Along with the pure and the bright!

CHORUS

4. What means such a gathering of people
    Upon such a cold stormy day?
    What means such a long line of hearses
    With tips plumed in feathery array?
    They're bound for the graveyard at Greenwood,
    Where the willow boughs bend with the breeze,
    'Tis there where the funerals is going,
    Their dear unknown dead for to leave.

CHORUS[16]

Mrs. Dodson's first stanza is similar to the second stanza of the Missouri variant, and her second stanza comprises the latter's chorus and the last part of the fourth stanza. This is reflected in the melodic material of the performance, that found at the beginning of the second stanza being quite different from that found at the beginning of the first, as would be the case were she singing a chorus.

The play being shown was *The Two Orphans*, a production popular at the time. It had been written in 1874 by a minor English playwright, J. Oxenford, who wrote nearly fifty plays during the second half of the century. Most of the plays produced at this time were pirated from English sources since the United States did not recognize international copyright until 1891, nearly seventy years after it had been established.

The actual cause of the Conway Theater fire was never determined. During this period theaters and homes were lit by gas lights. In theaters the footlights and border lights, the latter being vertical strips placed just back of the proscenium, were formed of what were called "gas tables." These

The New-York Times.

VOL. XXVI.....NO. 7873.

NEW-YORK, THURSDAY, DECEMBER 7, 1876.—WITH SUPPLEMENT.

THE BROOKLYN CALAMITY

The Extent of the Disaster Underestimated.

Two Hundred and Eighty-three Bodies Recovered.

Over Three Hundred and Fifty Lives Probably Lost.

The Accounts Given by those who Escaped.

TWO ACTORS AMONG THE VICTIMS.

Widespread Grief in the City of Churches.

Scenes and Incidents at the Ruins of the Theatre.

Early yesterday morning the people of Brooklyn realized the fact that the destruction of the Brooklyn Theatre by fire on Tuesday night had involved a considerable loss of life. Up to 6 o'clock the general public understood that the loss of life, if any, had been very small, but soon the rumor reached the public ear that the dead bodies of fifty persons had been exhumed by the firemen. When the "extras" announced this fact, the wildest excitement was created, both in Brooklyn and this City, and hopes were expressed that the worst was known. Men, women, and children went rushing to the site of the ruined theatre and to the Morgue in eager search for missing friends. The city put on an air of mourning, and ... one hundred bodies had been taken from the ruins, the excitement grew more intense, and sympathy for the friends and relatives of the victims was generally expressed.

Again came the news that 150 bodies had been recovered, and soon that number was increased to 190. Never before in the history of Brooklyn was public feeling so much aroused. The City Fathers met promptly to express the feeling of the people on the great calamity which had deprived Brooklyn of so many of its citizens. As many of the victims are working men, steps have been taken to extend relief ...

GROUND PLAN OF THE THEATRE.

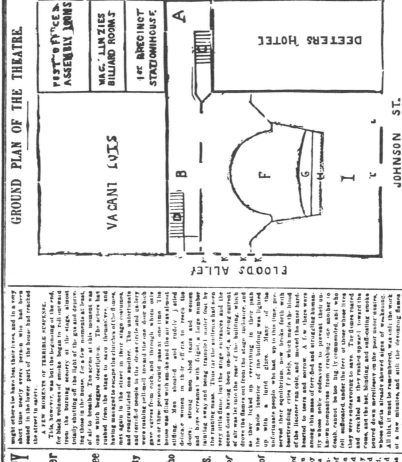

WASHINGTON ST.

POST OFFICE & ASSEMBLY ROOMS

MAG...LINZIES BILLIARD ROOMS

1st PRECINCT STATIONHOUSE

VACANT LOTS

DEETERS HOTEL

FLOODS ALLEY

JOHNSON ST.

A.—Washington-street entrance, twenty feet wide.
B.—Lobby, sixteen feet wide.
C.—Stairs to family circle, seven feet wide.
D.—Stairs to dress circle, eight feet wide.
E.—Stairs from lobby to dress circle, eight feet wide.
F.—Orchestra chairs, 250.
G.—Orchestra.
H.—Curtain.
I.—Stage.
K.—Doors opening into Flood's alley.
L.—Stage doors opening into Johnson street.

A.—Dress circle, 450 seats.
B.—Lobby, sixteen feet wide.
C.—Stairs to family circle, seven feet wide.
D.—Stairs from lobby to dress circle, eight feet wide.
E.—Stairs to Washington street entrance, seven feet wide.
F.—Orchestra.
H.—Curtain.
I.—Stage.

A FEW MOMENTS OF TERRIBLE SUSPENSE.

This, however, was but the beginning of the end, for black volumes of smoke began to roll outward from the burning scenery of the stage, almost totally shutting off the light of the gas and depriving those in the house, for a few moments at least, of air to breathe. The scene at this moment was one which beggars description. The actors had rushed from the stage to save themselves, and having managed to escape the clutches of the flames, met again in the street in their stage costumes, and congratulated one another. The unfortunate and terrified people in the dress circle and gallery were rushing pell-mell toward the one door which gave egress from each, and through which only two or three persons could pass at one time. The house was filled with smoke and the air was almost stifling. Men shouted and rudely jostled delicate women in their efforts to reach the doors; strong men shed tears and women were being trampled under foot ...

THE FIRE DEPARTMENT ON THE GROUND.

The Police of the First Precinct, under the command of Sergts. Eason and Cain, were on the ground within three minutes after the breaking out of the fire, and did very effective work in quieting the fears of the populace. To much praise cannot be bestowed on these two officers. These gallant men, devoting themselves to their arduous duties ...

had been almost completely consumed before the fire could be stopped, leaving a mass of fine charcoal, which emitted occasional volumes of smoke mingled with steam. The large gas-pipe through which all the gas used in the building was received, and which had donations been broken by the falling of the roof, was blazing fiercely until late in the ...

were rows of gas jets in boxes of reflecting metal. When lit, they were, of course, open flames.

The fire was first seen creeping along the flies on the left side of the stage, and it was believed that one of the drops was ignited by a border light. The flames spread rapidly to all curtains and drapery. The stage crew was prevented from immediately reaching the fire by the roof of a mimic house which had been erected in center stage as part of the set. The actors on the stage endeavored to keep the audience calm, but there was a rush for the exits and many were trampled to death by others fighting to get out of the theater.

The Greenwood Cemetery mentioned in the ballad was the fashionable burying place for the wealthy of the period. The cemetery was a model of Victorian architecture. It contained many elaborate tombs and was the only cemetery in the country dignified by the work of Sanford White, the outstanding architect of the time.

In 1898 over forty songs were composed concerning the sinking of the *Maine* in Havana Harbor. The song given below is not one of these, but apparently was written later.[17] Many of these songs were still in the oral tradition in the twentieth century, and one was published in a well-known collection in 1950.[18]

TR 94 Did the *Maine* Go Down?

Sung by Virgil Sandage, Uniontown, 12 June 1963.

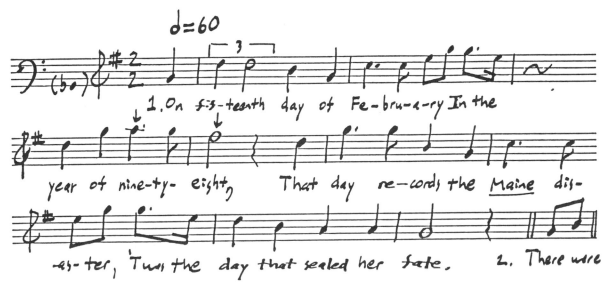

those on board that noble vessel That we ne'er shall see a-gain. Their proud homes are draped in mourning For they went down on the Maine.

1. On fifteenth day of February
   In the year of ninety-eight,
   That day records the *Maine* disaster,
   'T was the day that sealed her fate.

2. There were those on board that noble vessel
   That we ne'er shall see again.
   Their proud homes are draped in mourning
   For they went down on the *Maine*.

3. Did the *Maine* go down? Yes the *Maine* went under
   And her loss was caused by Spain.
   Shall the Spaniards laugh at our misfortune
   And the lives lost on the *Maine*?

4. "I will make this trip," said Captain Sigsbee
   As he started out to sea.
   "But danger's in those Spanish waters,
   Spain has planted it in the sea."

5. "But I'll go wherever my duty calls me;
   With my comrades I'll remain."
   But fortune made him a survivor
   Of the victims of the *Maine*.

6. At ha' past eight when the sea were ruffled
   By a quiet, saucy breeze,
   And all on board were soundly sleeping
   Or were gazing out to sea.

7. When, hark! I hear such shrieks of horror
   They seem to reach heaven's high domain.
   And rifles in those Spanish chambers
   All went down on the *Maine*.

8. Said a brave, young lad to his loving mother,

"I must go on board the *Maine*.
She will take us to Havana Harbor
But we'll soon return again."

9. So he kissed her while sadly weeping,
   For her tears fell down like rain.
   And now she mourns for her lost darling
   For he went down on the *Maine*.

This disaster was the most important incident leading to the outbreak of the Spanish-American War. Two powerful newspapers, the *New York Journal*, owned by William Randolph Hearst, and the *New York World*, owned by Joseph Pulitzer, made use of this incident to promote a war which would increase the circulation of the papers. War with Spain was accomplished by what became known as "yellow journalism," the description of events which were outright fabrications and which were presented to the public in lurid red banner headlines, accompanied by drawings based upon imagination rather than fact.

Of the two publishers, the immensely wealthy Hearst--his father had owned shares in America's richest mining venture, the Comstock Lode, as well as the Homestead and Anaconda mines--was by far the more bellicose. Pulitzer expressed himself privately to the effect that "a small war would be useful to the circulation of the *World*." Hearst, on the other hand, wanted all-out war. When his illustrator, Frederic Remington, could find no atrocities in Cuba, Hearst is reputed to have wired him, "Please remain. You furnish the pictures and I'll furnish the war."

Under pressure from Hearst and Pulitzer--the *Journal* had been printing incendiary reports of rebellion in Cuba, although it had no representative there--the weak William McKinley administration dispatched the battleship *Maine* to protect "American interests," of which there were few. The *Maine* entered Havana Harbor 15 January 1898, was saluted by the guns at Morro Castle--not shot at by them--, and the *Maine* replied with its own salute. Its place of anchorage was designated by the harbor authorities, as was the custom.

On the night of 15 February the *Maine* blew up, and 260 men lost their lives. On 17 February the *Journal* carried a story with the headline, "The Warship Maine Was Split in Two by an Enemy's Secret Infernal Machine!" The paper carried pages of drawings of imaginary portrayals as to how

BRAVE AMERICANS READY TO RESPOND TO THE FIRST CALL TO AR[MS]

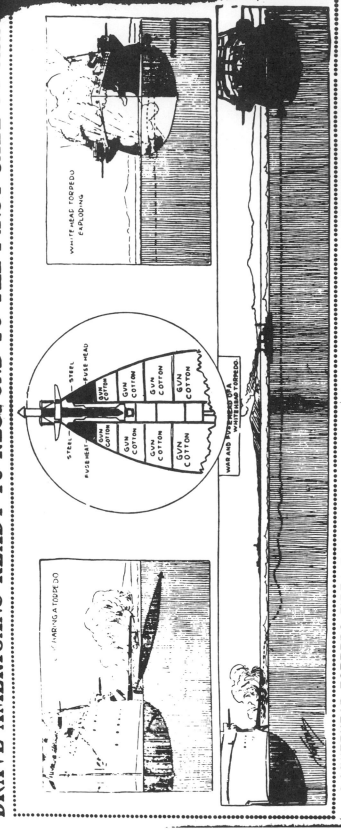

A WHITEHEAD TORPEDO FIRED FROM AN OVERHEAD TORPEDO TUBE, AND ITS PROGRESS UNDER WATER.

THE torpedo is expelled from its tube by means of a small charge of powder. On striking the water the torpedo is propelled with great speed by means of an engine contained in its main body. In the forward portion of the weapon is carried an explosive charge of one hundred and fifty pounds of gun cotton. This mass is exploded by a percussion fuse, fitted into the nozzle of the weapon. The effect of one hundred and fifty pounds of gun cotton exploded at a depth of fifteen feet would be fatal to the strongest ship afloat.

WAR SPIRIT SPREADS RAPIDLY WITH THE BELIEF THAT SPANISH TREACHERY DOOMED THE BATTLE SHIP MAINE.

President W. J. O'Brien, of the Board of Walking Delegates, Declares Organized Labor Is Ready to a Man to Take Up Arms Against Spain--Buffalo, in Mass Meeting, Cries to McKinley for War.

SUGGESTS NATIONAL MOURNING FOR DEAD.

ZALINSKI SAYS IT LOOKS LIKE A MINE.

But the Dynamite Expert Urges Suspension of Judgment, as It Is Not Proven Yet.

Here Is the FIRST ACTUAL PHOTOGRAPH of the Wreck

A Matanzas paper rejoices almost openly and the Spanish merchants of Sagua La Grande drank cases of champagne behind closed doors the day after.

On Havana's streets the Spanish shopkeepers' faces are on the sly grin constantly. The difference from their usual aspect is remarkable and is noted by everybody. This is common talk.

It is now known that the Maine had only swung into the position she occupied at the time of the explosion but once before. Then it was on a bright night. Tuesday night, when the explosion occurred, was dark.

Each succeeding fact is more and more sombre. So far there is not a fragment of proof to indicate that the original explosion was internal or that there was a later explosion of anything in the Maine.

Several insulting circulars have been gotten out. One, published just before the explosion, stated clearly that the Maine should be destroyed. Another, of yesterday, supposedly against autonomy, glories in the sinking of the Maine.

Pen and ink sketches of Pelayo sinking the whole American fleet multiply all over town. The little lighthouse tenders and the Fern are really thought by the lower classes to be the real kind of vessels the United States Navy has.

Politeness to Americans on the pavements and in the theatres is much decreased.

The disavowal of any intention to prejudice is now repeated and complete, and the question should be dropped. In the Cabinet to-day there [is] no one who, in view of the accumulating evidence, does not believe that the men of the Maine met their death at the hand of Spanish treachery, and belief is growing that the verdict of the inquiry will not be an indecisi[ve] one and every effort is being made to prepare to carry out the line of action which will then be inevitable when the people of the country will deman[d] with one voice.

PRESIDENT IN TOUCH WITH PEOPLE.

There should be no hysterical utterances and no frenzied action. I am convinced from what I have seen since reaching Washington that the President is in close touch with the people, and that when the evidence to b[e] produced shall have been passed upon by the cool, calm judgment of th[e] naval board and the common sense and the patriotism of all self-respecting Americans, he will enter upon the course which circumstances and a patriotic sense of duty may then demand, without delay and without hesitation. In the meantime, we should be patient under the necessity for delay.

The assurance that I am able and authorized to give that it has been decided not to lose a single moment more and, that what can be done in this, the eleventh hour, to advance our state of preparedness, is being done night and day, should help to curb the signs of national restiveness which have reached Washington, and this state of public excitation is adding another anxiety to those in authority, at a moment when the outlook is already anxious and full of many uncertainties.

Activity Displayed in All Departments.

While reserving judgment and hoping now almost against hope that th[e] catastrophe to the battle-ship may yet be ascertained to be due to [some] cause, the preparations that are being made in the active departments of the Government to-day are being made without a precedent within the m[emory] ...

STEPHEN BONSAL.

the explosion might have been accomplished. Captain Charles D. Sigsbee of the *Maine*, a fortunate survivor of the catastrophe, considered these diagrams to be proof that there had been a plot and that the *Journal* knew of it. However, exactly what happened has never been determined. Even after the hulk was towed out of the harbor in 1911 and buried with honors at sea, the cause of the explosion could not be determined.

Perhaps because of some accident the magazine of the ship blew up or it may have been mined by the *insurrectos*, although they were unlikely to have had the means of accomplishing this without outside aid. They were a small group without wide support among the population and had never attempted to attack even Spanish installations. Spain has been completely exonerated by history.

A tug was sent to Havana Harbor by the *World* and divers sent down in an attempt to discover what had happened. The *Journal* launched a subscription campaign to build a memorial to the dead sailors. The circulation of both newspapers rose above a million daily.

The two papers, and the *Journal* in particular, continued to work up war sentiment in every way possible, even printing false statements attributed to members of the War Department. Congress appropriated $50 million for "national defense." President McKinley expected complete capitulation from Spain to every American demand and, indeed, the Spanish agreement to these demands had been dispatched, and the administration knew this when war was hastily declared.[19]

At the turn of the century newspapers were the principal means of communication. The song, "Did the *Maine* Go Down?," reflects the attitude of a multitude of American citizens who believed what they read in newspapers merely because it was in print.

The songwriters were as much at fault as the newspapers and carried forward their own form of jingoism. At least ten songs were published in 1898 with the title, "Remember the Maine." One song of this title, date unknown, ends "To Hell with Spain!"[20] "Did the *Maine* Go Down?" includes most of the motifs employed by other writers of *Maine* songs: the description of the horrid event, the placing of the blame on Spain (in this case the rifles from Morro Castle were supposed to have fired on the ship), the general mourning, and the individual lament of the about-to-be-bereaved mother. The *Maine*'s commander, Captain Sigsbee, is made to have intimations of disaster. He received his share

334

WILLIE WILDWAVE'S
THE
BATTLESHIP
MAINE

From the NEW YORK WORLD.

SONGSTER

PRICE, 25 CENTS.

Published by WM. W. DELANEY, 117 Park Row, N. Y.

of attention; one Navy march was dedicated to him and another march composed at the time is entitled "The Sigsbee Maine-March."[21]

The tune to which "Did the *Maine* Go Down?" is sung is the same as the Vernon Dalhart 1924 Victor Black Seal recording of "The Wreck of the 97."[22] I had a copy of the record when I was in high school and played it incessantly. On the flip side Dalhart sang "The Prisoner's Song," for which I developed almost as strong a predilection.

"The Indiana Hero," more frequently known as "Fuller and Warren," is the only ballad which Indiana can claim completely as its own. Like other murder ballads, of course, it has spread to other parts and has been collected not only in neighboring states such as Michigan and Kentucky, but also in others as distant as Maine and Texas.[23]

The incident upon which the ballad is based occurred in 1820, only four years after Indiana became a state, in the southeastern town of Lawrenceburg on the Ohio River. A change of mind by a young woman as to whom she would wed resulted in both a murder and a hanging. The ballad is believed by some to have been composed soon after the event by Moses Whitecotton, a Scotsman who was not only a justice of the peace but also a painter and a poet.[24] The patriotic opening, the biblical allusions, and the high-flown imagery may seem stilted today but were much appreciated at the time.

TR 95 The Indiana Hero

(Laws AM F 16, Fuller and Warren)

Sung by Anna Sandage Underhill, Uniontown, 12 June 1963.

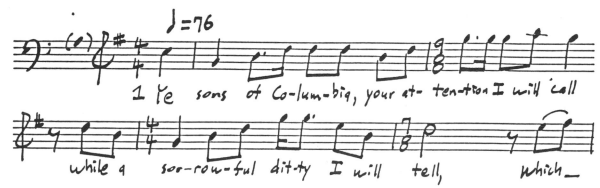

336

hap-pened of late in the In-di-a-na State To a
he-ro which none can ex- cel, 2. Like Sam-son he
cour-ted his choice of the fair And in-ten-ded to make her his
wife, But— like De-li-lah fair, Oh, she did his heart ensnare, which— cost him his ho-nor and his life

1. Ye sons of Columbia, your attention I will call
   While a sorrowful ditty I will tell,
   Which happened of late in the Indiana state
   To a hero which none can excel.

2. Like Samson he courted his choice of the fair
   And intended to make her his wife,
   But like Delilah fair, oh, she did his heart ensnare,
   Which cost him his honor and his life.

3. A gold ring he gave her in token of true love,
   And the flower was the image of a dove;
   They mut'ally agreed to get married in speed
   And had promised by the Power above.

4. Now this feeble-minded maiden was again for to wed
   To young Warren, a liver of the place;
   Fuller's heart did overflow, and he struck the fatal
        blow,
   Which ended in shame and disgrace.

5. When Fuller came to find he was depreeved of his love
   Which had promised by the Powers to wed,
   With heart full of woe, straight to Warren he did go
   And smiling, to Warren, he said:

6. "Oh, Warren, you have wronged me to gratify your cause
   By relating I had left a prudent wife.
   Acknowledge you have wronged me; although I break the
       laws,
   Oh, Warren, I'll depreeve you of your life."

7. "Now, Fuller, your request, it must be denied,
   For my heart unto your darling it is bound,
   And I can safely say that this is my wedding day
   In spite of all your heroes in town."

8. Now Fuller in a passion of hate and anger high
   Which has caused many a man to die,
   With one fatal shot, he killed Warren on the spot
   And smiling, said, "I'm ready now to die."

9. Now Fuller was condemned by the honorable court
   At Lawrenceburg, and sen'ced to die
   An ingremious [sic] death to hang above the earth,
   Like Haman, on the galleys so high.

10. The morning, it came when young Fuller was to die,
    And smiling, he bade this world adieu;
    Like an angel he did stand, for he was a handsome man,
    On his breast he wore a ribbon of blue.

11. Ten thousand spectators were smote on the breast
    And the guard dropped a tear from his eye,
    Saying, "Cursed be she who has caused this misery,
    For she in his stead ought to die."

12. Now, from all this ancient history that I can
        understand,
    And what's more, that I'm bound to believe,
    That women are essentially the downfall of men
    As Adam was beguiled by Eve.

13. Now marriage is a lottery and few win a prize,
    Though it's pleasing to the heart and to the eye;
    And you that never marry may well be called wise,
    So, gentlemen, excuse me, goodbye!

TR 96 Fuller and Warren

Sung by Mary Vandora McNeely Bryant, Evansville, 8 or 9 April 1938.

1. Ye sons of Columbia, 'tention I crave
   Whilst a sorrowful ditty I do tell,
   Which has happened of late in the Indiana state
   Of a hero who many [*sic*] did excel.

2. Like Samson he courted, made choice of the fair,
   And intended to make her his wife,
   But she, like Delilah, when she did his heart ensnare,
   Oh, she cost him his honor and his life.

3. A golden ring he gave her in token of his love;
   On the . . . was an image of a dove;
   They a-mutually agreed to get married in speed,
   And was promised by the powers above.

4. But this feeble-minded maid she did vow again to wed
   Unto Warren, a liver of the place;

Oh, it was a fatal blow, for it caused his overthrow,
And added to her shame and disgrace.

5. When brave Fuller came to hear he was deprived of
    his dear,
And was promised by the powers to wed,
Unto Warren he did go with his heart full of woe,
And smiling, unto him thus he said:

6. "Young man, you have wronged me to gratify your cause
By reporting I left a prudent wife;
Oh, Warren, you have wronged me! Although I break
    the law,
Oh, Warren, I'll deprive you of your life!"

7. At this Warren replied, "Your request must be denied,
For what I said was true renown;
And farther I can say that this is my wedding day
In spite of all the heroes in town."

8. And then by the anger of love and passion bound,
Which has caused many a hero to cry,
And at one fatal shot he killed Warren on the spot,
And smiling, says, "I'm willing now to die."

9. Brave Fuller was condemned by the court of
    Lawrenceburg,
Condemned in Durban [sic] for to die,
To die an ignominious death, for to hang above
    the earth,
Like Haman on the gallus so high.

10. The time was drawing nigh when brave Fuller was to die;
He most cheerfully bid the audience adieu.
Like an angel he did stand, for he was a handsome man;
On his bosom wore a ribbon of the blue.

11. The smiling gods of love looked with anger from above,
While the rope flew asunder like the sand;
Two doctors for their prey did the murder, we must say,
For they hung him by the main strength of hand.

12. One pleasing consolation must well remembered be;
While the gallus hung over his head,
He had been baptized and from all sin set free,
And his spirit unto glory had fled.

Mrs. Underhill learned the ballad from her father and said that it was his favorite song.

Mrs. Bryant learned it from her step-grandfather, Stephen Cox. She heard him sing it when she was a

very small child.

The ballad casts Fuller as a hero both for his actions and for his demeanor under stress. This seems to have been the view of most of the county's population since one writer states, "The people in Dearborn almost in mass signed a petition to the Governor for the pardon of Fuller."[25] However, newspaper accounts of the tragedy are scanty and somewhat contradictory. In one account emanating from Cincinnati dated 25 March 1820, it is stated that the governor of Indiana had granted Fuller a reprieve, which was expected to lead to a pardon. According to this report public indignation ran high that Fuller should be reprieved, and "the guards at the jail, upon hearing the news, discharged their pieces and refused to serve any longer."[26] However, the supreme court upheld the verdict of the lower court, and Fuller's public hanging, as customary at the time, was witnessed by thousands.

According to one family's oral tradition, Fuller was a Kentuckian and a large group of armed men from that state decided to rescue him from the gallows. Unfortunately, when they reached the Ohio River the ferry was on the other side. By the time they had forded the river they were too late to effect the rescue; Fuller had already been hanged.[27] The reproduced article from *The Indiana Republican* of 16 March 1820 was taken from the *Indiana Oracle* of Lawrenceburg.

Mrs. Bryant's variant records one of the more fantastic aspects of the execution, the breaking of the rope and the subsequent improvised hanging. The first ten stanzas of both variants are similar in subject matter, and the eleventh stanza of each is related. The remaining stanzas differ, the two in Mrs. Underhill's variant concentrating on the original sin of womankind and the last stanza of Mrs. Bryant's variant on Fuller's redemption from sin. In both variants the young woman is described as "feeble-minded." In other variants she is described as "fickle-minded." This last is probably the original term. As a matter of fact, Mrs. Bryant sent Paul Brewster a written copy of her song in 1935, which he published in his 1940 volume. In this he prints the term "fickle-minded" instead of "feeble-minded."[28]

The word "gallus" in "gallus so high," as sung by Dora Bryant, is an older term for "gallows." In the plural, "galluses," it signifies "suspenders." Language often links the gruesome with the pedestrian. Mrs. Underhill pronounces it "galleys." Her pronunciation of other words is also

The Indiana Republican.

"WHERE LIBERTY DWELLS, THERE IS MY COUNTRY"

MADISON, INDIANA, THURSDAY, MARCH 16, 1820.

Bank of Maryland ditto,
Union bank of Baltimore
Mechanics bank "
Merchants bank of Baltimore,
Franklin bank of "
Commercial & Farmers do.
Farmers & Mechanics do.
Bank of Colum. Dist. of Col.
Union bank of Georgetown do.
Farmers & Mechanics bank
Patriotic do. of Washington
Bank of Washington
Bank of the Metropolis
Union Bank of Alexandria ,,
Bank of Alexandria, ,,
Bank of Potomack, ,,
Farmers bank of ,,
New York bank - New York,
Manhattan Company ditto
Mechanics Bank ,,
Merchants Bank ,,
Union Bank of ,,
Bank of America ,,
Farmers and Mechanics bank
Bank of Chillicothe,
State bank of Ia. Vincennes,
Bank of Illinois at Shawnee-
town,
Bank of Missouri St. Louis,
Bank of Mississippi Natchez,
Bank of Orleans, Orleans,
Bank of Louisiana,
Planters Bank do.

Except notes of a less deno-
mination than five dollars.
(CORRECTED WEEKLY.)

From the Indiana Oracle.

TRIAL FOR MURDER.

The circuit court for Dearborn county closed its session
Saturday last—the whole of the
term was consumed by the trail
of *Amasa Fuller*, on an indict-
ment for the murder of *Palmer
Warren*. Few trials have excited more general interest, as
well from the character and ap-
pearance of the prisoner, as
from the circumstances which
led to the atrocious deed. The
circumstances were briefly these:
Fuller had, for a considerable
time prior to the murder of
Warren, been attentive to a
young lady who was residing
with her uncle in Lawrenceburg,
about the last of November
1819, Fuller left this place for
Brookville; while there, the
unfortunate deceased compenc-
ed an intimacy with the young
lady to whom Fuller had been
before attached; their intimacy
resulted in an engagement of
marriage, which was to have
been consummated on the fatal
10th of January, 1820. It appeared in evidence, that about
the middle of December, Fuller, then at Brookville, received a letter in the hand writing
of Warren, and signed by the
young lady, enclosing a ring, in
which she renounced all feelings
of attachment towards him, & returned him the ring which she had
received from him in pledge; that
after the receipt of this letter, F.
appeared gloomy and melancholly, and on Friday, 7th January,
he left Brookville on foot, and
arrived at Lawrenceburgh in
the evening of that day; after
changing his wet clothes (having
rained) he went into the house
of the young lady's uncle, next
to Mr. Coburn's hotel, where
he put up, and was there frequently between the time of his
arrival from Brookville and
the day of the murder, meeting Warren at the house, he
several times attempted to
quarrell with, which Warren as
often declined; on Saturday 8th
January, it appeared that Fuller
borrowed a pair of pistols with
the avowed design of shooting

at a mark, in which amusement
he requested several young men
to participate; on the afternoon
of that day he asked a Mr.
Hitchcock if he would go out
and hunt with him, he replied,
that he would, and would go
for his gun; Fuller answered, I
do not hunt with guns, but
with pistols. On Sunday 9th
January, Fuller seemed cool and
collected, talked on various
subjects with his fellow boarders;
and declared he had no pretentions to the young lady in question. On Monday morning
10th January he asked Mr. Hitchcock, when up in his room at
the Hotel, what was the
best way to load a pistol
and the surest way to kill? and
observed, I am afraid that this
pistol has not enough of powder in it, how shall I shoot it off
so as not to be heard? (It must
be observed that Warren's office is under the same rooff with
Coburn's hotel.) Fuller went
down stairs, and shortly after
came up saying, I have shot it
off, and no person heard me.
Fuller then loaded the pistols
with powder and four slugs
each—Hitchcock told him he
hoped he had no evil designs—
Fuller replied, "I have not, but
I will shew you some fun;" Fuller
then put on a great coat which
he had borrowed from Mr. Coburn, and feeling it it had pock-
ets, he put one pistol in each
pocket of the coat, and walked
down stairs, having previously
asked Hitchcock if he could
discover that he had pistols. It
appeared further in evidence,
that Fuller left the house, came
back and went out again; he
was seen by Mr. Farrar, who
was standing in the door of his
house, next but one to Warren's
office, to come out of Coburn's
bar room about a yard behind
Warren, who unlocked the door
of his office and entered followed by Fuller; in about 3 4's of a
minute Mr. Farrar heard the
report of a pistol in Warren's
office, instantly ran there, and
attempting to open the door, it
was stopped by something, and
looking down he discovered
the body of Warren lying cross-
wise the door; he pushed open
the door, and upon entering the
office discovered Fuller standing
beside the body, and the room
filled with smoke and the smell
of powder; Warren was not
yet dead but was struggling in
the last agonies. Mr. Farrar
seized hold of Fuller, exclaim-
ing "Good heavens, Fuller, is
it possible you have done this?"
Fuller replied, "I am a man, and
have acted the part of a man! I
have been ridding the earth of a
vile reptile! I glory in the deed!!!"
The pistols were found lying on
the counter in the office, one
discharged of its contents, the
other still charged; a writing was
was found on the floor, the sub-
stance of which was, that Warren,
in the presence of Almighty God,
swore to renounce all pretentions
to the young lady, and acknowledge himself to be a base liar
and scoundrel! Fuller said, after his arrest, that he had presented this paper to Warren de-
siring him to sign it; he refused—he then offered him a pistol,
bidding him defend himself like
a man; that Warren also refused
—and that he then shot the
cowardly rascal. The body of
Warren was pierced with a
wound just below the pap of the

left breast. It does not appear
that Warren had ever taken a-
ny undue advantage of Fuller,
or even spoke a disrespectful
word of him to the young lady,
or any other person.

The prosecution was conducted by Amos Lane and John Test,
esquires; the prisoner was ably
defended by Charles Dewey,
Joseph S. Benham, Daniel J.
Caswell, William C. Drew, S.
Q. Richardson, and Merritt S.
Craig esquires. The counsel for
the prisoner moved to continue
the trial, until the next term of
this court, on an affidavit of
the absence of two material witnesses. This motion was overruled by the court, because not
stating the facts to be proved
by those two witnesses. A-
nother motion was then made
for continuance by the counsel
for the prisoner, on affidavit of
the fact that popular prejudice
ran so high that the prisoner
could not have a fair trial. The
opinion of the court was: That
if the fact thus stated came to
the knowledge of the prisoner
subsequent to the former motion for a continuance, we
would listen to it; but as it does
not appear that it did, the motion is overruled. The defence
set up on the trial was insanity.
It, however, appeared in evidence that the prisoner had
been thought by those witnesses
who had seen him, to be more
gloomy and melancholly than
usual, and as if something disturbed his mind; but nothing
like insanity was made out. After a long and patient hearing
of the testimony, which was
very consistent and positive, and
after an able defence by the prisoner's counsel, the jury retired
—and in about two hours returned with a verdict of Guilty.
On Saturday morning the sen-
tence of the court was passed,
by his honor Judge Eggleston,
That the prisoner at the bar be
remanded to his place of con-
finement, & be thence conducted,
on Friday 31st March, next to
the place of execution, and be
there hanged by the neck until
he be dead! Fuller preserved
throughout his trial, and at the
time the judge pronounced to
him his awful doom, that his
days were numbered, a stern
inflexible countenance.

VIRGINIA LEGISLATURE.
House of Delegates.

On Thursday, February
10th, the resolutions submitted
to the H. of D. some weeks a-
go, on the U. S. bank and the
opinion of the Supreme Court
thereon, were taken up.

Mr. Smith of the I. of Wight
moved a postponement of them
till the 31st of March.—Mr. S.
ascribed the excitement against
the U. S. bank to the influence
of the state banks; declared his
opposition to all banks, both
national and state; objected to
narrowing down all antinadver-
sions to the national bank, &c.

Messrs. Bassett, Rives Cham-
berlayne, Selden, Gordon, Stevenson, and Baldwin, opposed
the postponement in the most
earnest manner; the five first
gentlemen expatiated upon the
unconstitutionality of the bank;
upon the alarming principles set
forth in its defence by the Supreme Court, which in fact
were calculated to prostrate every state right; upon the necessity of making a stand in the

interesting. Thus "deprive" is pronounced "depreeve" and the first syllable of "Haman" as "ham." She also pronounces "ignominious" as "ingremious." All these mispronunciations or corruptions may have been passed down to her as she learned the song.

The following, which may at least be partially claimed by Indiana, celebrates the sensational and rather brutal murder of Pearl Bryan, a daughter of a wealthy farmer in Greencastle. Pearl, a young woman of eighteen or nineteen, became pregnant. Whether the father of the unborn child was William Wood, a second cousin, or Scott Jackson, whom he had introduced to Pearl, was never established. Pearl left Greencastle, telling her parents she was going to visit friends in Indianapolis. She was seen off at the station by Wood who did go to Indianapolis. Pearl, instead, traveled to Cincinnati to meet Scott Jackson. He was at the time a student at the Ohio College of Dental Surgery, and through him she apparently hoped to secure an abortion. She arrived late and registered in a hotel under an assumed name. She was last seen alive on 29 January 1896 as she left the hotel with Scott Jackson and a fellow dental student, Alonzo Walling. On 1 February her decapitated body was found near Ft. Thomas, Kentucky.

The body was identified by her shoes, which had been purchased in Greencastle, and by her clothing, which was recognized by her parents and friends.

Jackson and Walling were arrested and each accused the other of the murder. Wood appeared only as a witness. In the autopsy a five-month-old fetus was discovered, which the doctors declared would have lived had the mother survived. It was thought that Pearl had died when she had been given chloroform. Her head, presumably, had been cut off to prevent identification of the body. However, later revelations leave this in doubt. Apparently, Jackson had carried the head around in the girl's own valise for a day before throwing it into a sewer or river. Jackson and Walling were extradited to Newport, Kentucky, convicted, and finally both were hanged.

TR 97 Pearl Bryan

(Laws AM F 2)

Sung by Oscar "Doc" Parks, Alton, 20 December 1963.

343

1. Come all of you young people,
   A sad story I will tell,
   That happened in Fort Thomas
   In the old Kentucky State.

2. Pearl went to Cincinnati;
   She had never been there before.
   She was stolen by Scott Jackson
   For to never see Mama no more.

3. They sent the bloodhounds hunting;
   At last an answer came,
   Saying, "Helen, we've found a dead woman's body
   But we can't find her head."

4. They telephoned for miles around;
   At last an answer came,
   Saying, "Helen, that woman's body,
   It must have been Pearl was slain."

5. Then in come Pearl . . . sister,
   Falling to her knees,
   Pleading to Scott Jackson
   For sister's head, "Oh, please!"

6. Scott Jackson set back stubborn;
   Those are the words he said,
   When we meet Pearl in Heaven
   There'll be no missing head."

TR 98 Pearl Bryan

Sung by Roxie South King, Bloomington, 16 April 1960.

345

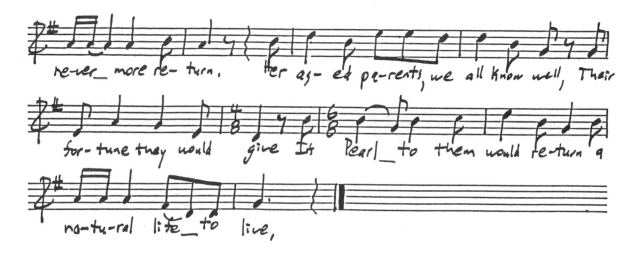

never more re-turn. Her ag-ed pa-rents, we all know well, Their
for-tune they would give If Pearl to them would re-turn a
na-tu-ral life to live,

1. Young ladies, if you'll listen, a story I'll relate.
   It happened near Fort Thomas in the old Kentucky State.
   It was January the thirty-first that dreadful deed was
        done
   By Jackson, Walling, and Pearl Bry[an], how cold the
        blood did run.

2. But little did her parents think, when she left her
        happy home,
   That their darling girl and youth would nevermore
        return.
   Her aged parents, we all know well, their fortune they
        would give
   If Pearl to them would return a natural life to live.

3. The driver is Jackson tells the tale of poor Pearl
        Bryan did moan
   From Cincinnati to the place where the dreadful deed
        was done.
   Next day a farmer passing by spied a lifeless form
   A-lying on the cold and sod where the blood had stained
        the ground.

4. Young ladies, now take warning, since you know young
        men are unjust.
   It may be your best lover yet you know not who to
        trust.
   Pearl Bryan died [far] from home and friends on that
        dark, lonely spot.
   My God! My God! Believe me, girls, don't let this
        be your lot.

Oscar "Doc" Parks explains how he came to learn the song at the beginning of Chapter 1. His

variant of the ballad is quite unusual. In only four of the seven stanzas is there rhyme, and one of

346

these is an assonant rhyme (came/slain). Parks is known to have composed ballads, and part of this rendition may be his own composition or improvisation.

Mrs. King's rendition is closer to the common line. Not only does the first stanza, as in the previous ballad, feature the commonplace plea for the auditors to listen but also there is in the last stanza a strong warning against trusting lovers.

Mrs. King apparently had a momentary loss of memory while singing the first line of the third stanza. She probably meant to sing, "The driver, Jackson." At the time of the recording she was eighty years of age. She stated that she had been married for sixty years. When asked to tell the story of the ballad and how it happened, she replied:

> Well, Pearl Bryan went from Greencastle, her home, over to Cincinnati to meet her boyfriend, this Jackson. . . . He was a cousin to her and he went over there and then her and Dr. Walling--she got a young doctor. . . . They let her out of the hotel, it was published in the paper at that time, and she had a grip . . . she was carrying the grip. And they cut her head off, that's the way the murder was done. . . . It was put in that grip and it was never found. They never found the grip nor her head. That's one thing they always surmised that it was throwed in the river. It happened close to the Ohio River near Ft. Thomas . . . and that's about all I know about it.

The driver mentioned in Mrs. King's variant did not come forward until several weeks after the investigation had been in progress. He was a black cabdriver coincidentally named Jackson. In the *Cincinnati Commercial Gazette* of 16 February 1896, he related:

> We were approached by a man who asked which one of us wanted to make five dollars. We asked him what service he wanted rendered and he said that he wanted a hack driven to Newport. The five dollars looked like a big pile to me, but I refused to take the job, as did also several others. The man finally called me to one side and talked to me a while and I finally agreed to drive the hack for him. I asked him where the money was and he said that he would give it to me when we returned; that he did not propose to pay until I had done the work. He then explained that he was a doctor and that he and another physician had a very sick patient whom they wanted to take to her home near Newport. He told me to wait about half an hour and he would drive the cab down George Street.
> I waited fully three quarters of an hour; it seemed longer than that to me and he surprised me by driving south on Elm street instead of coming down George. I also noticed when he drove up that he had a surrey and not a cab. He directed me to get in the front seat, and he then entered the back part of the vehicle, where, I learned, later, there was another man and a woman. I was directed to drive rapidly toward Newport, and this I did. When I reached the other side of the bridge I

347

CINCINNATI COMMERCIAL GAZETTE

Editor:
Northwesterly Winds.

CINCINNATI, SUNDAY FEBRUARY 16, 1896.

24 PAGES

PRICE FIVE CENTS.

GEORGE H. JACKSON THE MAN WHO DROVE PEARL BRYAN TO HER DEATH.

SOLVED.

THE CABMAN FOUND.

COMPLETE

SOLVED.

The Mysterious Cabman
Is Found,

Though It Was Not in
a Cab

That Pearl Bryan and Her
Murderers

Took That Fateful Ride to
Fort Thomas.

George H. Jackson, a Col-
ored Coachman,

In the Employ of William S.
Winfield,

Was Hired for the Sum
of Five Dollars

To Drive the Rockaway They
Had Secured,

Tried to Get Away Back of
Newport,

But Was Compelled at the
Point of a Revolver to
Complete the Journey.

GEORGE H. JACKSON, DRIVER OF THE CAB.

COMPLETE

Is Jackson's Identifica-
tion of Walling.

Picked Him at Once in a
Large Crowd,

In the Corridor of the County Jail.

His Identification of Jackson Not So Good,

First Picking Out a Covington
Reporter

Who Happened to Stand by
Walling's Side.

His Story Believed by All
Who Heard It.

Now to Find the Vehicle and
the Head,

Though Neither Necessary to
Assure Conviction.

Happy Are the Mayor, the Detectives and All Who Have
Followed the Case.

CINCINNATI, MONDAY, FEBRUARY 17, 1896.   PRICE 2 CENTS.

THE SURREY,

Or, Rather, a Coupe
Rockaway,

Believed to Have Been
Found on Walnut Hills,

At Chester Mullen's McMillan
Street Stable.

George Jackson Identifies the
Outfit

As That He Drove the Night
of the Murder.

Its Floor Carpet Stained with
Spots Like Blood,

But Which Failed to Pan Out
Under Examination.

Who Was the Man Who
Hired the Rig?

Suspicion Again Points to
Barber Albion,

But the Chances Are Walling
Was the Man.

MAP OF ROUTE TAKEN BY THE CAB THE NIGHT OF THE MURDER.

Cincinnati Commercial Gazette, *16 and 17 February 1896*

348

could not understand the directions and did not know which way they wanted me to go and one of the men, the same one who had engaged me for the job, came around and sat on the front seat with me. About this time the woman began to moan and cry in an undertone and there a sort of whispered conversation between her and the other man. This continued for some time and finally I discovered there was something wrong. The woman acted as though she was suffering great agony, and, although I could not see her nor the man with her, her cries and moans frightened me. I got so scared that I finally said to the man next to me, "Here, I don't want any more of this job; there is something wrong with that woman back there and I don't want to have anything more to do with this." I handed the lines to him, but instead of taking them and allowing me to get out, he placed a gun at my head, and, calling me a terrible name, said that if I did not drive on he would put a bullet in my head and drive me to hell.

I was directed to stop. I pulled up to the side of the road near the entrance to the lane, and the man in the back seat got out and lifted the woman. He had to drag her from the buggy, and she seemed unable to stand on her feet.

After he got her out and was holding her in his arms the man who was on the seat with me said, "Now, you damned black nigger, you turn around here, and when we are ready for you we will whistle. If you try to get away or ever say anything to anyone about this job we will kill you, and you know we are prepared to do it. If we ever hear anything about this we will know you have told it, and your life won't be worth a fig."

He then got out and walked about behind the carriage, and the two men carried, or rather, dragged, the woman down the lane. I followed directions, drove up the road a little ways and turned around. I then heard some funny noises coming from the direction in which they had gone, which sounded like they were scuffling in the leaves. I could hear the cries of the woman, which, as before, seemed to be smothered, but it was so dark that I could see nothing.

I got so scared at this point that I made up my mind to get away from there just as quick as I could. There was a hitching weight in the carriage; I threw this out on the ground, fastened the horses to it, and started down that road walking about as fast as I could. I hadn't gone very far when the men discovered what I was doing and bellowed at me. I then started to run as fast as I could and didn't stop until I got clear back to Cincinnati.

According to the *Greencastle Banner Times*, William Wood, not Scott Jackson (as Mrs. King says), was Pearl Bryan's cousin. Such errors commonly occur in oral transmission. In the numerous articles published concerning this sensational affair, I could find no mention of the "Helen" found in Parks's variant. As ballads spread, dramatic incidents are frequently invented and added. A sister begging Scott Jackson for Pearl's head at the end of the variant is another case in point.

The melody sung by Roxie King is parallel in almost all respects to that employed by Garland South in singing TR 85, "Brennan on the Moor," in the previous chapter. Roxie was, of course, Garland's aunt, and it is not surprising to find the same melody used by members of the same family in singing different texts.

349

THE STAR.

BLOOMINGTON - INDIANA

Popular Science.

Dr. Busey says that school-children should sing an hour a day, as a preventive of consumption. Vocal music is gymnastic exercise of the lungs by development of the lung tissue itself.

Lieut. Finley finds that there were 141 tornadoes in Illinois in the fifty-four years ending with 1883. The month of greatest frequency was May, no month being free from the storms.

The professor of geology in the University of West Virginia declares that the rumors of failure of natural gas are idle, and have no foundation. From his protracted study and investigation of these regions, aided by the best scientific light on the subject, he asserts that the production will largely increase for years to come.

From a recent study of the bones of anthropoid apes, it appears that the gorilla and chimpanzee approach nearest to man, but in different degrees, the orang-outang holding the third place. But great differences exist between the proportions of the human frame and those of all the apes.

Under all circumstances the temperature of the healthy body is about the same, not varying much from 99°. If, from sickness or any cause, the temperature rises a few degrees above this point. death soon occurs, and one of the most important matters in cases of fever is to reduce the bodily temperature; but, usually, the wonderful vital processes regulate the internal fires very accurately, and the bodily temperature is constant, whether exposed to the rigors of an Arctic winter, or to the extreme heat endured by the iron smelters in their daily toil.

The Consequences of Overwork and Exposure.

From the News, Wanatah, Ind.

At Wanatah, La Porte County, Ind., lives Samuel Atwater, who for many years lived a life of such suffering as seemed well nigh impossible for man to bear.

To a reporter who called upon him Mr. Atwater willingly told the story of his deliverance, which is here given in his own language.

"For many years I have been a sufferer from the most excruciating pains in the back of my head and neck, and also in the small of my back. These pains were caused by overwork and exposure, and were so intense at times as to be almost unbearable. I would toss upon my bed at night suffering untold agony. I tried every remedy which I or my friends thought would give even temporary relief, but all to no purpose. I was able to attend to my work at times, but suffered greatly while doing so. Last spring I began using Dr. Williams' Pink Pills and now after six months' trial can say that they have done more for me than all the medicine I have ever taken. The pain is all gone and I feel like a new man. I have worked at the hardest kind of farm work all summer and have gained in weight and feel better than I have before for many years.

I have also been troubled with scrofulous sores, but through the wonderful cleansing properties of the Pink Pills I have been partially freed from this ailment also.

As a blood purifier and nerve builder they cannot be equaled. I feel it a duty to recommend Dr. Williams' Pink Pills to everyone suffering from any of the various forms of disease for which they are prepared, for they have certainly done wonders for me."

(Signed)   SAMUEL ATWATER.

Sworn and subscribed to before me this 30th day of September, 1895.
(Seal.)   EDWARD F. MITZNER,
Notary Public.

Dr. Williams' Pink Pills contain, in a condensed form, all the elements necessary to give new life and richness to the blood and restore shattered nerves. Pink Pills are sold in boxes (never in loose bulk) at 50 cents a box or six boxes for $2.50, and may be had of all druggists, or direct by mail from Dr. Williams' Medicine Company, Schenectady, N. Y.

Mr. Tyron of Ballston, Ore., celebrated recently his one hundredth birthday. He settled in Oregon in 1852 and has seventy-eight direct descendants.

ATROCIOUS CRIME.

Indiana Boys Gain Unenviable Notoriety.

Story of the Murder of Pearl Bryan—Partial Confession by Jackson—Wood and Walling Implicated.

A Cincinnati special, Feb. 6, says: All day the city has been nervously excited over the hourly development of the now famous story of the mysterious death of Pearl Bryan, the Greencastle, Ind., farmer's daughter. What is called a confession of two of the young men implicated as her murderers is only a strange sort of half-defiant wincing under the semi-torture of a police examination. So far it is known that Pearl Bryan, about to become a mother, and desirous of hiding her shame, left Greencastle, Ind., Tuesday, Jan. 28, ostensibly to visit Mrs. Fisher in Indianapolis. That William Wood saw her to the train; that she came directly to Cincinnati, tried to see Scott Jackson at

SCOTT JACKSON.

the dental college that night, but could not; that she registered at the Indiana House as "Mabel Stanley, city," and was assigned to room 114. Alonzo M. Walling, the roommate of Scott Jackson, both of whom were arrested last night, says that Jackson saw Miss Bryan on Wednesday and that he went about the city with her and finally on Friday completed the crime of murder, cutting off the girl's head and bringing it to Cincinnati in her own valise, which he kept until Monday, when he cast the head into a sewer and threw her clothing into the Ohio river. On the other hand, Jackson, in a stolid manner, placed the entire burden on Walling. According to his story the condition of Miss Bryan was attributed to William Wood, who applied to Jackson to help him cover up the girl's shame.

Wood did this, Jackson says, because he (Jackson) was a dental student and supposed to have access to means for procuring an abortion. Jackson denied having such knowledge, but recommended Walling, who had told him how he had assisted two girls from Hamilton, O. Thereupon Wood sent Miss Bryan to Cincinnati, where Jackson turned her over to Walling. He said that Walling took the girl away from the hotel on Wednesday, and that was the last he saw of her. But under the spur of persistent questioning he made many more admissions, as that he left the girl's valise at a barber shop empty, where the police found it. The chief of police asked him to open the valise and had him describe the ghastly blood stains made, as Jackson naively argued, by the dissevered head of his victim. But he denied that he had carried the valise with the girl's head in it. His "confession" was, in shreds and patches, accusations against Walling and denials of what incriminated him. But the evidence against these men does not depend on their own statements. This bloody valise is shown by other witnesses to have been left at a barber shop by Jackson. He couldn't have been 'innocent of its ghastly use, when he admits that it belonged to the poor girl. A saloon keeper has identified the men as having been in the saloon with two women.

The main facts of the time, manner and place of the girl's death remain unrevealed. It is reasonably clear she met her death Friday night. The theory that a bungling mechanical operation caused her death is clearly disproved by the coroner's

MISS PEARL BRYAN.

investigation. So, also, is the theory of death from drugs, as the analysis of her stomach showed no such conditions. It is clear she was either brutally beheaded or was killed by an anaesthetic. As death from the latter cause can only be determined by the condition of the blood, and as decapitation depleted the veins, that question can only be settled by the testimony of a witness. Imagination staggers at the suggestion of cold-blooded murder by decapitation and leaves the only plausible theory that the girl died under the influence of an anaesthetic, and that the subsequent treatment of her body was to hide the cause of death.

William Wood was brought here tonight from South Bend, Ind., by Sheriff Plummer, of Newport, Ky., and Detectives Crim and McDermott under arrest as an accomplice of Scott Jackson and Alonzo Walling in aiding and abetting their alleged abortion on Pearl Bryan. Wood is not yet of age, bright looking, with florid face cleanly shaved, light hair and finely dressed. He is accompanied by his father, the Rev. D. M. Wood, presiding elder of the Methodist church in the district where he resides at Greencastle; the Rev. A. A. Gee, pastor of the Methodist church at South Bend; A. N. Grant, attorney of Indianapolis, who is counsel of Wood, and A. R. Colburn, a lumber merchant of Michigan City who came to go on the bond of young Wood. Although a warrant had been issued charging Wood with aiding and abetting an abortion, yet he was held on suspicion without bond.

During the time that Walling made his confession Scott Jackson was present and heard it all and denied everything as his roommate proceeded with the story. They called each other liars and were with difficulty prevented from creating a disturbance. Meantime a large crowd surrounded the place and both the boys expressed their apprehension for their safety. They are not anxious to be taken to Newport, Ky., for trial, but as soon as the preliminary examination is cleared up requisition papers will be issued and the prisoners will be turned over to Sheriff Plummer of Newport, Ky.

Later—William Wood was released on his own recognizance and went to the hotel with Sheriff Plummer.

A Much Married Man.

Texas Siftings.

"That man has had five wives."

"Tandem or simultaneously."

"I don't understand."

"Is he a Mormon or a Chicago man?"

Not in That Business.

Texas Siftings.

Mendicant—Can't you give me a few pennies for my poor family at home, sir?

Merchant—No, no, man, I don't want to buy any poor family.

Fits Jas. All stopped free by Dr. Kline's Great Nerve Restorer. No fits after first day's use. Marvelous cures. Treatise and $2 trial bottle free to Fit cases. Send to Dr. Kline, 931 Arch St. Philadelphia, Pa.

The Phenix Insurance Company has agents everywhere, and always the best man in the business represents that company.

Florida Facts.

February and March are two of the best months of the year to visit Florida. The climate is fine and the social features at their height of interest. When you have made up your mind to go you naturally want to get there as soon as possible and in the most comfortable manner. No matter whether you live in St. Louis, Chicago, Peoria, Indianapolis, Columbus, Cleveland, Buffalo, New York or Boston, you can take one of the magnificent trains of the "Big Four Route" from any one of these cities to Cincinnati, and with only one change of cars continue your journey to Jacksonville. Direct connections made in Central Union Station, Cincinnati, with through trains of all lines to Florida. Call on or address any agent "Big Four Route," or address E. C. McCormick, Passenger Traffic Manager, or D. B. Martin, General Passenger and Ticket Agent, Cincinnati Ohio

Bloomington Star, *15 February 1896*

"Atrocious Crime"

In the minds of singers of American ballads the name "Pearl Bryan" seems to have become attached to any murdered woman. Many ballads have been collected, for example, in which the material of "Florella" or "The Jealous Lover" have been combined with that of "Pearl Bryan." Below is such a ballad collected in Indiana.

Pearl Bryan

1. Way down in yonder valley
    Where the violets fade and bloom,
    Our own Pearl Bryan slumbers
    In a cold and silent tomb.

2. She died not broken-hearted,
    Nor lingering ill befell,
    But in an instant parted
    From the one she loved so well.

3. One night the moon shone brightly,
    The stars were shining too,
    When to her cottage window
    Her jealous lover drew.

4. "Come, Pearl, and let us wander
    In the valley deep and gay;
    Come, Pearl, and let us ponder
    Upon our wedding day."

5. Deep down into the valley
    He led his love so dear;
    She said, 'T is for you only
    That I have wandered here.

6. "The way seems dark and dreary,
    And I'm afraid to stay.
    Besides, I'm worn and weary;
    I would retrace my way."

7. "Retrace your way? No, never!
    These woods you'll roam no more.
    No one on earth can save you;
    Pearl Bryan, you must die!"

8. Down on her knees before him
    She pleaded for her life;
    Deep in her snow-white bosom
    He plunged a fatal knife.

9. "What have I done, Scott Jackson,
    That you should take my life?

You know I've always loved you,
And would have been your wife.

10. "Farewell, my loving parents,
My happy peaceful home;
Farewell, my dear old schoolmates;
With you no more I'll roam.

11. "Farewell, my dear, dear sister,
My face you'll see no more;
Long, long you'll wait my coming
At the little cottage door."

12. And while the birds were singing
So gaily all around,
A stranger found Pearl Bryan,
Cold, headless, on the ground.[29]

Categorizing such a hybrid is not an easy task. Brewster includes it under "Pearl Bryan" and lists it as variant C. George Malcolm Laws, on the other hand, incorporates it in his listing for "The Jealous Lover" (F 1). This combination of "The Jealous Lover" and "Pearl Bryan" is F 1B, while "Pearl Bryan" is F 2.

There can be nothing more American than the old West. It has been the inspiration not only of hundreds of stories, books, and motion pictures, but also of ballads. Here is one set in Texas.

TR 99 The Texas Rangers

(Laws AM A 8)

Sung by Virgil Sandage, Uniontown, 12 June 1963.

352

me, My name 'tis no-thing ex-try; to you I will not

tell. I was a jol-ly ran-ger; I'm sure I wish you

well, 2. when at the age of eight-een I joined this

jol-ly band, we marched from San An-to-nio un-

to the Rye-o Grande, Our cap-tain he in-formed us-per-

-haps he thought it right— "Be-fore you reach that

Sta-tion I'm sure you'll have to fight."

1. Come all you Texas Rangers, wherever you may be.
   I'll tell you all the story that happened unto me.
   My name 't is nothing extry; to you I will not tell.
   I was a jolly ranger; I'm sure I wish you well.

2. When at the age of eighteen I joined this jolly band,
   We marched from San Antonio unto the Rye-o Grand.
   Our captain he informed us--perhaps he thought it
      right--
   "Before you reach that station I'm sure you'll have
      to fight."

3. We saw the Indians coming, I heard them give the yell.
   My heart it sank within me; my courage almost fell.
   I saw the smoke ascending; it seemed to reach the sky.
   My feelings at that moment: this is my time to die.

353

4. We fought for nine long hours until the strife
     was o'er.
  The sight of the dead and wounded I'd never seen
     before.
  There were six and good old Rangers as ever travelled
     west
  I buried with their comrades. May sweet peace be
     their rest.

5. Perhaps you have a mother, likewise a sister, too.
  Or it may be a sweetheart who will weep and mourn
     for you.
  If this be your condition and you feel inclined to
     roam.
  I'll advise you by experience you'd better stay at
     home.

Note the excellent advice offered in the final stanza.

The Texas Rangers trace their beginning to 1823 when Stephen F. Austin employed ten men to "range" around his settlement to prevent depredations by the Indians. This force proved so effective that in 1836 a small battalion of armed Rangers, rather than an army, was established by the new Texas Republic to protect its frontiers. Indian fighting and scouting were always their main tasks until their last battle with the Indians in 1881 in the Diablo Mountains of west Texas. Later they became a division of the Department of Public Safety, and a few are still active. As such, they are the oldest continuously active law enforcement group in the United States. The battle upon which the above ballad is based probably occurred in the middle part of the last century.

TR 100 The Cowboy's Lament

(Laws AM B 1, The Dying Cowboy)

Sung by Garland "Jack" South, Monroe County, May 1956.

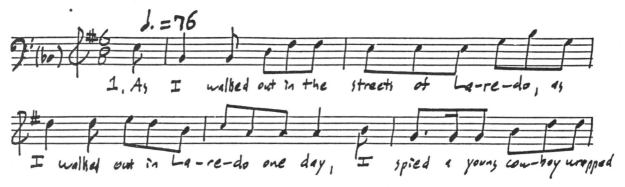

354

up in white lin-en, Wrapped up in white lin-en as cold as the clay.

5. "Oh, beat the drum slow-ly and play the fife low-ly And

play the dead march as you car-ry me a-long. Take me to some

grave-yard and lay the sod o'er me, For I'm a wild cow-boy, I

know I've done wrong."

1. As I walked out in the streets of Laredo,
   As I walked out in Laredo one day,
   I spied a young cowboy wrapped up in white linen,
   Wrapped up in white linen as cold as the clay.

2. "I see by your outfit that you are a cowboy,"
   These words he did say as I boldly stopped by.
   "Come, sit down beside me and hear my sad story,
   For I'm a poor cowboy and I know I must die."

3. "Oh, once in the saddle I used to go dashing,
   Once in the saddle I used go gay.
   First took to drinking, then took to card playing,
   Got shot by a gambler and I'm dying today."

4. "Go write me a letter, to my gray-haired mother,
   And write another to my sister so dear,
   Yet there's another, she's dearer than mother,
   I know it would grieve her to know that I'm here."

5. "Oh, beat the drums slowly and play the fife lowly
   And play the Dead March as you carry me along.
   Take me to the graveyard and lay the sod o'er me,
   For I'm a wild cowboy, I know I've done wrong."

6. "Oh, get me some water, a drink of cold water,
   To cool my parched lips," this cowboy then cried.

'Fore I could get it his soul had departed,
And gone to its maker; the cowboy had died.

TR 101 The Wild Cowboy

Sung by Vern Smelser, Paoli, 16 February 1964.

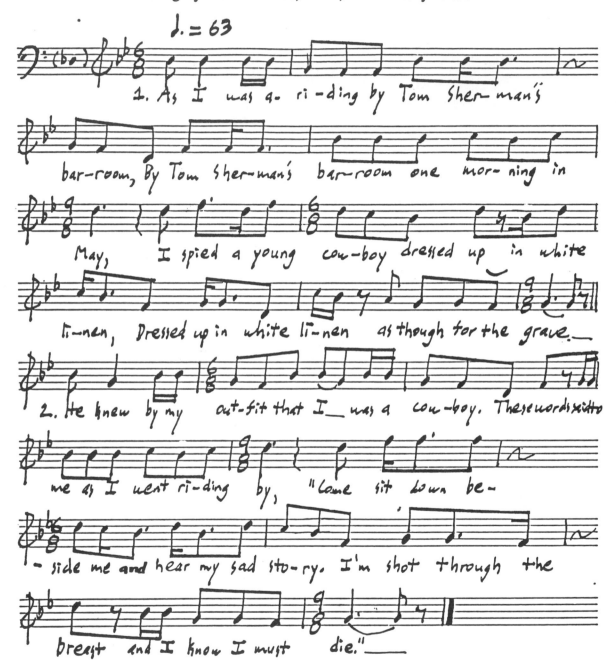

1. As I was a-riding by Tom Sherman's barroom,
    By Tom Sherman's barroom one morning in May,
    I spied a young cowboy dressed up in white linen,

Dressed up in white linen as though for the grave.

2. He knew by my outfit that I was a cowboy.
   These words [he] said to me as I went riding by,
   "Come sit down beside me and hear my sad story.
   I'm shot through the breast and I know I must die."

3. "So beat your drum lowly and play the fife slowly
   And play the Dead March as they bear me along.
   Take me to the graveyard 'n' throw the sod o'er me,
   For I'm a wild cowboy and I know I've done wrong."

4. "Oncet in the saddle I used to go dashing:
   Oncet in the saddle I used to feel gay.
   I first took to drinking and then to bad comp'ny
   And then took to fighting and now to my grave."

5. "Break the news softly to my gray-haired mother;
   Break it as softly to my sister dear.
   And not a-one word of this place do you mention
   When they gather around you my story to hear."

6. "And then there's another more dearer than a sister.
   Oh, how she will weep when she hears I am gone.
   But there'll be another to gain her affections,
   For I'm a wild cowboy and know I've done wrong."

7. "Go and get me a glass of cold water
   To cool my hot temples," this cowboy he said.
   And when I returned he had gone to the Giver;
   This one lonesome cowboy lay senseless and dead.

8. "So beat your drum lowly and play the fife slowly
   And play the Dead March as they bear me along.
   Take me to the graveyard and throw the sod o'er me,
   For I'm a wild cowboy and I know I've done wrong."

I have transcribed the melody of the first and fifth stanzas of TR 100 rather than the first and second, since there is a variation in the internal cadence that takes place only in stanza 5. This will be discussed further in Chapter 9 (p. 381).

This song is thought of as typical of the American West, yet it actually originated in England. This version is its second metamorphosis. In its original English form it was a broadside known as "The Unfortunate Rake" or "The Unfortunate Lad." The protagonist is a young man who has contracted syphilis and is dying of its effects.

The Unfortunate Rake

1. As I was a-walking down by St. James' Hospital,
   As I was a-walking down by there one day,
   What should I spy but one of my comrades
   All wrapped up in flannel though warm was the day.

2. I asked him what ailed him, I asked him what
       failed him,
   I asked him the cause of all his complaint.
   "It's all on account of some handsome young woman,
   'Tis she that has caused me to weep and lament.

3. "And had she but told me before she disordered me,
   Had she but told me of it in time,
   I might have got pills and salts of white mercury,
   But now I'm cut down in the height of my prime.

4. "Get six young soldiers to carry my coffin,
   Six young girls to sing me a song,
   And each of them carry a bunch of green laurel
   So they don't smell me as they bear me along.

5. "Don't muffle your drums and play your fifes merrily,
   Play a quick march as you carry me along,
   And fire your bright muskets all over my coffin,
   Saying: There goes an unfortunate lad to his home."[30]

Mercury was often prescribed as a cure for venereal disease. There is evidence that this ballad existed in oral tradition in the eighteenth century, but the first full texts are found in English and Irish broadsides of the subsequent century. Since he asks for a military funeral, the unfortunate lad cut down in his prime is apparently a member of the armed forces. This is made more apparent in later variants in which he is described as a trooper, a soldier, or a sailor.[31]

At some point in the process of oral transmission the sex of the protagonist was changed. In this new form it is entitled "The Bad Girl's Lament" or "One Morning in May." Below is a variant of the former.

The Bad Girl's Lament

1. As I walked down to St. James' Hospital,
   St. James' Hospital early one day,
   I spied my only fairest daughter
   Wrapped up in white linen as cold as the clay.

CHORUS:

> So beat your drums and play the fife lowly,
> And play the dead march as you carry me along;
> Take me to the churchyard and lay the sod over me,
> For I am a young maid and I know I've done wrong.

2. Once in the street I used to look handsome;
   Once in the street I used to dress gay;
   First to the ale house, then to the dance hall
   Then to the poor house and now to my grave.

CHORUS

3. Send for the preacher to pray o'er my body,
   Send for the doctor to heal up my wounds,
   Send for the young man I first fell in love with,
   That I might see him before I pass on.

CHORUS

4. Let six pretty maidens with a bunch of red roses,
   Six pretty maidens to sing me a song,
   Six pretty maidens with a bunch of red roses
   To lay on my coffin as they carry me along.

CHORUS[32]

The paraphernalia of a military funeral has now become part of the chorus, and she asks for maidens, rather than men, to carry her coffin. The cause of death is no longer explicit, but in some variants, as in the following stanza from "One Morning in May," the listener is clued in by the fact that she is salivating. Mercury, when employed in the treatment of venereal disease, causes an excess flow of saliva.

> Go send for the preacher to come and pray for me;
> Go send for the doctor to heal up my wounds;
> My poor head is aching, my sad heart is breaking,
> My body's salivated, and Hell is my doom.[33]

Variants of "The Bad Girl's Lament" were sung in the United States[34] and formed the basis for the second metamorphosis of the ballad. When "The Bad Girl's Lament" is compared with TR 100, "The Cowboy's Lament," or TR 101, "The Wild Cowboy," it will be seen that the English and American ballads have much in common.

The chorus of "The Bad Girl's Lament" is now incorporated almost as a whole, and the following stanza from the American form of the ballad:

"Oncet in the saddle I used to go dashing:
Oncet in the saddle I used to feel gay.
I first took to drinking and then to bad comp'ny
And then took to fighting and now to my grave."

closely parallels this stanza from the English form:

Once in the street I used to look handsome;
Once in the street I used to dress gay;
First to the ale house, then to the dance hall
Then to the poor house and now to my grave.[35]

It was the morning of 2 July 1881. President James A. Garfield was chatting with his friend and companion, Secretary of State James G. Blaine, as they slowly walked through the nearly deserted Baltimore and Potomac Station toward their train. At their rear there suddenly appeared a slight young man with a dark beard. He pulled a revolver from his pocket and fired two shots into Garfield's back. As the president slumped to the floor his assailant pocketed his revolver, turned, and walked hurriedly toward the exit. He might have escaped had not a Washington policeman, Patrick Kearney, been standing on the sidewalk outside the station. Hearing the shots, Kearney rushed to the entrance and, pulling open the door, collided with the dark-bearded young man. "I have a message to send to General Sherman," he told the officer in an agitated tone. But Kearney would not let him pass since he had come from the direction of the shooting. Almost immediately the depot watchman and the ticket taker ran up and joined forces with Kearney. Charles Julius Giteau, twenty-five, assassin of the twentieth president of the United States, was caught.

TR 102 Charles Giteau

(Laws AM E 11)

Sung by Roxie South King, Bloomington, 15 April 1960.

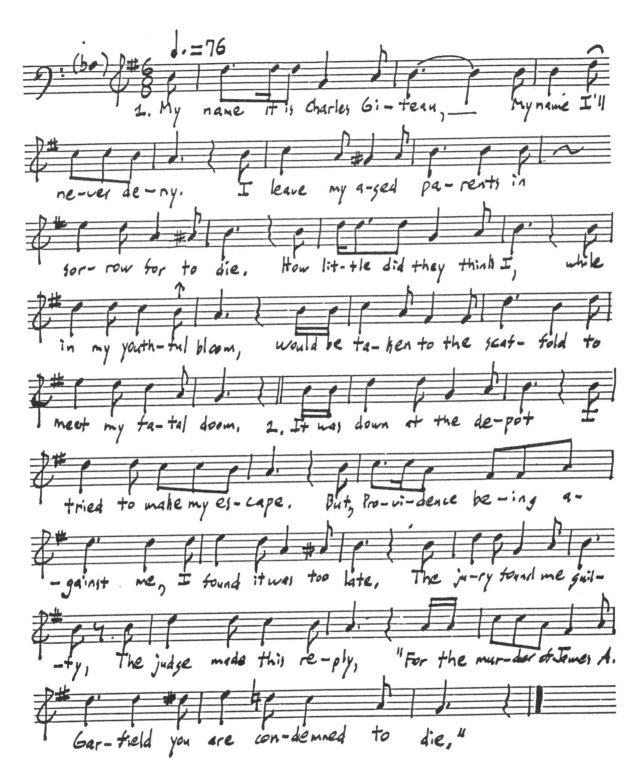

1. My name it is Charles Giteau, my name I'll never deny.
   I leave my ancient parents in sorrow for to die.
   How little did they think I, while in my youthful
      bloom,
   Would be taken to the scaffold to meet my fatal doom.

2. It was down at the depot I tried to make my escape
   But, Providence being against me, I found it was
      too late.
   The jury found me guilty, the judge made this reply,
   "For the murder of James A. Garfield, you are condemned
      to die."

3. My sister came to the prison to bid her last farewell.
   She threw her arms around my neck and wept
      most bitterly.
   Says she, "My darling brother, today you'll surely die
   For the murder of James A. Garfield upon the
      scaffold high."

Charles Giteau had been a very nervous and hyperactive child who had difficulty in learning to speak. His mother died when he was seven, and his father remarried. He was primarily raised by his sister, Frances, who was almost six years his senior.

His father, Luther, was a religious fanatic and a convert of John Humphrey Noyes, who in 1840 founded the controversial Oneida Community in New York. The community was based on "Bible Communism," which apparently applied not only to property and work but also to child rearing and sexual relations. For various reasons Luther never joined the community, but Charles twice went in and out of the Oneida. Giteau spent much time at YMCAs and camp meetings; he married a young woman he met under these circumstances, but they were divorced five years later.

Unsuccessful as a lawyer or as a lecturer on theology and politics, he tried to secure a political patronage appointment, buttonholing politicians in the corridors of the White House and writing to Secretary of State Blaine proposing that he be made a consul at Vienna or Paris.

He considered himself a Stalwart, one of the wing of the Republican party that believed in patronage, and was bitterly opposed to Garfield's movement toward civil service. Continually frustrated in his search for a political appointment, Giteau finally felt called by God to kill Garfield so that the Stalwarts could return to power. The following letter addressed to General William Tecumseh Sherman was found on his person when he was apprehended at the railway station:

To General Sherman:

I have just shot the President. I shot him several times, as I wished him to go as easily as possible. His death was a political necessity. I am a lawyer, theologian and politician. I am a Stalwart of the Stalwarts. . . . I am going to the jail. Please order out your troops, and take possession of the jail at once.

Very respectfully,

Charles Giteau

Giteau's was the first sensational American murder trial in which insanity was an important aspect of the defense. The trial soon became an arena in which the differing schools of psychiatry aired their conflicting concepts of mental health and of how the law should deal with issues of insanity, problems which are still with us.[36] Giteau was ambivalent, at times claiming to be insane and, at others, sane. This is reflected in a stanza from another variant of the ballad:

> I tried to be insane
> But I found it ne'er would do.
> The people were all against me,
> To escape there was no clue.
> Judge Cox, he read my sentence,
> His clerk he wrote it down,
> I'd be taken to the scaffold
> To meet my earthly doom.[37]

During this period the American public would probably have not been satisfied with anything less than a guilty verdict, and Charles Giteau was hanged on 30 June 1882.

The ballad seems to have been based on an earlier model, requiring only a change of name:

> My name it is John T. Williams,
> My name I'll never deny,
> I'll leave my dear old parents
> To suffer and to die,
> For murdering . . . .
> Upon the scaffold high.[38]

This was apparently sung in Iowa, Nebraska, and Canada in the 1870s before Garfield was assassinated.

TR 103 The Battle of Stone River

Sung by Oscar "Doc" Parks, Alton, 30 December 1963.

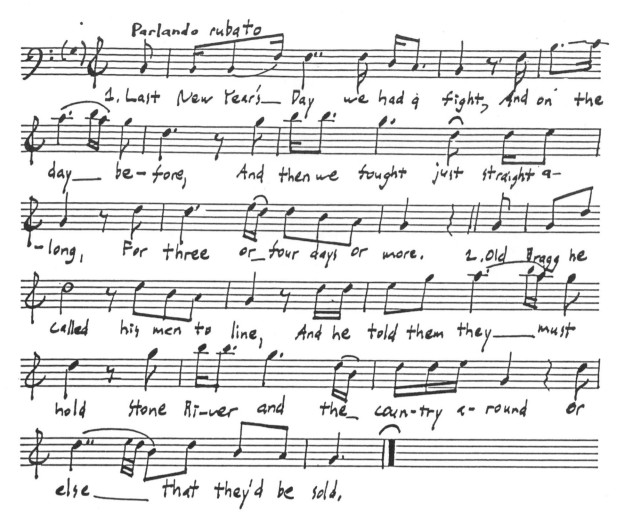

1. Last New Year's Day we had a fight,
   And on the day before,
   And then we fought just straight along,
   For three or four days or more.

2. Old Bragg he called his men to line,
   And he told them they must hold
   Stone River and the country around,
   Or else that they'd be sold.

3. Hardee was in the cedar swamp,
   That line just on the right,
   Our general had his men in line
   All ready for the fight.

4. When General Johnson saw their force,
   He told them men to run,
   He said that it was in vain to fight
   Them rebels ten to one.

5. But when Rosecrans saw their scheme,

He understood their plot,
And he reinforced General Van Cleves,
And made them rebels hot.

6. I never will forget that day,
    The ground all stained with blood,
    When hundreds of our gallant men
    Lie weltering in the mud.

7. We fought full five hours or more,
    Them rebels would not yield,
    Until our dead and wounded men
    Lied piled upon the field.

8. They swore they would not leave the field,
    And Breckenridge rolled in.

9. He took advantage of the night
    While everything was still,
    And he brave[ly] dashed into the fight,
    And there fell General Sills.

10. In wild confusion they left the ground,
    Stone River they plunged through,
    And they never stopped to look around
    For Yankees as they flew.

Parks was seventy-one at the time the recording was made, but was still able to maintain his high-pitched, ornamented, mountaineer style of singing. He paused to clear his throat after stanza 7 and in continuing apparently omitted the first two lines of stanza 8.

The ballad is a most vivid description by a foot soldier of one of the fiercest battles that occurred during the greatest period of civil strife in our history. It is imbued with the fervor of one ready to die for the Northern cause. All the generals mentioned were actually present, and General Joshua Woodrow Sills was indeed killed in action, as were numbers of common soldiers, many from Indiana. But like many ballads it is hardly accurate history.

The battle, known as Stone's River or Murfreesboro, began on New Year's Day of 1863 in Tennessee and was characterized more by carnage than by victory. The Northern Army of the Cumberland, commanded by Major General William S. Rosecrans, and the Southern Army of the Tennessee, commanded by Major General Braxton Bragg, were nearly equal in forces. There was mismanagement and bad luck on each side, which cost both sides almost nineteen thousand dead and wounded. After four days of fighting both armies were exhausted. Bragg had little choice but to retreat. Rosecrans was in a much better position to secure reinforcements than Bragg, and the river was rising behind him so that he might have been cut off had he waited. There was no real pursuit. The cut-up Army of the Cumberland stumbled into Murfreesboro and spent several months recuperating.[39] Of such stuff are heroic ballads made.

Commentary

During the First World War Cecil Sharp, the eminent student of English folk song, came to the United States, where he did extensive fieldwork in our Southern Highlands, the results of which were published in his superb collection, *English Folk Songs from the Southern Appalachians* (1932). On 13 and 14 April 1915 he offered two lectures in Chicago at the Quadrangle Club and the Little Theater. According to Leah Jackson Wolford, who was in attendance:

> Mr. Sharp said that the United States had no folk-lore of its own, for all of that which at first seemed to have originated here could be traced back to some other country. Although he deplored our barren fate, he did suggest that Americans turn for inspiration to the folk-music of England "for," to use his own words, "the songs are at least in your own tongue." [40]

After making this authoritative statement, typical of a representative of the then flourishing British Empire, Sharp spent parts of 1916, 1917, and 1918 in our Southern Highlands, where he collected numerous songs which had prototypes in England and carefully ignored those which had not.

Nowhere in the two volumes resulting from these investigations does he as much as mention the existence of songs of American origin, although they obviously were being sung in the region. In his work Sharp provides a map of the counties in which he collected during the forty-six weeks of field-work. One of these was Harlan County, Kentucky, famous for its feuds. In this same county the team of Loraine Wyman and Howard Brockway collected the words and melodies respectively of "Little Mohee," an American ballad of which two examples are given in Chapter 4 (TR 50-51). The Harlan variant of this song was published with piano accompaniment by Brockway in 1916 in *Lonesome Tunes: Folk Songs from the Kentucky Mountains*.[41]   As it happens, I was enrolled in a course concerning the larger musical forms under Brockway at the Juilliard School of Music in 1933. When analysis of the intricacies of the music of Richard Strauss' opera, *Elektra*, became wearisome, Brockway would both refresh and delight students by playing some of his arrangements of these Appalachian melodies.

Songs Sung in the Southern Appalachians (1934) by Mellinger E. Henry contains a number of texts of American ballads sung in the area. From Sevier County, Tennessee, where Sharp also worked, comes "The Santa Barbara Earthquake," collected in 1929.[42] From Avery County, North Carolina, where according to Sharp's map he did not work, but which forms part of the highland area and borders three counties in which he did collect (Unicoi, Tennessee; Yancey and MacDowell, North Carolina), comes "Shady Valley (The Jealous Lover)," collected in 1933,[43] of which two examples are found in this chapter (TR 89-90), "Gladys Kincaid," collected in 1932,[44] and "Old Smokey,"[45] collected in 1930. These five American ballads are listed or mentioned in George Malcolm Laws's *Native American Balladry*.[46]

The "Little Mohee" collected by Brockway in 1916 and "The Jealous Lover" collected by Henry in 1933 have had a wide distribution, the former from Nova Scotia to Mississippi and the latter from Nova Scotia to Arkansas. There is a difference of twelve to fifteen years between the Sharp and Brockway collections and that of Henry, but it is unlikely that the bulk of the American tradition could spring into being in such a short period. As a matter of fact, Henry also collected in Avery County a variant of "The Orphan Girl" (TR 68-69), which undoubtedly dates back to the Victorian period of the last century.[47]

As pointed out previously, there are many other signs of the Victorian influence. The ballads are no longer impersonal; the first person pronoun appears with some frequency. The ballads are more sentimental, and there is a greater emphasis upon mourning for the dead. There is also more evidence as to the songs' origins than there is for the older ballads from Britain. The moralizing or advice offered at the end of a song is occasionally found in the older British ballads, as in that of which TR 2-3, "Two Babes in the Woods," are curtailed variants. And if the sample offered in this chapter is at all representative, such endings multiply in the American tradition.

367

The forms in which the songs are cast are much more varied than those found in the previous chapter. With two exceptions the British ballads were cast in the common or ballad meter. In one of these two exceptions the poem could have been written in quatrain form in common meter, except for the requirements of the melodic stanza. In this chapter only five out of the sixteen songs included are in quatrains in common or ballad meter. The others are in eight-line stanzas which, if one ignored the musical stanza, could be broken down into quatrains in ballad meter. The other poems are in quatrain form, but in long meter. The remaining five songs are characterized by lines of three or six stresses. Musically these are in most cases in triple meter and reflect the omnipresent influence of the waltz in the latter part of the last century. (TR 97, "Pearl Bryan," as sung by Oscar "Doc" Parks, is not one of the latter.)

There are no choruses and no repetitions of last lines or of the last two lines. Repetition takes the form of the reprise of stanzas or of lines as, "Pray, Edward, take me home" in TR 90, "The Jealous Lover." Certain words or ideas occur in a number of songs. The verb "to ramble" and the noun "tomb" occur frequently. Those who mourn always included the mother, often gray-haired, and in several instances the sister and sweetheart as well.

As far as can be determined, all but one of the ballads offered in this chapter had their origin in America. The ballad represented here by TR 100-101, "The Cowboy's Lament," or "The Wild Cowboy" (Laws lists this ballad as "The Dying Cowboy") had its origin in England, but has been so modified that it can now only be considered American in character. Returning to Sharp's comments, he would have been more correct if he had stated that since the majority of the population of the United States was descended from immigrants of the British Isles, American folk songs would naturally have been based upon British models. It is therefore not strange to find similar themes being pursued.

CHAPTER 8   THE BALLAD IN RETROSPECT

Throughout the last few chapters I have at times commented on the lack of expository material, especially that explaining motivation, in ballad poems. These are not new insights on my part. MacEdward Leach characterizes the ballad as follows:

> A ballad is a story. Of the four elements common to all narrative--action, character, setting, and theme--the ballad emphasizes the first. Setting casual; theme is often implied; characters are usually types and even when more individual are undeveloped, but action carries the interest. . . . The ballad practices rigid economy in relating the action; incidents antecedent to the climax are often omitted, as are explanatory and motivating details. The action is usually of a plot sort and the plot often reduced to the movement of climax; that is, of the unstable situation and the resolution which constitutes plot.[1]

Leach notes that many ballads omit almost all expository material and give the listener only the crisis and resolution. Tristram Coffin has attempted to explain how and why this occurs. He suggests that "plotting is vestigial, rather than vital, in the make-up of Anglo-American ballads. . . . Generally, the folk tend to discard plotting in favor of something one might call 'impact' or 'emotional core.'" Coffin does not believe that it is action per se which interests folk, but that they "retain, in the long run, only enough of the original action or plot unity to hold this core of emotion in some sort of focus."[2]

Coffin postulates that the Anglo-American ballad goes through three stages:

> Stage 1. A poem, created by an individual, enters or is retained in the oral tradition. This poem has . . . an emotional core, details of action, and frills of a poetic style which are too "sophisticated" for the folk. . . .
> Stage 2. This is the "ballad" stage. The frills of subliterary style have been worn away by oral tradition; some of the action details have been lost. . . .
> Stage 3. In this final stage the ballad develops in one of two ways. Either unessential details drop off until lyric emerges, or essential details drop off until only a meaningless jumble, centered about a dramatic core, is left.

This latter form is usually known as a "degenerate ballad," although Coffin describes this term as "poor."[3]

Coffin offers "Mary Hamilton" (Child 173) as an example of a ballad which has developed to the third stage and which is in lyrical form. Unfortunately I did not find a variant of it in the Indiana repertory. Francis James Child's variant A has eighteen stanzas. The first five deal with Mary Hamilton's out-of-wedlock pregnancy and her drowning of her child, the fifth through tenth stanzas with her trial. The last eight reflect her feelings, especially those concerning her parents, as she waits on the scaffold to be hanged. It is this snuffing out of the life of a young and beautiful girl by the law which Coffin believes to be the "emotional core" of the ballad. As an example of this ballad in its third stage, he reproduces the following variant collected by Phillips Barry:

1. Yestre'en the queen had four Maries,
   This nicht she'll hae but three;
   There was Mary Beaton, an' Mary Seaton,
   An' Mary Carmichael an' me.

2. Last nicht I dressed Queen Mary
   An' pit on her braw silken goon,
   An' a' thanks I've gat this nicht
   Is tae be hanged in Edinboro toon.

3. O little did my mither ken,
   The day she cradled me,
   The land I was tae travel in,
   The death I was tae dee.

4. They've tied a hanky roon me een,
   An' they'll no let me see tae dee:
   An' they've pit on a robe o' black
   Tae hang on the gallows tree.

5. Yestre'en the queen had four Maries
   This nicht she'll hae but three;
   There was Mary Beaton, an' Mary Seaton,
   An' Mary Carmichael an' me.

Of the above Coffin writes:

Here is a lyric poem with but the merest suggestion of a plot. Only the facts that the girl was one of the Queen's favored maidens and is now about to die remain clear. Yet the emotional core, girlhood and its beauty snuffed out by law, is as clear as it was in Child A.[4]

Coffin is interested in the ballad as art. The article which I am discussing is titled, "Mary

Hamilton and the Anglo-American Ballad as an Art Form." Coffin is primarily concerned with variants of ballads, which, often by mere chance, measure up to Western European aesthetic standards. This Coffin believes to be the case in the variant of "Mary Hamilton," reproduced above, and of a number of others which are commonly found in anthologies. He states that the American ballad, "Charles Giteau" (TR 102), has also reached the third and lyrical stage, but he finds its text inferior as poetry.[5]

My purpose here has been to give a representative sampling of folk songs sung in southern Indiana, including ballads, and to offer as much of their historical and sociological background as possible. I have attempted, in general, to refrain from making artistic judgments. The cultural process by which ballads become as truncated as they do is, of course, of interest. TR 86, "The Hangman Song," certainly offers nothing but crisis and resolution. Whether it is "lyrical," as Coffin views this quality, I cannot say. It is, like "Mary Hamilton" and a very few other of the old British ballads, couched in the first person. TR 2-3, "Two Babes in the Woods," is another ballad truncated to the merest of crisis and resolution. Children who listened to it found it "sad," but I doubt if it expresses "intense emotion," which is the dictionary definition of "lyric." Perhaps it would be more proper to speak of "emotional impact" rather than "emotional core" in discussing such ballads. Some ballads could be reduced to the crisis and resolution only and still have emotional impact. Others perhaps cannot.

Certainly it is the crisis and resolution which has the greatest impact on the folk, for this seems to be the part of the ballad they most easily remember. I give below, in a slightly modified form, the results of a comparison of transcriptions of recordings of Child 4, "Lady Isabel and the Elf Knight," as found in the Archives of Traditional Music. To these I apply a type of analysis derived to some extent from concepts applied by the French classical dramatists. TR 76 of Chapter 6 is so analyzed below. To save space I have omitted the repeated last line of each stanza and the added syllables preceding it.

Exposition

1. "He followed me up and he followed me around
   And he followed me around all day.

371

I had not power to speak a word,
Nor tongue to answer nay."

2. "Go bring me some of your father's gold
And some of your mother's fee
And I'll take you to the salt sea sands
And there we'll marry at sea."

First Episode

3. She mounted upon a milk white steed
And he the iron gray,
And they rode till they came to the salt sands,
Three hours before 'twas day.

Crisis and Resolution

4. "Alight, alight, my pretty Polly Ann,
Alight, alight," said he,
"For six kings' daughters have I drownded here
And the seventh one you shall be."

5. "Take off, take off those fine, fine clothes
And lay them on this rock,
For they are too fine and costelly
To lie in the sea and rot."

6. "It's turn your face three times around,
Your back to the leaves on the tree."
Then she picked him up most manfully
And plunged him into the sea.

7. "Help me out, help me out, my pretty Polly Ann,
Help me out, help me out," said he,
"And we will go to the next sea sands
And there we'll marry at sea."

8. "Lie there, lie there, you false-hearted one,
Lie there instead of me.
If six kings' daughters you have drownded here
The seventh one you shall be."

Second Episode

9. She mounted up on her milk-white steed,
And led the iron gray,
And she rode till she came to her own father's door,
Three hours before it was day.

Secondary Crisis and Resolution

10. "Hush up, hush up, my pretty parrot,
Don't tell no tales on me.

Your cage shall be lined with beads of gold
And hung on a willow tree."

The entire Exposition may be, and often is, omitted, as is the First Episode. The same is true of the Second Episode and the Secondary Crisis and Resolution. The Crisis and Resolution is the drama proper, without which the history is lost.

The table below gives the total number of stanzas of text of each variant transcribed and the number of stanzas of each variant which fall within the five indicated sections of the narrative. TR 76 is Variant I in this table.

Table 1. Comparison of eleven variants of Child 4

VARIANT NO.	NUMBER OF STANZAS IN EACH SECTION					TOTALS
	Exposition	Episode	Crisis & Resolution	Episode	2nd Crisis & Resolution	
I	3	1	5	1	2	12
II	2	1	5	1	1	10
III	3	1	4	1	1	10
IV	2	1	4	1	2	10
V	2	1	4			7
VI			6			6
VII			4	1	1	6
VIII			5			5
IX			3			3
X			1		1	2
XI			1			1
Totals	12	5	42	5	8	72

In most cases the Crisis and Resolution section contains more stanzas than the other four sections added together. Even when the ballad is reduced in length some part of this central section, of this gist of the plot, always remains. The one stanza of XI, for example, consists of the order to undress:

> "Take off, take off, your silken gown,
> Deliver them unto me.
> For six pretty maids I've drownded here
> And the seventh one you shall be."

Variant VI contains the full Crisis and Resolution and nothing else. It begins with the villain's announcement of his intention and proceeds in logical order to the maid's taunt. After performing it the singer commented, "There are two more verses and two before it commences but I can't recollect them." What he does remember is the entire Crisis and Resolution in approximately the same order as found in I. The same is true of the eighth variant given in the table.

A singer may not remember material from all five sections listed in the analysis but, as mentioned above, all the renditions analyzed contain at least part of the Crisis and Resolution. In four cases, VI, VIII, IX, and XI, elements from no other sections are found in the rendition. When the performance contains only a small number of stanzas, as in IX, or one stanza only, as in XI, the stanzas performed represent part of this central section and are sufficiently characteristic to identify the incomplete text as part of this particular ballad.[6]

Since it is the Crisis and Resolution aspect of the ballad, or at least part thereof, that singers remember, this is the section which carries the emotional impact, or, in Coffin's words, the emotional core. The emotional impact may be produced not only by an exploration of the feelings of the character or characters but also by the situation itself, that is, by the gist of the plot. When a ballad wears down and reaches Coffin's third stage it is the situation or plot which remains, not only the expression of feelings by the characters.

In Chapter 7 mention was made of the frequent emphasis on death, mourning, and motherhood in the native American ballads, as well as their tendency to have moralizing endings. Since most American

374

ballads seem to have had their origin in the nineteenth century, perhaps these phenomena can be explained by the examination of the historical trends during the period, both specific and general.

Mark Tristram Coffin has studied the American narrative obituary verse, which was written to be sung or recited at funerals in rural communities in the Northeast in the eighteenth and nineteenth centuries. He is of the opinion that this verse had considerable influence on the development of native American balladry. These narrative poems were cast in quatrain form and in long meter. The rhyming scheme was *a a b b*. A further characteristic is the use of a subtitle, a device also found in early ballads and broadsides. The poem emphasizes the mourning of the friends and relatives of the deceased, while simultaneously indicating that he or she has moved to a better afterlife. The poems were never composed in the first person, but are full of clichés, stock phrases, and repetition of the same sentiments.

Moralizing also is a common characteristic of this genre. Only a few native American ballads are based on narrative obituary poems, and none are found in this volume. However, according to Coffin, the style of the narrative obituary poem has affected many such ballads. Among these he mentions "The Jealous Lover" (TR 90), "Pearl Bryan" (TR 97-98), "Fuller and Warren" (TR 95-96), and "Young Charlotte" (TR 91-92).[7] These, he writes, "are more closely tied to the traditions of the broadside composers than to the folk habit of composing narrative funeral verses," but have been affected by their style. The ballad is usually about sensational events which capture the public interest, while the narrative obituary poem is in most cases composed concerning average individuals.[8]

The narrative obituary poem was necessarily a reflection of the culture of its time. The general character of society during the Victorian period must have produced the emphasis upon death, mourning, and moralizing. In *The Feminization of American Culture* (1978), Ann Douglas discusses the changes which occurred in American society between 1829 and 1875. Her thesis is that with the weakening of Calvinism the ministry lost much of its prestige, and ministers turned to middle- and upper-class women, who had leisure for pious activity, as allies. A literature developed in which women writers and editors combined with the liberal clergy to produce works of diluted religious content. With the rise of taboos against the discussion of bodily functions such as procreation and birth, literature turned to death and illness as its principal subjects. This led to moralizing and the glorifica-

tion of motherhood, without mention of its physical aspects. From the fascination with death grew the

cemetery movement, with its tombs covered with winged angels, extravagant mausoleums, and halls of fame

for the dead. As Douglas puts it:

> Barred by external taboos and internal anxieties from elaboration on the overtly
> sexual acts of impregnation and childbirth, they concentrated on illness and death:
> they were more interested in the moments at which crude energy failed than in those
> at which it accelerated.[9]
>
> In the midst of the transformation of the American economy into the most powerful-
> ly aggressive capitalist system in the world, American culture seemed bent on es-
> tablishing a perpetual Mother's Day.[10]

Thus through the writing of the upper-class women and the liberal clergy there was a thorough

sentimentalization of the American culture during the latter part of the Victorian period. These writ-

ings affected the general public as well, and the results can clearly be seen in many of the native

American ballads offered in Chapter 7.

When the data has been available I have endeavored to ascertain the origin of the numerous

ballads offered in this volume. In no case was there evidence that a ballad had originated as an impro-

visation by a particular individual. James H. Jones has postulated that ballads could have come into

being in this manner by the use of well-known formulaic devices.

According to Jones's theory the many variants existing for the same ballad may not be due to

the processes of oral transmission, that is, slow changes due to lapses in memory and changes in taste

and environment and the semiconscious artistic impulses of the singer. Rather, the experienced singer

of ballads keeps in mind only a broad outline of the narrative, which he or she then relates through

the use of commonplace stanzas, half stanzas, lines, and phrases.[11]

Jones's theory is based on Albert B. Lord's analysis of the formulaic improvisation of epics

by Serbo-Croatian singers. These *guslars* were able to improvise an epic employing only a general

plan of the narrative and a traditional stock of formulas and themes.[12]

Jones offers some intriguing evidence in applying the theory of formulaic composition to Scottish and English ballads as published by Child. For example, the visit of a lover is often described by one variation or another of the following commonplace stanza:

> He is on to Annie's bower-door,
> And tirled at the pin:
> "Oh sleep ye, wake ye, my love, Annie,
> Ye'll rise, lat me come in."

This is stanza 5 in Child 71, "The Bent Sae Brown," and is also found, with some change of detail, in at least half a dozen other Child ballads. Both halves of this fourteen-stress commonplace stanza, or seven-stress two-line half-stanzas, may be commonplaces in their own right. The first half is found in stanza 2 of 70B, "Willie and Lady Maisry" as well as in at least five other Child ballads:

> But he is on to Maisry's bower-door,
> And tirled at the pin:

This, or any other seven-stress commonplace, can be combined with another half-stanza to form a different commonplace stanza. Here is such a combination, stanza 2 of 74B, "Fair Margaret and Sweet William":

> Sweet William came to Lady Margaret's bower,
> And knocked at the ringe,
> And who so ready as Lady Margaret
> To rise and let him in.

Now let us look at some of the texts transcribed in Chapter 6.

The same commonplace stanza forms stanza 4 of TR 78:

> He rode till he came to Eleanor's bower,
> And rattled at the ring,
> And who was there so ready as she,
> To rise and let him in.

And in incremental repetition as stanza 11:

> She rode until she came to Lord Thomas' bower

377

And rattled at the ring,
And none was there so ready as he
To rise and let her in.

In TR 79 it also forms stanza 4:

He rode until he came to fair Ellender's gate.
He jingled at the ring,
And who so ready as fair Ellender, herself,
To rise and let him in?

And in incremental repetition stanza 9.

Jones offers other examples. In many plots there is the need to greet an individual who is bringing a message, as in this seven-stress commonplace in stanza 8 of Child 87B, "Prince Robert":

"What news, what news, my bonnie boy?
What news have ye to me?"

This can be seen in stanza 5 of TR 78:

"What news, what news, Lord Thomas," she said,
"What news have you brung to me?"

And in the same stanza in TR 79:

"What news, what news, Lord Thomas," she cried,
"What news have you brought to me?"

Jones also cites examples of one-line commonplaces, such as the following from Child 20B, "The Cruel Mother," and elsewhere:

She's taen out her little pen-knife,

In Chapter 6 this is found as stanza 14 of TR 78:

The brown girl she had a little pen knife.

Albert B. Friedman has pointed out flaws in Jones's theory of formulaic improvisation. He notes that the Serbo-Croatian epics recorded by Albert B. Lord and Milman Parry run from six hundred to thirteen thousand lines. "Every improvised epic is unique: none resembles another in the way that a given ballad text is a version or a variant of another." The remarkable similarity among variants and versions in the Child ballads makes it inconceivable that these are recorded from improvisation. Friedman concludes, "memorization, not improvisation by means of commonplaces, is the basic vehicle of oral tradition."[13] I should add that the Serbo-Croatian epics were sung to a series of melodic formulas adapted to the requirements of the singers, while the ballad is sung to a more or less fixed stanzaic melody, which, incidentally, because of its stability, aids in the memorization of the text.

W. Edson Richmond has taken an intermediate position. In his study of the Norwegian ballads he has found one, "Den utrue egtemann," of which only four variants are known, and which seems without an exact parallel in Scandinavia or the remainder of Europe. Nevertheless, it would be difficult to imagine a more typical ballad plot, and it is replete with commonplace stanzas. "It is almost as though someone familiar with great numbers of folksongs had decided to compose a song using only stanzas frequently found in other ballads, settling upon a new if commonplace plot." He thus finds that the possibility exists that either an archetype upon which the four variants of this ballad are based or one of the variants was composed by formulaic improvisation, and the other variants derived from it. Although transmission by memorization may be the more common process, he believes one cannot rule out the possibility of the composition of a ballad by formulaic improvisation.[14]

Richmond's assertion of formulaic composition of this particular Norwegian ballad is heavily documented with cognate stanzas from other ballads in the Norwegian repertory. He is of the opinion that any stanza in a traditional European ballad can be matched with a similar stanza from another ballad.[15]

As I see it, formulaic improvisation may have been the origin of some special English or Scottish ballads in past centuries when this was a living, flourishing tradition. What I have offered in this volume are the remains of that tradition, as remembered by individuals who were born in the last century or early in this century. Ballad singing was no longer a living tradition when they were recorded, and all the items transcribed were probably transmitted by memory.

379

CHAPTER 9 THE TUNES

A folk song has both a text and a tune. These two aspects of song show some relationship. Melodic and verbal phrases normally coincide in length, but at times two verbal phrases may be sung to one musical phrase. The text may also be extended to fit a tune by the addition of nonsense syllables. Thus, should a singer wish to employ a four-phrase melody in singing a couplet, nonsense syllables can be inserted to extend the length of the text. This may be the origin of the nonsense syllables in TR 46, "The Two Lovers." Tune and text also show a relationship as far as musical accent and verbal stress are concerned. This was discussed in the commentary of Chapter 2, pp. 117-19. However, the text and tune of folk song do not necessarily remain in association. In addition, the tune is abstract while the text is lexically meaningful. The two are therefore best discussed separately.

Performance Practices

The great majority of the singers represented in this volume could not read music. Even in the case of the daughters of the Bryant family, who were trained to sing in choirs, it can be assumed that the tunes were sung by ear without reference to music notation. Thus many phenomena occur which would not if a professional musician were singing from a written or printed score. The most obvious of these are the pauses of uneven length which occur between the end of one stanza and the beginning of the subsequent one. A trained singer would move from stanza to stanza without losing a pulse. The folksinger feels himself under no such compunction. He or she may pause for half a pulse, or for as long as three pulses or more before moving on. This is such a common occurrence that I have not usually indicated it in detail. However, when the wait is of considerable length I have marked its occurrence by placing a fermata over the double bar at the end of the stanza after which the pause occurs. Less frequently, similar waits or pauses occur between the phrases of a stanza. In most cases I have indicated these with notated rests.

In traditional folksinging the tempo is not slowed down at the close of a song to indicate that it is coming to an end. Nevertheless, this device is employed occasionally by the singers and, in particular, by Albert J. Fields. When it is employed it can be assumed that the singer has been influenced in making such *ritardandos* by his or her hearing of art music.

Some of the songs, particularly the old ballads, are sung in the "parlando rubato" style (see Introduction, p. xxvi). Here there is no meter and no regular pulse. They are sung as much in prose as in musical rhythm. Even here, however, I have indicated the pauses between stanzas with the usual fermata.

When a song accompanies physical motion, such as a game or dance, or is accompanied by guitar, the pulse is usually adhered to rather strictly. Waits or pauses do not occur between phrases. Singers who are accustomed to accompanying themselves on the guitar, such as Lotus Dickey and Vern Smelser, show this influence in singing songs even without guitar. Their pulse in such songs is usually quite regular.

Even when the pulse is regular, a musical phrase may be lengthened or shortened by a folksinger. In TR 92, "Young Charlotte," Vern Smelser lengthens the second phrase of each stanza by one beat. In TR 93, "The Brooklyn Theater Fire," Viola Dodson curtails each melodic phrase by a short duration, represented by a quarter rest in the transcription.

Occasionally a singer may alter the common sequence of phrases in a song, probably not knowing that he or she has done so. This can be seen in TR 100, "The Cowboy's Lament." In all stanzas but the fifth, the midcadence occurs on the second degree of the scale, while in the fifth stanza it occurs on the first degree (this was briefly alluded to following the transcription). The pitches of the final cadence of a stanza may also be modified, as in TR 1, "Go Tell Aunt Rhody." The pitches of the cadence in the first stanza are 2 1 3 2 1, while those of the second are 2 4 3 2 1.

Finally, I should mention the few performances which are sung in the "ornamented" upland style. In this style the melody is elaborated, extending syllables by singing them on several pitches of short duration. This can be seen in the two performances of "Barb'ry Allan" by Oscar "Doc" Parks (TR 80-81) and, to a lesser extent, in his performance of "Pearl Bryan" (TR 97), and TR 77, Francis

Marion Stogdill's performance of "Six Kings' Daughters." That this type of singing is at least partly improvised is demonstrated by the fact that the singers do not perform the same number of pitches to a particular syllable in the melismata of each stanza. Parks is also the only singer to use falsetto to reach his high notes (TR 97, "Pearl Bryan").

Rhythmic Considerations

Table 2. Metric Organization

Type of Meter	Number of TRs
Duple simple	55
Duple compound	24
Triple simple	6
Triple compound	1
"Waltz time"	6
Duple simple with a "waltz time" chorus	1
"Parlando rubato" or frequent meter changes	10

In the above metrical analysis I have omitted consideration of an occasional change in meter. With this in mind, it can be stated that a majority of the transcriptions, 55 out of 103, are in duple simple meter (4/4 is counted as duple meter). The next most common meter is duple compound, of which there are 24 examples. Only one song is cast in triple compound meter. Six other songs have been classified as "waltz time." These could, with some logic, be written in duple compound meter (6/8 for example), but in these songs I felt the strong influence of the waltz tempo which was so common in the latter part of the last century. One transcription, of a popular song of the period, has a simple duple verse and a "waltz time" chorus.

A number of songs cannot be described as being in any particular meter. There are eight in which the meter is somewhat irregular, but a fairly regular pulse is maintained. These have been classified according to what I perceive as the dominant meter and are included under "Duple simple," etc. There are nine in "parlando rubato" style. Here no meter is indicated and there is no regular pulse. There is one (TR 74, "In the Baggage Coach Ahead") in which the meter changes are so frequent that it is all but impossible to detect the "waltz time" of the original sheet music, although the beat itself is reasonably steady.

There are a number of songs which display a fairly consistent change in meter. In TR 7, "Soldier, Soldier, Won't You Marry Me?," the first measure of each stanza is in 3/4, while the remainder is in 2/4. TR 99, "The Texas Rangers," is in 2/4, but in each stanza measures 2, 10, and 14 are in 5/8. Other TRs which exhibit a consistent change of meter are 39, 66, 68, 72, 82, 88, 89, 93, and 101. All are classified in the table by their dominant meter.

Considerations of Pitch

Table 3. Range

Range	Number of TRs
3rd	1
4th	4
5th	4
6th	11
7th	10
8ve	29
9th	26
10th	11
11th	7

The songs display a wide variety of ambitus or range. The children's songs exhibit a range as small as a 3rd and the adult songs as large as an 11th. The most common range is that of an octave, that of a 9th running a close second. The songs showing a range of an octave or a 9th total 55, which is over half of the corpus. Combining these with songs with a range of a 10th or 11th we have a total of 73. Thus songs with a range of an octave or larger make up the majority.

Table 4. Pitch Inventories

Pitch Inventory	Number of TRs
Tritonic	
G B^b C	6
G A B^b	1
Tetratonic	
G A B D	3
G B^b C D	1
Pentatonic	
G A B D E	10
(One of these does not end on G1)	
G A B D F$^\#$	1
G B^b C D F	2
G A C D E	1
G A C D F	1
Pentatonic with chromatic tone(s)	
G A B D d$^\#$ E	1
Pentachordal	
G A B C D	3
D E F$^\#$ G A	1
Pentachordal with chromatic tone(s)	
G A B C c$^\#$ D	1
G A B C D	1

(with e^b and f$^\#$ in a "tag"

unrelated to principal

melody)

<u>Hexatonic</u>

G A B D E F$^\#$ 9

G A B C D F$^\#$ 2

G A B^b C D F   2

G B C D E F   1

G A B D E F   1

G A C D E F   1

<u>Hexatonic with chromatic tone(s)</u>

G A B D e^b E F$^\#$ 1

G A B^b C c$^\#$ D F$^\#$ 1

<u>Hexatonic with modulating chromatic tone(s)</u>

G B C <u>c</u>$^\#$ D E F$^\#$ 1

    (This, TR 61, also ends on the

      third scale degree)

<u>Hexachordal</u>

G A B C D E   8

<u>Hexachordal with chromatic tone(s)</u>

G A B C D d$^\#$ E   1

<u>Heptatonic</u>

G A B C D E F$^\#$ 26

    (major scale)

G A B C D E F   3

    (mixolydian mode)

G A B^b C D E^b F   1

385

(aeolian mode)

G A B$^{\flat}$ C D E F   3

(dorian mode)

<u>Heptatonic with chromatic tone(s)</u>

G A a$^{\#}$ B C D E F$^{\#}$ 2

G A a$^{\#}$ B C c$^{\#}$ D E e$^{\#}$ F$^{\#}$ 1

G g$^{\#}$ A a$^{\#}$ B C D d$^{\#}$ E F$^{\#}$ 1

G g$^{\#}$ A a$^{\#}$ B C c$^{\#}$ D E e$^{\#}$ F$^{\#}$ 1

<u>Heptatonic with modulating chromatic tone(s)</u>

G A B C <u>c</u>$^{\#}$ D E F$^{\#}$ 2

(One clearly modulates, the

other is debatable)

G A B <u>c</u>$^{\#}$ D d$^{\#}$ E F$^{\#}$ 1

<u>Heptatonic with unclassifiable chromatic tone(s)</u>

G A B$^{\flat}$ B C D E F F$^{\#}$ 1

(Pitch inventories are classified as pentatonic, hexatonic, etc., by the number of principal scale tones contained therein. Chromatic tones are excluded for this purpose. Principal scale tones are indicated in CAPS. Chromatic tones which do not establish a modulation, but serve a passing or neighboring function, are indicated in lowercase letters. Chromatic tones which do establish a modulation are indicated in <u>underlined</u> lowercase letters.)

The variety of scales, or pitch inventories, displayed is very large. At one end are the tritonic scales of the children's taunts, and at the other end the heptatonic major scales with several chromatic tones. The most common scale is the major without chromatics. There are 26 examples of this out of the total of 103 songs. Next in importance, with ten examples, is the pentatonic scale G A B D E.

Nonheptatonic scales form about 59 percent of the corpus. Among the heptatonic scales are seven which are modal, three mixolydian, three dorian, and one aeolian. Only one song can be considered to be in the minor mode, TR 55, "Her Name Was Lil." This song is obviously an attempt to imitate a blues. There are ten pitch inventories which exhibit nonmodulating chromatic tones and three which modulate. One of the latter is TR 61, "The Cookery Maid," which also ends on the third scale degree. A fourth inventory, that of TR 2, "Two Babes in the Woods," may or may not contain a modulation. Finally, there is TR 49, "John Riley," the scale of which contains both a B-natural and a B-flat, as well as an F-natural and an F-sharp. The mode thus cannot be determined.

TR 53, "The Big Fat Rooster and the Little Red Hen," is basically pentachordal. A "tag" is added which contains a chromatic tone, plus the seventh scale degree, neither of which is found in the song proper.

The distribution of pitch inventories seen above is fairly typical of those in any fair-sized body of folk song. Cecil Sharp in his *English Folk Song: Some Conclusions* (1907) found the major mode to be the most common of all folk scales, but recovered no song couched in the minor mode.[1] He found a number of heptatonic scales cast in the "church" modes, mixolydian, dorian, and aeolian. He discusses various pentatonic modes,[2] and an examination of the tunes he collected readily reveals many songs with pentatonic and hexatonic scales.

However, Sharp's definition of folk song was much more restricted than that applied in this volume. His informants came almost entirely from rural areas. They were the remains of English peasantry, whose melodies had been little affected by urban popular and art music. These influences are much stronger in this corpus, which contains one song in the minor mode, several which modulate, and a large number which contain chromatic nonscale tones.

Table 5. Cadence Patterns

Pattern	Number of TRs
1 7 1	5
1 5 1	2

387

1 5 1	1
1 2 1	5
1 4 1	1
1 <u>6</u> 1	1
2 <u>7</u> 1	3
2 1	1
3 2 1	34
3 <u>7</u> 1	3
4 2 1	13
4 <u>7</u> 1	3
4 3 1	1 + 6 taunts
5 3 1	2
5 4 3	1
<u>5</u> <u>6</u> 1	1

Pattern	Count
<u>5</u> 2 1	2
5 2 1	3
5 3 2	1
<u>5</u> <u>7</u> 1	3
<u>6</u> <u>7</u> 1	9
<u>6</u> <u>5</u> 1	1
<u>7</u> <u>5</u> 1	4
<u>7</u> 2 1	2
Spoken	1

(In the above table, 1 represents g^1, 2 a^2, etc. When a number is underlined, this represents a pitch *below* g^1. Thus 5 would indicate D above g^1, while <u>5</u> would indicate D below g^1. No consideration has been given as to whether the intervals above or below g^1 are major or minor. Hence, for example, 3 would represent either B-natural or B-flat.)

When two stanzas of a song are transcribed they may have different cadence patterns. A song may also have a chorus which, in turn, may display a different cadence pattern. Thus for the 103 TRs there are actually 116 cadence patterns counted above.

The most common pattern by far, with 34 examples, is 3 2 1. Next, with 13 examples, is 4 2 1, followed by nine examples of <u>6</u> <u>7</u> 1. The taunts plus one other of the children's songs produce seven examples of 4 3 1. There are five examples each of two other patterns, 1 <u>7</u> 1 and 1 2 1.

Commentary

Certain melodic phenomena impress my ear as being characteristic of the Victorian period. They may also be considered influences of the Romantic movement in art music. The first of these is the use of the diminished 5th in the cadence pattern 4 7 1. This is found in three of the TRs, 50, 62, and 90. Another characteristic of the period is the beginning of a song with the sixth degree of the scale, as seen in TR 93, "The Brooklyn Theater Fire." (For another example of this see Stephen Foster's "Jeanie with the Light Brown Hair.")

Another melodic trait, which seems characteristic of the later Victorian period, is the upward leap of a 6th or 7th. Such leaps are found in TR 41, 49, 68, 90, and 93. Alternatively this can be considered a Scottish influence. Such large leaps, whether upwards or downward, are considered characteristic of Scottish folk song by Ann Dhu Shapiro.[3] The Scotch snap or syncopation (as in "Coming Through the Rye"), another trait of Scottish folk song offered by Shapiro, is rare in the songs offered in this volume.

TR 7, "Soldier, Soldier, Won't You Marry Me?" seems to be in the major mode since it outlines the tonic triad of this mode. However, the song ends on the second degree of the scale. This type of cadence, according to Shapiro, is also characteristic of Scottish folk song.[4] Sharp has a theory concerning such tunes. Many are dance tunes and are repeated over and over again, and it would be inappropriate to end each repetition on the tonic. Each stanza but the last, therefore, ends on a pitch different from the tonic and would "thus allow the repetition to be effected without break of continuity." According to Sharp the proper conclusion, which would only be performed once at the end of the song, would fall into disuse and be forgotten. Thus the tune would be "perpetuated in an incomplete form."[5]

In 1955 Bruno Nettl published an article concerning the tunes of British ballads collected in southern Indiana by Alan Lomax for the Library of Congress. This is the only previous study of folk music of the region. Nettl transcribed twenty-seven of the British ballads, but provided only six of these in the article and did not identify them. Any comparison of the present study and his is there-

390

fore difficult. However, Nettl did indicate that the range of the melodies he transcribed was between an octave and an 11th. The same is true for the melodies of the British ballads found in Chapter 7 of this work. Further, he comments on the ornamented singing style of Oscar "Doc" Parks and Marion Stogdill.[6] Thus in two aspects, at least, the two studies are in agreement.

Songs or chants, such as the taunts or other simple songs of children, which make repetitive use of melodic formulas limited in compass and pitch material, are widespread and in common use in Europe and America. George Herzog notes that the repertory of children often contains tunes of this simplicity. He lists as one of these simple formulas the pattern E G A (G B^b C in my transcriptions) and indicates that this is the melody to which "A Tisket, A Tasket" is sung. However, he finds that melodies composed of a repeated pattern of 2-5 pitches are also heard in the songs of European adults. They are more common in eastern and southern Europe than in the north or west and are found most frequently in calendric or seasonal songs concerned with the agricultural year, work songs, and songs of rural ceremonies such as marriage and burial. On the other hand, such simple melodies are rare in European adult songs with lyrical or narrative texts, such as ballads and romances. The music to which these genres are sung is usually more highly developed. The simpler melodic type, which he believes the child learns from an adult or older child, is therefore representative of the songs intimately connected with the functional life of the village. Herzog concludes that these simple melodies represent a primitive and archaic stratum of folk song.[7]

Children's tunes of this simple type, like TR 13-19, have been little studied, and Herzog offers little concrete evidence to validate his broad generalizations. However, on the basis of Herzog's own exposition I will venture the opinion that the particular form taken by this little melody is more common in, or is peculiar to, America.

NOTES

Chapter 1

1. Emma Lou Thornbrough, *The Negro in Indiana: A Study of a Minority* (Indianapolis: Indiana Historical Bureau, 1957) and Emma Lou Thornbrough, ed., *This Far by Faith: Black Hoosier Heritage* (Indianapolis: Indiana Committee for the Humanities, 1982, pamphlet accompanying photo exhibit).

2. Gregory S. Rose, "Upland Southerners: The County Origins of Southern Migrants to Indiana by 1850," *Indiana Magazine of History* 82 (September 1986): 244.

3. John D. Barnhart and Donald F. Carmony, *Indiana, from Frontier to Industrial Commonwealth*, 4 vols. (New York: Lewis Historical Publishing Co., Inc., 1954), 1:178.

4. Rose, "Upland Southerners," 249-50.

5. Ibid., 259-60.

6. Robert La Follette, "Interstate Migration and Indiana Culture," *Mississippi Valley Historical Review* 16 (1929): 347.

7. Howard Henry Peckham, *Indiana: A Bicentennial History* (New York: W. W. Norton Co., 1978), 65.

8. Craig Carver, *American Regional Dialects: A Word Geography* (Ann Arbor: University of Michigan Press, 1987), 248.

9. Arthur Rosenbaum, booklet for *Fine Times at Our House: Traditional Music of Indiana* (Folkways Records No. FS 3809).

10. Dillon Bustin, *If You Don't Outdie Me: The Legacy of Brown County* (Bloomington: Indiana University Press, 1982).

11. Rosenbaum, *Fine Times at Our House*, 3.

12. Herbert Halpert, "A Group of Indiana Folksongs," *Hoosier Folklore Bulletin* 3 (March 1944): 4-7.

Chapter 2

1. Vance Randolph, *Ozark Folksongs*, 4 vols. (Columbia: The State Historical Society of Missouri, 1946-50), 2:347-49.

2. George Pullen Jackson, *White Spirituals in the Southern Uplands: The Story of the Fasola Folk, Their Songs, Singings, and "Buckwheat Notes"* (Chapel Hill: University of North Carolina Press, 1933; Hatboro, Pa.: Folklore Associates, Inc., 1964), 173-74.

3. Ibid., 174.

4. Randolph, *Ozark Folksongs*, 2:347.

5. Thomas Percy, *Reliques of Ancient English Poetry, Consisting of Old Heroic Ballads, Songs, and Other Pieces of Our Earlier Poets, Together with Some Few of Later Date*, 3 vols. (London: S. Sonnenchein, Lebas and Lowrey, 1886; New York: Dover Publications, Inc., 1966), 3:170.

6. Ibid., 3:175-76.

7. Albert H. Tolman and Mary O. Eddy, "Traditional Texts and Tunes," *Journal of American Folklore* 35 (October-December 1922): 348-50.

8. Paul G. Brewster, *Ballads and Songs of Indiana* (Bloomington: Indiana University Folklore Series No. 1, 1940; New York and Philadelphia: Folklorica, 1981), 313.

9. Henry Martin Belden, *Ballads and Songs Collected by the Missouri Folk-Lore Society* (Columbia: University of Missouri Studies, 1940. Reprint, 1955), 107.

10. Percy, *Reliques*, 3:171.

11. Alice Bertha Gomme, *The Traditional Games of England, Scotland, and Ireland with Tunes, Singing-Rhymes, and Methods of Playing According to the Variants Extant and Recorded in Different Parts of the Kingdom*, 2 vols. (London: D. Nutt, 1894-98; New York: Dover Publications, Inc., 1964), 2:233-55.

12. Ibid., 2:234-35.

13. Paul G. Brewster, "Game-Songs from Southern Indiana," *Journal of American Folklore* 49 (July-September 1936): 258.

14. Ibid., 258.

15. Mabel Evangeline Neal, *Brown County Songs and Ballads* (Master's thesis, Indiana University, 1926), 46.

16. Leah Jackson Wolford, *The Play-Party in Indiana* (Indianapolis: Indiana Historical Commission, 1916), 52.

17. Ibid., 53.

18. Gomme, *Traditional Games of England*, 2:251.

19. Charlotte Sophia Burne, *Shropshire Folk-Lore: A Sheaf of Gleanings* (London: Trübner and Co., 1883), 517.

20. Iona Archibald Opie and Peter Opie, *The Singing Game* (Oxford and New York: Oxford University Press, 1985), 79.

21. William Wells Newell, *Games and Songs of American Children* (New York: Harper and Brothers Publishers, 1883; New York: Dover Publications, 1963), 49.

22. Gomme, *Traditional Games of England*, 2:251.

23. Newell, *Games and Songs*, 47-49.

24. Burne, *Shropshire Folk-Lore*, 517.

25. Newell, *Games and Songs*, 39-46.

26. Burne, *Shropshire Folk-Lore*, 516.

27. Opie, *Singing Game*, 86-87.

28. Newell, *Games and Songs*, 47-49.

29. Gomme, *Traditional Games of England*, 2:253.

30. Ibid., 1:204-5.

31. Ibid., 1:322.

32. Ibid., 2:167.

33. Ibid., 2:199.

34. Ibid., 1:322.

35. Newell, *Games and Songs*, 94.

36. Columbia Records 15589-D.

37. Opie, *Singing Game*, 240.

38. Gomme, *Traditional Games of England*, 1:177.

39. Newell, *Games and Songs*, 242.

40. Gomme, *Traditional Games of England*, 1:171.

41. Ibid., 1:172, 176.

42. Ibid., 1:177-81.

43. Ibid., 1:182.

44. Newell, *Games and Songs*, 242.

45. ATM Pre 54-155-F, ATL 428.1.

46. Newell, *Games and Songs*, 71.

47. Don Blair, *The New Harmony Story* (New Harmony: New Harmony Publications Committee, 1967), 10.

48. Opie, *Singing Game*, 404.

49. Ibid.

50. Ibid., 474-75.

51. Ibid., 409-11.

52. Gomme, *Traditional Games of England*, 1:32.

53. Burne, *Shropshire Folk-Lore*, 516-17.

54. Ibid., 513.

55. Gomme, *Traditional Games of England*, 2:248.

56. Ibid., 2:249.

57. Ibid., 2:275.

58. Wolford, *Play-Party in Indiana* (1916), 52.

59. Newell, *Games and Songs*, 93-94.

60. Gomme, *Traditional Games of England*, 1:322, 205; 2:199.

61. Opie, *Singing Game*, 314.

62. Barrie Thorne, "Girls and Boys Together but Mostly Apart: Gender Arrangements in Elementary Schools," in *Relationships and Development*, ed. Willard W. Hartup and Zick Rubin (Hillsdale, N.J.: Lawrence Erlbaum Associates, 1986), 167.

63. Ibid., 177.

64. Ibid.

65. Ibid., 180.

Chapter 3

1. Leah Jackson Wolford, *The Play-Party in Indiana*, (Indianapolis: Indiana Historical Commission, 1916), 34-35.

2. B. A. Botkin, *The American Play-Party Song* (Lincoln: University Studies of Nebraska, 1937; New York: Frederick Ungar Publishing Co., 1963), 296-97.

3. William Wells Newell, *Games and Songs of American Children* (New York: Harper and Brothers Publishers, 1883; New York: Dover Publications, 1963), 245.

4. Wolford, *Play-Party in Indiana* (1916), 68.

5. Newell, *Games and Songs*, 102-3.

6. Iona Archibald Opie and Peter Opie, *The Singing Game* (Oxford and New York: Oxford University Press, 1985), 314.

7. Paul G. Brewster, "Game-Songs from Southern Indiana," *Journal of American Folklore* 49 (July-September 1936): 250.

8. Newell, *Games and Songs*, 103.

9. James J. Fuld, *The Book of World-Famous Music: Classical, Popular and Folk* (New York: Crown Publishers, Inc., 1971), 591-92.

10. Ibid.

11. Mabel Evangeline Neal, *Brown County Songs and Ballads* (Master's thesis, Indiana University, 1926), 164.

12. Ludwig van Beethoven, *Ludwig van Beethoven Werke* (Leipzig: Breitkopf and Haertel, posthumous), 24:21.

13. Alice Bertha Gomme, *The Traditional Games of England, Scotland, and Ireland with Tunes, Singing-Rhymes, and Methods of Playing According to the Variants Extant and Recorded in Different Parts of the Kingdom*, 2 vols. (London: D. Nutt, 1894-98; New York: Dover Publications, Inc., 1964), 1:289-90.

14. Wolford, *Play-Party in Indiana* (1916), 72.

15. Newell, *Games and Songs*, 91.

16. Gomme, *Traditional Games of England*, 2:289.

17. Wolford, *Play-Party in Indiana* (1916), 28.

18. Lester S. Levy, *Flashes of Merriment: A Century of Humorous Songs in America, 1805-1905* (Norman: University of Oklahoma Press, 1971), 321.

19. Ibid., 345.

20. Wolford, *Play-Party in Indiana* (1916), 80-81.

21. Leah Jackson Wolford, *The Play-Party in Indiana*, rev. ed., Indiana Historical Society *Publications*, vol. 20, no. 2 (Indianapolis: Indiana Historical Society, 1959), 288.

22. Wolford, *Play-Party in Indiana* (1916), 89.

23. Ibid., 90.

24. Ibid.

25. Botkin, *American Play-Party Song*, 53.

26. Vance Randolph, *Ozark Folksongs*, 4 vols. (Columbia: The State Historical Society of Missouri, 1946-50), 3:287.

27. E. C. Perrow, "Songs and Rhymes from the South," *Journal of American Folklore* 26 (April-June 1913): 136.

28. Neal, *Brown County Songs and Ballads*, 7.

29. James Orchard Halliwell-Phillipps, *The Nursery Rhymes of England,* (London: For the Percy Society by T. Richards, 1842; London: The Bodley Head, 1970), 177.

30. Wolford, *Play-Party in Indiana* (1916), 66.

31. Newell, *Games and Songs*, 125.

32. John Richard Alden, *The American Revolution, 1775-1783* (New York: Harper and Brothers, 1954), 52-58.

33. Wolford, *Play-Party in Indiana* (1916), 66.

34. *The Frank C. Brown Collection of North Carolina Folklore*, ed. Newman Ivey White, 7 vols. (Durham, N.C.: Duke University Press, 1952-64), 1:118.

35. Botkin, *American Play-Party Song*, 352.

36. Wolford, *Play-Party in Indiana* (1916), 22.

37. Ibid., 23.

38. Ibid., 19.

39. Ibid., 23.

40. Fuld, *Book of World-Famous Music*, 231.

41. Ibid.

42. Paul Nettl, "First of the Song Hits," *American German Review* 14 (April 1948): 17-19.

43. Paul Nettl, "Marlborough: Two Centuries on the Hit Parade," *Musical Digest* 28 (August 1947): 42.

44. Fuld, *Book of World-Famous Music*, 232.

45. Emelyn E. Gardner, "Some Play-Party Games in Michigan," *Journal of American Folklore* 33 (April-June 1920): 91.

46. Wilhelm Tappert, *Musikalische Studien* (Berlin: I. Guttentag, 1868), 61.

47. William Chappell, *Old English Popular Music* (London: Chappell, 1893; New York: Jack Brussel, 1961), 84.

48. Wolford, *Play-Party in Indiana* (1916), 13.

49. Ibid., 104-5.

50. Newell, *Games and Songs*, 80.

51. Mari Ruef Hofer, *Children's Singing Games Old and New: For Vacation Schools, Playgrounds, Schoolyards, Kindergartens and Primary Grades* (Chicago: A. Flanagan and Co., 1901), 38.

52. Emma Bell Miles, "Some Real American Music," *Harper's Monthly Magazine* 109 (June 1904): 121.

53. James Hogg, *The Jacobite Relics of Scotland; Being the Songs, Airs, and Legends, of the Adherents to the House of Stuart* (Edinburgh: W. Blackwood, 1821), 76.

54. Wolford, *Play-Party in Indiana* (1959), 290.

55. Hogg, *Jacobite Relics of Scotland*, 92-93.

56. Brewster, "Game-Songs from Southern Indiana," 246.

57. E. C. Perrow, "Songs and Rhymes from the South," *Journal of American Folklore* 26 (April-June 1913): 136.

58. Botkin, *American Play-Party Song*, 104-11.

59. Wolford, *Play-Party in Indiana* (1916), 72.

60. Ibid.

61. Wolford, *Play-Party in Indiana* (1959), 260.

62. Ibid.

63. Ibid., 259-60.

Chapter 4

1. Vance Randolph, *Ozark Folksongs*, 4 vols. (Columbia: The State Historical Society of Missouri, 1946-50), 4:234.

2. Ibid.

3. Grover Rann and Harry Ayers, "They Tell Me Love's a Pleasure," Columbia Records 15600-D.

4. Personal Communication from Guthrie T. Meade.

5. Sigmund Spaeth, *A History of Popular Music in America* (New York: Random House, 1948), 259-62.

6. George Malcolm Laws, *Native American Balladry: A Descriptive Study and a Bibliographical Syllabus* (Philadelphia: American Folklore Society, 1964), 278.

7. Randolph, *Ozark Folksongs*, 4:222-24.

8. W. K. McNeil, *Southern Folk Ballads*, 2 vols. (Little Rock, Ark.: August House, 1987), 1:165.

9. Paul G. Brewster, *Ballads and Songs of Indiana* (Bloomington: Indiana University Folklore Series No. 1, 1940; New York and Philadelphia: Folklorica, 1981), 307.

10. Buster Carter and Preston Young, "A Lazy Farmer Boy," Columbia Records 15702-D and Folkways FW FA-2951.

11. Cecil J. Sharp, *English Folk Songs from the Southern Appalachians*, 2 vols. (London: Oxford University Press, 1932; London: Oxford University Press, 1973), 2:93-95 and John Harrington Cox, *Folk-Songs of the South* (Cambridge, Mass.: Harvard University Press, 1925; Hatboro, Pa.: Folklore Associates, Inc., 1963), 489.

12. Albert H. Tolman, "Some Songs Traditional in the United States," *Journal of American Folklore* 29 (April-June 1916): 188.

13. Randolph, *Ozark Folksongs*, 1:291.

14. Sigmund Spaeth, *Read 'Em and Weep: The Songs You Forgot to Remember* (Garden City, N.Y.: Doubleday, Page and Co., 1926; rev. ed., New York: Arco Publishing Co., 1959), 63-64.

15. Frank Crumit, "Get Away, Old Man, Get Away," Victor Records 20137.

16. Francis James Child, *The English and Scottish Popular Ballads*, 5 vols. (Boston: Houghton, Mifflin and Co., 1882-98; New York: Cooper Square Publishers, Inc., 1965), 1:13-14.

17. Jane Yolen, *Favorite Folktales from Around the World* (New York: Pantheon Books, 1986), 33-40.

18. Lucy E. Broadwood and J. A. Fuller Maitland, *English Country Songs: Words and Music* (London: The Leadenhall Press, Ltd. and New York: Charles Scribner's Sons, 1893), 12-13.

19. Paul Simon and Art Garfunkel, "Are You Going to Scarborough Fair?," Columbia CS 9363.

20. Elizabeth Eliot, *Heiresses and Coronets: The Story of Lovely Ladies and Noble Men* (New York: McDowell, Obolensky, 1959).

21. Carter Family, "My Heart's Tonight in Texas," Bluebird B5908; Montgomery Ward M4549; and Camden LP CDN-5111.

22. George Malcolm Laws, *American Balladry from British Broadsides: A Guide for Students and Collectors of Traditional Song* (Philadelphia: American Folklore Society, 1957), 212-13.

23. 25276.19+ v.4, Harvard University Houghton Library, Cambridge, Mass.

24. Fannie Hardy Eckstorm and Mary Winslow Smyth, *Minstrelsy of Maine: Folk-Songs and Ballads of the Woods and the Coast* (Boston and New York: Houghton Mifflin Co., 1927), 233.

25. Henry Martin Belden, "Balladry in America," *Journal of American Folklore* 25 (January-March 1912): 16.

26. Harvey Lewis Carter, *The Life and Times of Little Turtle: First Sagamore of the Wabash* (Urbana and Chicago: University of Illinois Press, 1987).

27. Albert H. Tolman and Mary O. Eddy, "Traditional Texts and Tunes," *Journal of American Folklore* 35 (October-December 1922): 408.

28. Phillips Barry, "The Miami Lass," *Bulletin of the Folk-Song Society of the Northeast* 6 (1933): 16.

29. William Roy MacKenzie, *Ballads and Sea Songs from Nova Scotia* (Cambridge, Mass.: Harvard University Press, 1928), 154.

30. Ibid.

31. Ibid., 155.

32. John Jacob Niles, *The Songs My Mother Never Taught Me* (New York: Gold Label Books, Inc., 1929), 144-46.

33. David Herd, *Ancient and Modern Scottish Songs, Heroic Ballads, etc.*, 2 vols. (Edinburgh: J. Dickson and C. Elliot, 1776; Edinburgh and London: Scottish Academic Press, 1973), 2:172.

34. Child, *English and Scottish Popular Ballads*, 5:88.

35. Francis Barton Gummere, *The Popular Ballad* (Boston: Houghton Mifflin, 1907; New York: Dover Publications, 1959), 90-92.

Chapter 5

1. Robert Ford, *Vagabond Songs and Ballads of Scotland* (Paisley, Scotland: A. Gardner, 1899; Norwood, Pa.: Norwood Editions, 1975), 137.

2. Willoughby Maycock letter in *Notes and Queries*, 12th ser., no. 3 (1917): 154.

3. Llewellynn Frederick William Jewit, *The Ballads and Songs of Derbyshire, with Illustrative Notes, and Examples of the Original Music* (London and Derby: Bemrose and Sons, 1867), 115-19.

4. John S. Gregson, *Gimcrackiana; or, Fugitive Pieces on Manchester Men and Manners Ten Years Ago . . .* (Manchester: W. H. Jones, 1833), 183-84.

5. Ford, *Vagabond Songs and Ballads of Scotland*, 135-37.

6. Albert B. Friedman, *The Viking Book of Folk Ballads of the English-Speaking World* (New York: Viking Press, 1956), 441.

7. Ford, *Vagabond Songs and Ballads*, 137.

8. Phillips Barry, "Some Traditional Songs," *Journal of American Folklore* 18 (January-March 1905): 52-53.

9. Gates Thomas, "South Texas Negro Work-Songs: Collected and Uncollected," *Texas Folk-Lore Society Publications* 5 (1926): 157-59.

10. Frank J. Gillis, "The Metamorphosis of a Derbyshire Ballad into a New World Jazz Tune," in *Discourse in Ethnomusicology: Essays in Honor of George List* (Bloomington, Ind.: Ethnomusicology Publications Group, 1978), 123.

11. Charles E. Stratton letter in *Notes and Queries*, 12th ser., no. 3 (1917): 309.

12. Gillis, "Metamorphosis of a Derbyshire Ballad," 136-38.

13. Ibid., 139.

14. Newman I. White, *American Negro Folk-Songs* (Cambridge, Mass.: Harvard University Press, 1928), 201-2.

15. Celestin's Tuxedo Jass Band, Southland SLP 206.

16. Gillis, "Metamorphosis of a Derbyshire Ballad," 144.

17. Ibid.

18. Ibid., 145.

19. Fiddlin' John Carson, "Papa's Billy Goat," Okeh 4994.

20. Albert H. Tolman and Mary O. Eddy, "Traditional Texts and Tunes," *Journal of American Folklore* 35 (October-December 1922): 394.

21. Ibid., 397-98.

22. Ibid., 399.

23. Vernon Dalhart, "Way Out West in Kansas," Edison 51459.

24. *The Roxburghe Ballads* (1869-1901; New York: AMS Press, Inc., 1966), 8:610.

25. Ibid., 8:611.

26. Tolman and Eddy, "Traditional Texts and Tunes," 391-92.

27. George Malcolm Laws, *American Balladry from British Broadsides: A Guide for Students and Collectors of Traditional Song* (Philadelphia: American Folklore Society, 1957), 252.

28. Francis James Child, *English and Scottish Ballads*, 8 vols. (Boston: Little, Brown and Co., 1857-58), 8:116.

29. Ibid.

30. Allan Cunningham, *The Songs of Scotland, Ancient and Modern*, 4 vols. (London: John Taylor, 1825), 2:124.

31. Louise Pound, "Traditional Ballads in Nebraska," *Journal of American Folklore* 26 (October-December 1913): 364.

32. Albert H. Tolman, "Some Songs Traditional in the United States," *Journal of American Folklore* 29 (April-June 1916): 174-77.

33. Paul G. Brewster, *Ballads and Songs of Indiana* (Bloomington: Indiana University Folklore Series, No. 1, 1940; New York and Philadelphia: Folklorica, 1981), 220-21.

34. *The Bannatyne Manuscript, Written in Tyme of Pest, 1568*, ed. W. Tod Ritchie, 4 vols. (Edinburgh: Printed for the Scottish Text Society by W. Blackwood and Sons, 1928-34), 2:320.

35. *Roxburghe Ballads*, 7:185.

36. Cunningham, *Songs of Scotland*, 2:123.

37. Pound, "Traditional Ballads in Nebraska," 365.

38. Tolman, "Some Songs Traditional in the United States," 174-75.

39. Ibid., 176.

40. Brewster, *Ballads and Songs of Indiana*, 220.

41. Frank Jenkins, "Wandering Boy," Gennet Records 6165.

42. The Stanley Brothers, "Wandering Boy," Rounder Records Special Series no. 10.

43. Henry Martin Belden, *Ballads and Songs Collected by the Missouri Folk-Lore Society* (Columbia: University of Missouri Studies, 1940; Columbia: University of Missouri Studies, 1955), 277.

44. Carl Sandburg, *The American Songbag* (New York: Harcourt, Brace and World, Inc., 1927), 316-19.

45. Riley Puckett, "The Orphan Girl," Columbia 150550-D.

46. Vance Randolph, *Ozark Folksongs*, 4 vols. (Columbia: The State Historical Society of Missouri, 1946-50), 2:393.

47. Arkansas Charlie, "We All Grow Old in Time," Vocalion 5367.

48. Sigmund Spaeth, *A History of Popular Music in America* (New York: Random House, 1948), 266.

49. David Ewen, *All the Years of American Popular Music* (Englewood Cliffs, N.J.: Prentice-Hall, Inc., 1977), 112.

50. Spaeth, *History of Popular Music in America*, 268.

51. Randolph, *Ozark Folksongs*, 4:163.

52. Spaeth, *History of Popular Music in America*, 267-68.

53. George Malcolm Laws, *Native American Balladry: A Descriptive Study and a Bibliographical Syllabus* (Philadelphia: American Folklore Society, 1964), 277.

54. Spaeth, *History of Popular Music in America*, 228.

Chapter 6

1. Francis James Child, *The English and Scottish Popular Ballads*, 5 vols. (Boston: Houghton Mifflin, 1882-98; New York: Cooper Square Publishers, Inc., 1965), 1:22-26; Tristram P. Coffin, *The British Traditional Ballad in North America* (Philadelphia: The American Folklore Society Bibliographical and Special Series, vol. 2, 1950, rev. ed. 1963; 2nd rev. ed., Austin: University of Texas Press, 1977), 25-28; Holger Olof Nygard, *The Ballad of Heer Halewijn, Its Forms and Variations in Western Europe: A Study of the History and Nature of a Ballad Tradition*, vol. 169 of *Folklore Fellows Communications* (Helsinki: Suomalainen Tiedeakatemia Academia Scientiarum Fennica, 1958); George List, "Toward the Indexing of Ballad Texts," *Journal of American Folklore* 81 (January-March 1968): 44-54; and others.

2. Nygard, *Ballad of Heer Halewijn*, 311.

3. Ibid., 315-16.

4. Ibid., 81-82.

5. Bertrand Harris Bronson, *The Traditional Tunes of the Child Ballads; with Their Texts, According to the Extant Records of Great Britain and America*, 4 vols. (Princeton, N.J.: Princeton University Press, 1959-72), 2:322-91.

6. Paul G. Brewster, *Ballads and Songs of Indiana* (Bloomington: Indiana University Folklore Series, No. 1, 1940; New York and Philadelphia: Folklorica, 1981), 99-121.

7. Ibid.

8. Ibid.

9. Gertrude [Schoepperle] Loomis, *Tristan and Isolt: A Study of the Romance*, 2 vols. (London: David Nutt, 1913), 1:65.

10. Child, *English and Scottish Popular Ballads*, 4:365.

11. Arthur Kyle Davis, *Traditional Ballads of Virginia* (Cambridge, Mass.: Harvard University Press, 1929; Charlottesville: University Press of Virginia, 1969), 446.

12. Brewster, *Ballads and Songs of Indiana*, 160.

13. Patrick Weston Joyce, *Old Irish Folk Music and Songs: A Collection of 842 Irish Airs and Songs Hitherto Unpublished* (London and New York: Longmans, Green, and Co., 1909), 186.

14. Norman Cazden, Herbert Haufrecht, and Norman Studer, *Folksongs of the Catskills* (Albany: State University of New York Press, 1982), 414.

15. Sabine Baring-Gould, "The Golden Ball," in *Notes on the Folk-Lore of the Northern Counties of England and the Borders,* ed. William Henderson (London: Longmans, Green, and Co., 1866), 333-35.

16. Lucy E. Broadwood and Anne G. Gilchrist, "Notes on Children's Game-Songs," *Journal of the Folksong Society* 5 (1915): 228-39.

17. Eleanor Long, *"The Maid" and "The Hangman": Myth and Tradition in a Popular Ballad*, Folklore Studies, Vol. 21 (Berkeley: University of California Press, 1971), 2-3.

18. Tristram P. Coffin, "The Golden Ball and the Gallows Tree," in *Folklore International: Essays in Traditional Literature, Belief, and Custom in Honor of Wayland Debs Hand*, ed. D. K. Wilgus (Hatboro, Pa.: Folklore Associates, Inc., 1967), 26-27.

19. Cecil J. Sharp, *English Folk Songs from the Southern Appalachians,* 2 vols. (London: Oxford University Press, 1932; London: Oxford University Press, 1973), 1:208-9.

20. *The American Songster: A Collection of Songs, as Sung in the Iron Days of 76* (Philadelphia: Fisher and Brother, 1840; Norwood, Pa.: Norwood Editions, 1974), 63-65.

21. W. Edson Richmond, "A New Look at the Wheel: An Essay in Defining the Ballad," in *The European Medieval Ballad: A Symposium*, ed. Otto Holzapfel (Odense, Denmark: Odense University Press, 1978), 91.

Chapter 7

1. Paul G. Brewster, *Ballads and Songs from Indiana* (Bloomington: Indiana University Folklore Series, No. 1, 1940; New York and Philadelphia: Folklorica, 1981), 211.

2. Ibid., 286.

3. Ibid., 248.

4. Ibid., 248-52.

5. George Malcolm Laws, *Native American Balladry: A Descriptive Study and a Bibliographical Syllabus* (Philadelphia: American Folklore Society, 1964), 191.

6. D. K. Wilgus, "A Type-Index of Anglo-American Traditional Narrative Songs," *Journal of the Folklore Institute* 7 (August-December 1970): 166.

7. Brewster, *Ballads and Songs from Indiana*, 181.

8. Ibid., 105.

9. Phillips Barry, "Fair Charlotte," *Bulletin of the Folk-Song Society of the Northeast* 8 (1934): 18.

10. Mabel Evangeline Neal, *Brown County Songs and Ballads* (Master's thesis, Indiana University, 1926), 172.

11. Phillips Barry, "Fair Charlotte," *Bulletin of the Folk-Song Society of the Northeast* 12 (1937): 26.

12. Samuel Warren, *Passages from the Diary of a Late Physician*, 2 vols. (Paris: Baudry's European Library, 1838), 1:166-69.

13. Barry, "Fair Charlotte," (1937), 26.

14. Barry, "Fair Charlotte," (1934), 18.

15. Vance Randolph, *Ozark Folksongs*, 4 vols. (Columbia: The State Historical Society of Missouri, 1946-50), 4:137.

16. Ibid., 4:137-38.

17. W. K. McNeil, " 'We'll Make the Spanish Grunt': Popular Songs about the Sinking of the Maine," *Journal of Popular Culture* 2 (1969): 537-51.

18. Randolph, *Ozark Folksongs*, 4:139.

19. Ferdinand Lundberg, *Imperial Hearst: A Social Biography* (New York: Equinox Cooperative Press, 1936; New York: Equinox Cooperative Press for Arno and the New York Times, 1970), 71-82.

20. McNeil, " 'We'll Make the Spanish Grunt,' " 548.

21. Ibid., 547.

22. Vernon Dalhart, "The Wreck of the 97," Victor 19427.

23. Phillips Barry, "Fuller and Warren," *Bulletin of the Folk-Song Society of the Northeast* 6 (1934): 12-13 and Phillips Barry, "Fuller and Warren," *Bulletin of the Folk-Song Society of the Northeast* 9 (1935): 14-16.

24. Brewster, *Ballads and Songs from Indiana*, 363-64.

25. O. H. Smith, *Early Indiana Trials and Sketches: Reminiscences* (Cincinnati: Moore, Wilstach, Keys and Co., 1858), 8-9.

26. Barry, "Fuller and Warren" (1935), 17.

27. Brewster, *Ballads and Songs of Indiana*, 363.

28. Ibid., 364-65.

29. Ibid., 286-87.

30. Kenneth S. Goldstein, booklet for *The Unfortunate Rake: A Study in the Evolution of a Ballad*, Folkways Records No. FS-3805, p. 4.

31. Ibid., 2.

32. Ibid., 5-6.

33. Ibid., 6.

34. George Malcolm Laws, *American Balladry from British Broadsides: A Guide for Students and Collectors of Traditional Song* (Philadelphia: American Folklore Society, 1957), 285-86.

35. Goldstein, *Unfortunate Rake*, 5-6.

36. Charles E. Rosenberg, *The Trial of the Assassin Guiteau: Psychiatry and Law in the Gilded Age* (Chicago and London: The University of Chicago Press, 1968).

37. Louise Pound, *American Ballads and Songs* (New York: Charles Scribner's Sons, 1922), 147-48.

38. Ibid., 251-52.

39. Bruce Catton, *Never Call Retreat*, vol. 3 of *The Centennial History of the Civil War* (New York: Doubleday and Co., Inc., 1965), 35-47.

40. Leah Jackson Wolford, *The Play-Party in Indiana* (Indianapolis: Indiana Historical Commission, 1916), 107, 115.

41. Howard Brockway and Loraine Wyman, *Lonesome Tunes: Folk Songs from the Kentucky Mountains* (New York: The H. W. Gray Co., 1916), 52-53.

42. Mellinger E. Henry, *Songs Sung in the Southern Appalachians: Many of Them Illustrating Ballads in the Making* (London: The Mitre Press, 1934), 86-87.

43. Ibid., 51-52.

44. Ibid., 57-58.

45. Ibid., 2-3.

46. Laws, *Native American Balladry*, 233, 272, 191, 296, 278.

47. Henry, *Songs Sung in the Southern Appalachians*, 124-25.

Chapter 8

1. MacEdward Leach, *Funk and Wagnalls Standard Dictionary of Folklore, Mythology, and Legend*, Maria Leach, ed., 2 vols. (New York: Funk and Wagnalls Co., 1949), s.v. "ballad," 1:106.

2. Tristram P. Coffin, "Mary Hamilton and the Anglo-American Ballad as an Art Form," in *The Critics and the Ballad*, ed. MacEdward Leach and Tristram P. Coffin (Carbondale: Southern Illinois University Press, 1961), 246.

3. Ibid., 248-49.

4. Ibid., 254-55.

5. Ibid., 255.

6. George List, "Toward the Indexing of Ballad Texts," *Journal of American Folklore* 81 (January-March 1968).

7. Mark Tristram Coffin, *American Narrative Obituary Verse and Native American Balladry* (Norwood, Pa.: Norwood Editions, 1978), 95-98.

8. Ibid., 76.

9. Ann Douglas, *The Feminization of American Culture* (New York: Alfred A. Knopf, 1977), 202.

10. Ibid., 6.

11. James H. Jones, "Commonplace and Memorization in the Oral Tradition of the English and Scottish Popular Ballads," *Journal of American Folklore* 74 (April-June 1961): 97-99.

12. Albert Bates Lord, *The Singer of Tales* (Cambridge, Mass.: Harvard University Press, 1960), 4.

13. Albert B. Friedman, "The Formulaic Improvisation Theory of Ballad Tradition—A Counterstatement," *Journal of American Folklore* 74 (April-June 1961): 114.

14. W. Edson Richmond, " 'Den utrue egteman': A Norwegian Ballad and Formulaic Improvisation," *Norveg* 10 (1963): 61-62.

15. Personal communication from W. Edson Richmond.

Chapter 9

1. Cecil J. Sharp, *English Folk Song: Some Conclusions*, 4th rev. ed. (London: Simpkin and Co., Ltd., 1907; Belmont, Calif.: Wadsworth Publishing Co., Inc., 1965), 54-55.

2. Ibid., 44-45.

3. Anne Dhu Shapiro, "Regional Song Styles: The Scottish Connection," in *Music and Context: Essays for John M. Ward*, ed. Anne Dhu Shapiro and Phyllis Benjamin (Cambridge, Mass.: Harvard University Department of Music, 1985), 408.

4. Ibid.

5. Sharp, *English Folk Song*, 62.

6. Bruno Nettl, "The Musical Style of English Ballads Collected in Indiana," *Acta Musicologica* 27 (1955): 79-84.

7. George Herzog, "Some Primitive Layers in European Folk Music," *Bulletin of the American Musicological Society* 9-10 (1947): 14.

BIBLIOGRAPHY

Alden, John Richard. *The American Revolution, 1775-1783*. New York: Harper and Brothers, 1954.

The American Songster: A Collection of Songs, as Sung in the Iron Days of 76. Philadelphia: Fisher and Brother, 1840. Reprint. Norwood, Pa.: Norwood Editions, 1974.

Bannatyne, George. *The Bannatyne Manuscript, Written in Tyme of Pest, 1568*. Edited by W. Tod Ritchie. 4 vols. Edinburgh: Printed for the Scottish Text Society by W. Blackwood and Sons, 1928-34.

Baring-Gould, Sabine. "The Golden Ball." In *Notes on the Folk Lore of the Northern Counties of England and the Borders*, edited by William Henderson. London: Longmans, Green, and Co., 1866.

Barnhart, John D., and Donald F. Carmony. *Indiana, from Frontier to Industrial Commonwealth*. 4 vols. New York: Lewis Historical Publishing Co., Inc., 1954.

Barry, Phillips. "Some Traditional Songs." *Journal of American Folklore* 18 (January-March 1905): 49-59.

_____. "The Miami Lass." *Bulletin of the Folk-Song Society of the Northeast* 6 (1933): 15-18.

_____. "Fuller and Warren." *Bulletin of the Folk-Song Society of the Northeast* 6 (1934): 12-13.

_____. "Fair Charlotte." *Bulletin of the Folk-Song Society of the Northeast* 8 (1934): 17-19.

_____. "Fuller and Warren." *Bulletin of the Folk-Song Society of the Northeast* 9 (1935): 14-17.

_____. "Fair Charlotte." *Bulletin of the Folk-Song Society of the Northeast* 12 (1937): 26.

Beethoven, Ludwig van. *Ludwig van Beethoven Werke*. Leipzig: Breitkopf and Haertel, posthumously.

Belden, Henry Martin. "Balladry in America." *Journal of American Folklore* 25 (January-March 1912): 1-23.

_____. *Ballads and Songs Collected by the Missouri Folk-Lore Society*. Columbia: University of Missouri Studies, 1940. Reprint. Columbia: University of Missouri Studies, 1955.

Blair, Don. *The New Harmony Story*. New Harmony, Ind.: New Harmony Publications Committee, 1967.

Botkin, B. A. *The American Play-Party Song*. Lincoln: University Studies of University of Nebraska, 1937. Reprint. New York: Frederick Ungar Publishing Co., 1963.

Brewster, Paul G. "Game-Songs from Southern Indiana." *Journal of American Folklore* 49 (July-September 1936): 243-66.

_____. *Ballads and Songs of Indiana.* Indiana University Folklore Series, No. 1. Bloomington: Indiana University, 1940. Reprint, with a new foreword by W. Edson Richmond. New York and Philadelphia: Folklorica, 1981.

Broadwood, Lucy E. and Anne G. Gilchrist. "Notes on Children's Game-Songs." *Journal of the Folksong Society* 5 (1915): 221-39.

Broadwood, Lucy E. and J. A. Fuller Maitland. *English Country Songs: Words and Music.* London: The Leadenhall Press, Ltd. and New York: Charles Scribner's Sons, 1893.

Brockway, Howard and Loraine Wyman. *Lonesome Tunes: Folk Songs from the Kentucky Mountains.* New York: The H. W. Gray Co., 1916.

Bronson, Bertrand Harris. *The Traditional Tunes of the Child Ballads; with Their Texts, According to the Extant Records of Great Britain and America.* 4 vols. Princeton, N.J.: Princeton University Press, 1959-72.

Brown, Frank C. *The Frank C. Brown Collection of North Carolina Folklore.* Edited by Newman Ivey White. 7 vols. Durham, N.C.: Duke University Press, 1952-64.

Burne, Charlotte Sophia. *Shropshire Folk-Lore: A Sheaf of Gleanings.* London: Trübner and Co., 1883.

Bustin, Dillon. *If You Don't Outdie Me: The Legacy of Brown County.* Bloomington: Indiana University Press, 1982.

Carter, Harvey Lewis. *The Life and Times of Little Turtle: First Sagamore of the Wabash.* Urbana and Chicago: University of Illinois Press, 1987.

Carver, Craig. *American Regional Dialects: A Word Geography.* Ann Arbor: University of Michigan Press, 1987.

Catton, Bruce. *Never Call Retreat.* Vol. 3 of *The Centennial History of the Civil War.* New York: Doubleday and Co., Inc., 1965.

Cazden, Norman, Herbert Haufrecht, and Norman Studer. *Folksongs of the Catskills.* Albany: State University of New York Press, 1982.

Chappell, William. *Old English Popular Music.* London: Chappell, 1893. Reprint. New York: Jack Brussel, 1961.

Child, Francis James. *English and Scottish Ballads.* 8 vols. Boston: Little, Brown and Co., 1857-58.

_____. *The English and Scottish Popular Ballads.* 5 vols. Boston: Houghton, Mifflin, 1882-98. Reprint. New York: Cooper Square Publishers, Inc., 1965.

Coffin, Mark Tristram. *American Narrative Obituary Verse and Native American Balladry*. Norwood, Pa.: Norwood Editions, 1978.

Coffin, Tristram P. *The British Traditional Ballad in North America*. Philadelphia: The American Folklore Society Bibliographical and Special Series, vol. 2, 1950. Rev. ed. 1963. 2nd rev. ed. Austin: University of Texas Press, 1977.

_____. "Mary Hamilton and the Anglo-American Ballad as an Art Form." In *The Critics and the Ballad*, edited by MacEdward Leach and Tristram P. Coffin. Carbondale: Southern Illinois University Press, 1961.

_____. "The Golden Ball and the Gallows Tree." In *Folklore International: Essays in Traditional Literature, Belief, and Custom in Honor of Wayland Debs Hand*, edited by D. K. Wilgus. Hatboro, Pa.: Folklore Associates, Inc., 1967.

Cox, John Harrington. *Folk-Songs of the South*. Cambridge, Mass.: Harvard University Press, 1925. Reprint. Hatboro, Pa.: Folklore Associates, Inc., 1963.

Cunningham, Allan. *The Songs of Scotland, Ancient and Modern*. 4 vols. London: John Taylor, 1825.

Davis, Arthur Kyle. *Traditional Ballads of Virginia*. Cambridge, Mass.: Harvard University Press, 1929. Reprint. Charlottesville: University Press of Virginia, 1969.

Douglas, Ann. *The Feminization of American Culture*. New York: Alfred A. Knopf, 1977.

Eckstorm, Fannie Hardy and Mary Winslow Smyth. *Minstrelsy of Maine: Folk-Songs and Ballads of the Woods and the Coast*. Boston and New York: Houghton Mifflin Co., 1927.

Eliot, Elizabeth. *Heiresses and Coronets: The Story of Lovely Ladies and Noble Men*. New York: MacDowell, Obolensky, 1959.

Ewen, David. *All the Years of American Popular Music*. Englewood Cliffs, N.J.: Prentice-Hall, Inc., 1977.

Ford, Robert. *Vagabond Songs and Ballads of Scotland*. Paisley, Scotland: A. Gardner, 1899. Reprint. Norwood, Pa.: Norwood Editions, 1975.

Friedman, Albert B. *The Viking Book of Folk Ballads of the English-Speaking World*. New York: Viking Press, 1956.

_____. "The Formulaic Improvisation Theory of Ballad Tradition—A Counterstatement." *Journal of American Folklore* 74 (April-June 1961): 113-15.

Fuld, James J. *The Book of World-Famous Music: Classical, Popular and Folk*. New York: Crown Publishers, Inc., 1971.

Gardner, Emelyn E. "Some Play-Party Games in Michigan." *Journal of American Folklore* 33 (April-June 1920): 91-133.

Gillis, Frank J. "The Metamorphosis of a Derbyshire Ballad into a New World Jazz Tune." In *Discourse in Ethnomusicology: Essays in Honor of George List.* Bloomington: Ethnomusicology Publications Group, 1978.

Glory Songs. Dalton, Ga.: A. J. Showalter Co., 1909.

Goldstein, Kenneth S. Booklet accompanying record album, *The Unfortunate Rake: A Study in the Evolution of a Ballad.* Folkways Records No. FS-3805.

Gomme, Alice Bertha. *The Traditional Games of England, Scotland, and Ireland with Tunes, Singing-Rhymes, and Methods of Playing According to the Variants Extant and Recorded in Different Parts of the Kingdom.* 2 vols. London: D. Nutt, 1894-98. Reprint. New York: Dover Publications, Inc., 1964.

Gregson, John S. *Gimcrackiana; or, Fugitive Pieces on Manchester Men and Manners Ten Years Ago* . . . Manchester, England: W. H. Jones, 1833.

Gummere, Francis Barton. *The Popular Ballad.* Boston: Houghton Mifflin, 1907. Reprint. New York: Dover Publications, Inc., 1959.

Halliwell-Phillipps, James Orchard. *The Nursery Rhymes of England.* London: For the Percy Society by T. Richards, 1842. Reprint. London: The Bodley Head, 1970.

Halpert, Herbert. "A Group of Indiana Folksongs." *Hoosier Folklore Bulletin* 3 (March 1944): 1-15.

Henry, Mellinger E. *Songs Sung in the Southern Appalachians, Many of Them Illustrating Ballads in the Making.* London: The Mitre Press, 1934.

Herd, David. *Ancient and Modern Scottish Songs, Heroic Ballads, etc.* 2 vols. Edinburgh: J. Dickson and C. Elliot, 1776. Reprint. Edinburgh and London: Scottish Academic Press, 1973.

Herzog, George. "Some Primitive Layers in European Folk Music." *Bulletin of the American Musicological Society* 9-10 (1947): 11-14.

Hofer, Mari Ruef. *Children's Singing Games Old and New: For Vacation Schools, Playgrounds, Schoolyards, Kindergartens and Primary Grades.* Chicago: A. Flanagan and Co., 1901.

Hogg, James. *The Jacobite Relics of Scotland; Being the Songs, Airs, and Legends, of the Adherents to the House of Stuart.* Edinburgh: W. Blackwood, 1821.

Jackson, George Pullen. *White Spirituals in the Southern Uplands: The Story of the Fasola Folk, Their Songs, Singings, and "Buckwheat Notes."* Chapel Hill: University of North Carolina Press, 1933. Reprint. Hatboro, Pa.: Folklore Associates, Inc., 1964.

Jewit, Llewellynn Frederick William. *The Ballads and Songs of Derbyshire, with Illustrated Notes and Examples of the Original Music*. London and Derby: Bemrose and Sons, 1867.

Jones, James H. "Commonplace and Memorization in the Oral Tradition of the English and Scottish Popular Ballads." *Journal of American Folklore* 74 (April-June 1961): 97-112.

Joyce, Patrick Weston. *Old Irish Folk Music and Songs: A Collection of 842 Irish Airs and Songs Hitherto Unpublished*. New York: Longmans, Green, and Co., 1909.

La Folette, Robert. "Interstate Migration and Indiana Culture." *Mississippi Valley Historical Review* 16 (1929): 347-58.

Laws, George Malcolm. *American Balladry from British Broadsides: A Guide for Students and Collectors of Traditional Song*. Philadelphia: American Folklore Society, 1957.

_____. *Native American Balladry: A Descriptive Study and a Bibliographical Syllabus*. Philadelphia: American Folklore Society, 1964.

Leach, MacEdward. "ballad." In *Funk and Wagnalls Standard Dictionary of Folklore, Mythology, and Legend*, edited by Maria Leach. 2 vols. New York: Funk and Wagnalls Co., 1949.

Levy, Lester S. *Flashes of Merriment: A Century of Humorous Songs in America, 1805-1905*. Norman: University of Oklahoma Press, 1971.

List, George. "Toward the Indexing of Ballad Texts." *Journal of American Folklore* 81 (January-March 1968): 44-61.

Long, Eleanor. *"The Maid" and "The Hangman": Myth and Tradition in a Popular Ballad*. Folklore Studies, Vol. 21. Berkeley: University of California Press, 1971.

Loomis, Gertrude [Schoepperle]. *Tristan and Isolt: A Study of the Romance*. 2 vols. London: David Nutt, 1913.

Lord, Albert Bates. *The Singer of Tales*. Cambridge, Mass.: Harvard University Press, 1960.

Lundberg, Ferdinand. *Imperial Hearst: A Social Biography*. New York: Equinox Cooperative Press, 1936. Reprint. New York: Equinox Cooperative Press for Arno and the New York Times, 1970.

MacKenzie, William Roy. *Ballads and Sea Songs from Nova Scotia*. Cambridge, Mass.: Harvard University Press, 1928.

McNeil, W. K. " 'We'll Make the Spanish Grunt': Popular Songs about the Sinking of the Maine." *Journal of Popular Culture* 2 (1969): 537-51.

_____. *Southern Folk Ballads*. 2 vols. Little Rock, Ark.: August House, 1987.

Malone, Bill C. *Country Music USA*. Rev. ed. Austin: University of Texas Press, 1985.

Maycock, Willoughby. Letter, *Notes and Queries*, 12th scr., no. 3 (1917): 154.

Miles, Emma Bell. "Some Real American Music." *Harper's Monthly Magazine* 109 (June 1904): 118-23.

Neal, Mabel Evangeline. *Brown County Songs and Ballads*. Master's thesis, Indiana University, 1926.

Nettl, Bruno. "The Musical Style of English Ballads Collected in Indiana." *Acta Musicologica* 27 (1955): 79-84.

Nettl, Paul. "Marlborough: Two Centuries on the Hit Parade." *Musical Digest* 28 (August 1947): 42.

——————. "First of the Song Hits." *American German Review* 14 (April 1948): 17-19.

Newell, William Wells. *Games and Songs of American Children*. New York: Harper and Brothers Publishers, 1883. Reprint. New York: Dover Publications, 1963.

Niles, John Jacob. *Songs My Mother Never Taught Me*. New York: Gold Label Books, Inc., 1929.

Nygard, Holger Olof. *The Ballad of Heer Halewijn, Its Forms and Variations in Western Europe: A Study of the History and Nature of a Ballad Tradition*. Vol. 169 of Folklore Fellows Communications. Helsinki: Suomalainen Tiedeakatemia Academia Scientiarum Fennica, 1958.

Opie, Iona Archibald and Peter Opie. *The Singing Game*. Oxford and New York: Oxford University Press, 1985.

Peckham, Howard Henry. *Indiana: A Bicentennial History*. New York: W. W. Norton Co., 1978.

Percy, Thomas. *Reliques of Ancient English Poetry, Consisting of Old Heroic Ballads, Songs, and Other Pieces of Our Earlier Poets, Together with Some Few of Later Date*. 3 vols. London: S. Sonnenchein, Lebas and Lowrey, 1886. Reprint. New York: Dover Publications, Inc., 1966.

Perrow, E. C. "Songs and Rhymes from the South." *Journal of American Folklore* 26 (April-June 1913): 123-73.

Plunket, E. M. *Merrie Games in Rhyme*. London: W. Gardner, Darton and Co., 1886.

Pound, Louise. "Traditional Ballads in Nebraska." *Journal of American Folklore* 16 (October-December 1913): 351-66.

——————. *American Ballads and Songs*. New York: Charles Scribner's Sons, 1922.

Randolph, Vance. *Ozark Folk Songs*. 4 vols. Columbia: The State Historical Society of Missouri, 1946-50.

Richmond, W. Edson. "A New Look at the Wheel: An Essay in Defining the Ballad." In *The European Medieval Ballad: A Symposium*, edited by Otto Holzapfel. Odense, Denmark: Odense University Press, 1978.

_____. " 'Den utrue egteman': A Norwegian Ballad and Formulaic Improvisation." *Norveg* 10 (1963): 59-88.

Rose, Gregory S. "Upland Southerners: The County Origins of Southern Migrants to Indiana by 1850." *Indiana Magazine of History* 82 (September 1986): 242-63.

Rosenbaum, Arthur. Booklet accompanying record album *Fine Times at Our House: Traditional Music of Indiana*. Folkways Records FS 3809.

Rosenberg, Charles E. *The Trial of the Assassin Guiteau: Psychiatry and Law in the Gilded Age*. Chicago and London: University of Chicago Press, 1968.

Roxburghe. *The Roxburghe Ballads*. Various editors. 1869-1901. Reprint. New York: AMS Press, Inc., 1966.

Sandburg, Carl. *The American Songbag*. New York: Harcourt, Brace and World, Inc., 1927.

Shapiro, Anne Dhu. "Regional Song Styles: The Scottish Connection." In *Music and Context: Essays for John M. Ward*, edited by Anne Dhu Shapiro and Phyllis Benjamin. Cambridge, Mass.: Harvard University Department of Music, 1985.

Sharp, Cecil J. *English Folk Song: Some Conclusions*. 4th ed., rev. and prepared by Maud Karpeles. London: Simpkin and Co., Ltd., 1907. Reprint. Belmont, Calif.: Wadsworth Publishing Co., Inc., 1965.

_____. *English Folk Songs from the Southern Appalachians*. 2 vols. bound as one. London: Oxford University Press, 1932. Reprint. London: Oxford University Press, 1973.

Smith, George Barnett, ed. *Illustrated British Ballads, Old and New*. 2 vols. London: Cassell, Petter, Galpin and Co., 1881.

Smith, O. H. *Early Indiana Trials and Sketches: Reminiscences*. Cincinnati: Moore, Wilstach, Keys and Co., 1858.

Spaeth, Sigmund. *Read 'Em and Weep: The Songs You Forgot to Remember*. Garden City, N.Y.: Doubleday, Page and Co., 1926. Rev. ed. New York: Arco Publishing Co., 1959.

_____. *A History of Popular Music in America*. New York: Random House, 1948.

Stratton, Charles E. Letter, *Notes and Queries*, 12th ser., no. 3 (1917): 309.

Tappert, Wilhelm. *Musikalische Studien*. Berlin: I. Guttentag, 1868.

Thomas, Gates. "South Texas Negro Work-Songs: Collected and Uncollected." *Texas Folk-Lore Society Publications* 5 (1926): 154-80.

Thornbrough, Emma Lou. *The Negro in Indiana: A Study of a Minority*. Indianapolis: Indiana Historical Bureau, 1957.

——————. *This Far by Faith: Black Hoosier Heritage*. Pamphlet accompanying photo exhibit. Indianapolis: Indiana Committee for the Humanities, 1982.

Thorne, Barrie. "Girls and Boys Together but Mostly Apart: Gender Arrangements in Elementary Schools." In *Relationships and Development*, edited by Willard W. Hartup and Zick Rubin. Hillsdale, N.J.: Lawrence Erlbaum Associates, 1986.

Tolman, Albert H. "Some Songs Traditional in the United States." *Journal of American Folklore* 29 (April-June 1916): 155-97.

Tolman, Albert H. and Mary O. Eddy. "Traditional Texts and Tunes." *Journal of American Folklore* 35 (October-December 1922): 335-432.

Twice 55 Plus Community Songs. Boston: C. C. Birchard and Co., 1919.

Urcia, Ingeburg. "The Gallows and the Golden Ball: An Analysis of 'The Maid Freed from the Gallows' (Child 95)." *Journal of American Folklore* 79 (1966): 463-68.

Warren, Samuel. *Passages from the Diary of a Late Physician*. 2 vols. Paris: Baudry's European Library, 1838.

White, B. F. and E. J. King. *The Sacred Harp*. Facsimile of 3d ed., 1859. Reprint. Nashville: Broadman Press, 1968.

White, Newman I. *American Negro Folk-Songs*. Cambridge, Mass.: Harvard University Press, 1928.

Wilgus, D. K. "Ballad Classification." *Midwest Folklore* 5 (1955): 95-100.

——————. "A Type-Index of Anglo-American Traditional Narrative Songs." *Journal of the Folklore Institute* 7 (August-December 1970): 161-76.

Wolford, Leah Jackson. *The Play-Party in Indiana*. Indianapolis: Indiana Historical Commission, 1916.

——————. *The Play-Party in Indiana*. Edited and revised by W. Edson Richmond and William Tillson. Indiana Historical Society *Publications*, vol. 20, no. 2. Indianapolis: Indiana Historical Society, 1959.

Yolen, Jane. *Favorite Folktales from Around the World*. New York: Pantheon Books, 1986.

Discography

TR 7   "Soldier, Soldier, Won't You Marry Me." Gid Tanner and His Skillet Lickers, Columbia Records 15589-D.

TR 40   "They Tell Me Love's a Pleasure." Grover Rann and Harry Ayers, Columbia Records 15600-D.

TR 43   "A Lazy Farmer Boy." Buster Carter and Preston Young, Columbia Records 15702-D and Folkways FW FA-2951.

TR 45   "Get Away, Old Man, Get Away." Frank Crumit, Victor Records 20137.

TR 46   "Are You Going to Scarborough Fair?" Paul Simon and Art Garfunkel, Columbia Records CS 9363.

TR 47   "My Heart's Tonight in Texas." Carter Family, Bluebird B5908, Montgomery Ward M4549, and Camden LP CDN-5111.

TR 57   "Didn't He Ramble." Celestin's Tuxedo Jass Band, Southland SLP 206.

TR 58   "Papa's Billy Goat." Fiddlin' John Carson, Okeh 4994.

TR 60   "Way Out West in Kansas." Vernon Dalhart, Edison 51459.

TR 67   "Wandering Boy." Frank Jenkins, Gennet Records 6165.

_____   "Wandering Boy." The Stanley Brothers, Rounder Records Special Series no. 10.

TR 68, 69   "The Orphan Girl." Riley Puckett, Columbia 150550-D.

TR 72 "We All Grow Old in Time." Arkansas Charlie, Vocalion 5367.

TR 94 "The Wreck of the 97." Vernon Dalhart, Victor 19427.

INDEX

Blaine, James G., 360, 362

Bloomington (Ind.), 16, 19, 24, 28, 29, 30, 35, 36, 39, 45, 59, 85, 86, 87, 88, 92, 100, 104, 105, 107, 109, 152, 165, 167, 174, 195, 208, 214, 221, 224, 230, 237, 238, 249, 255, 298, 308, 313, 324, 345

Blountsville (Ind.), 36

Boatman family, 39

"Bobby Bingo," 114

Bohannan, Anna L., 27

"Bonnie Prince Charlie," 160

"Bonny Barbara Allan," 281, 287

Boone, Daniel, 20

Boonville (Ind.), 21, 37

"Boots and Leggings," 173

Botetourt County (Va.), 13

Both men and women, listen well, 235

Botkin, B. A., 123, 162

Bourbon County (Ky.), 38

"Boyne Water," 303-4

Bracket, William W., 215

Braden family, 25

Bradford County (Pa.), 23, 326

Bragg, Braxton, 365, 366

"Break the News to Mother," 168

"Brennan on the Moor," 41, 295-98, 306, 307, 349

Brewster, Paul, 11, 34, 44, 63, 66, 67, 160, 172, 281, 287, 313, 341, 352

"Bring Back My Boy," 238

Broadsides, 2, 186

Broadwood, Lucy, 300

Brockway, Howard, 366-67

Bronson, Bertrand, 281

"The Brooklyn Theater Fire," 324-29, 381, 390

Brown County (Ind.), 14, 15, 16, 17, 18, 41, 42, 50, 120

Brownstown (Ind.), 14, 15

Bryan, Pearl, 343, 347, 349

Bryant, Dan, 126

Bryant, Kathleen, 315, 320

Bryant, Mary Vandora McNeely (Dora), 11-14, 47, 82, 85, 216, 266, 270, 271, 285, 287, 291, 338, 340, 341

Bryant family, 11-14, 47, 48, 49, 50, 380

Bryantsville (Ind.), 34, 35

Buchan, David, 271

Buckley, Bruce, 10

Bufkins, Russell, 12, 13

Bullitt County (Ky.), 200

"The Burglar Man," 224

Burne, Charlotte Sophia, 114

Burris family, 21

Bush family, 17, 41

Bustin, Dillon, 18, 19

Butler family, 45-46

"By the Silvery Rio Grande," 183

Calcott, Dr., 209

Calumet region, 4

"The Cambric Shirt," 12, 177

Camp family, 12, 14

Campbell, Alexander, 156

Campbell, Frank, 175

Campbell, Thomas, 156

Campbellites, 131, 155

"Capitals of the States," 80

"Captain Jinks," 133-35

"Captain Jinks of the Horse Marines," 135-37, 176

Carson, John (Fiddlin'), 215, 241

Carson family, 23

Carter, A. P., 238

Carter, Buster, 172

Carter, William Lorenzo, 321

Carter family, 2, 183, 238

Carthage (Ind.), 26

Carver, Craig, 8, 50

Carver family, 37

Casanova, 301

Casselberry family, 23

Celestin's Tuxedo Jass [sic] Band, 213

Chapbooks, 2, 186

Chapman family, 36, 37

Charles II, 278

Charles III, 159, 160

"Charles Giteau," 12, 41, 360-63, 371

Charley, he's a nice young man, 156

"Charley Is My Darling," 159, 160

"Charlotta," 320

"Charlotte," 320

Chetham Library (Manchester, England), 233

Child, Francis James, 32, 177-78, 204, 270, 271, 277, 281, 290, 291, 293, 294, 300, 306, 370, 377, 379

Churchill, John (Duke of Marlborough), 149

Churchill, Lord Randolph, 181

Churchill, Sir Winston, 149, 181

"The Churlish Husband Turn'd Nurse," 234, 236

Cincinnati Commercial Gazette, 347-48

Cincinnati Conservatory, 252

Clayton family, 46

Clemens family, 11

Clinton (Mo.), 19

"Coffee Grows in a White Oak Tree," 121-23, 141

Coffin, Tristram P., 300, 369, 370, 371, 374, 375

Cole, Robert "Bob," 213

Collier, John William, 14-15, 41, 42, 50, 230, 231

Collier family, 14-15

Columbus (Ind.), 42

Come a-listen, you young folks, to my song, 171

Come all of you young people, 344

Come all you Texas Rangers, wherever you may be, 352

Come all young maids and lend attention, 308

Come boat me o'er, come row me o'er, 159

[Come] get you down, you Pretty Polly, 268

"Come Over, Playmate," 94-95, 99

Comer, Imogene, 257

"Coming Through the Rye," 390

Conway Theater, 324, 327

"The Cookery Maid," 221-22, 264, 387

"A Corpse Going to a Ball," 321-23

"Couplets, Sur la morte de Mr. Malbrourk," 150, 163

"The Cowboy's Lament," 41, 354-56, 359, 368, 381

Cox, Stephen, 340

Cox family, 12

Craddock, Elizabeth, 78

Cramer, J. B., 58

Crawford County (Ind.), 19, 20, 31, 32, 45, 46, 50

Crawford family, 46

"Crazyhead, Michael," 86

Crews family, 46

Crider family, 41

Cripple Creek (Ind.), 41

Croshaw, C., 234

Crow, Linda, 85, 86

"The Cruel Mother," 378

Crumit, Frank, 176

"Crybaby, Crybaby," 85-86

Cuba, 331

Cunningham, Allan, 234

Curry, Orpha Mae Hopper, 16-18, 59, 61

Curry, Patricia "Patty" Elaine, 16-18, 85, 86, 88

Curry family, 16-18

Custer, George Armstrong, 192

Daganhart family, 11

Dale (Ind.), 34

Dalhart, Vernon, 2, 176, 215, 221, 336

"The Darby Ram," 211

"Dark and Dreary Weather," 166

Darke County (Ohio), 19, 20

Davis, Gussie, 252, 257, 260

Dear, don't you know, a long time ago, 59

"Death at the Toilet," 321, 323

Delaware County (Ind.), 36, 37, 38

Delmore brothers, 241

De Pauw University, 26

"The Derby Ram," 208-14, 263

Derbyshire (England), 209, 211

Deuchars (Ind.), 31, 32, 158, 172, 281

Dickey, Quentin Lotus, 18-20, 49, 242, 244, 381

Dickey family, 18-20

"Did the *Maine* Go Down?," 329-36

"Didn't He Ramble?," 211, 212, 213

Dills, Charlotte, 321

419

Kixmiller family, 11, 12
Klapmeyer, J. M., 260
"The Knights Out of Spain," 70, 114
Ku Klux Klan, 45

Labree, Lawrence, 321
"Lady Isabel and the Elf Knight," 270, 281, 371
"Lady Jinks of the Foot Dragoons," 135
"Lady on the Mountain," 72, 73, 115
Laing, David, 234
Lancaster County (Va.), 27
"The Lass of Mohee," 193, 194
Last New Year's Day we had a fight, 364
Lawrence County (Ind.), 25, 26, 34, 45, 46
Lawrenceburg (Ind.), 336, 341
Laws, Malcolm, 32, 170, 188, 197, 224, 241, 260, 313, 352, 367, 368
"A Lazy Farmer Boy," 172
"The Lazy Young Man," 171
Leach, MacEdward, 369
Lee, Henry "Light-Horse Harry," 20
Lee, Robert E., 20
Leesville (Ind.), 45
L'Estrange, 278
Let the air blow in upon me, 261
Levenworth (Ind.), 46
Library of Congress, 11, 30, 390
Lightwood, James T., 58
Lilleston family, 21-22
Lincoln, Thomas, 14
Lincoln County (Ky.), 13
Lindsey, David, 29-30, 50, 246, 255, 260
Lindsey family, 29-30
Lingard, William Horace, 135
Linsville (Ind.), 12
List, Amanda Joan (Mandie), 30, 85, 87, 105, 106, 107, 109, 113
List, George, 200
List, Michael, 116
List family, 30

Liston (British comedian), 219
"The Little Graves," 321
"The Little Green Valley," 221
"The Little Mohea," 37, 191-92
"Little Mohee," 366, 367
Little Turtle, 192
Livingston (Ind.), 1
Livingston (Ky.), 19, 32
Logan County (Ky.), 13
Lomax, Alan, 10, 11, 14, 20, 23, 24, 28, 31, 32, 41, 42, 44, 45, 47, 48, 85, 156, 173, 390
Lomax, Dr. Claude, 34
Lomax, Elizabeth, 11, 24, 43, 85
"London Bridge," 133, 162
Long, Eleanor, 300
Loogootee (Ind.), 34, 215, 222
Lopez, Vincent, 197
Lord, Albert B., 376, 379
"Lord Lovell," 307
"Lord Thomas and Fair Annett," 287
Lord Thomas he was a bold for'ster, 272
Louisville (Ky.), 30
"The Love-Sick Frog," 219
"The Lowland Sea," 291-94, 306
Lynchburg (Va.), 31

McCary's Bluff (Ind.), 1
MacDowell County (N.C.), 367
Mack, E., 262
McKinley, William, 331, 334
Maclagan, T., 135
McLendon, Altha Lea, 162, 163
McMurtry family, 43-44
McNeely family, 11-14
Macon, Dave, 215
McReynolds family, 44
Madison (Ind.), 36
Madison County (Ky.), 13
Mahalisville (Ind.), 39
"Maids When You're Young Never Wed an Old Man," 173

421

422